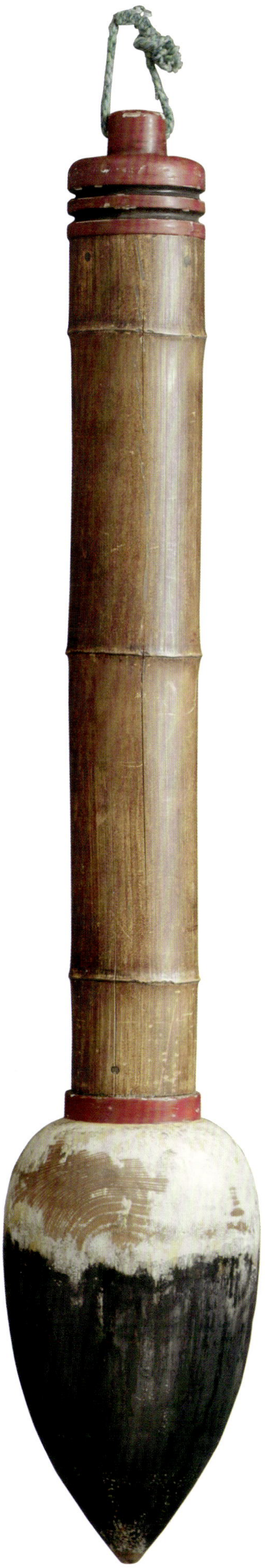

KANBAN

Traditional Shop Signs of Japan

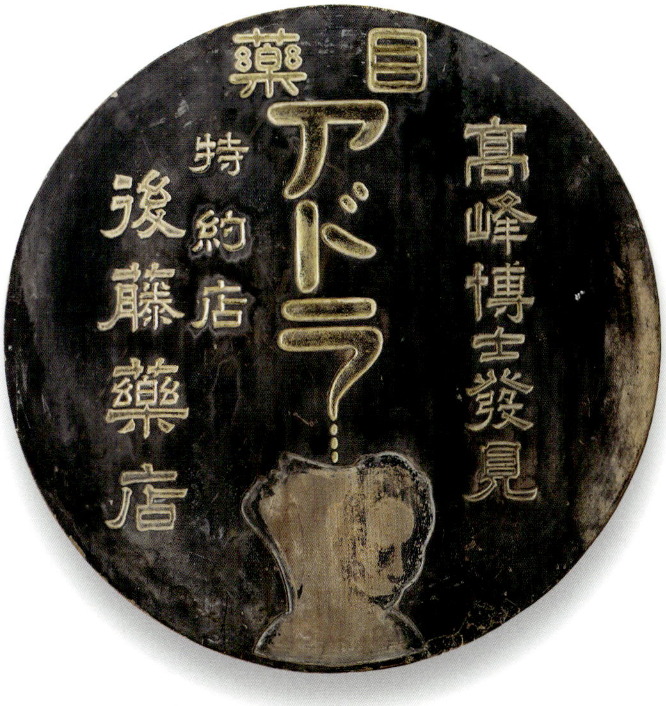

Alan Scott Pate

MINGEI INTERNATIONAL MUSEUM
SAN DIEGO

PRINCETON UNIVERSITY PRESS
PRINCETON AND OXFORD

7 Foreword—Rob Sidner

9 Introduction

- The Neon Scramble
- Kanban: Signs of the Times

19 Chapter 1 **Fingerprints of the Artisan**

- Visual Records
- Scenes in and around the Capital
- Woodblock Prints

37 Chapter 2 **The Kanban of Nihonbashi**

47 Chapter 3 **The Way of the Merchant**

55 Chapter 4 **Kanban and Kabuki: Product Placement and the Edo Stage**

61 Chapter 5 **Collectors and Collections**

- The Sugiura Collection
- The Peabody Essex Museum Collection
- The Shôwa Neon Takamura Kanban Museum Collection

69 Chapter 6 **Categorizing Kanban: The Catalogue**

- Medicine
- Tobacco Shops
- Mokei Kanban: Shop Signs as Sculpture
- Yôki Kanban: Container Shop Signs
- Consumer Goods: Kanban and Daily Necessities
- Kanban and Specialty Trades
- Kanban and Pastimes

161 Notes

165 Glossary

168 Bibliography

174 Index

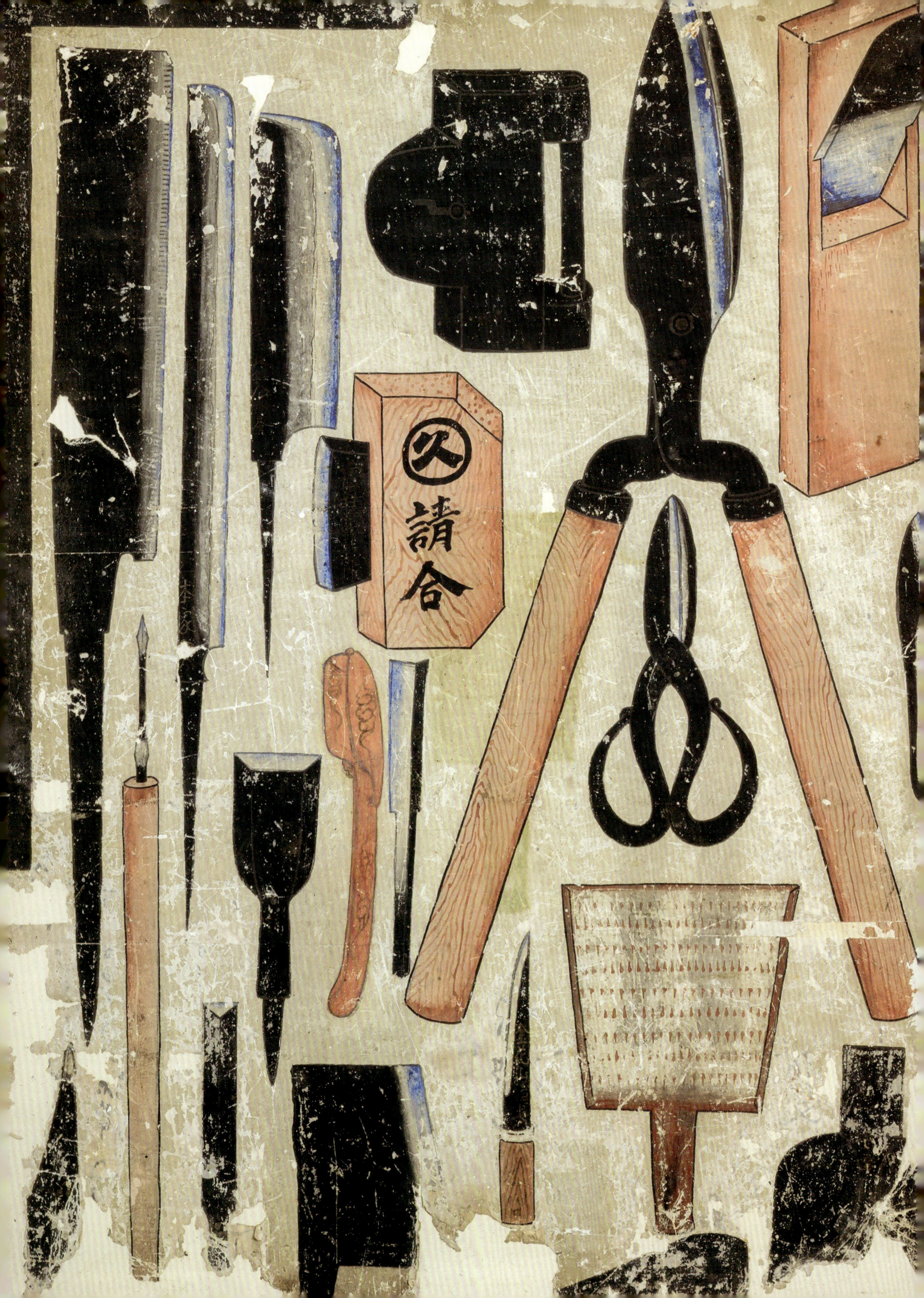
久
請合

FOREWORD

SIXTEEN YEARS AGO the *Mokei Kanban for Brush Shop*, pictured on the first page of this book, entered Mingei International Museum's collection—the generous gift of board member Jeaninne Helmstetter and her husband, Richard. The first kanban acquired by the Museum, it was a powerful introduction for me to this unusual corner of Japanese folk art, and I was immediately enamored. This calligraphy brush is a completely believable, large-scale example of what a nineteenth-century shopper would have found inside the store where it hung. Two- and three-dimensional shop signs, with no words or few, came onto the scene as a fresh and lively means of communication in support of commerce, which flourished during the Edo period amid the rise of the merchant class. Such kanban are greatly admired by aficionados of traditional Japanese art and culture for their straightforward yet artful visual language.

Though Mingei International Museum got a late start collecting kanban, the Museum has been able to build a worthy, growing collection of these alluring trade signs over the past sixteen years. The collection has expanded to the point that it seemed possible, with the significant addition of borrowed kanban, to mount an important exhibition of them with a publication that could add significant information and insight. Here we build on *Kanban: Shop Signs of Japan*, the groundbreaking book of 1983 published by the Japan House Gallery of the Japan Society and the American Federation of Arts in association with what was then the Peabody Museum.

Our eager collaborator in this project, from the very idea of it, has been longtime Museum friend Alan Scott Pate. A respected authority on Japanese dolls and the author of three definitive books on the subject, Alan also researched and wrote Mingei International's publication *Maneki Neko: Japan's Beckoning Cats, from Talisman to Pop Icon* (2011), and he served as guest curator for the exhibition of the same title. A prodigious researcher, Alan has developed around these kanban a lively, visually rich context of commercial life in Edo-period Japan and later.

Bruce Silverstein, M.D., a professor at the University of Washington School of Medicine in Seattle, is also a passionate collector of traditional Japanese arts, most notably kanban. With generosity and joy, he has from the beginning supported the Museum's desire to develop this publication and exhibition.

We are honored to have six kanban on loan from the Peabody Essex Museum in Salem, Massachusetts. It is the oldest continuously operating museum in the country, with a vast and distinguished collection of the arts of Asia and the most important public collection of kanban outside of Japan.

With hearty thanks we recognize other public and private lenders of kanban to the exhibition:

Shôwa Neon Takamura Kanban Museum, Tokyo
John Joseph Schloss and Dieuwke Eijer, New York
David M. Kahn, New York
Kate Leonard, San Diego
Robert Mangold, Kyoto
The late Mary Jean Nelson, Denver

Shôji Hamada, the great folk potter of Mashiko, Japan, used to counsel people not to "speak of art and money in the same sentence," as he was convinced that valuing something according to its market price often made for skewed judgments about its inherent worth. Good advice for all of us, I think. Yet, here we present a book and exhibition whose very subject matter is commerce—clever, artful signage that was intended to be alluring to potential buyers of various products. The exception, then, proves the rule once again. It is said that good poets need good audiences. So, too, do good products need good kanban.

Rob Sidner
Director, Mingei International Museum

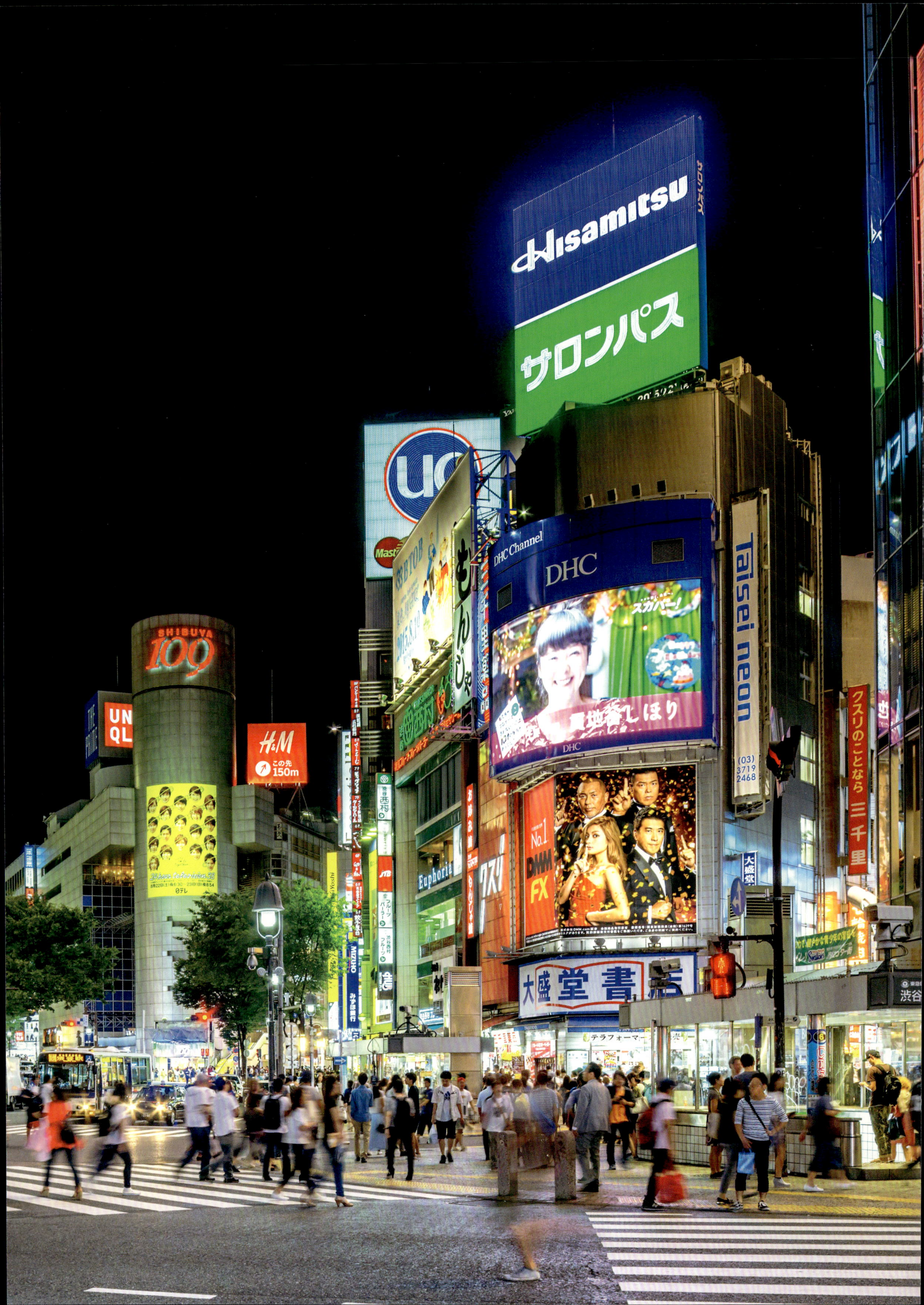
Hisamitsu
サロンパス
SHIBUYA
109
UNI
QL
H&M
この先
150m
DHC Channel
DHC
スカパー!
Taisei neon
(03)
3719
2468
No.1
DMM
FX
Euphoria
クスリのことなら
三千里
大盛堂書店

INTRODUCTION

The Neon Scramble

IN TOKYO, A COVERED CEMENT STAIRWELL rises up out of the pavement and disgorges you onto an intersection filled with people. A spectacular number of people. A surreal number of people: suited salarymen off for a round of drinks and slurred karaoke; commuters rushing for their trains or searching for a last-minute dining option; lovers meeting lovers; friends meeting friends; ubiquitous *gyaru* girls perched atop impossibly high-heeled shoes, meeting up with other gyaru girls or gelled-hair *gyaru-o* boys and doing whatever it is that they do; tourists gawking and stumbling. The entire frenetic scene is bathed in brilliant, colorful, pulsating neon light. Vivid, multi-story jumbotron images of a famous American actor touting a wristwatch, or another equally famous figure advocating a brand of cognac, flash and wink at you from on high. Glowing texts and kaleidoscopic imagery advertising department stores, pachinko parlors, bookstores, clothing stores, wedding boutiques, love hotels, purveyors of electronics, purveyors of luxury brands, restaurants, and cafes all rise vertically, virtually obliterating the night sky. As you surge forward with the tidal crowd, you try not to stare and you try not to trip. Welcome to Shibuya Crossing, also known as the "Scramble" (fig. 1).

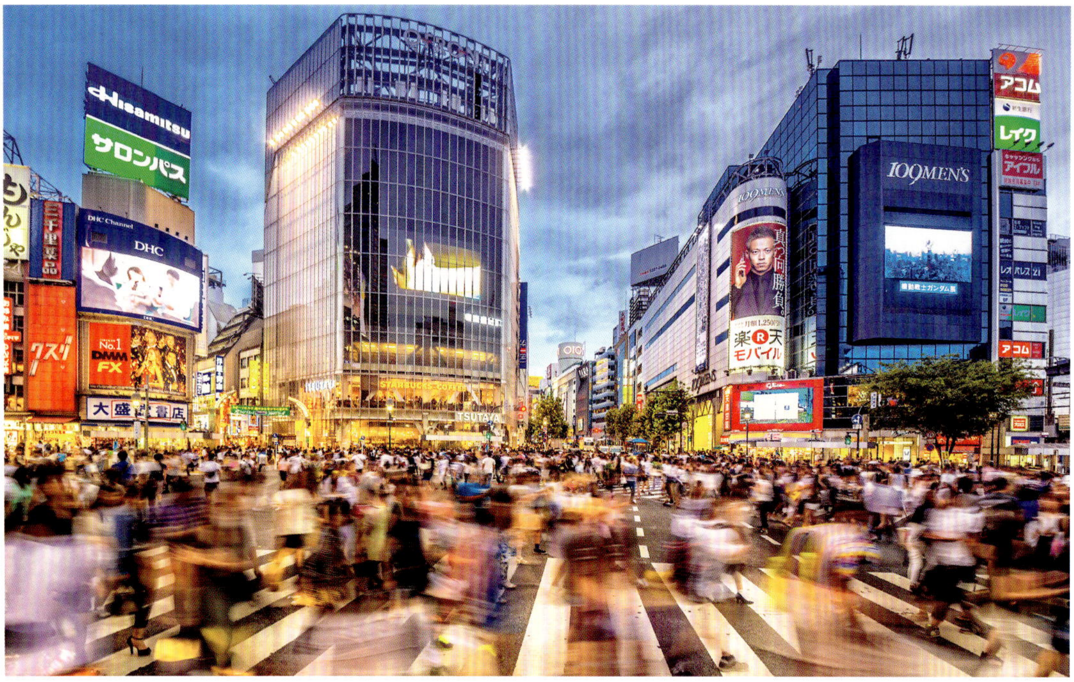

Thought to be one of the busiest pedestrian intersections on the planet, Shibuya Crossing is invariably listed as one of the top ten things to experience on a visit to Japan. At peak hours it is estimated that more than a thousand people make the scramble with each sixty-second signal sequence. At night the crossing is singular in its intensity, as the pedestrian signals turn from red to green and thousands of evening revelers and workers from the area's thriving IT community converge in an attempt to cross the street—from all directions, at once, moving, milling, and progressing through the multi-pronged intersection in front of Shibuya Station. It is a complicated dance, one performed well by the habitué, falteringly by the novitiate, and catastrophically by the faint of heart. In the daytime the area is crowded but benign, with office workers out on their breaks, students transiting between school and cram sessions, and other assorted locals waiting for the signal and petting the paw of the statue of Hachikô, the famous dog who waited in vain for ten years for his master to return home from his daily commute. Or they might head to the Starbucks on the second floor of the QFRONT building, with its prime view of the Shibuya scene. But at night, the crossing becomes one of the hippest (and brightest) locales in the world.

Shibuya Crossing also boasts the world's highest density of neon advertising. From building-enveloping mega screens to tiny flickering accent marks in a plethora of scripts, fonts, and languages, all vying for attention, the signs brighten the night and point the way to hopeful commercial ventures—advertising by "liquid fire." Of course, Shibuya is not the only iconic center for neon advertising. Take the Las Vegas Strip or New York's Times Square, for example, or the neon signs and video screens of London's Piccadilly Circus, or the parade of neon along Shanghai's Nanjing Road. But while neon as a favored advertising medium has penetrated nearly every corner of the globe, in Japan it has perhaps attained its highest articulation, and the spectacular montage at Shibuya Crossing is unquestionably the peak of that ultimate.

The invention of the now-common neon sign is attributed to the French scientist Georges Claude (1870–1960) as a happy by-product of his experiments with liquefying air in 1902. The first commercial sign application was designed for a barbershop in Paris and erected in 1912. In America, there remains some controversy over who first employed the neon sign as commercial advertisement. Earle C. Anthony (1880–1961), a Packard car distributor in Los Angeles, has long

FIG. 1 Night scene of Tokyo's Shibuya Crossing, also known as the "Scramble." iStock 88283039.

FIG. 2 Utagawa Sadahide (1807–1878/9), *Tôtô Ryôgokubashi natsu keshiki* (Panoramic view of the Ryôgoku Bridge in the summer), 1859. Triptych of polychrome woodblock prints, ink and color on paper. Image (a): 13¾ × 9½ in. (34.9 × 24.1 cm); Image (b): 13¾ × 9½ in. (34.9 × 24.1 cm); Image (c): 14 × 9½ in. (35.6 × 24.1 cm). Metropolitan Museum of Art, Bequest of William S. Lieberman, 2005, 2007.49.294a-c, www.metmuseum.org.

been accorded this bragging right for a large red sign, simply reading "Packard," that he had mounted high atop a hotel at the corner of 7th and Flower Streets, supposedly in 1923. However, recent research has shown that Anthony was not given a construction permit until late 1924 and did not actually erect the sign until January 1925, leaving a brightly lit question mark over who may actually lay claim to this particular American first.[1] But it is clear that, by the mid-1920s, neon had arrived in America in all its lurid color, hawking myriad wares and services while illuminating the night sky from coast to coast.

Japan followed quickly on the heels of this American love affair with neon and the "architecture of light," installing its first domestically produced signs in Hibiya Park in Tokyo in 1926. But Japanese neon literally hit the big time in 1957 with Sony's dramatic and massive neon sign installation at the Sukiyabashi intersection in the Ginza. Measuring 32 by 36 feet (10 by 11 meters), with each brightly glowing letter of the Sony name weighing over 580 pounds (263 kg), the sign itself weighed in at 4,960 pounds (2,250 kg). Crowds gathered to witness its first illumination, which helped secure Sony's impression on the Japanese and global consciousness as a brand name to be remembered. The rest, as they say, is glowing history. And now, images of Japan's neon street scenes, from the Ginza, Shinjuku, and Shibuya in Tokyo to Shinsaibashi in Osaka, have become singularly emblematic of modern Japan itself.

Advertising is perhaps the world's second oldest profession. Visual and written records of the development of Tokyo, originally called Edo, reveal that this city—already one of the largest in the world by the dawn of the eighteenth century, with over 1 million people—has long been noted for its intense push and clash of pedestrians and the merchants trying to attract them. Unsurprisingly, pedestrian density was highest in the principal market areas. Commercial centers such as Nihonbashi and the marketplace at the base of

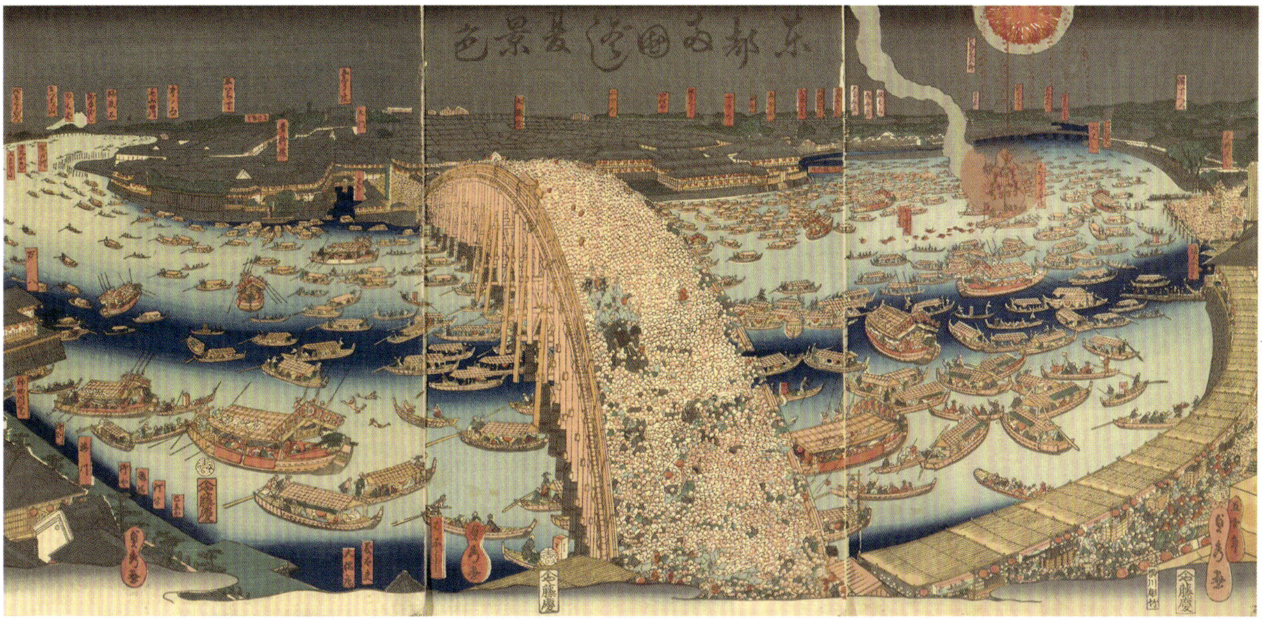

the Ryôgoku Bridge were among the most congested, blending vendors, travelers, and residents in their own form of scramble.

A woodblock print by Utagawa Sadahide (1807–1878/9) depicting the Ryôgoku Bridge on a summer evening gives us an effective look at Edo crowds in 1859 (fig. 2). In this triptych, boats clog the Sumida River as it curves around the midsection of the capital on its way to Edo Bay. The foreground shows a continuous line of vendor stalls, with their thatched roofs solidly filling the banks as fireworks explode in the distance. The crowds are so densely packed along the approaches of the Ryôgoku Bridge and across its span that the artist has made no attempt to render individualized faces, just circular blobs depicting head after head after head after head. This is the Edo version of the Shibuya Scramble—over water. Famously, in 1807 the Eitai Bridge, located further downstream, collapsed under the weight of similar crowds passing over it on their way to the Fukagawa Hachiman festival at Tomioka Hachimangu Shrine; 1,400 people were killed.

While neon may have only a hundred years of history under its gaseous belt, advertising by signage is not at all a new concept. For as long as there has been a merchant or artisan trying to sell his wares in either a fixed or floating location, a sign has been sure to accompany him. Whether it was a white banner (*zhi*) fluttering atop a bamboo pole announcing the presence of a wine shop in China during the Warring States period (475–221 BCE), or an Egyptian papyrus wall poster advertising a cure for hangovers for an Alexandrian apothecary 1,900 years ago, signs and signage have historically formed the bedrock of commercial culture.[2] Advertising signs thus are a shared part of a truly global culture, with each period, region, and people practicing and expressing themselves in this particular medium based on the tastes, proclivities, and technologies of a specific time and place.

Researchers in the development of shop signs in Japan point to the practice of prominently displaying actual objects on sale as a nascent form of advertising and a precursor to our subject here, *kanban*.[3] Known specifically as *jitsubutsu kanban* (actual-object signs), this form of advertising has a documented history dating from the Nara period (710–794). One can easily imagine a marketplace where erstwhile companionable merchants and traders become intense competitors vying for customer attention and patronage, using all available means. A seller of *ashiginu* (rough silk), for example, would hang a colorful array of samples from the eaves of his assigned booth to attract the eye and coin of a customer.

This exact scene is captured in a verse recorded in Japan's oldest poetry anthology, the *Man'yôshû*, compiled around 759; it reads:

Nishi no ichi ni
Tada hitori idete
Menarabezu
Kaite shi kinu no
Akiji kori kamo

Matsumiya Saburô, in his work *Edo no kanban*, has liberally translated this verse as:

At the Western market, colorful silks are lined up at the shop,
So beautiful to look at
But since I bought some without taking a close look
And I was alone and could seek no advice
I did not buy very well.[4]

In the case of this particular customer, the colorful arrangement may have softened his judgment, and the poem introduces us perhaps to a particularly early example of false advertising.

The markets and market mechanisms of the Nara period have been well documented, with goods flowing in and out of the capital city through sophisticated road, river, and canal networks extending far into the archipelago. And the silks described in the *Man'yôshû* represent only one commodity among many that were purchased, traded, and bartered at the formally established and closely regulated Eastern and Western Markets (*tôzai ichi*). Other products included used clothing, cotton, bast fiber, white rice, black rice, wheat, soybeans, azuki beans, salt, miso, vinegar, sesame oil, sugar, sake, firewood, charcoal, construction timber, medicines, paper, brushes, ink, wooden shoes, hardware, bamboo tools, pottery, iron, seaweed, fish, vegetables, and fruit. Additional products and transactions—though more veiled, due to strict Buddhist consumption laws—would have included horse and boar meat, weapons, and saddles.[5] A brisk trade with China would have ensured not only local staples and daily necessities such as those listed above, but also more exotic fare, such as finished silk brocades, ivory, jade, and rhino horn. All reflected a vibrant economy and marketplace, not unlike any Japanese market today (except for maybe the weapons, and, hopefully, the ivory and rhino horn). One can easily imagine that vendors employed or devised their own methods for advertising their goods and attracting the eye of potential customers, much like the silk merchant and his disappointed customer poetically immortalized above.

It is a long road from the Nara-period silk merchant's stall to the neon jumbotron of the Shibuya Scramble. And yet there is a distinct commonality between them: communication, a fundamental desire to transmit a message from seller to buyer. For the art historian, the lover of Japanese folk art, as well as the consumer, there is a shared delight in marveling at the signposts stationed along this meandering road—namely, the kanban that Japanese merchants used to advertise their products and services.

Kanban: Signs of the Times

Kanban, a distinctive fusion of art and commerce, refers to the traditional signs Japanese merchants and craftsmen displayed street-side to advertise their presence, denote the products or services found inside, and give individual identity and expression to the shop itself. Created from wood, bamboo, iron, paper, fabric, lacquer, or even stone, kanban form a rich visual vocabulary of traditional advertising. Elongated panels of lacquered wood ornamented with elegantly inscribed calligraphy; whimsically carved three-dimensional scenes of carp climbing waterfalls (cat. 1) or munificent deities presiding over hoards of bounty; oversized but functional Buddhist prayer beads; stencil-dyed segments of colored cloth fluttering in front of an open doorway; *geta* clogs strung in rows; sword scabbards mounted proudly on finely etched wooden plaques; iron furniture fittings of assorted sizes exploding from large wooden panels; gigantic combs; oversized parasols; Brobdingnagian writing brushes; colorfully rendered images of seductive courtesans with painted faces and coiffed hair; massive silk thread skeins—all of these are signs and images that would have been a familiar sight on traditional Japanese commercial streets.

Shop signs are an iconic folk art form, found in nearly every culture around the world. Yet, the Japanese seem to have excelled at this early take on Madison Avenue, creating a multi-faceted inventory of symbol and meaning designed to engage the viewer and entice the customer. From a hand-carved sign made by the shopkeeper himself, hanging over the doorway to his modest shop in the smallest of back-country hamlets, to a sumptuous and professionally rendered virtuoso of a sign mounted atop a tall post in the booming capital city of Edo, kanban were an integral part of Japanese trade culture.

Bustling commercial sectors were lined with kanban of varying descriptions, creating a potentially dizzying montage of imagery and signage,

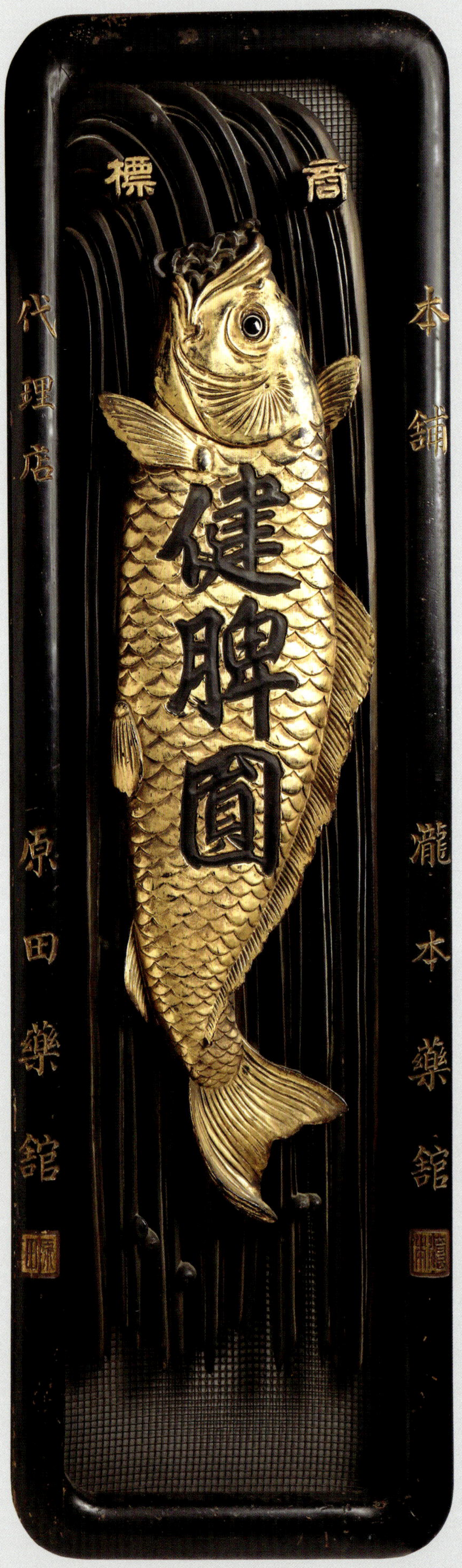

1

Sage kanban for pharmacy selling Kenpien
Early twentieth century
Wood, pigment, lacquer, glass
66 × 20 × 4 in. (167 × 52 × 10 cm)
Mingei International Museum Purchase, 2012-40-001

Shop owners frequently spent significant sums of money on kanban for their shops. They used these carefully crafted signs to convey prestige, solidity, and reliability to their customers; ego may have also played a role. While some shop owners were content with kanban that conveyed a bare minimum of information, others sought out aesthetic testimonies that employed extravagant materials, resulting in beautiful works of art worthy of admiration in their own right. Here, a sage kanban of a carp climbing a waterfall is rendered with a high sense of realism and covered in gold lacquer; the characters on the fish's body advertise Kenpien medicine. Water fills and slides out of the carp's open mouth. His large eye, inset with glass, possesses an iridescent quality. A wire mesh background suspends the carved wooden strands simulating cascading water and communicates an added sense of altitude, as if the carp is climbing to great heights. The characters "tôroku shôhyô" are placed at the top of the falls, indicating that the ascending carp is a registered trademark. Along the right margin of the frame is the text "Honpo Takimoto Kusuri Kan" (Main Office of Takimoto Medicinal), followed by the Takimoto seal. The left margin reads, "Dariten Hirada Kusuri Kan" (Agent for Hirada Medicinal), followed by the Hirada seal.

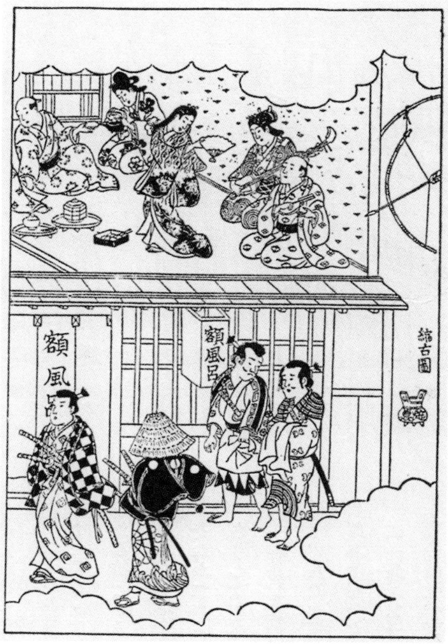

FIG. 3 Edo-period woodblock print depicting a kanban of an arrow-notched bow in the upper right, indicating a bathhouse. Reproduced from Tsuboi, *Kôshô gigei kanban kô.*

all vying to attract and seduce the potential customer. *Noren* curtains fronting the shop bore individual designs or stencil-dyed text indicating the shop name or services. *Yane* or *noki kanban* were suspended from under the eaves of the building and could be viewed from far down the street (if not blocked by a neighbor's even larger kanban). *Sage kanban,* or single-sided, hanging kanban, were flush against the side of the building. *Hako kanban* were placed on the street immediately at the entrance to the shop, resting on a light framework box with a stretched-paper upper section upon which the image of the product sold, or the name of the proprietor or shop itself, would have been professionally written. *Yôki kanban,* or container signs, simple silhouettes carved in the shape of the commodity's container, hung outside, creating a direct means of communication for purveyors of tea or vinegar, whose distinctive container shapes made them readily identifiable to even the illiterate in the community. Taking this concept further, *mokei kanban,* or model signs, featured mounted display carvings replicating in three dimensions the objects sold. Painted or relief-carved renderings on double-sided signs, called *shitta kanban,* hung just beside the door and were brought in each night in order to protect these valuable advertisements. A quick peek inside a more upscale shop might have revealed a gilded and mother-of-pearl-encrusted freestanding *oki* or *tsuitate kanban* functioning as both advertisement and room divider, shielding a customer or shopkeeper from prying eyes. *Andon kanban* or *chochin kanban,* made in a lantern style, would have been lit at night to broadcast the presence of a restaurant, tea shop, theater, or pleasure house.

For the playful Edo mind, kanban frequently functioned in code, presenting abstracted, distilled, or obliquely referential imagery to communicate to the savvy, in-the-know buyer. These brainteaser signs relied on puns (known as *hanji mono* or *goro awase*), hidden meanings (*nazo*), and parodies (*mitate*) that challenge the uninitiated today, but delighted the worldly Edo community that prided itself on sophistication. For example, a simple herring shop might have been named Yuki no Tsuki (Moon of Karma), perhaps using a giant moon as its kanban. This is a puzzling choice, unless one is versed in the classic song composed for the samisen by Tsuruyama Koto (act. mid-eighteenth century). Then one just might glimpse the wordplay in which the classic lyric, "*Honna ennishi ga konimo aroka?*" (Is there a sweeter fate [*en*] than this?) could easily be substituted with "*Honna iinishin ga konimo aroka?*" (Is there sweeter herring [*nishin*] than this?").[6] Another, more common example of wordplay kanban is found in the tradition of using an arrow as a symbol for a bathhouse (fig. 3). This obscure image captures the similarity between the phrases *"yûmi iru"* (to shoot an arrow) and *"yû iru"* (to get into a bath).[7]

A common *nazo* (hidden meaning) example is the use of imagery from *hanafuda,* or playing cards, to sell deer, boar, and horse meat. Due to traditional Buddhist prohibitions against eating meat, purveyors of these commodities tended to remain low-key in their advertising. Code names developed: deer was referred to as *momiji* (autumn leaves), boar was *botan* (peony), and horse was *sakura* (cherry blossom). Cards from the hanafuda deck with these symbols became convenient substitutes when advertising these somewhat controversial, but not outlawed, products.[8] Interestingly, when hanafuda cards themselves became proscribed by the government for their abuse as a game of chance, similar *nazo* elements were employed for shops dealing in the cards. The term *hanafuda* literally means "flower cards" but can alternatively be read as "nose cards," so images of the long-nosed *tengu* goblin became a popular code for the shops (cat. 2).[9] Beef cattle were not introduced into Japan in large number until 1843, and the first public meat market appeared in the Takamatsu area of Osaka in 1851, at a time when Buddhist prohibitions lacked the force of earlier periods.[10] As a result, shop owners advertising beef did not have to resort to such clever subterfuge, but they did tend to write the word *gyûniku* (beef) in red letters, symbolizing red meat.[11]

An example of a *mitate,* or parody, was the common practice of a needle shop simply advertising its presence with an image of pine needles. Stylized pine needle designs were emblazoned on the shop's noren, or sometimes a shop owner would place potted pine plants on the street. Pine needles referred to the tale of Kichibi Daijin, who supposedly traveled to China in early antiquity and learned the art of sewing. When he returned to Japan, he found no metal needles and so resorted to pine needles as a substitute.[12]

Today, isolated from their surroundings, kanban have become objects to be appreciated in their own right. One can marvel at the intricacy of the carving or titter at the humorous take on a revered deity. One can puzzle over a sign's meaning or clearly imagine the shop and the wares it proffered. To explore the world of kanban is to delve into Japan's commercial and artistic roots, the evolution of trade, the emergence of mass consumer culture, and the ploys of advertising. Kanban have long been admired by collectors of traditional Japanese folk art, and examples of relevant kanban are frequently included in museum exhibitions and treatises on specific Japanese industries or craft traditions. But little effort has been made to look more deeply into their history, to examine their role in the development of Japan's now-formidable advertising industry, or, on a more basic level, to become acquainted with the talented artisans who made them.

2

Sage kanban for Oishi Tengudo playing card shop
Twentieth century
Wood, pigment
30 × 6 in. (76 × 14 cm)
Shôwa Neon Takamura Kanban Museum

This shop sign for the Kyoto-based Oishi Tengudo playing card shop features a tasseled mask of a long-nosed *tengu* goblin, surmounted by the tôroku-shôhyô (registered trademark). In the center, boldly rendered characters read, "Hana karuta ya," bearing traces of their original gilt treatment, with the black lacquer under layer showing through. Three playing cards cascade down the sign. The top one is *matsu* (pine) for January, with a crane and pine boughs; the middle one is *sakura* (cherry blossoms) for March, with a blossoming cherry tree glimpsed behind a field curtain; and finally the card for August shows a full moon with a red sky, as part of the *susuki* (grass) series. The Oishi Tengudo, established in 1800, remains an important manufacturer of various forms of *karuta*, or playing cards. It retains the tengu as its corporate symbol.

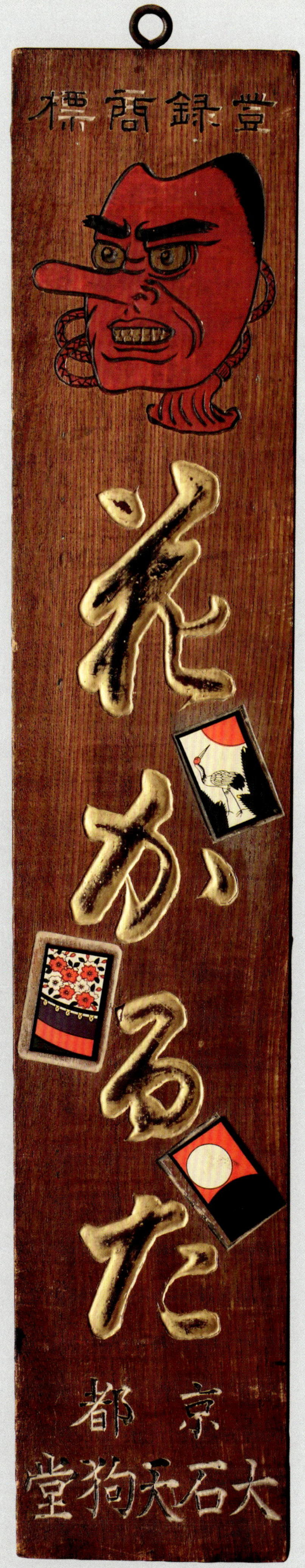

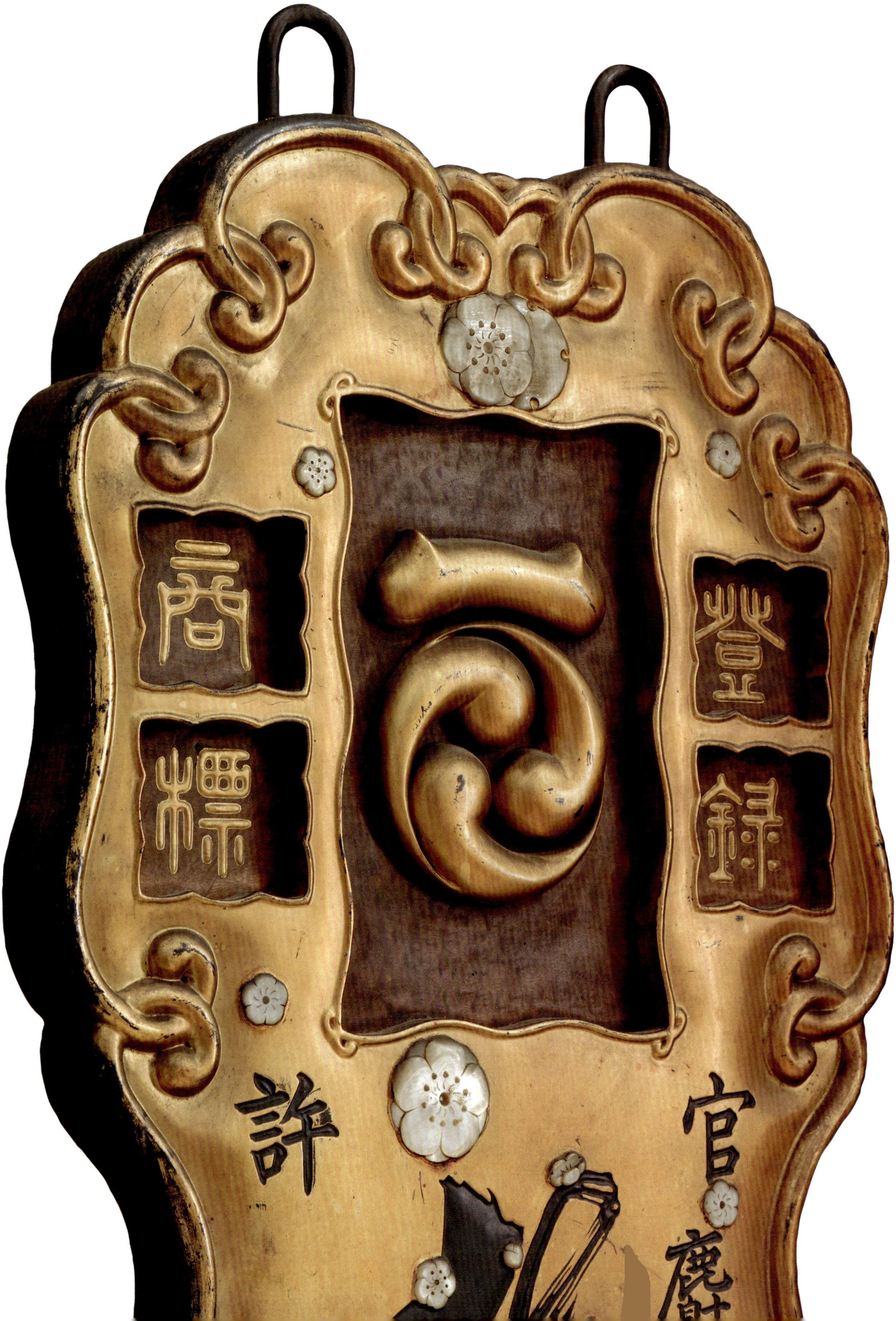
商標
登録
許
官

FINGERPRINTS OF THE ARTISAN

1

KANBAN ARE INEXTRICABLY CONNECTED with Japan's artisanal and merchant traditions. By their very nature, they contain elements both crassly commercial as well as subtly artistic. Shop signs were first and foremost advertisements, a method of attracting customers. They were designed and intended as moneymaking tools, helping to expand a given shop's market reach within its community. But many kanban were also intrinsically artistic expressions, capable of conveying a shop's self-image, communicating through a deft combination of shape, imagery, and words the nature and character of the goods sold, and, by extension, the sellers themselves. Or, in modern parlance, they helped to create a brand identity.

Kanban were also, in many instances, collaborative efforts between merchants and the craftsmen employed to create the signs. A purveyor of Bikkuri megusuri (Astonishing eye medicine), for example, would have had little of the skills required to carve a sign advertising the benefits of this popular patent medicine. He would have had to call on the services of a *kanban-shi* (kanban carver) or a *kanban-gaki* or *mono-gaki*, specialists in calligraphy for kanban. Or perhaps he would have engaged an *on-gaku* who specialized in carving frames and name signs. Together they would have arrived

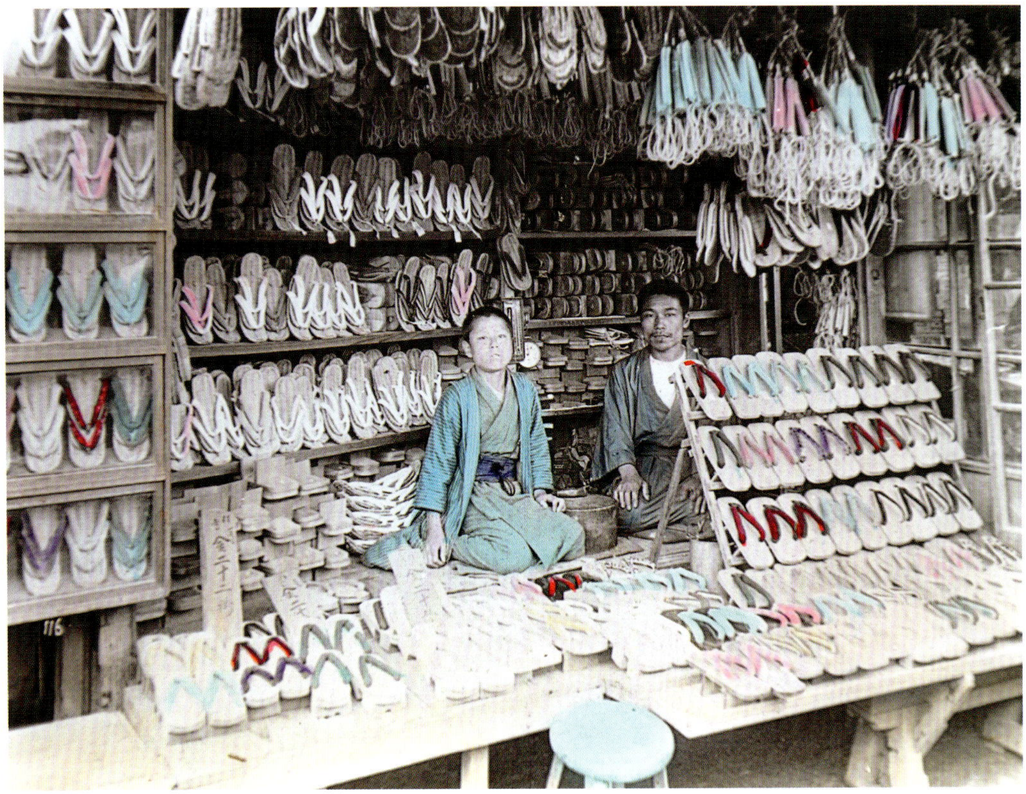

at the most effective way to communicate the desired message. The type of kanban and the degree of ornamentation would have depended on both the technical skills of the kanban-shi and the depth of the pockets of the merchant employing him.[13]

Conversely, a raw lacquer seller (*urushi-ya*) would also not typically have had the skills necessary to create an elaborate kanban, but by tradition would merely have suspended five to seven of his lacquer barrels along the front of the shop as advertising, effectively indicating his presence and trade.[14] Such use of actual objects as kanban was generally referred to as *jitsubutsu kanban*, such as with the Nara-period silk merchant, and made an easy go of it for merchants and artisans dealing in materials that lent themselves to such displays. Other common jitsubutsu kanban included *kasa* and *hi-gasa* (umbrellas and parasols), *juzu* (Buddhist rosaries), *kasa* (sedge hats), *kaga* (palanquins), *kagami* (mirrors), and *geta* (wooden clogs) (fig. 4). Similarly, rice merchants would have arrayed the distinctive straw- and rope-encased bundles of this precious commodity along the street fronts of their shops, and the ubiquitous purveyors of sake had only to arrange stacked series of *sakadaru* (sake casks), a sight still common today.

Only a fraction of the kanban made during the Edo and Meiji eras survive. Time, the rigors of duty, the inherent fragility of some of the materials employed, and the carelessness of indifferent handlers all have conspired to significantly reduce the potential gene pool of signs from which to draw upon for study and enjoyment. This has left a yawning chasm in our ability to firmly identify the shops that displayed them, the proprietors who commissioned them, and, perhaps, more importantly from an art-historical perspective, the artisans who made them. Overall, it is rare to find a signed kanban, one clearly announcing and recording the hand that made it. When found, they are typically kanban executed in an elegant, ornate, and ostentatious style and known as *shôkei kanban*. These luxurious kanban were rarely displayed outside and typically graced only the inner sanctum of shops, where proprietors met more privately with their clientele. The quality of the sign, its beauty, and the extravagance of its materials emphasized the prosperity and, hence, reliability, of the shop. Such signs might have also carried the inscribed

FIG. 4 A merchant selling wooden *geta* and various styles of *zori* sandals is surrounded by his merchandise. Archival photograph. Peabody Essex Museum.

characters "*kobu-gôyo*," indicating that the shop was a supplier for samurai and imperial nobility, a designation akin to the Royal Warrant system in Great Britain. Bold graphics, elegant calligraphic inscriptions, and exceptional detailing were frequently hallmarks of these valuable signs—signs onto which the artisans proudly affixed their names.

A richly carved shôkei kanban for the medicine Ume no yuki (Plum blossoms in snow) is a prime example (cat. 3). The sign itself is stunning, with a sensual and undulating silhouette and an extensive use of gold leaf and gold lacquer. The vibrant calligraphy in the center reads, "Ume no yuki," while, above, carved in deep relief and set in a cartouche, are the characters for "*ichi*" (one) over the ancient *mitsudomoe* design of swirling sacred gems (*magatama*). Adding greatly to the effect of the sign is the scattering of eponymous plum blossoms of varying sizes, fashioned from mother-of-pearl; these fleck the surface of the sign like snowflakes falling from the sky. The business aspect of the sign indicates that the medicine has a registered trademark (*tôroku shôhyô*), that it is made from deer musk (*jako sei*), and that it is designed to help cure nervousness (*kitsuke*) and hangovers (*yoisamashi*). The proprietor's name is listed as Ishida Katsuhide.

On the reverse is a lengthy inscription dating the sign to the sixth month of Meiji 22 (1889); it also includes a poem that reads:

Hiromareshi kusuri
shirushoya
arawashite
umeni furitsumu
yuki mo kaoreri

"Snow covering the blossoms is like medicine covering the need for medicine," a poetic turn of phrase alluding to the medicine's general effectiveness.[15] The poem is carved into the back in a particularly beautiful flowing script. The inscription also includes three names: Takegawa Tomohiro, Tamatsukasa Kogyokudo, and Shimizu Kôjirô. Takegawa Tomohiro is assigned the title *gaku*, a term usually referring to a carver specializing in framing and lettering, while Shimizu Kôjirô is listed as the kanban-shi, responsible for the overall sign itself.

A slightly earlier and nearly identical example of a sign for Ume no yuki medicine is found in the collection of the Peabody Essex Museum (PEM), exhibiting the same silhouette and lettering. Though elegant in its overall design, this sign is much more modest in execution, bearing no evidence that it ever held gilt or gold-lacquer treatments, much less mother-of-pearl inlay. Its one nod to expense and ostentation is that it was created from a single slab of *keyaki* (*Zelkova serrata*) measuring 19 by 13 inches (73 by 33 cm). This type of elm was much prized for its rich grain pattern, and this detail is left in its natural state. Traces of pigment, however, can be seen around the raised edges of the frame. Carved in much lesser relief are the familiar "ichi" and "mitsudomoe" symbols found on the later sign. Flanking this symbol is the term "tôroku shôhyô" (registered trademark), indicating that this sign was produced after 1884. The lightly carved Ume no yuki name, highlighted in black *sumi* ink, can still be easily read in the center, along with the owner's name, Ishida Katsuhide. Helpfully, the shop's address, a detail not included in the first sign, is listed as Kyôto, Gôjôbashi Higashi nichôme—that is, just east of the Gojo Bridge in Kyoto. However, there are no artist signatures included on this more basic version. The sign itself was acquired by the PEM in 1913 through the auspices of the important Japanese art dealer Yamanaka & Co.[16] Although the sign has long been considered a kanban for an incense shop, through comparisons with the Shimizu Kôjirô example, it is now clear that the sign represents a Meiji-era kanban for Ume no yuki.

Two additional signs for Ume no yuki can be found in the Naito Museum of Pharmaceutical Science and Industry at Kakamigahara in Gifu

3

Shôkei kanban for pharmacy selling Ume no yuki, made by Shimizu Kôjirô

Dated Meiji 22 (1889)

Wood, gold leaf, lacquer, ink, metal fittings

40½ × 17¾ × 2 in. (102.9 × 45.1 × 5.1 cm)

Private Collection

Shôkei kanban are noted for their elegance and for the great expense of the materials employed. Not designed to be displayed outside, they functioned more as private testimonials to the character of the shop and the quality of the goods sold. Though possibly viewed from the street, they were intended for the established customer, who, upon entering the shop and engaging in business, would be comforted and assured by the presence of such a beautiful and costly kanban. Here, a wonderfully worked gold-lacquer shop sign with cascading plum blossoms worked in mother-of-pearl advertises Ume no yuki (Plum blossoms in snow) medicine; it was crafted by the noted Meiji-era kanban maker Shimizu Kôjirô.

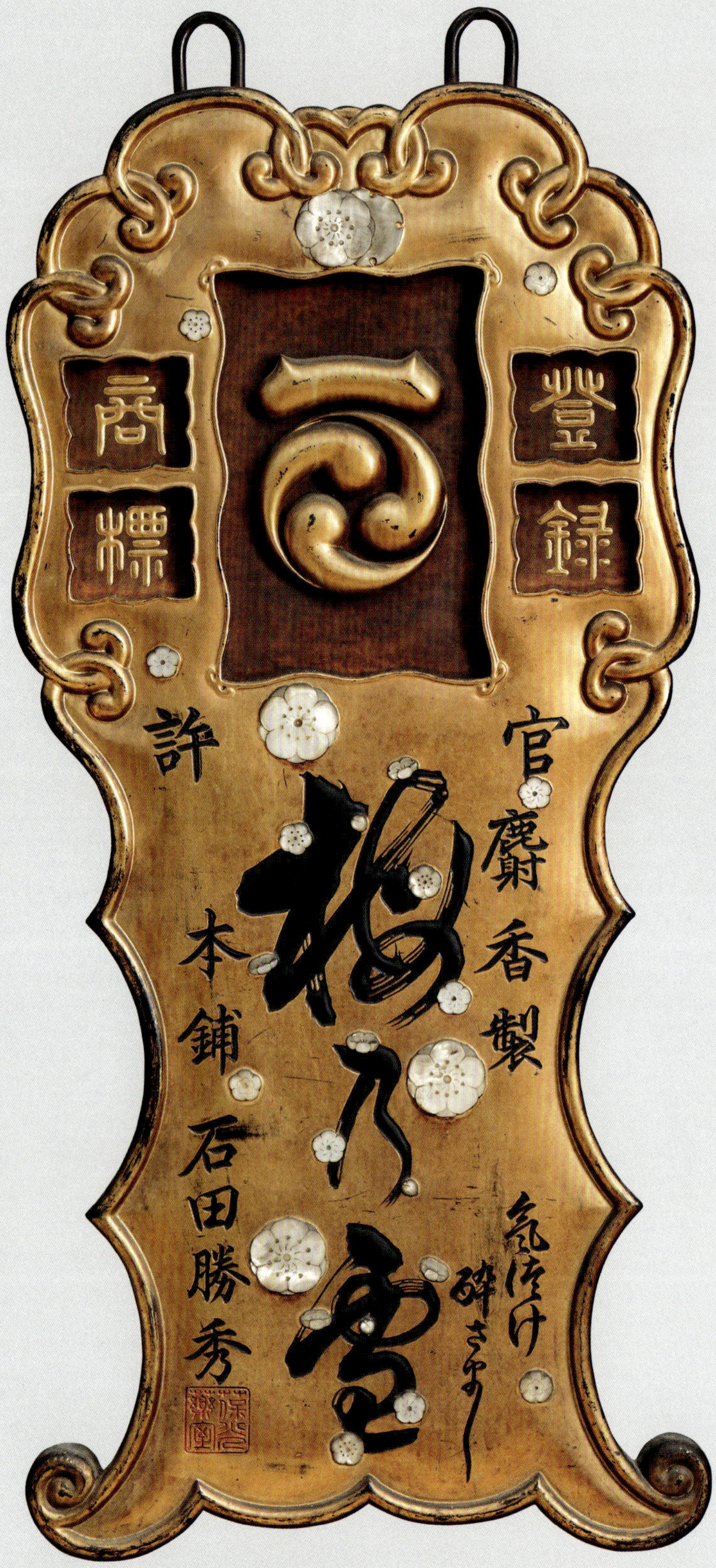

Prefecture. They mirror in nearly every way the two signs already discussed. One is a gold-lacquered sign measuring 39 by 19 inches (99 by 49 cm), studded with mother-of-pearl plum blossoms, for a shop named Tori Chosuido, listed as a wholesaler for Ishida Katsuhide's Ume no yuki. The other is a sign measuring 29 by 13 inches (74 by 34 cm), made of keyaki and stained black, with gold lettering and details. This second sign matches the PEM example almost identically and lists Katsuhide's home shop address in Kyoto.[17] Neither of these beautiful kanban bears the signature of the craftsman who made them. But the larger sign is so nearly identical to the one in the present exhibition that it can be safely assumed to be the work of Shimizu Kôjirô of Kyoto. An additional sign in the shape of a large lotus blossom in the Naito Museum of Pharmaceutical Science and Industry bears Ishida Katsuhide's trademark ichi mitsudomoe design and Kyoto address and advertises the product Kaigigan, a purgative for congenital syphilis.[18]

Though little is known about his career or life's work, Shimizu Kôjirô was one of the more noted kanban-shi in Kyoto active during the late Meiji era. A wonderful turtle-shaped kanban advertising the healthful benefits of ground turtle shell soup, also from Ishida Katsuhide's Kyoto shop, bears the date of the eighth month of Meiji 39 (1906) and the signature of Shimizu Kôjirô (cat. 4). This kanban is carved from a single block of keyaki, with its lively grain showing through the black lacquer and gold-leaf ground. The calligraphy on the right reads, "*Hoketsu jiyôhin*" (Nutritious article that replenishes the blood supply), and Katsuhide's name is on the left. The bold calligraphy in the center reads, "*Suppon no kau saimatsu*" (Ground suppon turtle shell), with accompanying phonetic *hiragana* characters on the right side, the undulating outline of the carapace serving as an elegant frame for the sign's lively calligraphic inscriptions. The reverse, bearing the date and artist's inscription highlighted in red lacquer, also reveals the turtle's clawed feet tucked up under the body (see p. 36).

Like the purveyors of patent medicines or parasols, or any other product, kanban-shi themselves were businessmen, with their own need to advertise. A second sign in the Peabody Essex collection is a rare example advertising the services of a kanban-shi or on-gaku.[19] This simple rectangular sign bears none of the stylistic flourishes of the mother-of-pearl example by Shimizu Kôjirô but is extremely straightforward in its presentation. With a simple cartouche at the top center with relief carved characters reading, "On-gaku," the only nod to extravagance is the remnant of cobalt blue and gilt still clinging to the well-worn lettering. Large characters carved in light relief and bearing similar traces of gilt and coloring read, "On-Gaku Kanban-shi." Here, the type of services rendered is clearly indicated, but no personal name of the craftsman is attached.

The kanban collection at the PEM is the largest outside of Japan, and it has for many years served as an invaluable resource for research on Japanese shop signs. A thorough survey of the inscriptions on the more than two hundred kanban in the PEM collection sheds very little light on the kanban-shi who actually made them, however. We learn that, in 1815, Harimaya Denuemon, at the age of seventy-three, created a sign for Kanda, a maker of temple implements.[20] Another sign advertises the services of Hakoshô, a goldsmith who did repair work (*senshûfuku*) to the gold leaf on kanban, as well as to Buddhist home altars.[21] A large, round wooden medallion with the bust of a Buddhist lohan—carved in relief, with elongated ears, a thin, drooping mustache, and an emaciated ribcage—announces the services of O Kojue, a carver of kanban (*chôkoku-shi*).[22] Another sign advertising the distributor for a patent drug called Kiôgan tells us that a sign maker (*kansei*) by the name of Kenchi Genkakudo was active in Osaka.[23] A competitor in the Osaka kanban market was Ozaki, a sign maker who

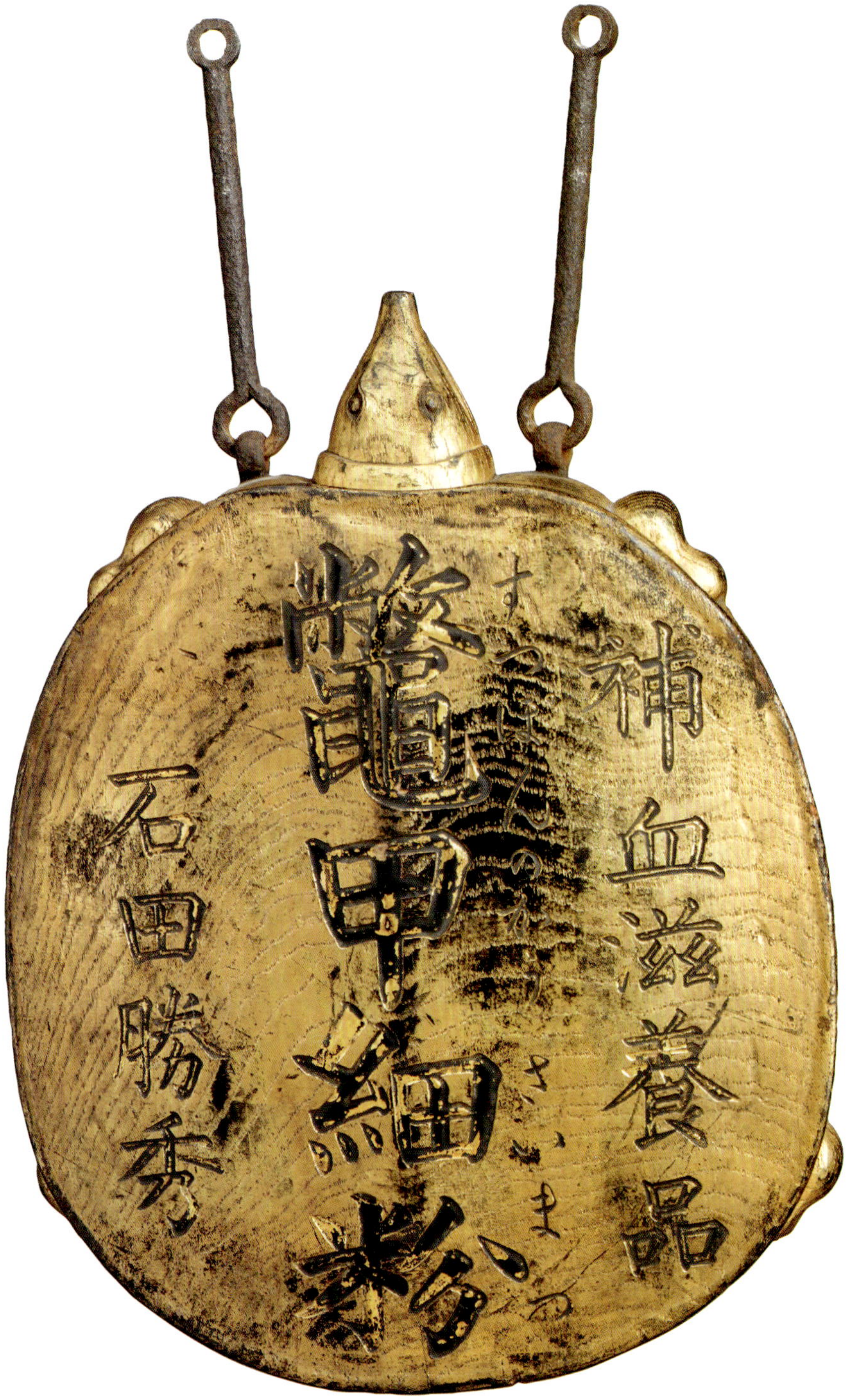

4

Mokei kanban for pharmacy selling ground turtle shell, made by Shimizu Kôjirô

Dated Meiji 39 (1906)
Wood, gold leaf, lacquer, ink, metal fittings
14 × 11 in. (36 × 27 cm)
Collection of John Joseph Schloss and Dieuwke Eijer

At its core, a sculptural mokei kanban was intended to replicate in three-dimensional form the product sold by a given shop. However, artistic license allowed for a wide range of interpretations, especially when the product itself might be a bit tricky to depict. Here, a mokei kanban for *suppon no kau saimatsu* (ground shell of suppon turtles) takes the carapace of the turtle as its template, using the broad shell as a visual space to communicate the particulars. The natural grain of the wood appears through the gold-lacquered surface, imitating to a degree the natural contours of the turtle's shell. Inscribed characters along the right side tout the suppon shell's medicinal benefits, reading, "*Hoketsu jiyouhin*" (Nutritious article that replenishes the blood supply). The characters on the left read, "Ishida Katsuhide." Katsuhide was the owner of a well-known pharmacy in Kyoto. The reverse bears an inscription by the noted kanban-shi Shimizu Kôjirô, dated Meiji 39 (1906). Kôjirô has included the soft-shelled turtle's pointed snout and clawed feet, just peeking out from underneath the shell (see p. 36). Suppon turtles (*Pelodiscus sinensis*) have been prized in China and Japan since prehistory for their flavor and medicinal benefits.

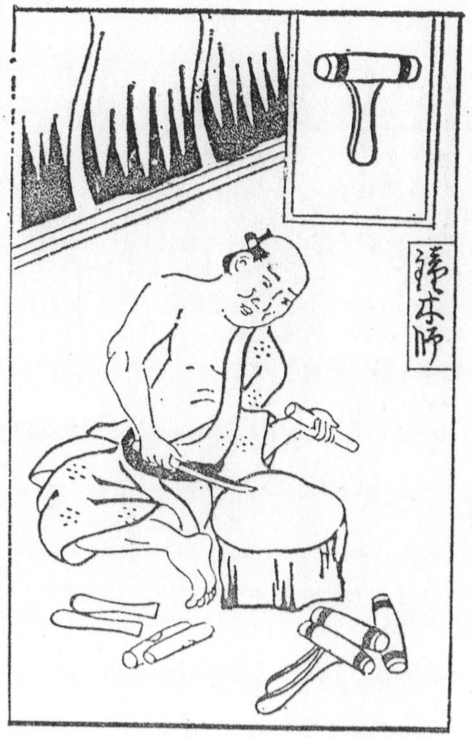

FIG. 5 Woodblock print of a mallet maker and his mokei kanban with a carved image of a mallet. Reproduced from *Jinrinkinmôzui* (1690), 191.

created a kanban for the druggist Higoya Takesuke, purveyor of the drug Shisen tenshinin.[24] In the Kojimachi district of Edo, an inn that was specially authorized to cater to members of the ruling Tokugawa clan commissioned a sign in 1757 by Iseya Kihei that prominently featured the three-leaf hollyhock (*mitsuba aoi*) crest of this powerful family.[25] The only signed example of a kanban done in the sculptural mokei kanban style, replicating an oversized version of the object being sold, is a large pipe and tobacco case (*tabako-ire*) bearing the name Toda Kinhodo Juraku, which is hidden on the interior flap of the large pouch.[26] But without a larger base of examples to compare, it is impossible to gain any true sense of the number of artists who were engaged as kanban-shi, their individual styles, or specialties. And for the most part, they remain the proverbial anonymous craftsmen.

Visual Records

To learn more about the artisans who made kanban, we unfortunately have to turn away from the signs themselves and look for alternative documentation. The *Jinrinkinmôzui*, an occupational dictionary first published in 1690, contains descriptions and illustrations of approximately 450 of the trades, crafts, and professions commonly encountered at that time. The book's simple woodblock prints of merchants and craftsmen not infrequently include kanban. For instance, a Buddhist rosary maker uses his finished product as a jitsubutsu kanban, hanging in rows alongside his noren.[27] A *shumakushi* (mallet maker) has a mokei kanban featuring the carved image of a mallet (fig. 5).[28] A *karuta-shi* (playing-card maker) has a noren bearing the image of the Buddhist deity Hotei happily engaged in this trivial pursuit.[29] The commentaries for these entries frequently provide useful details and insights into various crafts and their practitioners, including the names of individual artisans. There are descriptions for Noh mask carvers, clock makers, miners, hairdressers, sword sharpeners, doll makers, and armorers, as well as exorcists, monkey trainers, porters, fishermen, and pearl divers, among other occupations.

The entry for "Gaku hori," or sign carver, shows an artisan seated at a low table industriously carving out the lettering for a framed sign (fig. 6). The description reads: "Gaku hori: Kanbyaô [the artisan's name, which can also be read as "Kanbe"] works in Takoyakushi, Yanaginobanba [Kyoto], and lives in Nakadachi, Horikawa Street. Kanbyaô also has another location in Edo at Udagawa, Kyohachi 2 Chome." (Udagawa is located just steps away from the Neon Scramble at Shibuya in modern-day Tokyo.)

From the PEM sign of an on-gaku kanban-shi mentioned above, we know that gaku specialists also worked as carvers for kanban and their lettering. Typically, gaku were framed signs bearing the inscribed names of temples or shrines. Placed prominently at the entrance gate, or under the eaves of the shrine itself, gaku were executed with a tremendous amount of skill and dexterity, with some signs obtaining truly impressive proportions. The beauty and power of the calligraphy

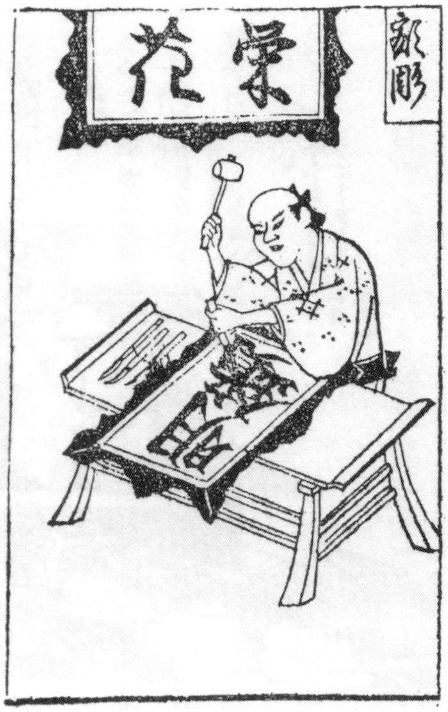

FIG. 6 Woodblock-printed image of a gaku hori (sign carver). Reproduced from *Jinrinkinmôzui* (1690), 176.

were essential elements in creating a gaku. Sometimes the name itself was brushed out by an important priest or known calligrapher, and the gaku hori had to transpose that inscription onto the chosen board for carving. Well versed in carving lettering as signage, gaku hori were also employed in the fabrication of kanban. The word *gaku* can also be written with the characters for "forehead"—relating to their position on the "face" of a temple or shrine. The fact that Kanbyaô had locations in both Kyoto and Edo indicates that he and his atelier carried on a brisk trade and were in high demand. The fact that he was featured in the *Jinrinkinmôzui* also tells us that he was probably one of the more renowned gaku hori working at this time. In addition to his listing in the *Jinrinkinmôzui*, the names of carvers such as Ogi Noto, Momo Kanbe, and Kane Moriko are recorded in the *Kokka manyô-ki* (Ten-thousand-leaf record of provincial flowers) of 1697.[30]

Documents such as the *Jinrinkinmôzui* are important for gaining a better understanding of the activities of Edo-period craftsmen, making them just slightly less anonymous. Although the *Jinrinkinmôzui* is exceptionally important in that it also includes written commentary, a vast reserve of visual records helps to penetrate the world of the Edo craftsman in general, and the creation and use of kanban in their various iterations more specifically.

The craftsman occupied a particular space within the social topography of traditional Japan. Placed below the farmer in terms of his contributions to society, but above the merchant, who was traditionally viewed in leech-like terms, the artisan was valued for his skills and his ability to provide much-needed items that made daily life better or, indeed, survivable. Beginning as early as the twelfth century, craftsmen held a certain fascination for the noble and samurai classes, who depended on them but led lives far removed from them. At this time it became fashionable to commission scrolls and paintings depicting craftsmen of various ilk (or noblemen masquerading as craftsmen) engaged in the ultimate elite pastime of poetry competition. The general term for craftsmen is *shokunin*, or people of skill, and these paintings, known collectively as *shokunin zukushi-e* (illustrations of various craftsmen), lionized the flourishing shokunin as a symbol of peace and prosperity for the age. A craftsman could only practice and excel in his given profession when the country was well governed. Thus, in the heavily Confucian-steeped social order of pre-modern Japan, a successful craftsman implied a prosperous rule or a virtuous ruling class.[31]

Essentially a parody of the well-established tradition of scrolls, paintings, and screens depicting courtiers engaged in poetry competitions called *uta awase*, these images initially did not situate the various trades- and craftsmen in contextual settings but depicted them floating in an open space, accompanied perhaps by some of the tools of their trade, with poems inscribed above that indicated, through allusion, their specific métiers.[32] These paintings were not designed to be accurate socioeconomic studies of the lives of a particular class. So while the idea of the shokunin was valued, the nobility expended little effort in familiarizing themselves with actual living circumstances or welfare. It was essentially a conceptual love affair, but these images do begin to introduce us to the world of the craftsman.

Over time, as the influence and effective power of the craftsmen and merchants increased, they began to commission images themselves. By the Edo period, shokunin were frequently shown in more realistic, fully rendered environments, actively engaged in their trades; these striking portraits were not so much of individuals but of trades and traditions. The most important of these later shokunin zukushi-e is a seventeenth-century example by the artist Kanô Yoshinobu (1552–1640) held in the collection at Kita-in Temple at Kawagoe, Saitama Prefecture. Now designated as an Important Cultural Property by the Japanese government, the Kita-in example depicts twenty-five professions individually rendered but mounted together as a pair of six-panel folding screens (*byôbu*). The right-hand screen includes images of a *busshi* (Buddhist sculptor), *kasa-shi* (umbrella maker), *yazaiku-shi* (arrow fletcher), *kacchû-shi* (armorer), *fude-shi* (brush maker), *kyôji* (Buddhist sutra transcriber), *ito-shi* (yarn maker), *kawa-shi* (leather tanner), *ôgi-shi* (fan maker), *himono-shi* (cypress wood crafter), *tôgi-shi* (sword polisher), *tatami-shi* (mat maker), and *oke-shi* (tub maker). The left-hand screen includes a *yumi-shi* (bow maker), *katana-shi* (sword maker), *juzu-shi* (rosary maker), *banjô* (house carpenter), *mukabaki-shi* (maker of hunting clothes), *makie-shi* (lacquerer), *nuitori-shi* (seamstress), *kôkechi-shi* (tie-dyer), *kataoki-shi* (textile stencil printer), *kaji-shi* (blacksmith), *hataori-shi* (weaver), and *raden-shi* (mother-of-pearl artist).[33]

The images set the craftspeople within their workshops and stores, actively engaged in the process of creating their products. The shops vary widely in terms of sophistication and general prosperity. The kanban illustrated in these images tend to be noren and jitsubutsu kanban. The image depicting the humble umbrella and parasol maker, for example, establishes him in relatively primitive surroundings. His workspace/home is a simple thatched-roof dwelling with a bamboo rush fence and coarse floor matting. It is a family affair. Remains of a meal can be seen in the background, with tools and materials related to the trade strewn haphazardly about the room. While his wife and child mix the glue, the umbrella maker himself is deep in concentration while he adheres strips of paper to an assembled bamboo frame. Two large completed parasols are mounted on the roof, serving as jitsubutsu kanban for his little enterprise. One is a simple umbrella, made of oiled paper to protect it from the rain and elements. The second is a more sophisticated hi-gasa parasol with chrysanthemum and paulownia designs (two crests closely allied with the imperial and samurai nobility), marking it as destined for a higher class of client. The artist has also helpfully included a series of images showing the umbrella in its closed, semi-open, and fully opened positions. In the painting these are depicted on a rack that is placed in what would be the street fronting the shop, so this may actually be another example of a street-level jitsubutsu kanban rather than a simple structural study of the opening of an umbrella.

A more successful business is illustrated in the silk yarn weavers and cord shop, which occupies a finely constructed tiled-roof building (fig. 7). A rich green (new) tatami mat serves as the floor of the workspace and shop. The scene is all of women, engaged in various aspects of production, from spinning the yarn, to braiding the threads, to fanning dry the dyed yarn. Completed skeins of yarn are arranged on the back shelves for sale. The shop is marked by the image of the *tachibana* (mandarin orange tree), which decorates the interior shop noren curtain, done in white, and by the larger banner-type noren in dark-blue indigo across the front, bearing the repeated tachibana design. Though no further specific information is provided or can be gleaned from the painting regarding the identity of this shop, the tachibana was directly related to the

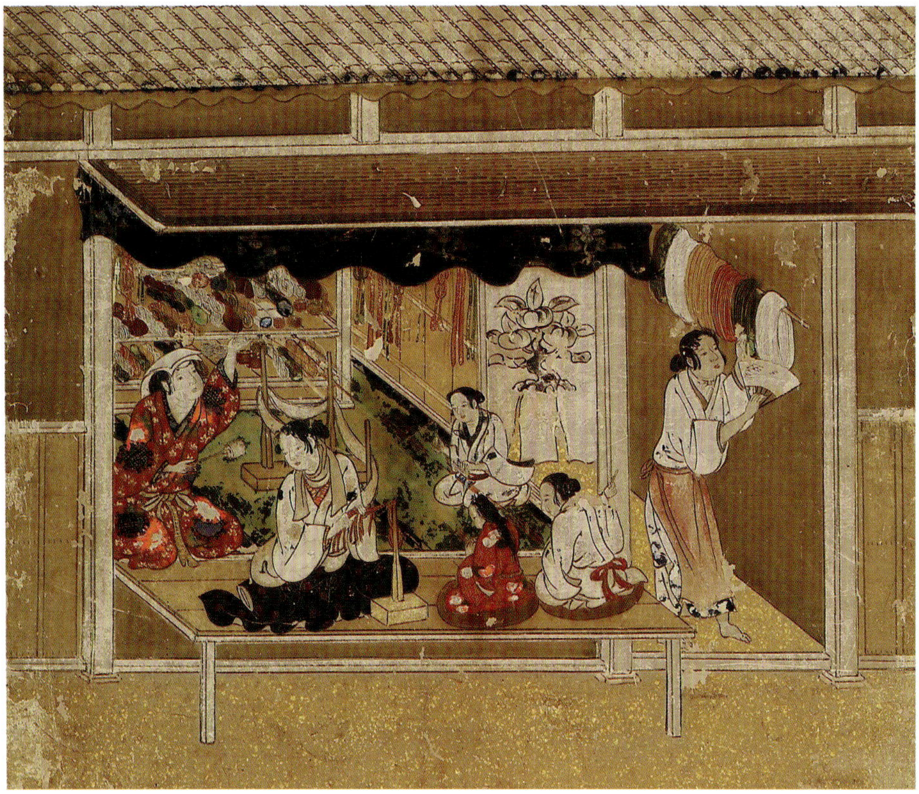

shop name or *yago*, likely the Tachibana-ya. The all-female aspect of this scene is all the more interesting when one considers that *ito gumi onna* (thread women) were frequently an attraction in and of themselves, with particularly beautiful women being employed to custom-plait cords while the customer waited and chatted. Like teahouse girls, certain ito gumi onna became celebrated in their communities as tourist attractions. And woodblock prints were created featuring these lovely *kanban musume*, or living kanban.[34]

An even more thriving enterprise is seen in the shop of a fan maker. This scene, too, is set in a fine, tiled-roof building, with a new tatami mat floor. The workspace is open to the street, as was common, and finished fans in both the *ôgi* (folding fan) and *uchiwa* (round fan) styles are lined up across the front to entice passersby. Fans were traditionally used as personal accessories year round, as opposed to seasonal cooling devices, and fan-shaped, predecorated sheets of paper were frequently purchased unmounted, and then mounted at home by the buyer. In this image, both completed fans and unmounted fan paper can be seen. To the right, the shop's noren is folded up to provide workspace for softening the paper by using a pestle-like weight attached to a flexing bamboo pole. Pounding the still-wet paper softens it sufficiently for application to the tines. As with the parasol maker, the business appears to be a family affair, with the master maker and his wife engaged in the more subtle aspects of the craft, such as painting and folding the fans. An elderly man applies glue to the fan paper, and a child prepares the painted fans for folding. Completed fans already in boxes line one wall. Finished fans in varying colors and designs are arranged on the side wall, serving as an attractive display. The shop's noren bears the image of an ôgi-style fan with a pine tree design, suggesting the yago of the shop might have been the Matsu-ya.

Yago are important to the development of Japanese kanban and, indeed, of modern corporate logos.[35] They represent the early origin of trade names. In their earliest iterations, shops were simply known by the names of what they sold, plus "*-ya*," meaning house or shop. *Su-ya*, for example, indicates a shop that sold vinegar. *Ha-cha-ya* was a common name for a shop selling leaf tea. Symbols and auspicious images were

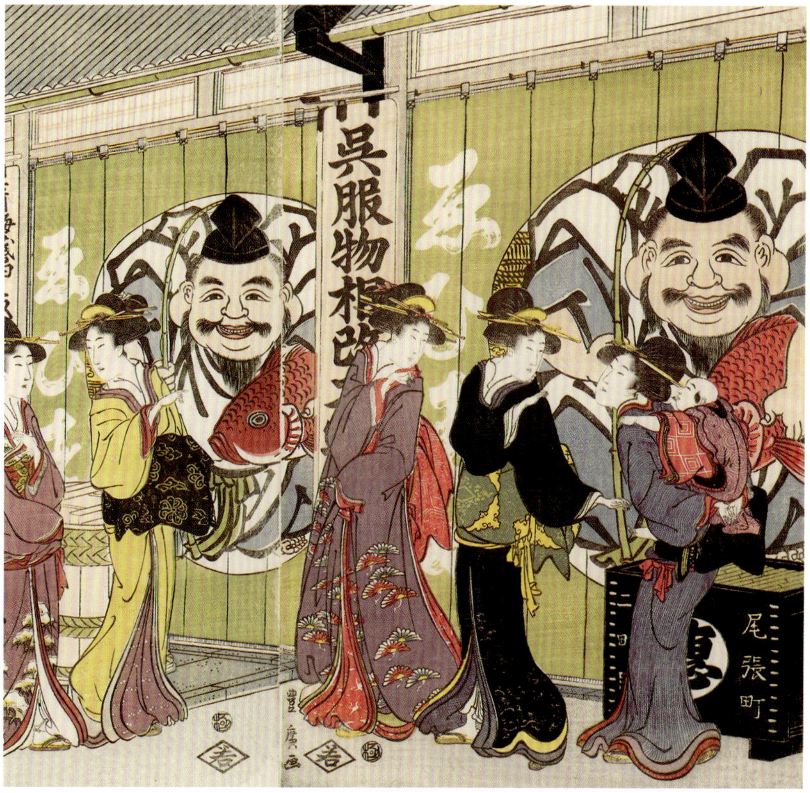

FIG. 7 Detail: Ito-shi (thread maker), as depicted in the shokunin zukushi-e screen by Kanô Yoshinobu (1552–1640). Kita-in Temple, Kawagoe, Saitama Prefecture.

FIG. 8 Detail: *The Ebisu-ya Dry Goods Store*, Utagawa Toyohiro (1773–1828), c. 1800. Vertical *ôban* triptych, woodblock print, ink and color on paper, 15 7/16 × 31 1/8 in. (39.2 × 79 cm). Museum of Fine Arts, Boston, William Sturgis Bigelow Collection, 11.14815-7. Photograph © 2017 Museum of Fine Arts, Boston.

also frequently employed, lending a more specific name to the shop but losing their immediate product recognition. These might have included one of the ever-popular Seven Gods of Good Fortune (*shichigofukujin*) or an established longevity symbol, such as the pine or tortoise. The Ebisu-ya dry goods store, for example, employed an oversize image of Ebisu, the god of daily provision, as its yago, and woodblock prints depicting this store along Owari-chô in Edo feature giant billowing noren with the face of this munificent deity staring back at passersby and beckoning them into this popular shop (fig. 8). In Kyoto the use of auspicious symbols followed by "-ya" dominated. Examples might include *shochiku-ya*, referring to the longevity symbols of pine and bamboo, or *fukuro-ya*, meaning lucky. In the first half of the nineteenth century, as part of a wave of fascination with China and its culture, shops frequently used the suffix *-ro* instead of *-ya*, lending the shop a sophisticated and successful air.[36] The use of yago is clearly derived from *ka-mon*, or house crests for the nobility, with *kanji* (Chinese-style) characters or symbols employed for either their meaning or their phonetic properties.

Scenes in and around the Capital

Rakuchû rakugai zu (Scenes in and around the Capital) is another genre of painting from the early Edo period that helps to shed light on craftsmen and their use of kanban. Typically executed in scroll format or in pairs of six-panel folding screens, these images accurately depict the streets of Kyoto, with its various shrines, temples, convents, theaters, palaces, samurai houses, as well as merchant shops. Originating in the early sixteenth century, these images helped to commemorate and document the rebuilding of Kyoto and its growing prosperity following essentially centuries of internecine conflict that had repeatedly destroyed many parts of the capital and greatly inhibited commercial and cultural growth.[37] Typically depicting the city from a slightly aerial viewpoint, filtered through golden clouds with generous applications of gold leaf and silk brocade borders, the screen format was particularly stunning and impressive to the viewer, truly communicating peace and prosperity.

Seen as an extension of shokunin zukushi-e, discussed above, rakuchû rakugai zu screens are filled with wonderful details that serve as sources

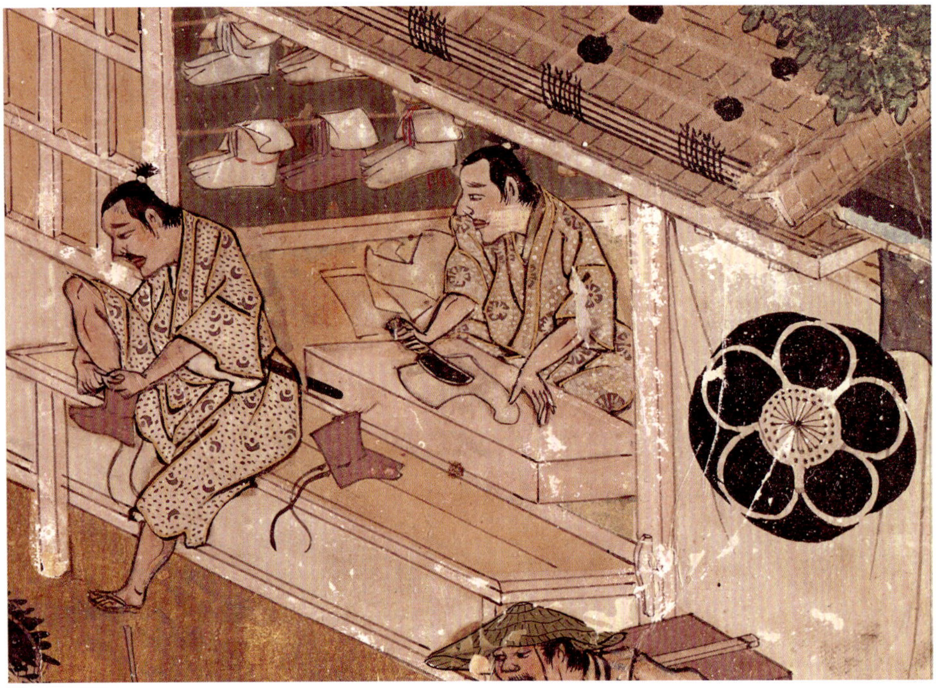

FIG. 9 Detail: A customer at a *tabi-ya* (sock shop) tests the shop's wares. *Rakuchû rakugai-zu* (Scenes in and around the Capital), Funaki screen attributed to Iwasa Matabei (1578–1650), Edo period, early seventeenth century. Pair of six-panel folding screens, ink, colors, and gold on paper, 64 × 135 in. (163 × 343 cm) each. Tokyo National Museum, A11168.

of information on life in Kyoto during the early Edo period—details that are as important as they are delightful. The large format of the screens, which can measure more than 5 by 11 feet (160 by 360 cm) each, allows one to almost enter the picture, tracing streets, crossing bridges over the Kamo River, visiting mountain temples, and witnessing the myriad festival processions that inundate the earthen streets with a merriment frequently bordering on chaos. We can watch children playing, mendicant monks asking for donations for temple rebuilding, builders carrying supplies, noblemen gambling on cockfights, monkey trainers and street entertainers, and an infinitude of other daily goings-on. Though these screens originated in Kyoto, their popularity and the growth of other cities quickly led to analogous interpretations for Edo and Osaka and other urban centers.

The growing importance and influence of the merchant class during this period, with many merchant houses sponsoring the screens themselves, assured that the business activities of the city were related in great detail. Commercial districts such as Sanjô and Gojô in Kyoto are exceptionally well delineated, and we can virtually peruse the various shops located there, eyeing the merchandise being offered as well as watching assorted craftsmen at work weaving and embroidering textiles, stitching *tabi* socks, painting fans, stringing bows, and carving Buddhist sculptures, among many other métiers. The majority of these shops boast noren along their fronts bearing stenciled designs frequently connected with their yago, as discussed above. In addition, we find more sophisticated kanban composed of wooden or paper panels with painted designs of the services rendered.

There are numerous sets of rakuchû rakugai zu screens in public and private collections, both in Japan and abroad. The most celebrated and well-studied are given names, frequently based on the collection they originally came from or the museum in which they now reside. So, for

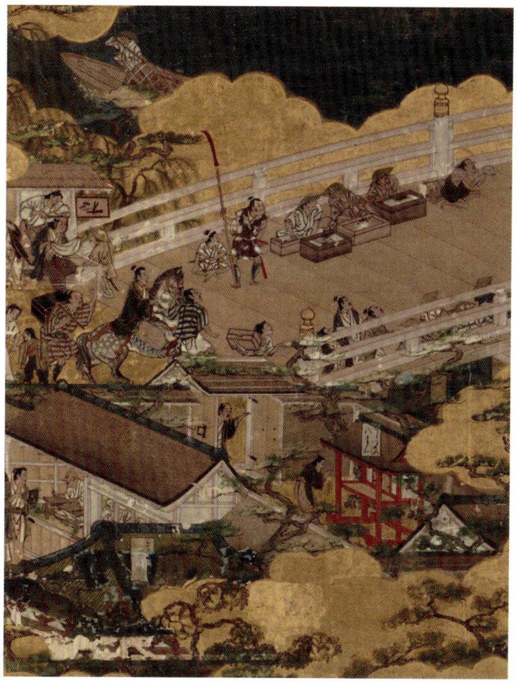

FIG. 10 Detail: *Kami yui dokoro* (barbershop) in upper left corner, as shown in Funaki screen attributed to Iwasa Matabei. Tokyo National Museum.

example, perhaps the earliest documented pair are known as "Sanjô screens," dating to the second quarter of the sixteenth century and held in the National Museum of Japanese History in Sakura.[38] There are the "Uesugi screens," perhaps the most famous of all sets, in the Yonezawa Uesugi Museum. And there is a particularly fine set of screens attributed to Iwasa Matabei (1578–1650) in the Tokyo National Museum, known as the "Funaki screens" because they were formerly in the collection of Dr. Funaki from Nagahama. Designated as an Important Cultural Property and dated to the seventeenth century, the Funaki screens devote an exceptional amount of care and detail to the pedestrians, artisans, and merchants of Kyoto.

In this version are a number of particularly animated scenes and a series of meticulously rendered shops on the western bank of the Kamo River at the foot of the Gojô Bridge. In the right-hand screen, for example, a cord maker engages in a lively discussion with an interested party who is fingering the work; a fan maker wearing a rich red and gold kimono proffers wares to an intent, would-be buyer; a stone mortar shop owner extols the virtues of his product while a customer experimentally turns the crank; a tabi sock maker cuts a template while a potential buyer laces up a pair (fig. 9), possibly to replace the straw sandal he still wears on his other foot; and a kimono shop owner tries to entice a passerby with his lavish product. Shifting to the left-hand screen, we find a potter working a vase while an assistant operates the wheel and, adding to the general diversity of the scene, we find a palanquin maker, a seller of *go* boards, booksellers, scroll dealers, and a money changer.

Most shops can be seen advertising their presence through their noren, with designs of red-capped cranes, pine trees, sacred jewels, and mountains with mist. But at the very base of the Gojô Bridge, a barber is at work, carefully shaving the pate of a customer who is carrying on an animated discussion with a pedestrian who is possibly asking for directions, as his right hand points east across the famous bridge. Above is a kanban with an image of a pair of scissors with a long red cord and a pair of combs. The sign itself is edged in red, with a dark outer frame, and it is suspended from a red cord from under the eaves of the roof line, protected from the weather but clearly visible to pedestrians crossing the bridge or approaching the river along Gojô-dôri (fig. 10). Images such as this one provide invaluable context for the environment in which kanban would have originally been displayed, adding a clear social dimension lacking from a signboard seen in isolation.

Woodblock Prints

Unquestionably, the richest mine for unearthing information on kanban, their makers, and consumers is to be found in woodblock prints. Frequently referred to as *ukiyo-e*, images of the "floating world," these prints often hold as their focus images and subjects taken from the lives of merchants, depicting them at leisure in the pleasure quarters of the demimonde, or before the stage boards of the kabuki theater, and embracing as well other, myriad forms of entertainment and subjects of interest. The world of the Japanese

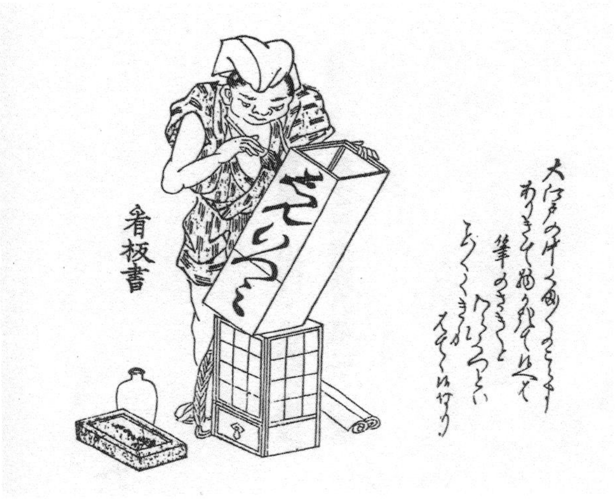

FIG. 11 Edo-period woodblock print showing a kanban-gaki at work. Reproduced from Hayashi, *Edo kanban zufu*, 339.

woodblock print is exceptionally well traveled, having caught the eye and interest of researchers and collectors of Japanese art from the nineteenth century onward. As such, it is also particularly well documented and a boon to explorers of many facets of traditional Japanese art and culture, including kanban.

Woodblock-print artists were frequently interested in the minutiae of life, providing intimate and telling details about their subjects that were frequently omitted from more formal media. These wonderful insights are often revealed through annotations, poems, and textual asides included within the printed image. For example, the simplest form of kanban would have been the *shoji kanban*, in which the name of the shop or product was simply written on the paper panels of the sliding doors opening into the establishment, or paper cutouts of the product sold would be affixed to a door's paper panels. Easily damaged by patrons entering or exiting, shoji kanban helped to spur an entire service industry developed around their repair. *Hako kanban*, written on framed paper boxes that were brought in and out of the shop each day, similarly suffered frequent damage, and early examples are left to us only through the infrequent woodblock print or painting that happened to capture them. Itinerant kanban-gaki would travel from town to town, carrying with them the small tool sets required for the job, making repairs as needed. An Edo-period woodblock illustration of a kanban-gaki shows him with brush in hand, studiously writing script on the side of a hako kanban, rolls of paper and a jar of glue at his feet (fig. 11). The accompanying phonetically expressive and delightful poem reads:

Oedo no nakka kuma guma nokorazu
Arikite mono kakkite tamaeba fudeno sakizakito
Waragutsu towa kottogottoku
Kirehatate soronari

As I travel around back and forth
from Edo and Osaka
writing letters for kanban
my shoes and brush have become worn out[39]

Perhaps the most famous illustration of a kanban-gaki was executed by the celebrated artist Katsushika Hokusai (1760–1849) in his series *Fugaku hyakkei* (One hundred views of Mt. Fuji). In this illustration, a kanban-gaki puts the finishing touches on the calligraphy for the teashop Fuji-ya, his traveler's pack and rolls of replacement paper resting to the side. A recently repaired shoji door panel sits to the side, with a distant Mt. Fuji peeking out from between the latticework of the door's unpapered upper frame (fig. 12).

If the shoji kanban was the most humble, conversely, the most imposing of all kanban would undoubtedly have been the enormous freestanding *tate kanban*. Mounted on posts in the street perpendicular to the flow of traffic, allowing the sign to be read from both sides, rising several stories into the air, and surmounted by a small roof for protection, this type of sign

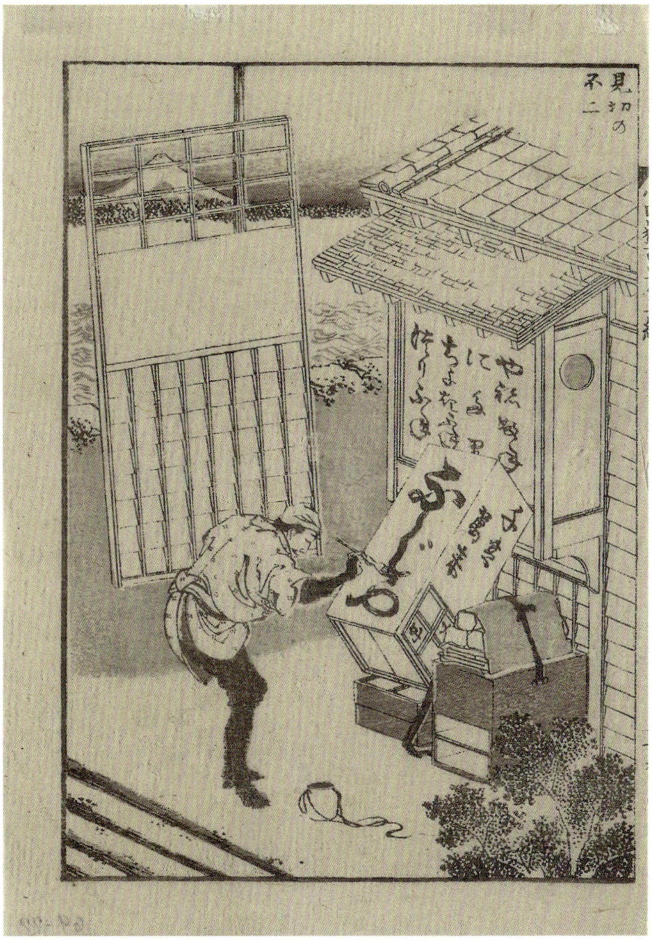

FIG. 12 *Mikiri no fuji* (A limited view of Mt. Fuji), Katsushika Hokusai (1760–1849), c. 1836. Woodcut, 8 × 6 in. (21.1 × 14.4 cm). Library of Congress, 2009615274.

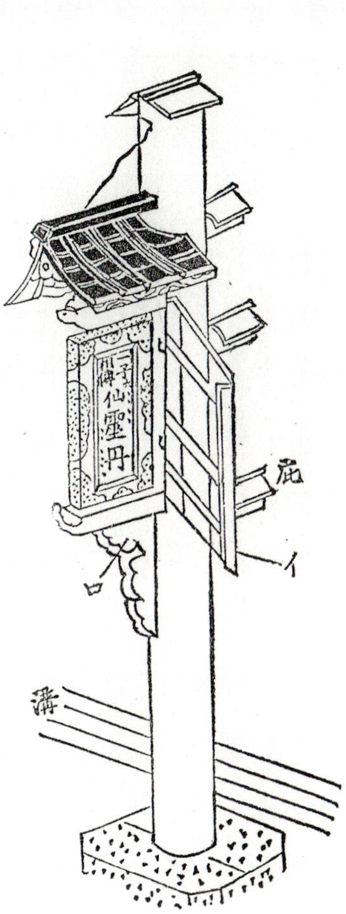

FIG. 13 Edo-period diagram of a tate kanban. *Morisada mankô.*

was usually commissioned by only the most successful of enterprises and could be easily and unmistakably seen from blocks away, creating a prestigious statement about the business and the individual proprietor (fig. 13). Significant sums were invested in the creation of this designed-to-impress form of advertisement. Tate kanban would have been unheard of in smaller Japanese towns or villages, but they were a noticeable fixture along the major thoroughfares in the urban capitals. While the narrow streets traditionally found in Kyoto and Osaka somewhat limited the popularity of tate kanban in the Kansai area, the broad avenues of the Edo commercial districts were especially conducive to this type of display.

Tate kanban were especially prevalent in the patent medicine industry, and diaries and documents of the day stress their architectural qualities. The important Edo-period text *Morisada mankô* (Morisada's miscellany), which documents many day-to-day aspects of life in Edo Japan during the period of 1830 to 1860, notes that even the most basic tate kanban cost upwards of 70–80 *ryô* (approximately 4.5 million yen), and that the more elaborate versions cost over 150 *ryô* (approximately 9 million yen).[40] Even if an exaggeration, these figures clearly speak to the intrinsic grandeur of these signs and the expense undertaken by the sponsoring merchants. By contrast, regulations regarding pharmaceutical kanban dating to 1884 list the following pricing schedule:

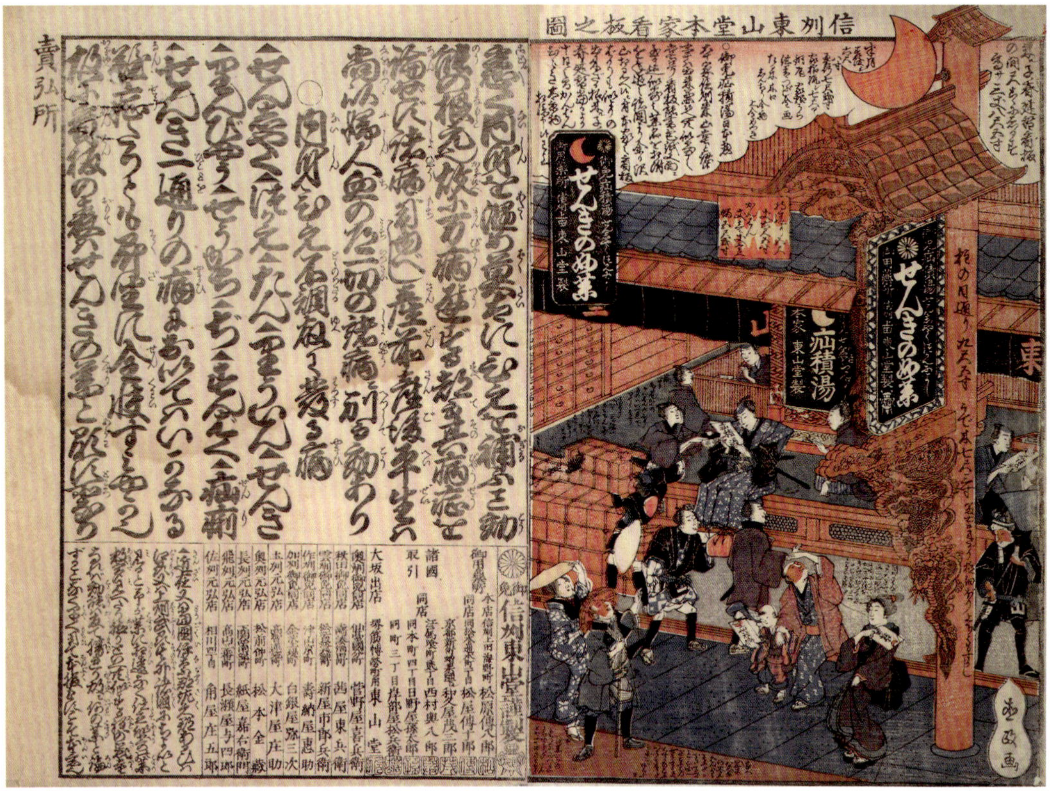

FIG. 14 *Hikifuda* (advertising print) for the Dôsandô (alt. Higashiyamadô) medicine shop in Shinshyû (Nagano). Polychrome woodblock print, ink and color on paper, 13 × 18 in. (34 × 45.4 cm). Reproduced by permission of the Nichibunken (International Research Center for Japanese Studies).

a small kanban (28 × 9 in.; 70 × 24 cm), black lacquered with gilded lettering, cost 1 yen per side. A normal-sized kanban (42 × 14 in.; 106 × 36 cm), black lacquered with gilded lettering, ran 2.7 yen for one side and 4.2 yen for both sides. A more elaborate yane kanban, placed under the roof eaves (43 × 24 in.; 109 × 61 cm), framed with the name of the medicine, cost 7.5 yen and 10 yen for both sides.[41] The exceptional and elaborate tate kanban were truly luxury items.

A woodblock advertising print depicting the *honpo,* or anchor store, of Dôsandô (alt. Higashiyamadô), the manufacturer of the immensely popular (and profitable) patent medicine Senkino myoyaku in Shinshyû (present-day Nagano), features a dramatic and imposing tate kanban. This behemoth of a sign is mounted on a stout wooden pillar rising above the height of the store itself, with a powerful, coiled dragon lurking beneath a secondary, supportive horizontal beam. The top of the post itself bears a small roof. The framed sign, reading, "Senkino myoyaku" just below a chrysanthemum roundel, is surmounted by a tiled roof boasting a second dragon underneath its eaves. Atop the roof is a large crescent moon, serving as an icon for the shop. Below its massive presence, pedestrians stop and gape at its magnificence. One man, holding the hand of a young boy, shields his eyes from the sun as he stares up at its impressive bulk, while in the background, staff at the Dôsandô service customers and tally profits (fig. 14).

Because this is a *hikifuda*, or advertising print, in addition to the bold graphics of the image itself, a running commentary and notations are included in the double-page spread. In tongue-in-cheek manner, comments by passersby show that, while they find the medicine adequate, it is the kanban that is the big draw. Part of the text is also given over to eulogizing the maker of the

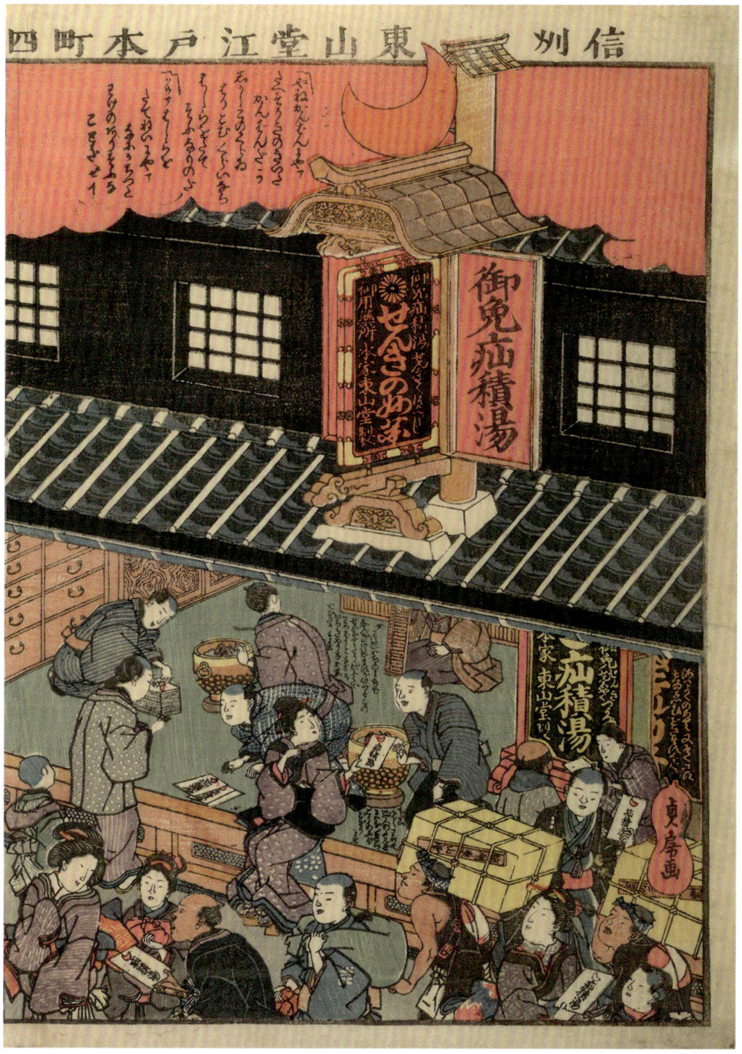

FIG. 15 Detail: *Hikifuda* (advertising print) for the Edo branch of the Dôsandô (alt. Higashiyamadô) medicine shop. Polychrome woodblock print, ink and color on paper, 13 × 9 in. (33.7 × 22.2 cm). Reproduced by permission of the Nichibunken (International Research Center for Japanese Studies).

kanban, Hayakawa Naokichi, a kanban-shi from the Honishimachi section of Edo. Hayakawa, it states, is the best kanban maker around, and he is famed throughout the country for his kanban and gaku.[42] The Dôsandô had a branch shop in Edo with an impressive yane kanban surmounted by the same large crescent moon. A separate advertising print focusing on the Edo branch features a similar spread depicting the shop front dominated by its kanban. In this case, however, people are disappointed that the famous Dôsandô shop would have spent so much money on a kanban that was "only" a yane kanban without a freestanding presence: "Surely there must be a reason."[43] Here, in addition to advertising the shop's most popular medicine, Senkino myoyaku, the kanban features a hinged double face that advertises another key product, Sen shakuto (fig. 15).

This brief survey of some of the visual records related to kanban helps us better appreciate the ways in which merchants deployed these powerful tools. Paintings and prints permit us to virtually "walk" the commercial streets of Edo Japan, to glimpse the merchants and craftsmen at work, to see how their products were arrayed and how their services were advertised. They allow us to better understand the myriad shapes and structures of the kanban themselves, how each style was related to a specific manner of display and method of communication to the potential buying public. A deeper exploration of one particular commercial venue, the Nihonbashi section of Edo, provides an even greater opportunity to see how kanban have played an essential role in Japan's commercial traditions.

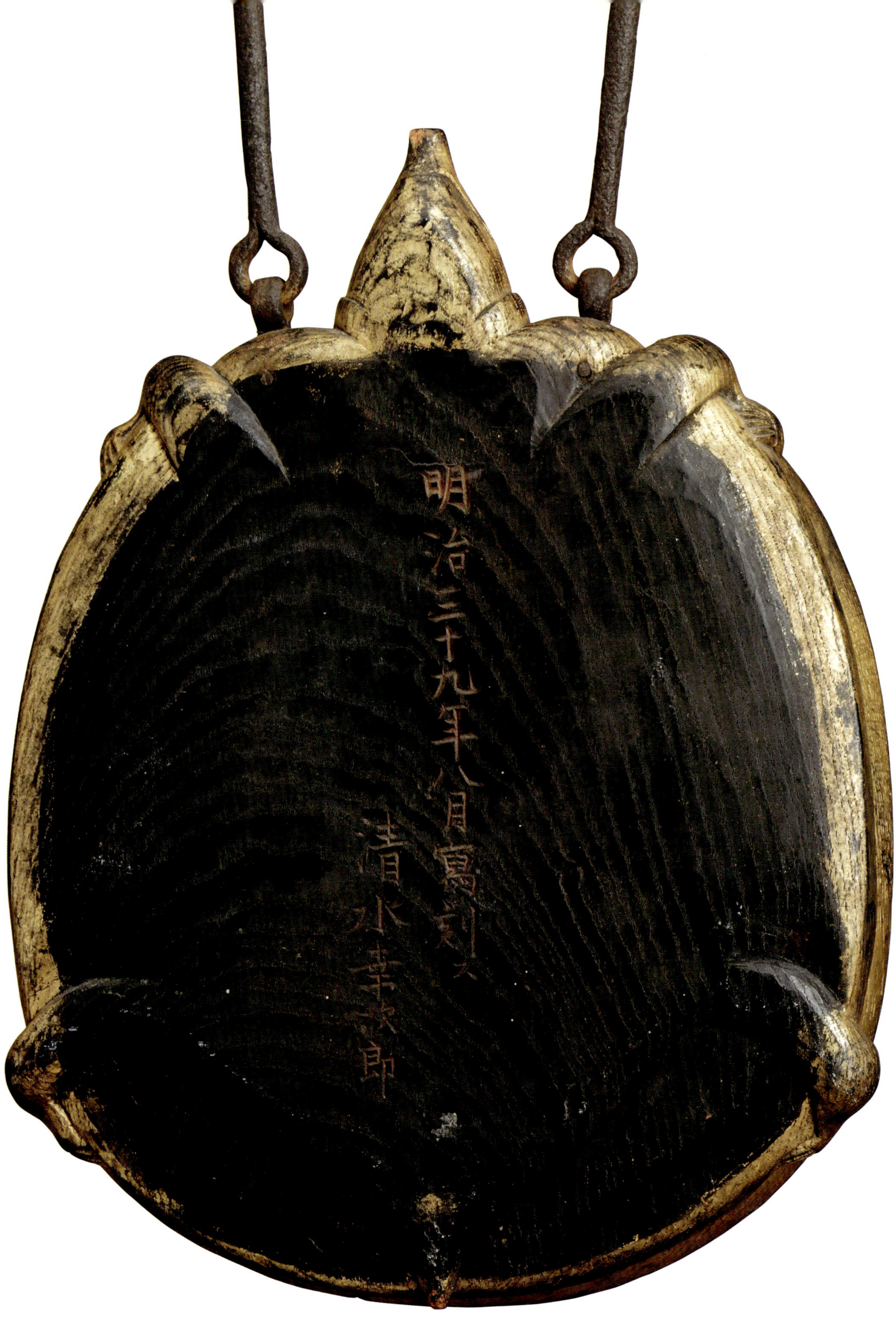
明治三十九年八月寫刻之
清水幸次郎

THE KANBAN OF NIHONBASHI

2

TATE KANBAN WERE THE EDO PERIOD'S VERSION of today's neon jumbotron screens. Their creation and erection would have involved multiple trades- and craftsmen, from the *hangi-gaki* who wrote the calligraphy, to the *kanban-shi* who executed the carving, to the *sashimono-shi* (wood joiner) who made the framework and bases. Other tradesmen would have created the small covering roof and placed and set the post within the street. The unveiling of a new and particularly imposing tate kanban in 1857 might have generated as much interest and excitement as Sony's neon sign did in the Ginza in 1957 or as a particularly interesting new screen display at Shibuya Crossing would today. At least the merchant who bankrolled it certainly hoped so.

One of the more graphic illustrations of an Edo-period tate kanban comes surprisingly not from a Japanese source but from a Prussian one. Following on the heels of the gunboat diplomacy of U.S. Navy commodore Matthew Perry (1794–1858), which had irrevocably opened Japan to the West in 1853, Western nations sought to capitalize on this new opportunity and market. Holland, Russia, Britain, and France soon rushed in. In 1860, Prussia's Count Friedrich Albrecht zu Eulenburg (1815–1881) sailed to Asia, with stops in Siam and China, but his main destination was Japan, where

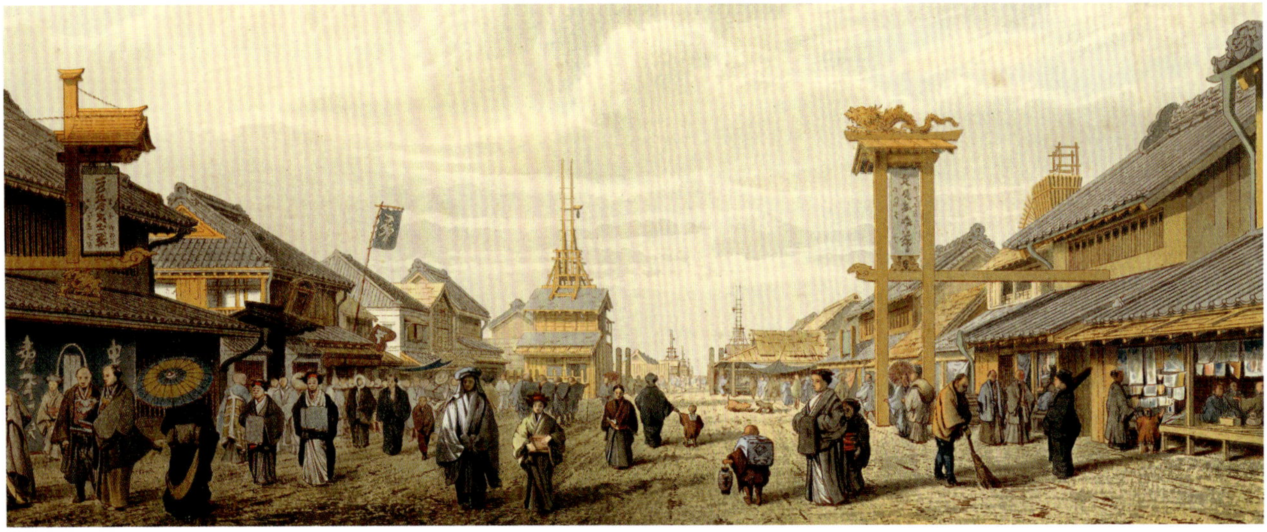

he hoped to secure a Treaty of Amity and Commerce. Eulenburg traveled with a team that included not only marines and diplomats but also geologists, zoologists, botanists, photographers, and artists, all intent on achieving their political and trade goals as well as documenting and collecting both objects and information pertaining to the East.

Albert Berg (1825–1884) was the lead artist attached to the expedition, which also included the colorful and controversial Wilhelm Heine (1827–1885). While Count Eulenburg struggled to secure the necessary concession from the increasingly resistant Japanese government, Berg and Heine worked to document various sites and scenes in and around Edo. Following the successful conclusion of the expedition in January 1861, Berg was commissioned to create a visual atlas of the journey. Over the next ten years he labored to translate his sketches and paintings into a grand artistic document. The final volume was entitled *Die preussische Expedition nach Ost-Asien: Ansichten aus Japan, China, und Siam* (The Prussian expedition to East Asia: Views from Japan, China, and Siam). It consisted of sixty photolithographs produced with the latest photomechanical technology in what was known as an imperial folio, measuring an impressive 22 by 28 inches (55 by 70 cm), issued in a limited edition of 500, and containing commentaries in German, English, and French.[44]

Thirty of the sixty scenes are taken from the expedition's stay in Japan and include numerous depictions of temples, shrines, gardens, and pastoral hamlets. Notably, Berg included two fascinating street scenes. One, plate 3 in the series, depicts the main road near the Akabane section of Edo, where the Prussian embassy was housed in a compound. The other, plate 18, "Yeddo: The Tokaido near the Bridge Nippon-basi," offers a stunning and dramatic mid-street view of the main commercial district, Nihonbashi (fig. 16). Men, women, children, monks, peddlers, beggars, merchants, porters, nobility, and commoners are all shown promenading down the broad earthen road. Shops line both sides of the street, which is depicted in the late afternoon, with heavy shadows beginning to obscure some of the buildings.

While Berg accurately and adequately conveys the hustle and bustle of Nihonbashi, unquestionably dominating the scene is a spectacular tate kanban rising from twin square posts and equaling the height of the rooflines of the surrounding buildings. Atop it rests a powerfully carved dragon, with an undulating, scaled body and gaping maw. It presides over a peaked tiled roof sheltering an enormous vertical sign, nearly one story in height. The sign itself is executed in the shape of a tall cylindrical *chochin* lantern, imitating in some ways the more humble *andon* and *chochin kanban*. But this sign is far from modest. It is so large that it has a lateral support beam attaching it directly to the shop's building.

A detailed scrutiny of the painting also reveals shops using noren, *hatta* flags, and yane kanban

FIG. 16 Detail: "Yeddo: The Tokaido near the Bridge Nippon-basi," no. 18 in Albert Berg (1825–1884), *Die preussische Expedition nach Ost-Asien: Ansichten aus Japan, China, und Siam* (The Prussian expedition to East Asia: Views from Japan, China, and Siam) (Berlin: Königlichen Geheimen Ober-Hofbuchdruckerei, 1864). Staatsbibliothek zu Berlin. Photo by Dietmar Katz. Art Resource, NY.

(roof kanban), among others. But clearly it is the tate kanban that has captured Berg's attention, with its dragon presiding over not only the shop but also seemingly the painting itself. The accompanying text, written by Berg, reads:

> The Nippon-bridge is the starting point, from which all distances of the Japanese empire are calculated, and is at the same time the centre of the commercial portion of Yeddo. All Japanese merchants of note have their offices and warehouses in this neighbourhood. The largest are the silk-shops, extensive buildings of elegant appearance, with long lines of street front, sometimes, as the one on the left of this drawing, consisting of open lattice-work, sometimes open in their whole length and hung with dark cotton curtains. Many young men are busy inside, but no goods are visible, they being only produced at the customer's demand. Visitors of distinction are shown upstairs and treated to tea and sweetmeats. —Upon the blue curtain hanging down over the entrance-door is inscribed the name of the firm in large white characters, while a signboard on the scaffolding above gives a more extensive account of the business. Sometimes these scaffoldings stand outside detached from the housefront, as the one with a dragon on the opposite side of this drawing; sometimes coloured flags are used instead of signboards.[45]

In Japanese, Berg's *Ansichten* is known as the *Oirenburuku ensei zuroku* (Eulenburg print compendium), and plate 18 depicting Nihonbashi is invariably included in publications related to kanban and Japan's commercial history. Although Berg's image is executed with Western one-point perspective and gives a sense of photorealism, his rendering of actual Japanese characters and script is not accurate enough to permit a reading of the tate kanban in question. And although no specific identity has been assigned to the shop connected to this imposing sign, it is generally assumed to be a pharmacy or patent medicine shop. A comparison of this image with the dragon-studded tate kanban created for the Dôsandô in Nagano about the same time suggests that this sign was also the work of Hayakawa Naokichi.

While the Nihonbashi image has legitimately commanded the lion's share of attention over the years, Berg's more modest Akabane lithograph, "Yeddo: A Street Close to Akabane," executed in a less-arresting black and white, also illustrates how kanban large and small factored into many street scenes, and not just the main commercial district. Akabane, where the Eulenburg contingent was housed, was on the outskirts of town. Yet, the short row of shops depicted at the intersection presents a surprising range of kanban types (fig. 17).

Again, using Berg's own description:

> From the landing-place for foreigners a straight road leads to the premises inhabited by the Prussian Embassy during the winter 1860–61, bearing the name of Akabane. . . . The corner-house in front, to the left, is a cook's shop and tea-house; next to it comes a shop, where fans, and another, where playthings are sold, to which the grotesque figure in the street, bearing an axe, serves as a sign-post. Further on are other shops, the contents of which are intimated to the initiated by various devices, as unintelligible to the stranger as the accompanying characters.[46]

The shops in this image are deeper in shadow than those in the Nihonbashi plate, and yet the strong visuals of the kanban for the fan shop, the toy shop, and a bast fiber textile (*asa-o*) shop (not

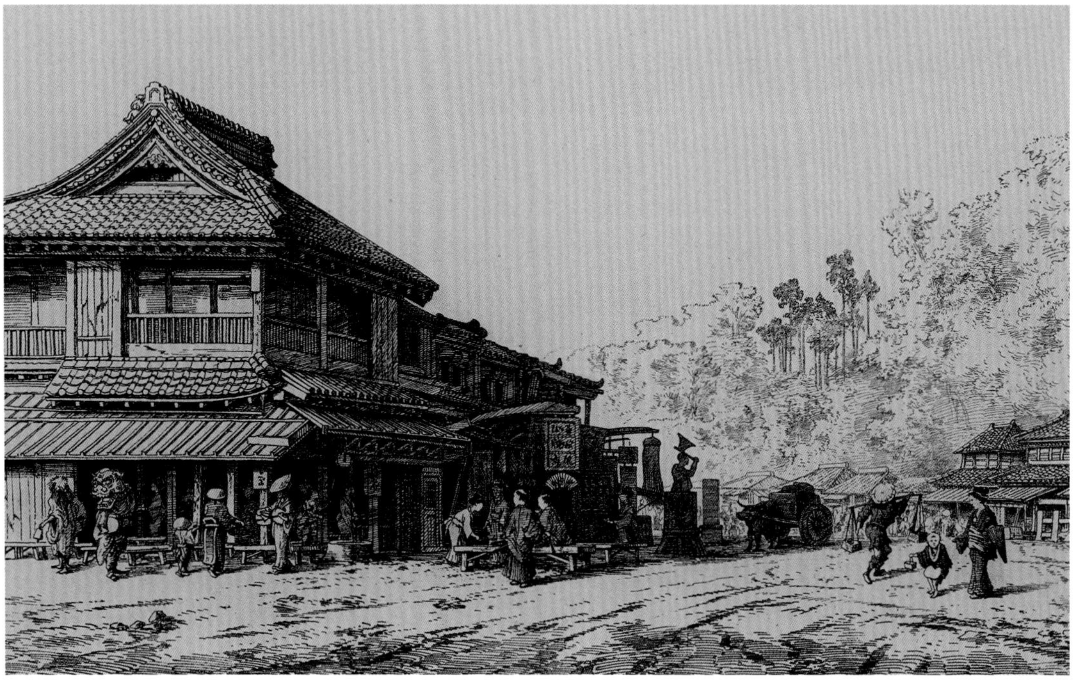

mentioned by Berg) are clearly visible and help to underscore the effectiveness of the kanban in catching the eye and proclaiming their intent, frequently at only a glance. The kanban for the fan shop is suspended from a pole extending from the building. Although the text is illegible, the bottom portion bears a separately formed open fan with its tines detailed by Berg, helping to denote its purpose. The slightly worrisome image of a figure wielding a giant axe is more perplexing, but according to Berg, served somewhat counterintuitively as a kanban for a toy shop—very Grimms' Fairy Tales in feeling. Behind that axe-wielding figure is another sign with a rounded cap and bundled strings hanging down. While Berg admits that he found this image somewhat "unintelligible," this was a common motif historically employed by bast fiber textile shops, which also sold fishing line, palm matting, and twine.[47]

Nihonbashi, indeed, tended to capture the imagination and notice of visitors to the capital, meriting mention in diaries and reports as well as visual documentation in the form of sketches and paintings. This applied to both Japanese and foreign visitors. Prior to Perry's arrival and the opening of the treaty ports, Japan exercised a strict "closed nation" policy, generally referred to as *sakoku*. Within this self-imposed isolation, trade and external influences were channeled through the Chinese and Dutch, who were permitted limited trading privileges. Based on the island of Deshima near Nagasaki, the Dutch operated a robust trade entrepôt and enjoyed a virtual monopoly on goods coming into and going out of Japan. Consequently, most foreign observations of Japan during the Edo period came through the Dutch.

For visitors, travel outside the trade compounds was strictly regulated. An annual trek to pay respects to the shogun in Edo was a rare opportunity to see more of the country. Official Dutch visitors to the shogunal court at Edo, such as Engelbert Kaempfer (1651–1716), Jan Cock Blomhoff (1779–1853), and J. F. van Overmeer Fischer (1800–1848), made special notice in their official reports and private journals and letters of the pressing crowds and merchant activity to be encountered on the streets of Japanese cities and along the roads leading to and from the capital. In 1692, Kaempfer, who was stationed briefly at Deshima island, made the long trip to Edo as part of the official Dutch mission. In describing his entry into Edo proper, Kaempfer recorded:

> At the beginning of the city we rode through the fish market, where a variety of seaweed, mussels, slugs, jellyfish, and fish

FIG. 17 Detail: "Yeddo: A Street Close to Akabane," no. 3 in Berg, *Die preussische Expedition*. Staatsbibliothek zu Berlin.

were collected and sold for human consumption. We stayed on the large central road, which runs through the whole city in a northerly direction, though with some curves. We crossed a number of handsome wooden bridges. . . . Among the bridges is one that is forty-two fathoms long and famous throughout the country, because it is used as the fixed central point from which the distance of all major roads and settlements is calculated. Because of the high esteem in which it is held, the bridge is called Nihonbashi, that is to say, the Japanese bridge. . . . On the main road, which is roughly fifty paces wide and runs through the whole city in a curve to the north, we came across an incredible turmoil of people: convoys of high-rank lords and courtiers, women in beautiful sedan chairs, and among others a procession of a company of firefighters of nearly one hundred men, on foot in European military formation, clad in local brown leather coats as protection against the fire. . . . We saw many fine stalls: those of merchants and cloth dealers, medicine dealers, traders in idols, book sellers, glass blowers, pharmacists, and people crying out their wares. The stalls were in the entrance of houses under the outer roof, and a few were on the street. They were half-covered with a black cloth suspended from above, and the goods were marked carefully with curious signs attached to them.[48]

Following the long-established route of transit from southwest to northeast, Kaempfer had entered Edo along the Tôkaidô highway, the nation's most important road. Upon entering the capital, he crossed over the celebrated Nihonbashi Bridge, marking the start and terminus of the Tôkaidô, and then passed along Edo's most prominent commercial district. Running generally from the Nihonbashi Bridge in the south to Imagawabashi Bridge in the north, this central district was famous for its half-mile (760-meter) stretch of closely packed shops with shared walls and tiled roofs. Kaempfer also documented his journey with sketches, but with much less skill and success than Berg would some two hundred years later. His words, however, are very evocative and allow us to travel down the Tôkaidô and enter Edo across the Nihonbashi Bridge, easily conveying the pulse and vitality of Japan's busiest city.

The Nihonbashi section of Edo was featured frequently in woodblock prints and paintings depicting daily life, symbolizing the vibrancy and commercial wealth of the city. Perhaps the most dramatic rendition is a 40-foot (12-meter) handscroll discovered in 1999 in the collection of the Museum of Asian Art in Berlin. Known as the *Kidai shôran* (An excellent view of our prosperous age), it depicts street by street, shop by shop, the entire length of Edo's Nihonbashi commercial district in exceptional detail. Dated to around 1805, a year before a massive fire obliterated this section of Edo, it depicts the fronts of over 88 houses and stores, illustrating 1,671 individual people, including 1,439 men, 200 women, and 32 children, along with 20 dogs, 13 horses, 4 cows, 2 falcons, and a monkey. Though the scroll was created over one hundred years and several fires after Kaempfer's visit, Nihonbashi had remained much the same, only more bustling and prosperous. While the artist of this impressive work is unknown, it bears a title inscription by the noted Edo-period calligrapher Sanô Tôshû. Interestingly, it also bears the character "*ten*," meaning "heaven," indicating that a companion scroll with the mark "*chi*" (earth) was likely painted at this time as well. In that the current scroll illustrates spring and summer, the second scroll would have likely depicted fall and winter.[49]

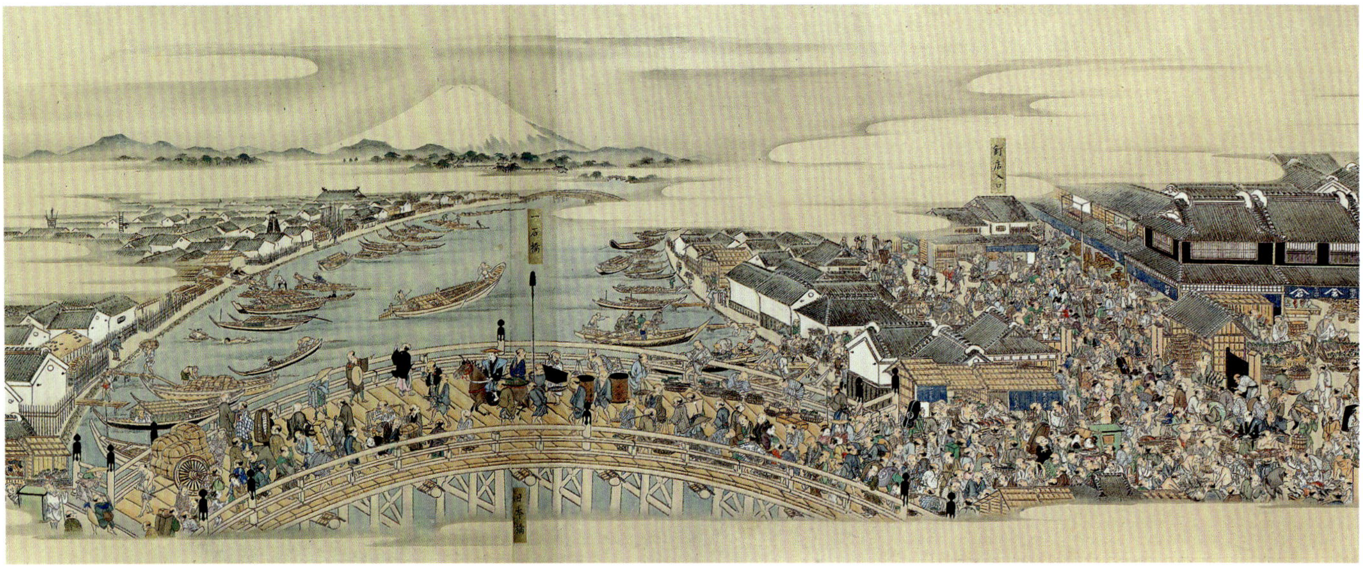

FIG. 18 Detail: The Nihonbashi Bridge, as depicted in the *Kidai shôran* (An excellent view of our prosperous age), Edo period, c. 1805. Handscroll, ink and color on paper, 17 × 485 in. (43.7 × 1232.2 cm). Museum of Asian Art, Berlin, 2002-17. © Museum für Asiatische Kunst der Staatlichen Museen zu Berlin–Preußischer Kulturbesitz. Photo by Jürgen Liepe. Art Resource, NY.

And as Kaempfer so wonderfully described, all manner of shops could still be found there. In addition to the ones listed, the *Kidai shôran* depicts pottery shops, candle shops, stores providing makeup, powder, lipstick, wooden dentures, combs, fans, mirrors, thread, parasols, sandals, dolls, toys, fish paste, tea, sushi, pipes and pipe pouches, raincoats, abacuses, stationery, ink stones, brushes, fruits and vegetables, miso, and candy. It also includes a fascinating depiction of the controlled chaos of the fish market at the base of the Nihonbashi Bridge, precursor to today's famous Tsukiji fish market (fig. 18). In keeping with the spring timeframe, the scroll also shows the famous Jukkendana doll market that spilled out into the middle of the road during the build-up to the March 3rd Hina-matsuri, or Girls' Day. The scroll depicts the shops as Kaempfer described them, with their fronts dressed with noren dyed with specific designs or crests, creating individualized images for the shops and frequently illustrative of their names.

With a vantage point that looks generally west, this significant handscroll offers a detailed broadside view of the shops along the western side of the street, with the eastern shops receiving a nominal outline. Scholars closely studying this image, looking at the positions of the various shops, inspecting the scroll's signage, reviewing the contents illustrated, and cross-referencing other archival documents, have been able to determine the historical names for a number of these businesses. And so, out of the depths of history re-emerge the names and shop indicators of such merchants and artisans as Nishimura Manya Ichibei, proprietor of a Buddhist altar shop, and Takashima Yosuke, who sold writing brushes and ink stones.

Studying the *Kidai shôran* also provides us with interesting information as to how these merchants, shopkeepers, and artisans marketed and branded themselves. For example, Nagai Kôemon, a purveyor of *mizuame* (a thick malt syrup), used a series of concentric circles, like ripples in a pond, for the design placed on his noren. The scroll treats us to a glimpse of the proprietor (Nagai Kôemon himself?) seated at a low table with a large vat of his delicious product, awaiting a customer (fig. 19). The oil-paper raincoat shop of Yamadaya Heizaemon is pictured with workers treating the fabric of his product, and while the small-paneled noren he selected bears no crest, two large kanban hang outside the shop, one protruding from under the eaves of the second story, and the other a tate kanban hanging from a pole mounted directly in the street, with a small shielding roof cover. All of this points to the eminent success and prosperity of Yamadaya Heizaemon's operations. The pipe store of Nakamuraya Genpachi is distinguished by not only his distinctive noren design of the character *naka* with a fan shape but also two elaborate kanban. One is a freestanding four-sided sign known as a hako kanban, featuring designs of his pipes painted on paper. The other is a very large and elaborate wooden sign with a painted and possibly carved image of a pipe on both sides. This valuable sign is shown fitted with a small tiled roof that would have protected it from the elements.

But undoubtedly the most famous and long-lived shop illustrated in the *Kidai shôran* is the Echigoya dry goods store, located prominently on the corner of Nihonbashi and Suruga-chô. Established by Mitsui Hachirôbei Takatoshi (1622–1694) in 1673, this illustrious company is known today as Mitsukoshi. Echigoya was originally noted for its fabrics, which were largely brought up from Kyoto, where the Mitsui family operated an important dry goods store. Their expansive Edo location occupied space on both sides of Suruga-chô. While the name "Echigoya" was a direct reference to the Mitsui family's home province of Echigo, their distinctive crest featured three lines (*mitsu*) within a measuring box surrounded by a circle, serving as a direct reference to their name. This crest can be seen prominently displayed on the long series of noren that starts on Nihonbashi and extends out of sight along Suruga-chô. It can also be seen worked into the peaks of the masonry and stucco buildings. The carrying sacks of two porters making their way east along the street also bear this crest. In addition, the crest tops each of the four tate kanban and one *nikai kanban*, or second-story sign, further announcing the presence of this landmark shop (fig. 20).

When the original shop on Nihonbashi Honcho burned down in 1673, Mitsui rebuilt, moving the shop to the Suruga-chô corner. He also took the opportunity to rebrand the store, introducing a line of affordable textiles accessible

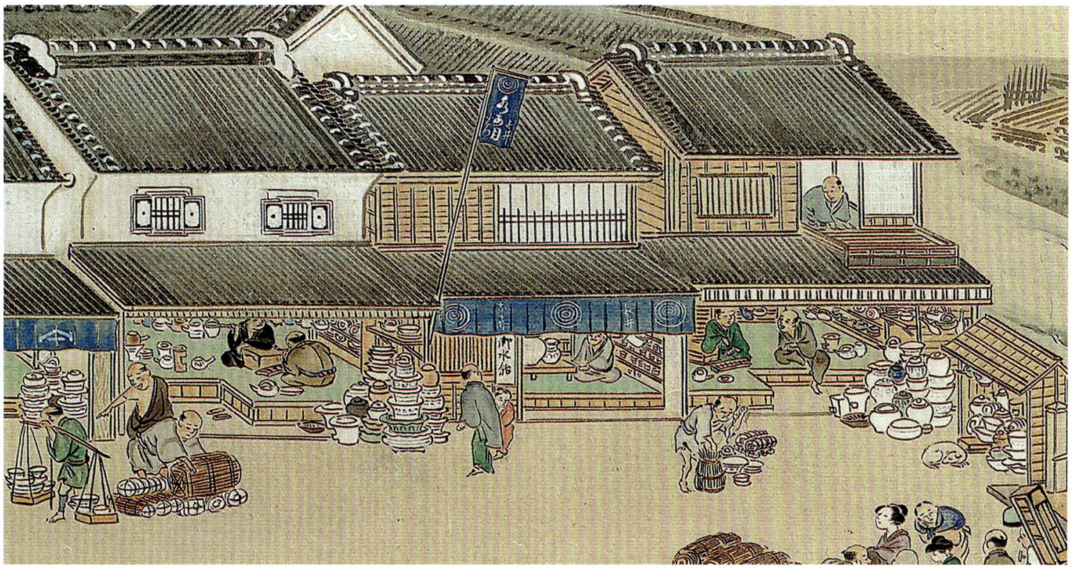

FIG. 19 Detail: The Nagai Kôemon mizuame (malt syrup) shop, as depicted in the *Kidai shôran*. Museum of Asian Art, Berlin.

FIG. 20 Detail: The Echigoya dry goods store located at the corner of Nihonbashi and Suruga-chô, as depicted in the *Kidai shôran*. Museum of Asian Art, Berlin.

to all classes of society, rather than just the nobility or rich samurai and merchant families, and he placed an emphasis on customer service. He also introduced a novel pricing and payment concept. Typical business policy of the period was to extend credit to customers throughout the year, with biannual collection around the O-bon festival in late summer and at New Year's, with only the smallest of businesses dealing in cash. During these festival seasons, customers were expected to come to the store to pay off their accrued debts. While firmly established as a business practice, this greatly hindered operations, and collections and unpaid balances severely affected the bottom lines of most concerns. Mitsui instituted an up-front payment policy, greatly enhancing the business's cash flow and prosperity. Also, it was rare for shops to establish and post prices; sums were traditionally arrived at through negotiation. Mitsui set fixed and visible prices for all of his inventory, eliminating the haggling aspect of the purchase, giving a sense of fairness for all customers, and streamlining the entire process. The new policy, known as *genkin kakane nashi* (cash only, fixed pricing), became a slogan that was prominently advertised on Echigoya's street-side kanban.[50] Other shops soon followed suit, and variations on the genkin kakane nashi model emerged, prefiguring the rise of the modern-day department store (cat. 5).

The study of the kanban of Nihonbashi transforms what might at first glance appear to be random remnants of trade practices into a coherent visual guide, leading us deeper into the individual identities of Japanese merchants from centuries past. Kanban speak not only of business transactions and product manufacture but also of a commercial milieu with deep roots and fascinating offshoots that lead to a broader understanding of Japan's celebrated merchant culture itself.

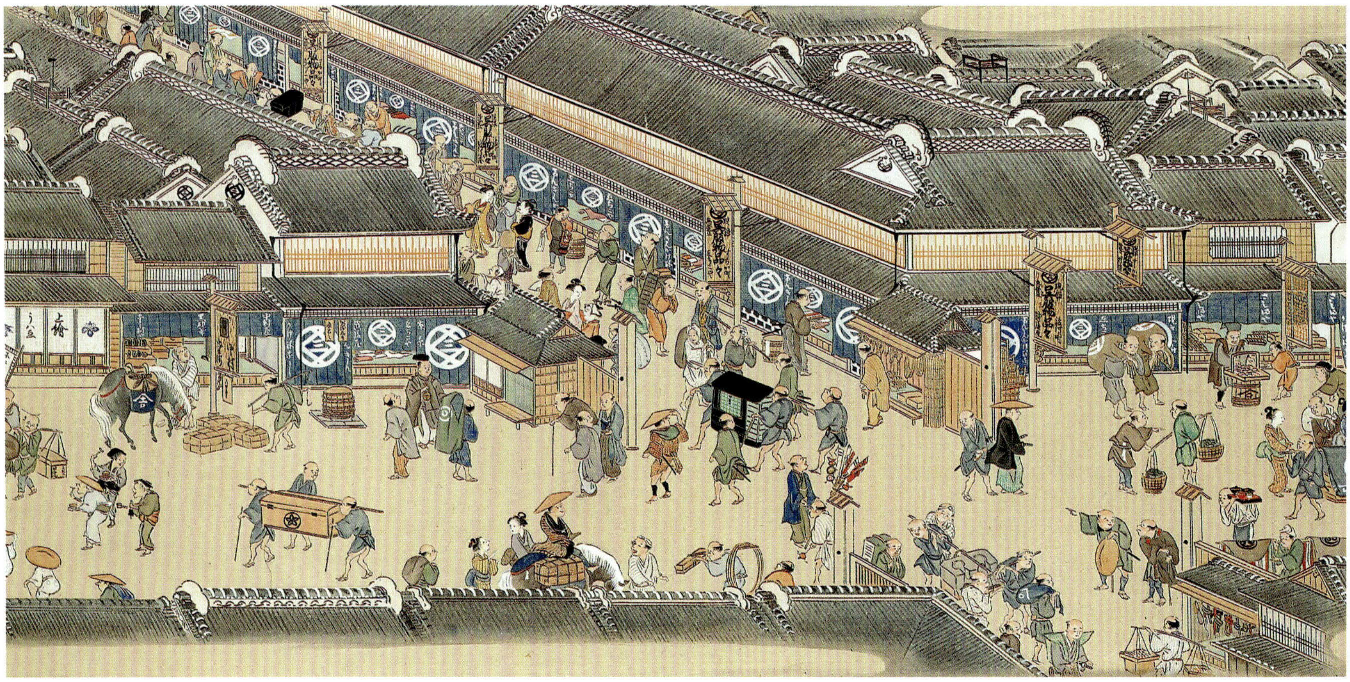

5

Shitta kanban for dry goods store with "fair pricing" slogan

Early nineteenth century

Wood, ink, metal fittings

68 × 20¾ in. (172.7 × 52.7 cm)

Private Collection

The kanban proved to be a versatile medium for communicating to potential customers. Here, a massive slab of keyaki (zelkova elm) announces, *"Genkin shohuda dokoro"* (Cash only, fair pricing), a slogan commonly employed by dry goods stores. This was a variation on the phrase *"Genkin kakane nashi"* (Cash only, fixed pricing), first introduced in the late seventeenth century by the hugely successful Echigoya dry goods store on Nihonbashi. The practices of Echigoya and the stores that closely emulated it anticipated those of the modern-day department store.

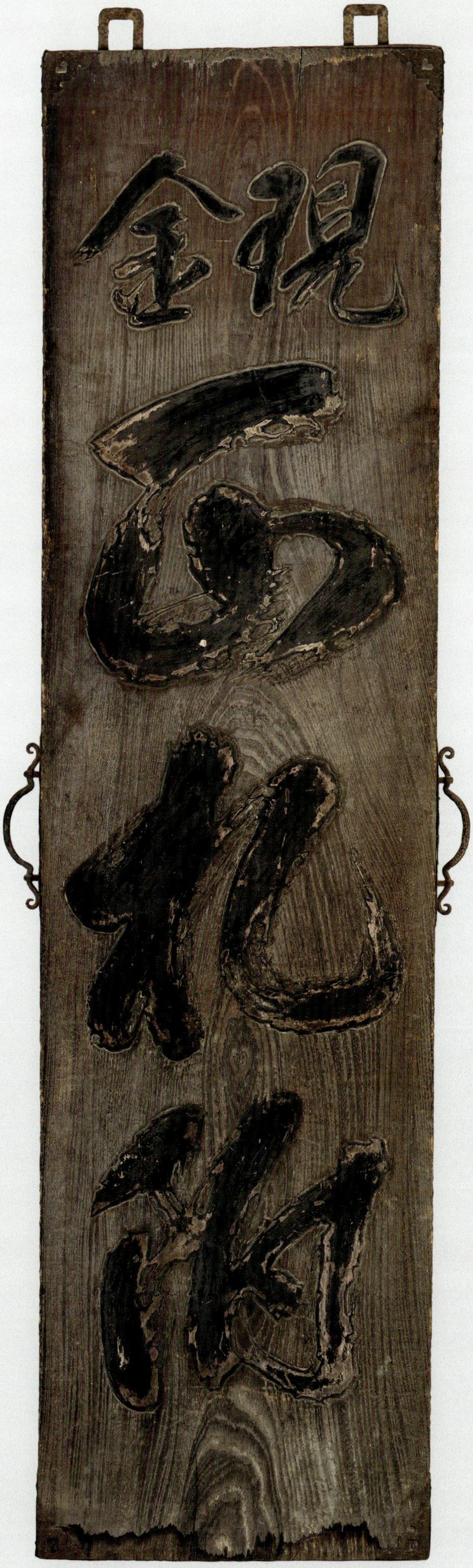

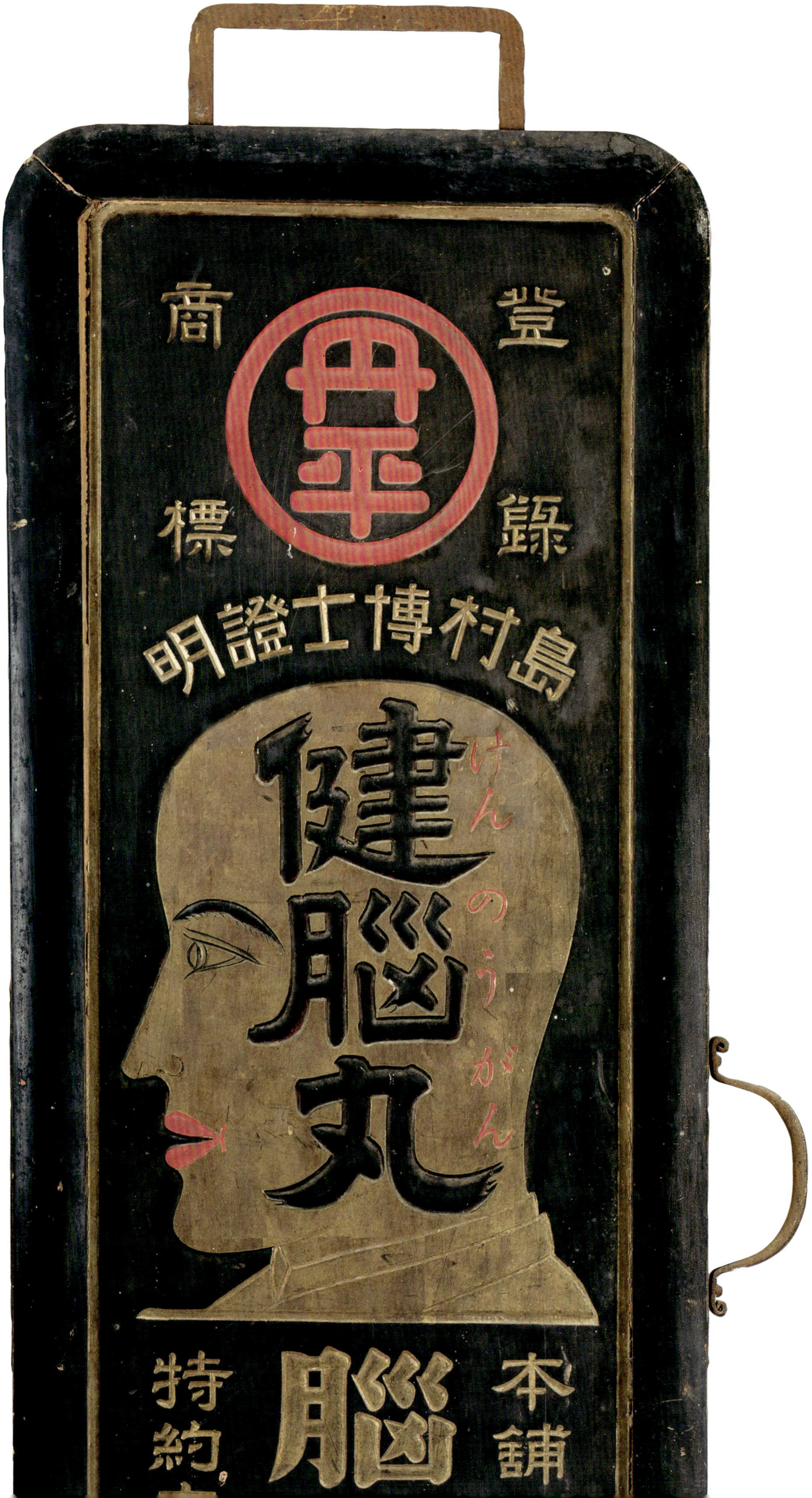

登錄商標
島村博士證明
健脳丸
けんのうがん
本舗
脳
特約

THE WAY OF THE MERCHANT

3

THE HISTORY OF JAPAN DURING THE EDO PERIOD is frequently described in terms of the rise of the merchant class (*chônin*) and its tastes and proclivities: from the growth of inter-region trade and the development of important infrastructure, to the efflorescence of the kabuki theater and the demimonde of the courtesan, to the veritable explosion of popular literature and the woodblock print as modes of social and artistic expression. Much has been written of the wealth accumulated by the rice and timber merchants, the moneylenders, the founders of great trade houses, the sake brewers, the copper kings, the cotton brokers, and any number of other economic avenues and the individuals who pursued them, rising to the apex of the financial pyramid by profiting from the various trends and vicissitudes of the period. Much has also been written of the social and political push back as the ruling classes tried to cling to their authority and power. Tending to view the economic and cultural pulses of their world through suspicious eyes, they cast the merchant into a role defined as exploitative and adventurist rather than beneficial to the land and its people. "The offspring of a toad is a toad; the offspring of a merchant is a merchant" was a frequently posited saying in Edo-period Japan, reflective of this bias.

An 1816 account by an anonymous "retired gentleman" writing under the nom de plume Buyô Inshi, entitled *Seji kembunroku* (Matters of the world: An account of what I have seen and heard) clearly reflected this negative attitude toward the merchant class. The author attributes the perceived slow demise of proper values and governance to the rise of the merchant class, stating:

> Merchants are people with no steady livelihood and without a steady mind. Their status is low to the extreme, and they are inferior to warrior houses, farmers, and all others. They make a living by stealing a profit from the process of buying and selling. In the course of more than two hundred years of peaceful government, the profits that they have embezzled have accumulated to such an extent that nowadays the financial means of the townspeople have become vast. There is a limit to the financial capacity of warriors, who offer their lives for the state. Farmers pay a large portion of their harvest, won by hard work in cold and hot weather, in annual land tax; they perform corvée labor, produce various kinds of goods, mingle with soil and excrement, and suffer all the hardships of the world. An artisan can only earn so much in a day's wages, and it is impossible for him to exceed that limit. For a merchant there is no such limit. His earnings depend solely on the profit he gains and on the extent of his greed. He is not affected by wind, flood, or drought, and he has no service obligations. Surely, he enjoys the greatest freedom of any in our world.[51]

Posted regulations (*ofurigaki*) attempting to moderate and guide nearly all aspects of commoner living constantly flowed from the governmental authorities, who were horrified by the tectonic shifts that were skewing the economy in favor of a class they saw as contributing nothing to the overall well-being and betterment of the world. Signposts along the major highways, written in easy-to-read hiragana script, declaimed: "*Mi no hodo wo shire!*" (Know your station in life!).[52] But the tide of history was truly against them, and officials were engaged in the futile effort of putting a legislative lid on an economic pot that was boiling over.

The social structure of Edo Japan was aptly reflected in the phrase *shinôkôshô*—referring to the Confucian-steeped hierarchical order of samurai-peasant-artisan-merchant. The ruling classes of samurai and nobility were imputed with the highest social worth, contributing most to the governing of society and providing a model of education and refinement. Farmers ranked second for laboring long and hard to provide essential foodstuffs and fulfilling needs basic to society and survival. Artisans fell into an awkward third rank—less noble and valuable to society than the farmer, but through skill and industry providing much-needed items desirable and even essential to the comfort and functioning of the population at large. Merchants were placed at the bottom, officially perceived as creating nothing and providing nothing of need or merit. They were described as *yûmin* (idlers), succubae that only ate away at society, perverting and corrupting.

An early Edo object lesson in this regard was the Yodoya House of Osaka, which garnered a truly vast fortune brokering the taxes paid in rice and received by the *daimyô* (landed samurai nobility). Yodoya Tatsugorô was instrumental in establishing the original rice market in Osaka, volunteering his warehouses on the banks of the Tosabori River to serve as the center of the exchange in 1681. To facilitate access, he had a bridge built leading directly to his compound, and it became known as the Yodoyabashi. The Yodoya family, through its wealth, influence, and connections, also involved itself aggressively in the lumber and construction industries, with a profitable sideline engaging in the silk trade from

China. However, in 1705 the government seized all of the Yodoya assets, citing the fact that the fifth-generation head of the family, Yodoya Saburôemon, lived a life far too extravagant for one of his lowly position. Saburôemon, who was only nineteen years old at the time, was noted for riding around in palanquins normally reserved for nobility, smoking silver pipes, and expending lavish sums courting a *tayû* (top-ranked courtesan) named Azuma from the Ibaragiya House in Shinmachi.[53] Conveniently, by stripping the Yodoya clan of its money, property, and position within the Edo economic food chain, the authorities also eliminated the tremendous debt burden of the government and individual members of the samurai class to the Yodoya family. As a result, the Yodoya name became virtually synonymous with conspicuous consumption and indelicate flaunting of wealth.[54] Interestingly, this cautionary tale would later be completely inverted, and Yodoyabashi would itself become a symbol of quality among merchants of tobacco-related products, particularly *tabako-ire* (tobacco pouches), in the late Edo and early Meiji eras (page 89).

But merchants had their own views and perspectives. Many of the most successful business leaders that government officials and critics aggressively decried perceived of their role and function in society in completely different terms. They, too, eschewed and condemned the greed and excess that so irked the samurai elite, behavior that only served to emphasize the vast gap between the highest and lowest levels of society. Many of the great merchant houses that

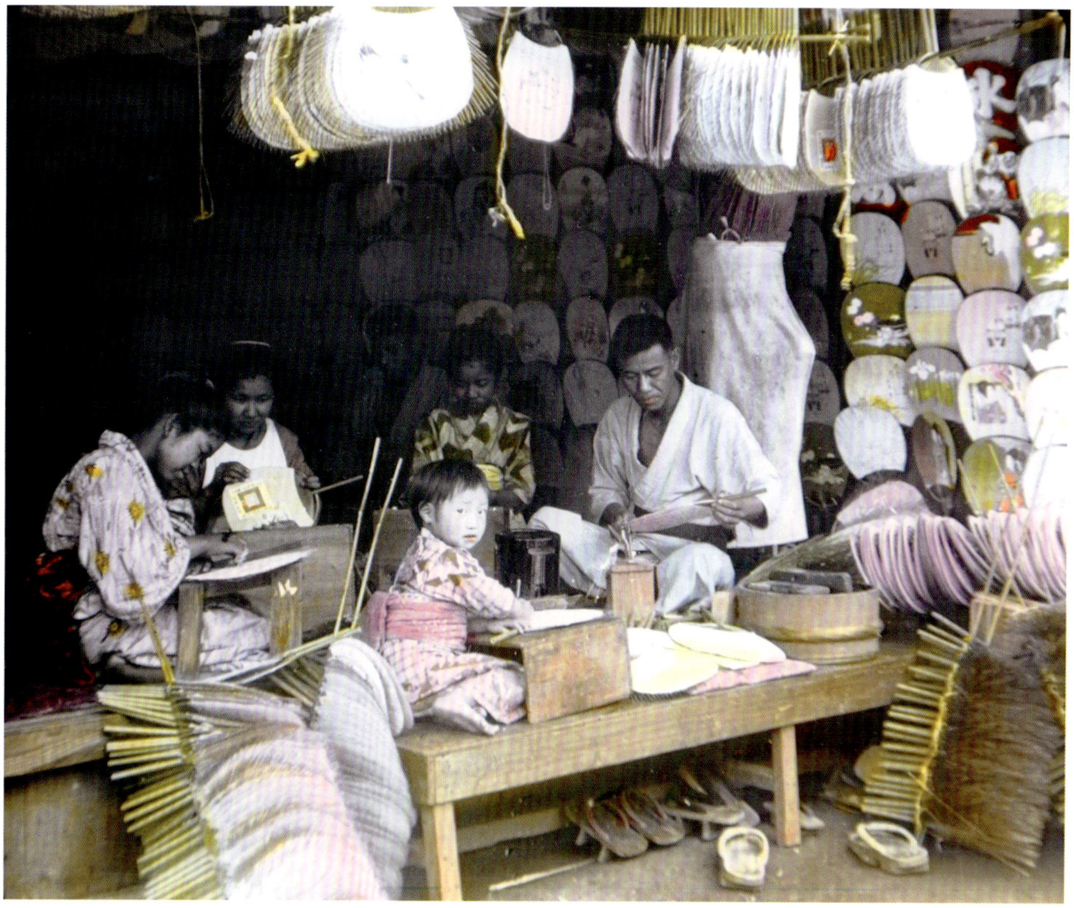

FIG. 21 A fan merchant. Archival photograph. Peabody Essex Museum.

FIG. 22 A line of shitta moji kanban announces the presence of doll shops on the street approaching Kiyomizu Temple in Kyoto. Archival photograph. Peabody Essex Museum.

flourished under the prolonged peace of the Edo period created stringent management systems for their financial fiefdoms. Frequently they established *kakun* (house codes) to govern the behavior of their successors and *tensoku* codes that were directed toward employees. These stated principles tended to espouse the value of hard work, frugality, obedience to the government, and attention to the reputation of the house.[55] Documented kakun exist for a wide variety of Edo-period businesses, ranging from the Shirokiya retailer headquartered in Edo, to the Mizuguchiya dry goods store in Nagoya, to the Enoguya drug store of Osaka and the Suminokura shipper based in Kyoto.

The world's longest continuously operating company was the Japanese construction firm Kongô Gumi. Founded in the year 578 by Kongô Shigemitsu, one of three Korean immigrants brought over to aid in the construction of Shintennô-ji in Osaka, Kongô Gumi operated uninterruptedly through fifty generations until

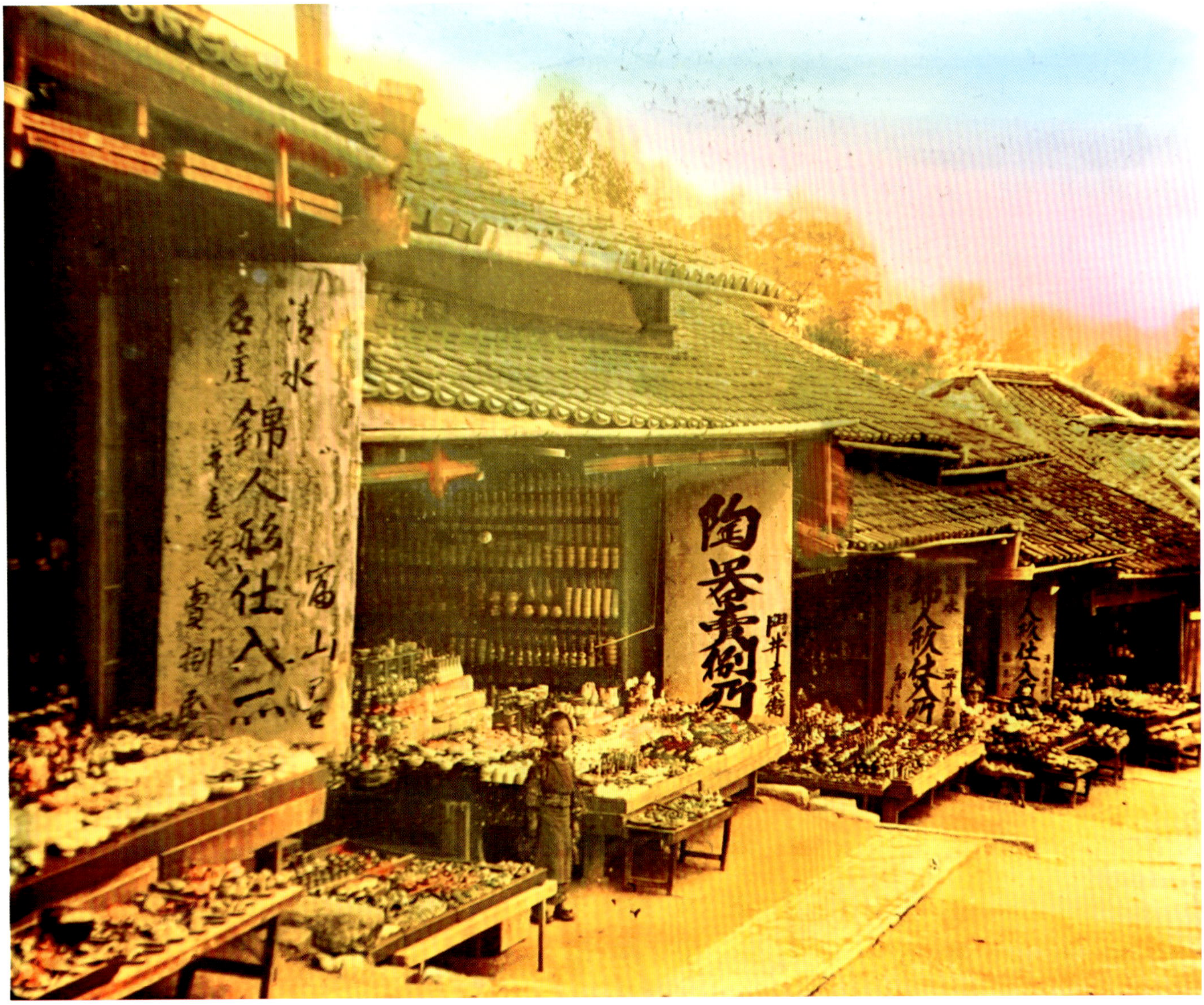

its unfortunate financial collapse in 2006, at which time it was bought by the construction behemoth Takamatsu. During the Edo period, the company's thirty-second-generation leader, Kongô Yoshisada, composed a will that included a kakun addressed largely to those who would follow him for generations to come. This kakun, referred to as the "Shokuke kokorenokoto," included sixteen points, ranging from an exhortation to listen to the customer, advice for carpenters to practice their training diligently, counsel not to drink alcohol too much, and admonition to dress according to station, speak politely, and submit honest bids. In summarizing the motto, Yoshisada wrote: "Have filial piety, needless to say, inherit the reputation of the family, take a wife, have children and educate them properly. Live long and follow Buddhism and Shintoism. . . . Receive the Buddha's blessings and attain enlightenment. It is important to look forward to the next life."[56] His statements would have rung true for the samurai nobility and governing Confucian elite as well as for his fellow merchants.

The Okaya Sasaya hardware store was founded in 1699 by Okaya Sôsuke Muneharu in the Teppo-chô area of Nagoya. The oft-quoted Okaya code stressed frugality as well as devotion to parents, attitudes that were in direct harmony with prevalent Confucian-based morality. But Okaya also stressed the legitimacy and fundamental "trueness" of the life of the merchant.[57] The Okaya kakun reads: "Samurai study martial arts and work in government. Farmers till their land and pay their taxes. Artisans labor at their family industries and pass on to their children family traditions. Merchants have trading as their duty and must trade directly and honestly. Each of the four classes has its own Way and that Way is the true Way."[58] Okaya was acknowledging an implicit "Way of the Merchant," equal in validity to the venerated "Way of the Samurai."

Nakai Ryosuke Genzaemon (1716–1805) began his career as an itinerant medicine peddler but quickly expanded into financing as well as sake, vinegar, and *shôyu* production. His astute sense of business allowed him to accumulate 87,255 *ryô* (approximately 9 billion yen) over his lifetime. Nakai famously published a family motto that he hoped would influence his heirs and set a moral tone and model for society at large. Nakai stated:

> Many people say that those who become rich are lucky. Saying, "I am not rich because I am unlucky" is silly and wrong. If we want to be rich, we should not expect fortune and there is no way to accumulate wealth, except to forbid excessive spending, to try and stay healthy, to practice thrift and to work hard at business. If we become greedy, our ancestors won't save us and we will violate the mind of the Deity. To be thrifty and to be mean are different. Ignorant people think there is no difference, but a mean person cannot provide sparkle. The sparkle of a person who has practiced thrift based on honesty can bring light to a great number of people and places.[59]

Economic ethics formed a solid creed for Nakai's modest but profitable empire. In his view, these ethics benefitted not only the house fortunes but also society at large. Nakai's "sparkle" carried an almost religious tone, and it was indeed closely allied with the Buddhist concept of *intoku*, which emphasizes anonymous philanthropy and economic virtue. And in this, Nakai echoed other merchants and some Neo-Confucian moralists.

Ishida Baigan (1685–1744), for example, founded an influential school of thought in the early eighteenth century known as Sekimon Shingaku (Heart-Mind Learning) that fused orthodox Neo-Confucian ideals with Buddhist and Shinto moral codes. To this he appended a merchant-friendly gloss countering government dispersions against the merchant classes by arguing for their fundamental importance and value to society. Ishida provided a philosophical

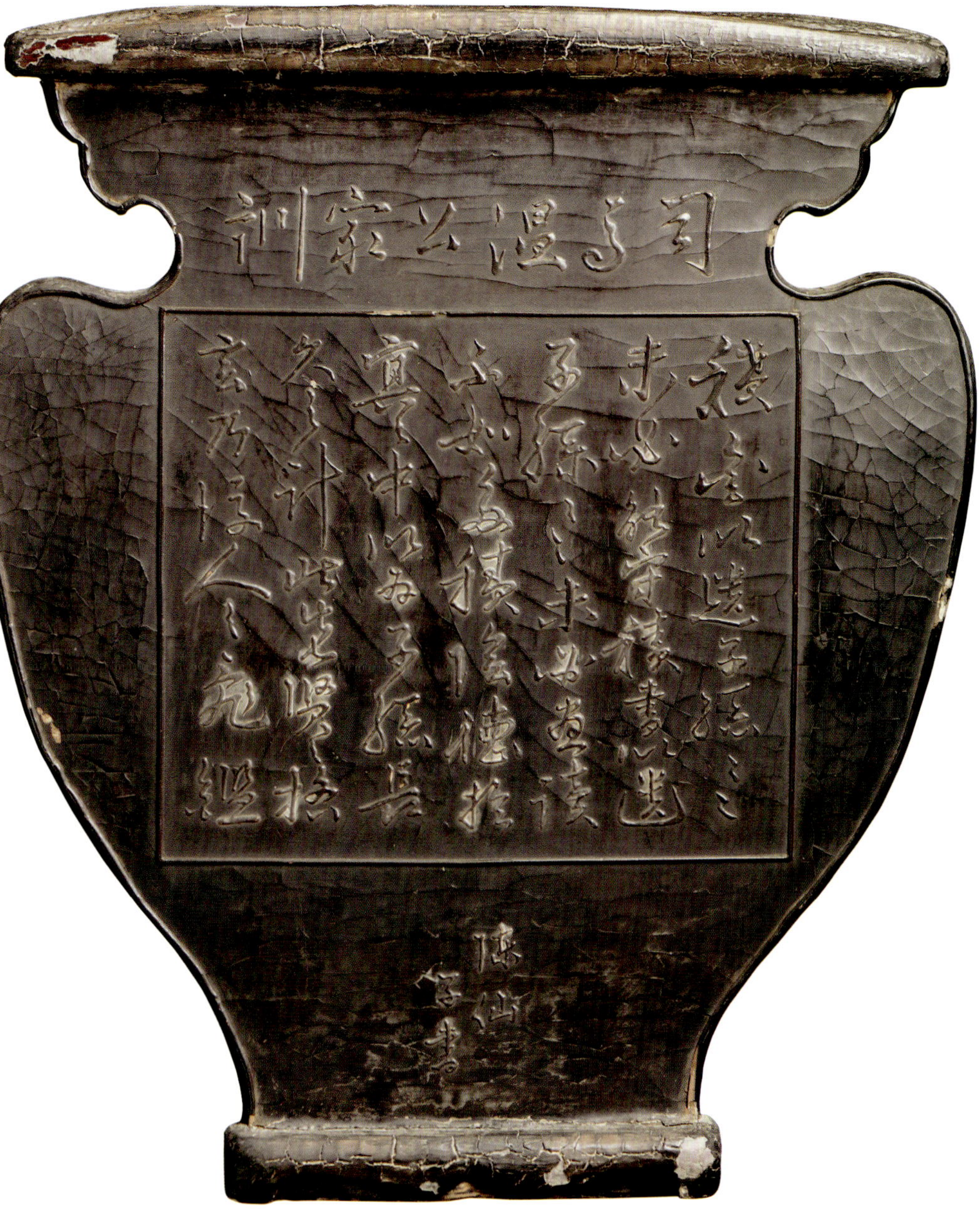

6

Yôki kanban for tea leaf shop

Nineteenth century

Wood, lacquer, ink

27 × 22½ × 2¼ in. (68.6 × 57.2 × 5.7 cm)

Private Collection

A kanban could be placed outside a shop to attract customers, or it could be situated deep within the interior to communicate messages to dedicated customers or staff members themselves. Here, a magnificent yôki kanban for a tea leaf shop bears a kakun (house code) in raised lettering, reading: "Accumulating wealth to pass on does not guarantee your descendants will have the sense to use and defend that wealth. Accumulating knowledge to pass on does not guarantee your descendants will have the wisdom or intelligence to make use of it wisely. If you would like to create a good world for your descendants, work for the people of the world you are in, accumulating good deeds and benefits that cannot be measured or counted. This is the foundation of your children's happiness."

framework for merchants, allowing them to reposition themselves within the social hierarchy; as a result, Sekimon Shingaku became a touchstone for many merchants during the Edo period.

Although the majority of preserved kakun come from such illustrious trading houses as Mitsui, Sumitomo, and Tomiyama, individual businesses intent on preserving family success, inculcating values to the next generation, and functioning as moral members of society also developed kakun. An exquisite yôki kanban in the shape of a tea container is embellished overall with a kakun for an unknown purveyor of tea, written in dense, staccato characters. It reads:

> Accumulating wealth to pass on does not guarantee your descendants will have the sense to use and defend that wealth. Accumulating knowledge to pass on does not guarantee your descendants will have the wisdom or intelligence to make use of it wisely. If you would like to create a good world for your descendants, work for the people of the world you are in, accumulating good deeds and benefits that cannot be measured or counted. This is the foundation of your children's happiness.[60]

A kanban such as this would have hung in the shop, serving as a private reminder to those who worked there of the values the business stood for, as well as communicating to customers the moral basis upon which the business was built, again projecting a particular image to the public (cat. 6).

As shown here, kanban reflected various aspects of Japanese merchants themselves, their values, principles, and aspirations. Not necessarily restricted to the physical walls, eaves, and support posts of shops, many kanban were designed to be portable, with metal handles attached to their sides. Ambulatory hawkers would parade through the streets, kanban in hand, singing the praises of a certain patent medicine or boasting of the quality of an item of clothing. And savvy merchants with means and access also used their kanban to tap into Edo Japan's most potent channel of mass communication—the theater.

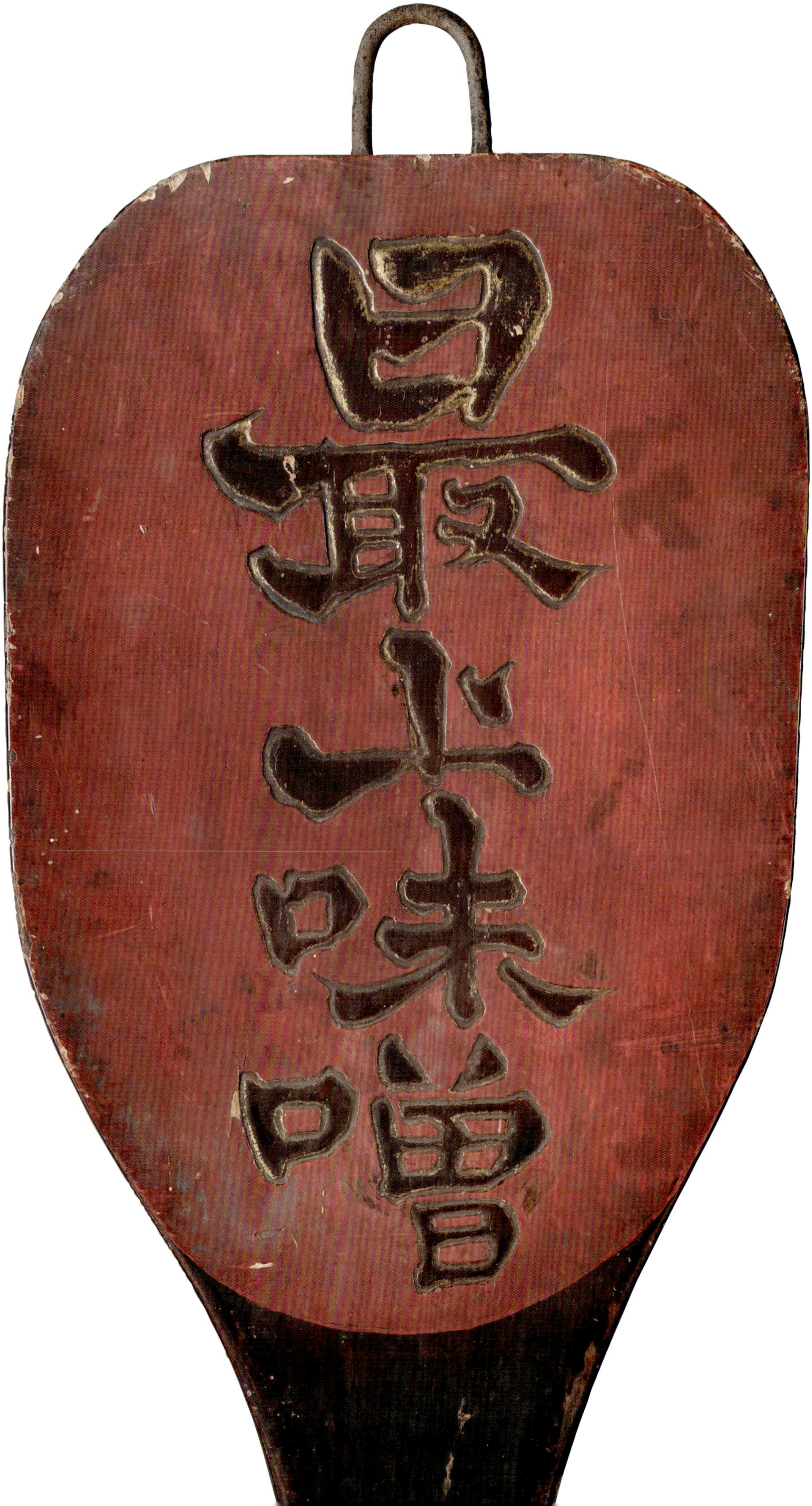
最上味噌

KANBAN AND KABUKI: PRODUCT PLACEMENT AND THE EDO STAGE

4

ONE OF THE KEY CULTURAL EMBLEMS of the Edo period is kabuki. This distinctive and internationally recognized form of theater had its surprisingly humble birth in Kyoto in 1603 when a mysterious woman named Okuni, a female attendant from the Izumo Shrine, began giving audacious and ribald performances on the banks of the Kamo River. Though kabuki essentially began as free-form female street theater with a certain amount of burlesque, it ultimately morphed into a cultural juggernaut. Through its deft ability to reinvent itself and remain closely aligned with the prevailing zeitgeist, over the next three hundred years kabuki evolved from coarse vaudeville with a prostitution endgame to an increasingly sophisticated theatrical experience exerting an incalculable influence on Edo society, shaping conceptions of heroism, beauty, tragedy, and morality.

Kabuki was many things. At its base, it was a story performed for entertainment—escapism pure and simple. But it was also high art, sophisticated in its presentation, with dynastic acting lineages, each with its own traditions and closely guarded teachings. Kabuki was social commentary, too, a way for a politically marginalized segment of society to take jabs at an oppressive government, flex its class muscles,

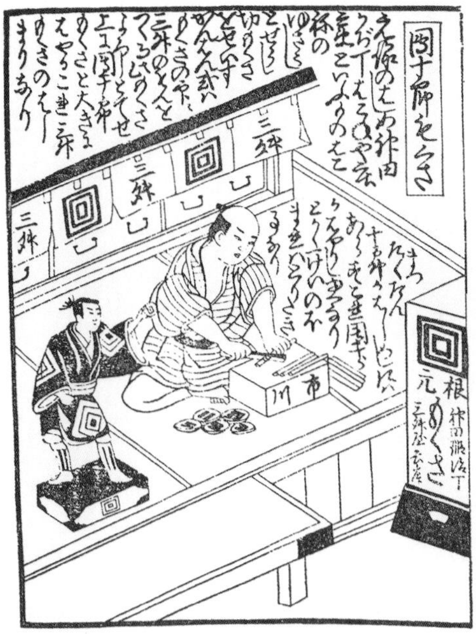

FIG. 23 Woodblock print of the moxa shop Mimasu-ya, which employed a doll of the actor Ichikawa Danjûrô II as a kanban. From Okumura Masafusa's (1686–1764) *Toshidama himachi banashi*, c. 1747. Reproduced from Matsumiya, *Edo no kanban*, 299.

and challenge societal norms and strictures. Finally, and most relevant to the present topic, kabuki provided the ultimate media outlet for merchants to connect with a million potential customers. And savvy Edo merchants, be they purveyors of makeup, tobacco pouches, patent medicines, combs, or dry goods, clearly recognized an opportunity when they saw one.

The commercial life of Edo Japan had many tendrils. Far from being restricted to storefront transactions between buyer and seller, it embraced and capitalized on many aspects of Edo culture. Popular writers, woodblock-print artists, and kabuki actors of repute were invested in a complex commercial mechanism that seamlessly blended popular culture and advertising. Plays were written about the founding of great merchant houses.[61] Actors operated their own shops, translating their fame and "good" names into successful commercial ventures and shamelessly peddling their own goods on the stage boards of the theater. For instance, Ichikawa Danjûrô II (1688–1758) sold *mogusa* (mugwort), used in a type of traditional medicine known as moxibustion. The popular late seventeenth-century *onnagata* (male performer of female roles) Uemura Kichiya sold cosmetics, the virile Matsumura Kôshirô IV (act. 1772–1801) sold wafers, and the hugely popular Sanogawa Ichimatsu II (act. 1767–81) sold incense and tooth powder.[62] Woodblock-print artists and authors of popular fiction interwove their own shops, or those of their friends or paying sponsors, into published works. This "lucrative constellation of advertising practices" also extended to restaurants, teahouses, courtesans, sumo wrestlers, and shop girls, all working in a loosely confederated way to promote specific products at specific times.[63] Manufacturers and purveyors of various services effectively used kabuki and its satellite phenomena to stimulate desire among consumers.[64]

Merchants, using an early form of "native advertising," cleverly smuggled product plugs and advertisements into stage performances. A particularly brazen example of what might be considered corporate advertising dates from a 1715 performance featuring a *kôjô* (declaimed announcement) lauding the new kimono patterns being offered by Echigoya in Nihonbashi that season. This was broadcast in all three of the principal Edo theaters, bespeaking a coordinated marketing blitz by the dry goods behemoth.[65] In a 1684 production of the play *Narukami*, Ichikawa Danjûrô I (1660–1704) inserted a small advertisement for a medicine known as *bôzu* (*Physalis pruinosa*, or ground cherry), a purported cure for beriberi; this effectively inaugurated a profitable lineage tradition of stage-based advertising.[66] Danjûrô II followed by promoting his own line of medicine, mentioned above, in addition to a brand of *shirazake* liquor.[67]

The most famous example of product insertion originated, again, with Danjûrô II. In a 1709 production of the play *Keisei hibari yama* (The prostitute's mountain of swallows), Danjûrô introduced the character of a fast-talking, itinerant peddler of moxa named Kumehachirô.[68] As the proprietor of a moxa shop himself, Danjûrô would likely have found this role particularly rewarding, in all senses of the word. The moxa peddler proved to be so popular that he was reprised in a number of plays over the ensuing theater seasons. These

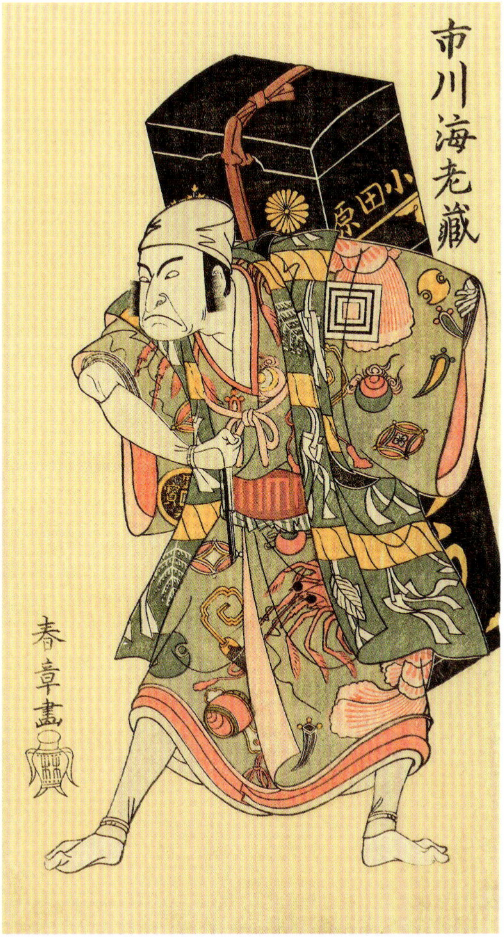

FIG. 24 *Memorial Portrait of the Actor Ichikawa Ebizo II (Ichikawa Danjûrô II) as a Peddler of the Medicine Urio*, c. 1768–70, Katsukawa Shunshô (1726–1792). Polychrome woodblock print, *hosoban*, ink and color on paper, 12 × 6 in. (31.2 × 14.2 cm). The Art Institute of Chicago, Frederick W. Gookin Collection, 1939.686.

characters boosted the popularity of moxa to such an extent that new shops appeared to meet the growing demand. The moxa shop Mimasu-ya in the popular Asakusa section of Edo used as its yago a crest identical to that of the Danjûrô lineage (*mi-masu*, or three nesting square rice measures). Capitalizing on Danjûrô's role, the Mimasu-ya started using as a kanban a *ningyô* (doll) depicting Danjûrô II in the role of the moxa peddler (fig. 23).[69] Given that kanban for moxa shops tended to be jitsubutsu in style, with a large metal vat used in preparing moxa placed on the roof, the use of the Danjûrô ningyô seems all the more unusual and directly indicative of the actor's influence on this particular market.[70]

In 1718 Danjûrô wrote and inserted a short segment involving his character into a larger drama; the segment came to be known as *Uriô uri* (The medicine peddler). The vignette still centered on an itinerant peddler (fig. 24) but introduced into the plot an actual Edo-period patent medicine known as Tonchinkô. Said to have originated in China some 1,400 years ago, Tonchinkô was brought to Japan in 1368 by a man named Chin Uriô, who had been in service to the Yuan emperor at the time of the Ming overthrow. The Japanese government, recognizing his value, allowed him to settle in Odawara. By the Edo period, Tonchinkô was sold exclusively by Toraya Fujiemon, a descendant of Chin Uriô, still living in Odawara. The short segment had little or nothing to do with the narrative of the larger play, but was a brief review of the product's illustrious history followed by a declaration and demonstration of the medicine's effectiveness. Danjûrô claimed to have personally benefitted from its use and wrote the scene specifically to thank Toraya.[71]

The centerpiece of *Uriô uri* features the most famous language sequence in all of kabuki, an extended 1,600-character-long tongue twister. Simulating the advancing restorative effects of the medicine, the actor's delivery accelerates as he progresses into the monologue, but with each word remaining clear and distinct, graphically demonstrating the effectiveness of Tonchinkô. So popular was this sequence that printed texts of the riff were produced, and aficionados of kabuki throughout the land attempted to master what was in essence an advertisement for Tonchinkô. Woodblock prints featuring Danjûrô in this scene included snippets of the complex speech in print and a peddler's pack emblazoned with the Uriô name in hiragana, effectively blurring the lines between celebration of the play, celebration of the actor, and celebration of the medicine. The overwhelming popularity of the *Uriô uri* scene led it to be incorporated into numerous dramas, ultimately becoming one of the signature pieces of the Danjûrô acting lineage, a bravura display of linguistic gymnastics. The device of employing a peddler within a play to promote a seemingly limitless array of products, from moxa to sushi, many of which were conveniently available from merchants in Nihonbashi and Ryôgoku, ultimately became stock and trade of the kabuki theater.[72]

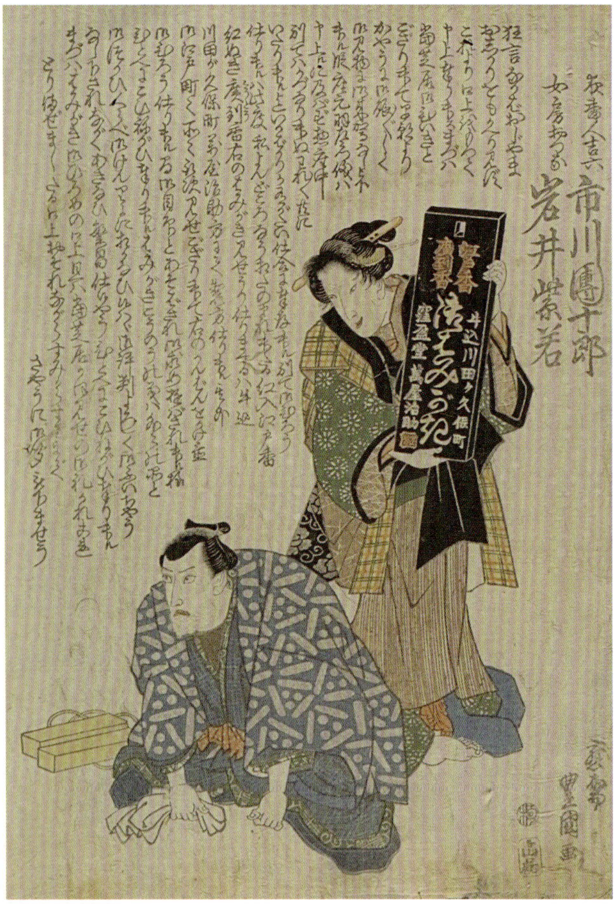

FIG. 25 The actor Ichikawa Danjûrô VII and the onnagata Iwai Murasakiwaka delivering a product placement pitch in the middle of a performance, as depicted by Utagawa Toyokuni II (1777–1835) in *Edokô kôtôko onhamigaki*, 1825. Polychrome woodblock print, ink and color on paper, 14 × 10 in. (36 × 25 cm). Advertising Museum of Tokyo, 1988-2489.

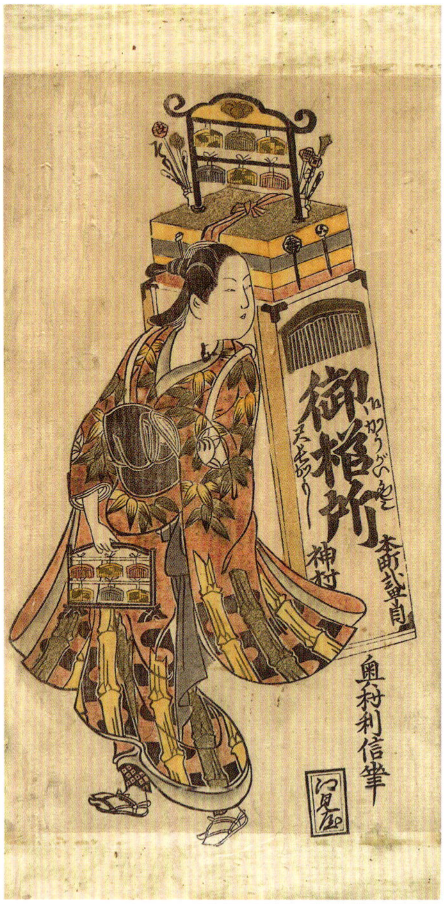

FIG. 26 The actor Ichimura Uzaemon (1699–1762) as a comb vendor, as depicted by Okumura Toshinobu (act. c. 1725–50), Edo period, c. 1730. Polychrome woodblock print, ink and color on paper, 12½ × 6 in. (31.8 × 15.4 cm). Metropolitan Museum of Art, H. O. Havemeyer Collection, Bequest of Mrs. H. O. Havemeyer, 1929, JP1608, www.metmuseum.org.

Stage-based advertising at times also included the blatant parading of a specific shop's kanban on stage for public edification, the Edo-period equivalent of "And now a message from our sponsor." A particularly noted example of this comes, again, from the Danjûrô family—an acting lineage that evidently excelled at both acting and marketing. In an 1825 performance, Danjûrô VII (1791–1859), in the role of the night watchman Kichiroku, stopped the performance to deliver a plug in the form of a ritual kôjô for Yorozuya Naosuke cosmetics and toothpastes, while his stage partner, Iwai Murasakiwaka, in the role of Kichiroku's wife, held up a kanban for the Aeidô shop in Kawatakubomachi in the Ushigome section of Edo. A woodblock print by Utagawa Toyokuni II (1777–1835) features the two actors at this precise moment in the production: Danjûrô kneels before the audience making his pitch, while the onnagata stands behind him proffering the shop's black-lacquered kanban for the audience's viewing pleasure. The accompanying text extols the virtues and benefits of the product (fig. 25).[73] The specific financial arrangements behind such an inclusion are unclear, nor do we understand yet how much relative weight rested on the playwright or the actors in deciding when and how to introduce a product so aggressively.

Audience members seem to have been perfectly comfortable with the arrangement as well and did not see these non-sequitur advertisements as necessarily disruptive to the overall theatergoing experience. On the contrary, it seems as if they embraced them wholeheartedly, even correcting actors when a shop's name, product, or address was given incorrectly. There was no impermeable "fourth wall" in kabuki, and there were numerous times and occasions in which an actor might step out of character to address the audience in a more personal vein. And, similarly, the audiences of kabuki, particularly those in the more boisterous Edo theaters, felt free to shout comments, praise, criticisms, or the random *bon mot* toward the actors on stage.[74] In this give-and-take environment, personal advertising and solicitation of products found a more natural setting than might be the case in the production of an Arthur Miller play, for example.

The stars of the kabuki stage were icons in the truest sense, their images replicated in the millions through the medium of the woodblock print and avidly worshipped and devoured by a consuming public, many of whom may never have actually attended a performance. The woodblock-print artist Okumura Toshinobu (act. c. 1725–50) made a subspecialty of images of actors in the stage roles of vendors, which were actually advertisements for shops. Extant examples show actors such as Ichimura Uzaemon (1699–1762) as a comb peddler (fig. 26) and the onnagata Sanogawa Ichimatsu (1722–1762), appropriately enough, as a cosmetics vendor, indicating that the Danjûrô lineage was not the only one participating in the rapacious marketing complex of Edo commercialism. Another print by the same artist, dated 1728, depicting an unknown actor selling textiles from Echigoya, also illustrates how advertising campaigns could have an extended run rather than one-time insertions and speaks to the success of this type of customer outreach.

Cheap to produce and easy to disseminate, woodblock prints proved to be a powerful advertising ally, trebly promoting actor, play, and product and functioning as an integral part of Edo's commercial machinery.[75] On the connection between kabuki and commercial advertising in the Edo period, David Pollack has stated: "The names of actual merchants, their shops, and the merchandise sold in them play so prominent a role in Edo-period art, fiction and drama to suggest that these media might usefully be understood as more narrowly focused modalities of a single general domain—advertising."[76] In essence, Pollack is posing the question, were kabuki and many other aspects of Edo popular culture merely entertaining delivery mechanisms for commercial advertisement? The same question might be asked of today's mass media, once more proving the adage "Everything old is new again." In this context, kanban and kabuki were essentially the same, art as advertisement.

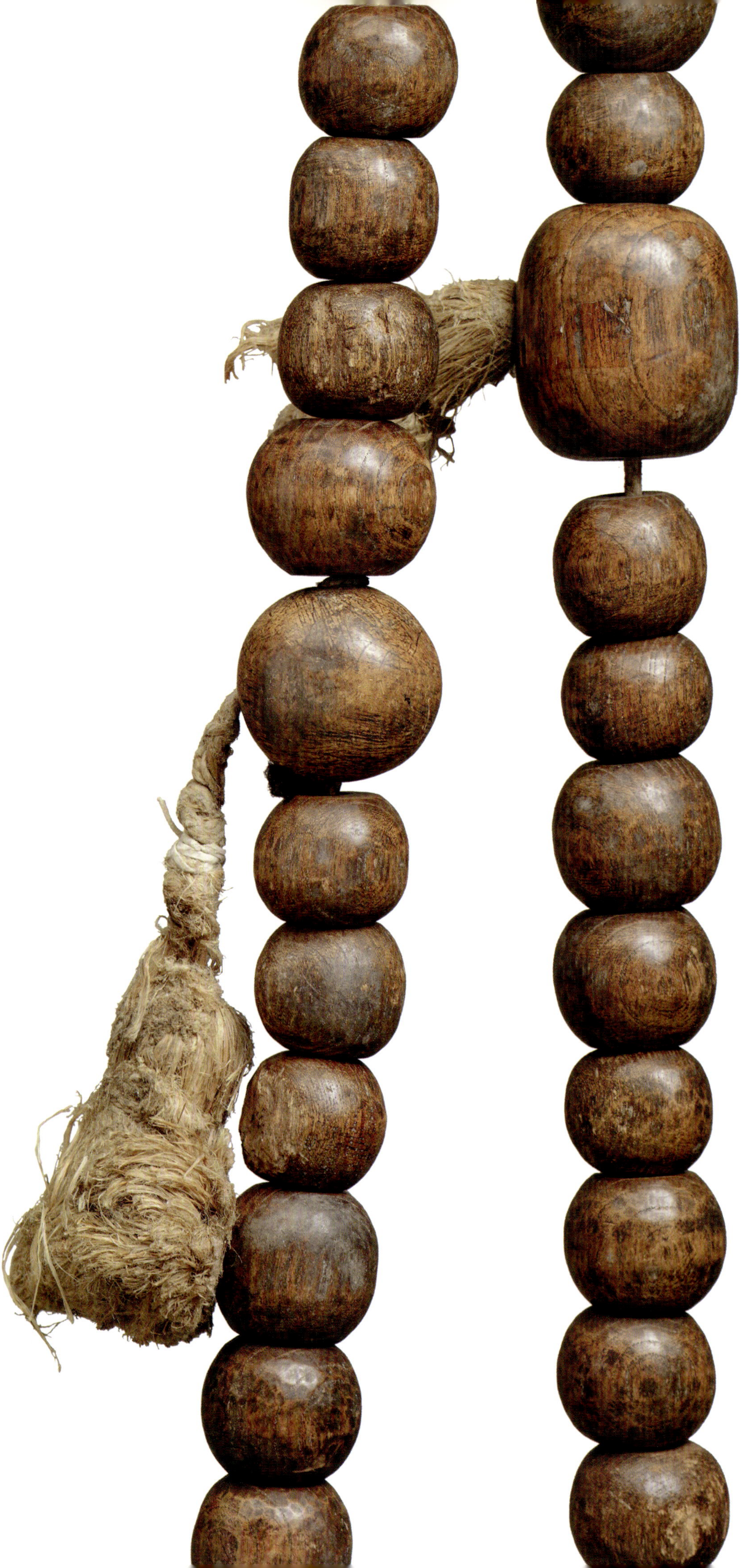

COLLECTORS AND COLLECTIONS

5

WITH THE ADVENT OF THE MEIJI ERA and its wholesale and, in many ways, forced conversion to things Western, with its attendant shocking loss and destruction of many of Japan's more traditional customs and arts, there was a parallel resurgence in tradition and nostalgia. This created a decided cultural push back in which formerly unnoticed objects suddenly became more interesting and important by virtue of their very absence. Their sudden loss also involved, counterintuitively, a rediscovery. This was particularly true with regard to native craft traditions. In the ningyô world, for example, this rediscovery took the form of study groups that would meet regularly and share regional examples of dolls and toys for study and mutual appreciation; lectures were given and publications were produced for both private and public consumption. This same trend was repeated in connection with a wide variety of traditional craft forms.[77]

One of the first individuals to draw attention to kanban (as well as, coincidentally, ningyô) during this period was Tsuboi Shôgorô (1863–1913). Widely considered one of the founding fathers of modern anthropology and archeology in Japan, Tsuboi published an in-depth illustrated study of Edo-period kanban in 1887, entitled *Kôshô gigei*

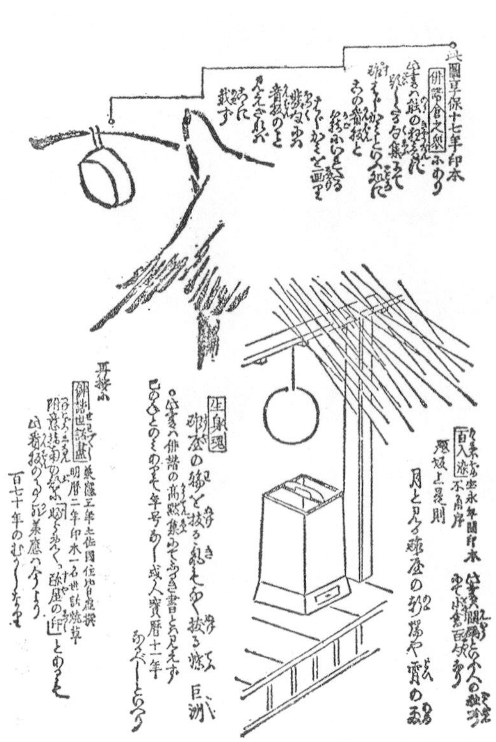

FIG. 27 Variations of kanban used for su-ya (vinegar shops) during the Edo period. Reproduced from Tsuboi, *Kôshô gigei kanban kô*, 40.

kanban kô.[78] Other observers had previously documented various aspects of daily life during the Edo period, including kanban. Kitagawa Morisada, mentioned above, published over a thirty-year period (1830–60) catalogs of daily ephemera collectively entitled *Morisada mankô* (Morisada's miscellany); these included a number of illustrations of kanban, both as a central focus as well as background material for other topics. Tsuboi, however, presented the first systematic study of kanban. Considered the earliest work to highlight the art, beauty, and inherent interest of Japanese shop signs, Tsuboi's study included numerous Edo-period woodblock-print illustrations of traditional kanban types, with notations of special features that might not be readily apparent to the casual observer.

Tsuboi, for example, introduced the *goro awase* or *hanji mono* (wordplay) signs frequently used for vinegar shops (*su-ya*). This is actually a twofold double entendre. *Su-ya* can also be written using the characters for "missed arrow." In keeping with this homonym, signs would frequently portray an archery target without any arrows (fig. 27). However, outdoor signs tended to degrade over time, and it was not uncommon for an unprotected sign of this type to devolve to the point where only the original bamboo circle framing the target was left. Eventually, this simple open circle itself became the symbol for a vinegar shop.[79] Tsuboi included a number of illustrated examples, such as an open circle hanging from a paddle used to stir miso, indicating that that particular shop sold both of these daily necessities.[80] Drawing directly from *Morisada mankô*, Tsuboi also helped to explain a stepped, box-shaped kanban with the image of a flying crane, used to advertise a facial makeup made from bird droppings, called *sei-san*.[81] A similar kanban can be seen in the *Jinrinkinmôzui* under the entry for *hakofunshi*, a Kyoto specialty.[82]

As a researcher, Tsuboi often did fieldwork related to kanban, trying to track down and document known examples of specific types. He described tromping through the back streets of Osaka trying to locate a *mokuba* (wooden horse) kanban representing a sweets shop. The curious marriage of a wooden horse with the face or mask of the goddess Okame is another wordplay kanban. The use of an image of a wild horse (*ara uma*) as a kanban for a sweets shop is a play on the phrase "*Ara! Umai!*" (How sweet!). Tsuboi ultimately located the Uma no Mochiya in the Shinsaibashi section of Osaka. The owner of the actual shop, however, claimed that his use of a mokuba was related to the phrase "*ashiga tsuyoi*" (strong legs), referring to the strong and long-lasting sweet taste of his particular *mochi* rice cake. Tsuboi illustrated the kanban with excerpts from a number of Edo woodblock prints. One print shows two men hard at work pounding mochi cakes under the watchful eye of the shop's mokuba kanban, which has an Okame mask. To the sounds of "*ton, ton*," the workers perform

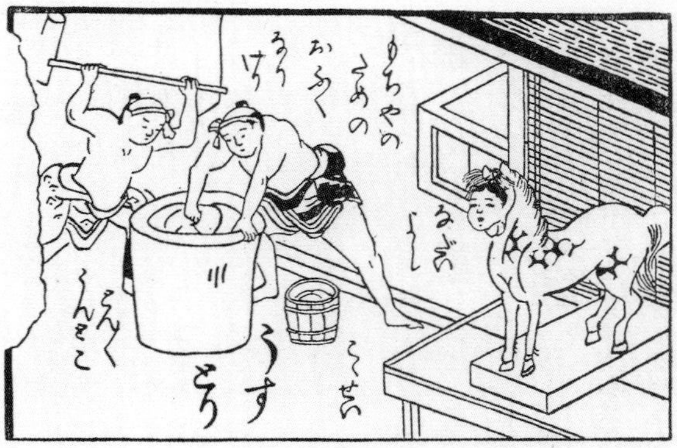

FIG. 28 Illustration depicting an Edo-period mokei kanban of a horse wearing a mask for the *mochi-ya* (rice cake shop) Uma no Mochiya. Reproduced from Tsuboi, *Kôshô gigei kanban kô*, 17.

usutori, adding water to the mochi mix, and they comment on the particular good luck that this kanban brings to their shop (fig. 28).[83]

The Sugiura Collection

Though Tsuboi researched, wrote, and promoted an appreciation of daily objects from Japan's rapidly disappearing past, he did not collect them in any intentional way. Perhaps the most famous and tragic of early kanban collections in Japan was assembled by Sugiura Seiburôbei (Kyûen) of Kyoto.[84] Although it is unclear as to what initially stimulated Sugiura's interest in kanban, he began his collecting efforts in 1897. This more or less passive activity transformed into a full-blown passion when he was presented with a copy of Tsuboi's work, *Kôshô gigei kanban kô*, which had been published a decade earlier. Sugiura remained dedicated to his collection for over thirty years, searching out particularly interesting kanban throughout the country. By 1940 he had amassed approximately four hundred examples of Edo- and early Meiji-era kanban. He published a book containing photostatic plates of 131 of his pieces, called *Kozô kanban zufu*. In addition, he periodically published images of special examples drawn from the collection in limited mimeograph form in what was known as *Unsensô sanshi*.

The war, however, was hard on the Sugiura family's finances, and in 1953 the entire collection was sold to the owner of a *ryokan* (traditional inn) called Nanahon Kisho, near the Sakai area of Osaka. It ultimately took six trucks to transport the entire collection of kanban from Kyoto to Sakai. The Nanahon Kiso functioned as a de facto private museum and contained at that time approximately 20,000 artifacts representing all aspects of traditional Japanese life and customs. Due to space considerations, however, many of the Sugiura kanban were stored outside and rapidly deteriorated. By 1963, new owners of the ryokan, either unable or unwilling to attend to the needs of such a vast repository, ultimately burned all but forty examples of the original Sugiura grouping of kanban. An undated image taken of the collection while it was still in Sugiura's Kyoto home was published in Hayashi Yoshikazu's *Edo kanban zufu*.[85] It shows a long corridor lined with wooden mokei and sage kanban mounted from floor to ceiling, with prominent examples advertising a fan shop, candle shop, tabi sock maker, rosary bead maker, thread shop, and samisen shop, among others. About sixty pieces appear in the image, all but a few now lost to us forever.

The Peabody Essex Museum Collection

One of the most significant collections of Japanese kanban to be found anywhere in the world is at the Peabody Essex Museum in Salem, Massachusetts. Originally organized in 1799 as a "cabinet of natural and artificial curiosities," the nascent museum was able to draw from the world's wealth as amassed by generations of sea captains and crew members who had spread out across the globe from this port city. The cabinet of curiosities grew rapidly into the Peabody Academy of Science, as its scope and vision expanded. Within its walls, basements, and assorted storage areas reposes a vast collection, reflective of Salem's

FIG. 29 Shitta kanban for a toy shop, late nineteenth century. Wood and pigment, 38 × 18 in. (96.3 × 44.5 cm). Peabody Essex Museum, E16481. © Peabody Essex Museum, Salem, MA. Photograph by Kathy Tarantola.

history as the center of the maritime world, augmented over the years through donations and acquisitions. The museum's Japanese holdings were largely built through the tireless collecting and scientific interests of Edward Sylvester Morse (1838–1925), who first went to Japan in 1877 to pursue his passion for studying shells and to lecture on zoology.[86] Ultimately, Morse would reside in Japan for a total of two and a half years, serving as professor at the University of Tokyo, where he helped to develop the zoology department. One of Morse's more promising students was, coincidentally, Tsuboi Shôgôro, discussed above.[87] Morse's impact on Japan and on the West's perception of that country would become indelible. He went on to serve as director of the Peabody Academy of Science from 1880 through 1916, with the museum formally changing its name to the Peabody Museum of Salem during his tenure.[88] His keen attention to the details of Japanese daily life and his insatiable collecting proclivities resulted in the development of a number of significant subcollections that now reside at the museum, ranging from fish hooks to tabi socks to kanban. Ultimately, Morse personally collected and donated 2,880 objects to the museum.[89]

Among the PEM's many collections is the single largest grouping of kanban to be found outside of Japan (fig. 29). The museum houses 212 individual examples of kanban, and over half of these, 133 pieces, were collected prior to 1920, corresponding to the period in which Morse and his direct collaborators were most actively involved in developing the institution's Japanese holdings. While Morse's journal and sketchbooks contain a number of images of kanban, including those for a tabi sock maker, a money changer, a comb maker, a parasol maker, a gold leaf artisan, a candle maker, a noodle restaurant and nori paste vendor, and a fabric shop, Morse himself only collected two examples.[90] And, surprisingly, neither of them can be considered kanban in the most orthodox sense of the word. One is a gaku for a Shinto shrine in Kyoto, reading "Sansusha" and dated 1730, given by Morse to the museum in 1902.[91] The second is a bit more difficult to classify. It is an elaborately painted wooden panel donated by Morse in 1898. It depicts the kabuki actor Ichikawa Danjûrô VII in a performance of *Shibaraku* with the Danjûrô crest of the mima-su featured at the top and a poem signed by the actor on the back.[92] Rather than a kanban, this might be more easily classified as an *ema*, or votive plaque.

Though kanban themselves were not a strong focus for Morse's collecting efforts, the attention he drew to the value and beauty of everyday Japanese objects did inspire others among the cultural elite of Boston who collected and donated to Morse's museum, including William Sturgis Bigelow (1850–1926), Dr. Charles Goddard Weld (1857–1911), Charles Freer (1854–1919), and Robert Charles Billings (1819–1899). Personal friends of Morse, Bigelow, Weld, and Freer traveled extensively in Japan and collected large quantities of art, antiques, and artifacts that form the basis of a number of important collections in U.S. museums today, including Boston's Museum of Fine Arts and the Freer Gallery at the Smithsonian. Following Morse's example, they also collected objects related to Japan's daily life, including kanban. The majority of early kanban in the PEM collection are credited as gifts from these individuals. In addition, Billings, upon his passing in 1899, left $3 million to 187 Boston-area institutions, including the Boston Public Library and the Peabody. The Billings Fund at the Peabody allowed for the acquisition of a number of particularly important kanban during the period of Morse's term as director and beyond, through such prominent Japanese art and antiques trading firms as Yamanaka & Co. as well as individual collectors.

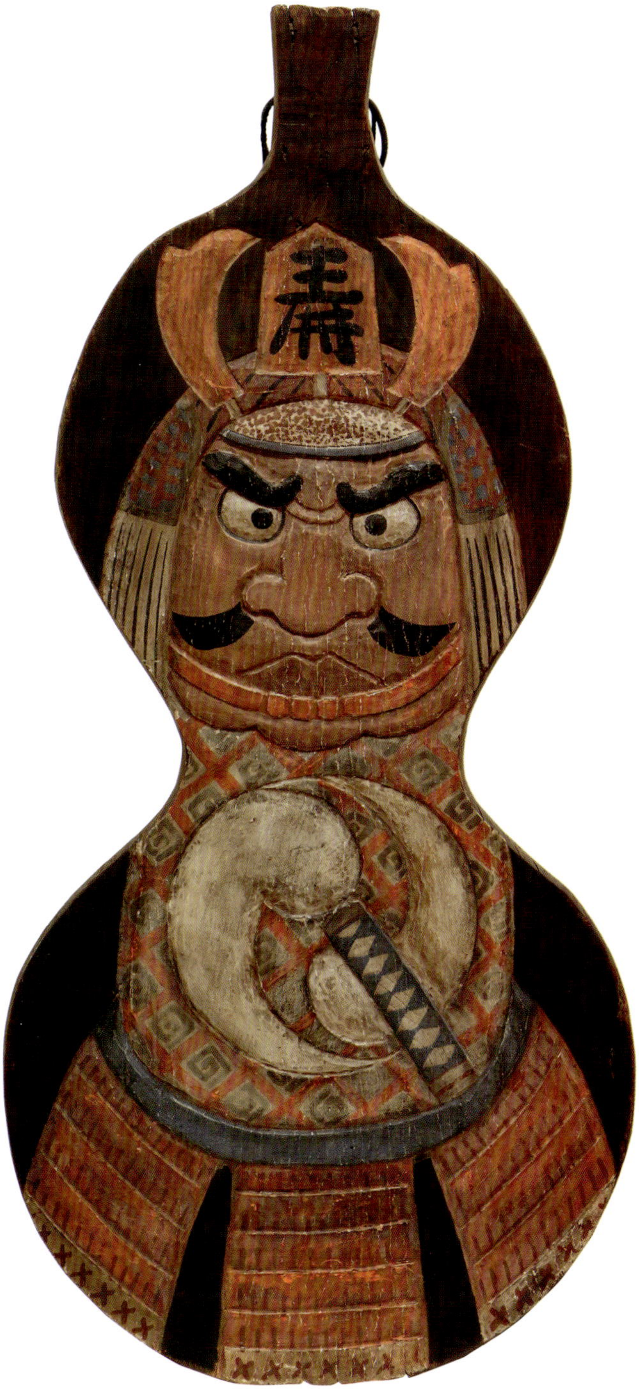

The Shôwa Neon Takamura Kanban Museum Collection

A wonderful marriage of old and new was found in the collecting habits of Takamura Gorô (d. 2003), former president of Shôwa Neon, a neon sign manufacturing company based in the Shinagawa area of Tokyo. The company itself started in 1921 as the Takamura Kanban Ten, a traditional kanban manufacturing company specializing in painted wood and tin signs. With the advent of neon in the late 1920s, the company moved in this direction, ultimately changing its name to Shôwa Neon. As part of a collaborative effort with the All-Japan Neon Sign Manufacturers Association, in 1977 Takamura Gorô embarked on a project to document the early evolution of neon signage in Japan by collecting and photographing old neon

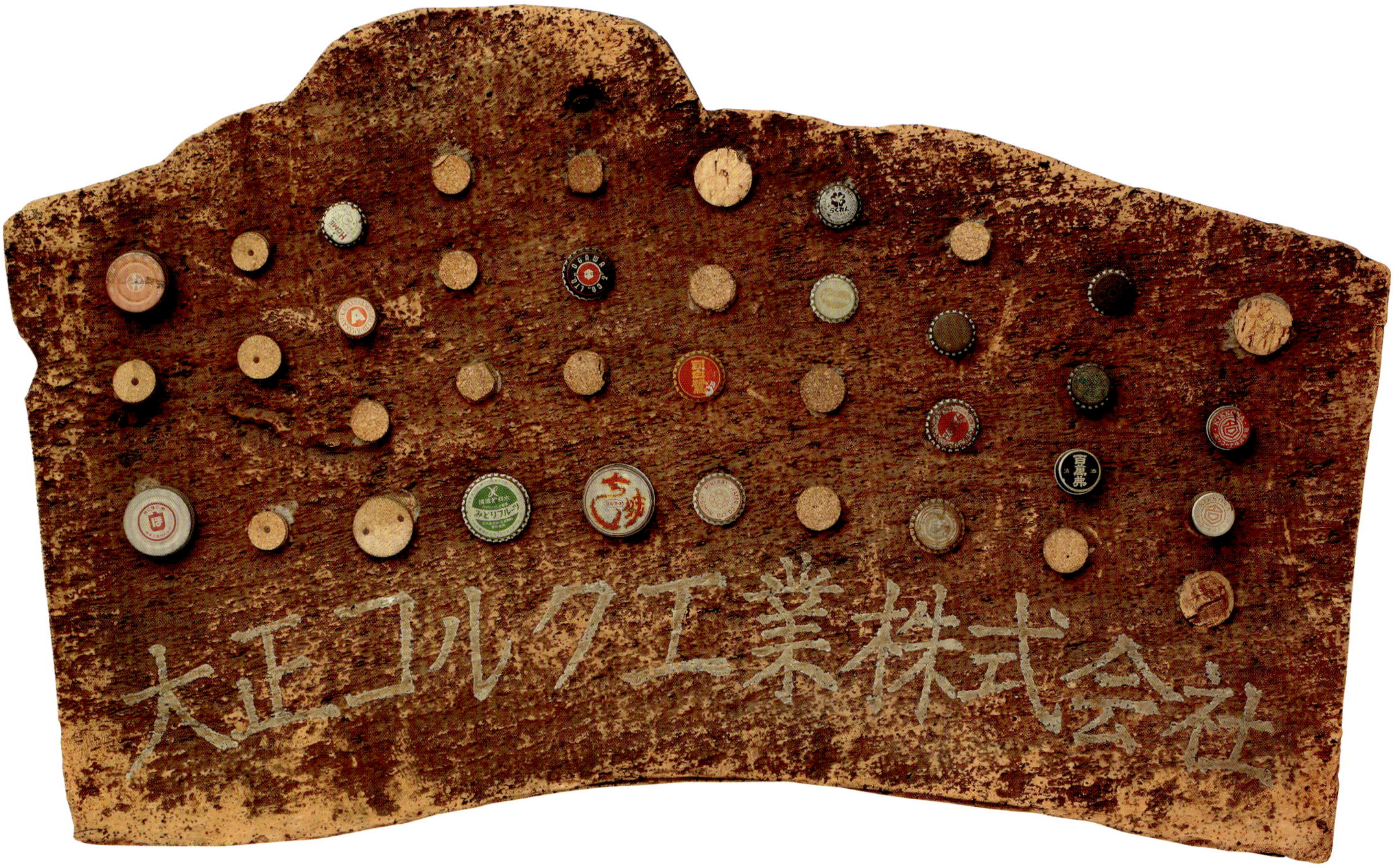

7

Jitsubutsu kanban for Taisho Cork Kôgyô Kakubishi Kaisha

Early twentieth century
Cork, metal, pigment
22 × 37 in. (57 × 94 cm)
Shôwa Neon Takamura Kanban Museum

Makers of kanban resorted to a wide variety of materials to realize their artistic visions and fulfill their commercial mandates. Although wood was the most common base material, paper, stone, bamboo, and iron were also used. Cork might at first seem to be an unusual choice for a kanban, but it was an appropriate choice for this sign, created for the Taisho Cork company. The jitsubutsu kanban features cork-backed bottle caps of various sizes manufactured by the Taisho Cork Kôgyô Kakubishi Kaisha, all mounted on a cork board. William Painter first patented the crown cork bottle cap in 1892. He created a fitted disposable metal cap backed by a thin wafer of cork to separate the liquid from the metal of the cap, revolutionizing the bottling and storage practices of soda and beer companies around the world. Here, an irregularly shaped cork panel is studded with bottle caps for beer, mineral water, and soda, with some of the metal crown caps themselves missing, leaving only their cork inner linings.

signs. He was dismayed to find that most of the older signs had been destroyed, so he shifted his focus to Edo- and early Meiji-period kanban.[93] Gorô eventually amassed over four hundred signs from these periods, a number roughly equivalent to the Sugiura Collection. In 2006, his son Takamura Toru fulfilled his father's vision by establishing a museum at company headquarters to display his collection to the public and to promote research into the history of kanban. Today approximately 180 signs are on display at any one time, and the museum holds what is arguably the largest kanban collection in existence. Highlights have been published in a lavish book entitled *Jidai o utsusu kanban*, which also features the results of a symposium on kanban held prior to Gorô's passing, entitled "Zadan kai kanban yomoyama banashi." It was moderated by Takamura Gorô and his son Toru, and it included the thoughtful participation of the celebrated potter and kanban collector Tsuji Seimei (1927–2008) and the kabuki actor Ichikawa Danjûrô XII (1946–2013).

The Shôwa Neon Takamura Kanban Museum has the added importance of having the only permanent display devoted exclusively to Japanese kanban. As we have seen, kanban form an integral part of Japanese commercial history as well as a much-respected aspect of *mingei* (folk art); as a result, selected examples can be found in many museums devoted to the arts and culture of Japan. Specialty museums such as the Naito Museum of Pharmaceutical Science and Industry in Gifu and the Tobacco and Salt Museum in Tokyo as a rule have kanban specific to their subjects on display. Japanese folk art museums and cultural history museums such as the Japan Folk Crafts Museum and the Edo-Tokyo Museum also display examples to illustrate certain industries or traditions. But Shôwa Neon's permanent, cross-industry collection and display makes it a unique institution and offers a wonderful opportunity to visually explore the world of kanban. Highlights include a 48 by 32 inch (121 by 82 cm) kanban advertising the services of the Sanoya metalsmith shop. This impressive kanban, previously in the Hosoda Collection of Tokyo, features a massive lock mounted to a board, with hand-forged metal lettering in an elegant script announcing the services available: *jômae* (locks), *hikite rui* (door pulls), and *migaki* (knife sharpening).[94] A unique sign from the Taisho Cork Kôgyô Kakubishi Kaisha, fashioned in a fan shape, is peppered with corks of various sizes as well as bottle caps, functioning as a jitsubutsu kanban (cat. 7).

To this list of noted public collections must be added the value and importance of kanban in private hands. Collections that are based on the proclivities, taste, and means of an individual collector can offer examples not found in more established institutions. For the study of kanban, it is important to examine as many of them as possible, as even redundancies can provide insight into the history and role of kanban in Japanese art and economic culture. Thus, for the purposes of this study, we look at representative kanban from such institutions as the Peabody Essex Museum, the Shôwa Neon Takamura Kanban Museum, and Mingei International Museum, as well as noted examples from several private collections.

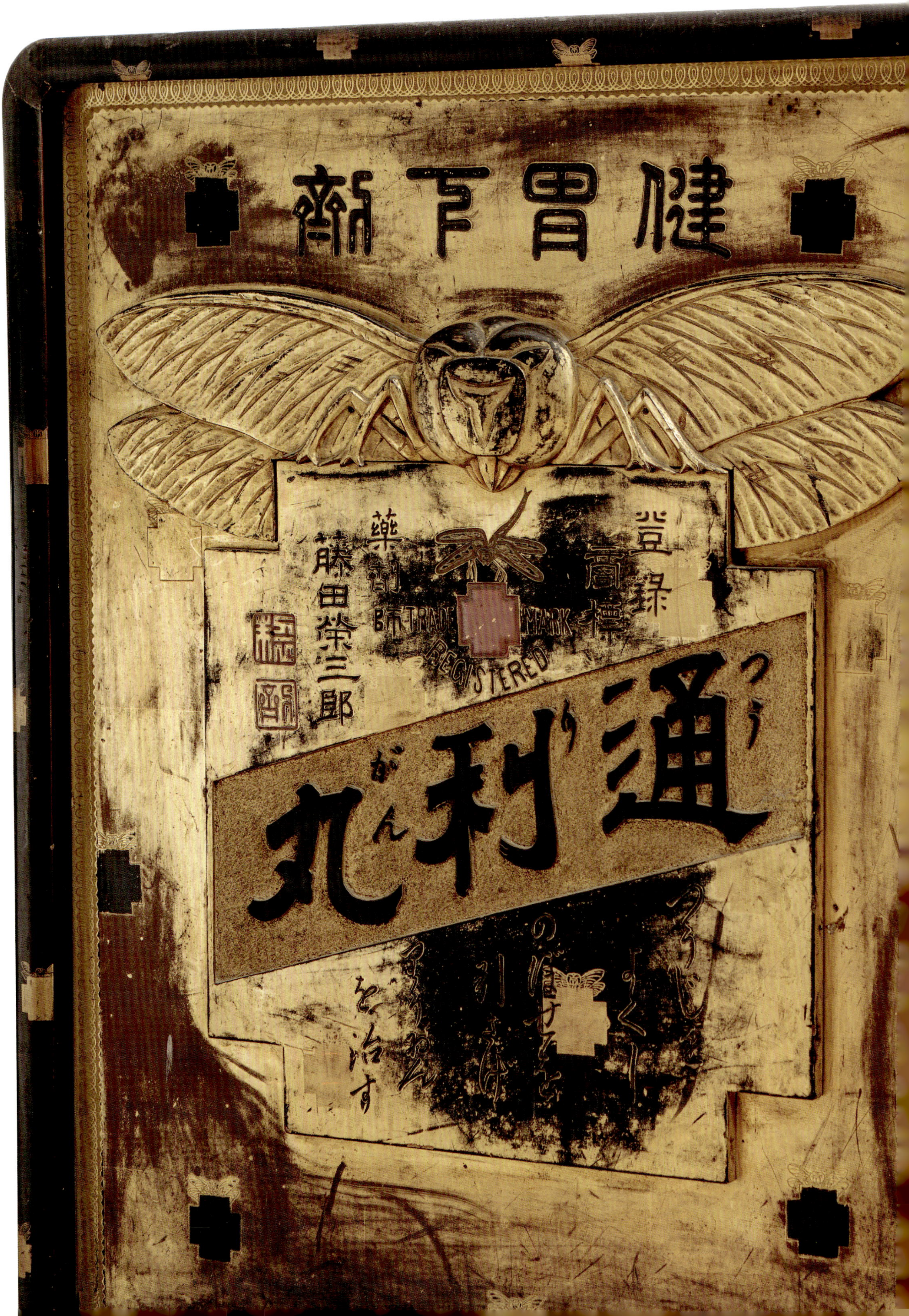

健胃下剤
登録商標
TRADE MARK
REGISTERED
薬剤師
藤田榮三郎
通利丸

CATEGORIZING KANBAN: THE CATALOGUE

6

KANBAN FUNCTIONED ON MANY LEVELS in traditional Japanese culture, responding to commercial as well as artistic exigencies. So how does one categorize and classify kanban? By material? By industry? By display modality? Tsuboi Shôgorô's pioneering book, *Kôsho gigei kanban kô*, takes a largely historical approach, focusing on the development of kanban, with explorations into subthemes. Wang Shucun's important work on shop signs in imperial China neatly divides signs into three broad categories: those that employ images, whether that be the object itself, a miniaturized study of the object, a carved image, or a painted image; those that employ symbols, which may or may not be obviously related to the product sold; and those that rely on text, the written word, to convey meaning.[95] Wang's system focuses strictly on the technique of presentation, with no implicit recognition of the type of product sold. By contrast, Tanabe Satoru's work on Japanese shop signs, "*Kanban no sekai*," delineates nine categories without regard to style of presentation: clothes/food/living; natural products; people/goods/information; trade; social life; religion; folk culture; sports/entertainment/brothels; and, finally, personal life/personal events.[96] A third approach, one taken by Matsumiya Saburô in his important work, *Edo no kanban*, and by Hayashi

Yoshikazu in his oft-quoted *Edo kanban zufu*, is to focus on the products depicted, but to place them in strict Japanese alphabetical order in an encyclopedic format, irrespective of subcategory or method of presentation. Drawing from a broad archival base and a number of earlier works, Saburô and Hayashi take their readers on a journey of kanban from A to Z, or from "A" to "*Wa*."

In the only previous work in English dedicated to shop signs in the Japanese tradition, *Kanban: The Art of the Japanese Shop Sign*, Dana Levy and Lea Sneider focus on the physical structure of kanban but divide their entries into categories similar to those used by Tanabe: food and drink; tobacco and related objects; household goods; clothes and accessories; martial arts; money and banking; medical; and, finally, arts and leisure.[97]

Kanban, like many examples of Japanese folk craft, function as windows into very rich and complex worlds that can make simple categorizations seem limiting and forced. A mokei kanban featuring an image of a large pipe, for example, is undoubtedly interesting as a visual object, a work of art, but it also clearly beckons us to explore the world of the *tabako-ya* and the culture of tobacco in early modern Japan. Similarly, a tsuitate kanban of a giant dragonfly advertising the benefits of the laxative Tsurigan not only presents an elegant and dramatic statement but also bids us enter into the fascinating world of Japanese *baiyaku*, or patent medicines (cat. 8). And a moji kanban advertising a *karuta* shop with the image of two playing cards, its pigments crackled with age, entices us to investigate Edo-period vice and the role of card games in traditional Japanese culture.

The present exhibition comprises approximately sixty prime examples of kanban from the Edo, Meiji, and early Taisho eras. Each piece, however, is in essence a world unto itself, filled with riveting backstories and surprising reveals. Many are also representative of living traditions, with ateliers and artisans devoted to preserving the lifeblood of these crafts and trades. Following a hybrid approach, the kanban are presented here in relation to product categories: medicine, tobacco, dry goods, household goods, personal items, consumer goods, specialty trades, and, finally, pastimes and entertainment. In addition, certain examples are more appropriately explored through kanban types—mokei kanban and yôki kanban, for example. And while the range of kanban presented is broad, it is clear that these are only the tip of the proverbial iceberg.

Medicine

Kanban related to medicine represent arguably the single largest such grouping. Early on, practitioners in the patent medicine industry embraced the need for branding and recognized the benefits of advertising through woodblock-printed broadsides, hikifuda, and kanban. Hikifuda were frequently handed out as gifts with the medicines as decorative calling cards. Sometimes these took the form of calendars that could be used for the entire year, greatly extending their appeal and advertising reach. It has been estimated that a full 50 percent of all extant Edo- and Meiji-period hikifuda are for patent medicines.[98] And a casual survey of collections in Japan and the United States shows that medical kanban make up the vast majority of Edo- and Meiji-era kanban still extant.

Ishida Katsuhide's Kyoto Pharmacy

The merchant Ishida Katsuhide, mentioned above, was an important purveyor of medicine in Kyoto. From the high quality of the signs we have seen, such as those produced by Shimizu Kôjirô, we can tell that the shop placed great emphasis on the power of effective advertising. Like the owners of many medicine shops, Katsuhide distributed a number of hikifuda to customers. The verb *hiku* means to distribute, and these colorful and often instructional broadsheets were a staple in the merchant's arsenal. A hikifuda in

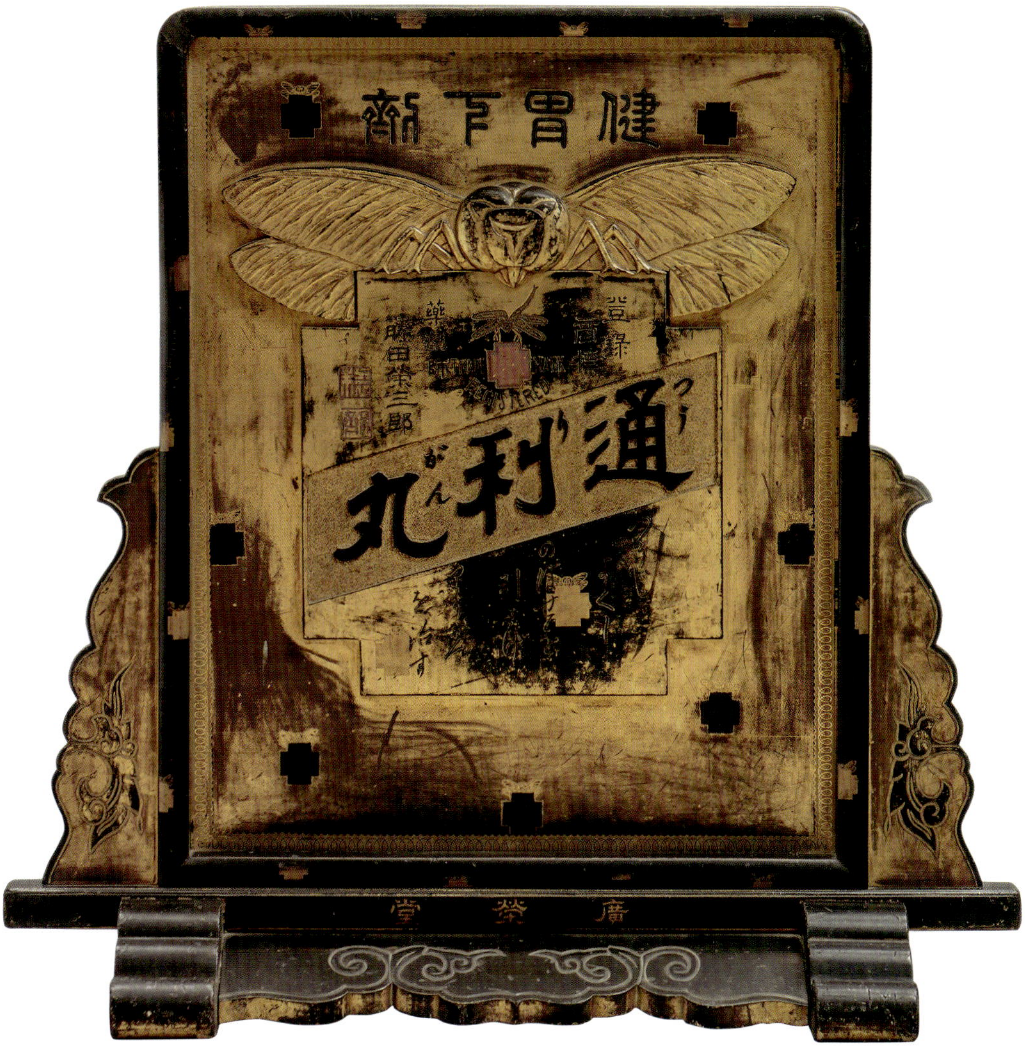

8

Tsuitate kanban for pharmacy selling Tsurigan laxative

Late nineteenth century

Wood, gold leaf, pigment, lacquer

43 × 42 × 11½ in. (109.2 × 106.7 × 29.2 cm)

Mingei International Museum Purchase, 2014-09-001

The tsuitate, or room divider, is an elegant and traditional decorative feature within Japanese homes and businesses, helping to define spaces and create areas of privacy. The tsuitate was also an excellent medium for the kanban maker, allowing the sign to serve two functions at once, as privacy screen and advertising surface. Its large size and the fact that it remained protected indoors made the tsuitate an ideal canvas for effectuating a client's vision. Woodblock-print mages from the Edo period show that tsuitate kanban reached impressive dimensions and were put to particularly effective use by kusuri-ya (medicine shops), which prized both ostentatious display and discretion—a delicate balance. Here, an elegant tsuitate kanban for the patent medicine Tsurigan, a stomach laxative, features the dramatic head and outstretched double wings of a dragonfly (*tombo*) alighting atop a four-sided cross. As with most Meiji-era kanban for patent medicines, the top features the phrase "tôroku shôhyô," registered trademark nomenclature mandated by the Meiji government beginning in 1884. Here it appears in both kanji and English. The central panel of the screen replicates the four-sided cross design and includes all of the pertinent information: "*Ken i gezai 'tsurigan'*" (Laxative pills for a healthy stomach), listing Fujita Eizaburô as the pharmacist (*yakuzaishi*). The lower section contains a recitation of the healthful benefits of Tsurigan: "*Tsuji yokushi nobose wo hikisage*" (Improves bowel movements and restores equilibrium) and "*tumariin wo naosu*" (corrects the cause of constipation). The dragonfly, an auspicious symbol, was known as the *kachimushi* (victory bug) based on its propensity to fly straight toward danger. It was also known as the "indestructible insect" and featured prominently in traditional samurai armor as a protective talisman. The very bottom of the sign bears the inscribed characters of the shop's name: "Koedô."

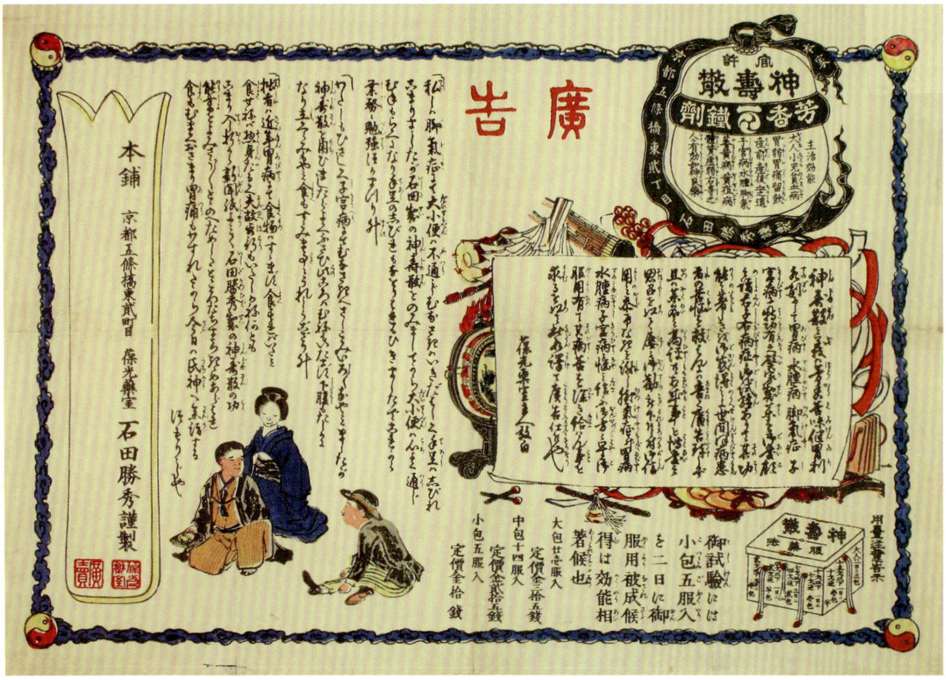

FIG. 30 Hikifuda (advertising print) for Ishida Katsuhide's pharmacy in Kyoto, featuring the Shinjusan image, early twentieth century. Polychrome woodblock print, ink and color on paper, 15 × 20½ in. (38 × 52 cm). Waseda University Library.

the collection of the Naito Museum of Pharmaceutical Science and Industry issued by Katsuhide bears his registered trademark with the ichi and mitsudomoe symbols. It describes and visually portrays the healthful benefits of a number of his medicines, including Kyôwasan (Chest ease powder), Seki no myôyaku (Miracle cure for cough medicine), and Hikanyakuôen, which was a cure-all with beneficial effects for the liver, spleen, kidneys, heart, and lungs. The illustrations depict a mother consulting with someone who might be Katsuhide and young children suffering from various maladies (fig. 30).[99] A number of hikifuda for Katsuhide's shop and various medicines, including his very popular strengthening medicine, Shinjusan, are also held in the Waseda Library collection.

Two nearly identical kanban for Katsuhide's Shinjusan hôkô tetsuzai (Fragrant iron pills) depict a jewel-like hanging *kôro* (incense container) swathed in a flowing ribbon surround (cat. 9). The incense-burner shape of the sign is a playful reference to the "fragrant" aspect of the name of this popular patent medicine. These double-sided signs are carved in the round, with the information repeated on both sides, making them mokei kanban as well as shitta kanban. A number of hikifuda exist extolling the virtues of Katsuhide's Shinjusan, and images of this type of kanban are used as a masthead of sorts for the advertisements.[100] The hikifuda in the Waseda Library collection advertising Katsuhide's Shinjusan includes a small printed image nearly identical to these two kanban. An explanatory note to the side encourages customers to look for this image when selecting Katsuhide products, to ensure their authenticity.[101] The flyer also lists information for Katsuhide's Osaka branch shop (*hokondo*), operated by Okamoto Kihei in the Yotsubashi section.

For the kanban, the details of Katsuhide's shop are inscribed into the ribbon, and the same address near the Gojo Bridge in Kyoto is listed as the home shop. The body of the sign itself is richly inscribed with ornate characters. At the very top, flanking the suspension hook, is the mark "*kankyo*,"

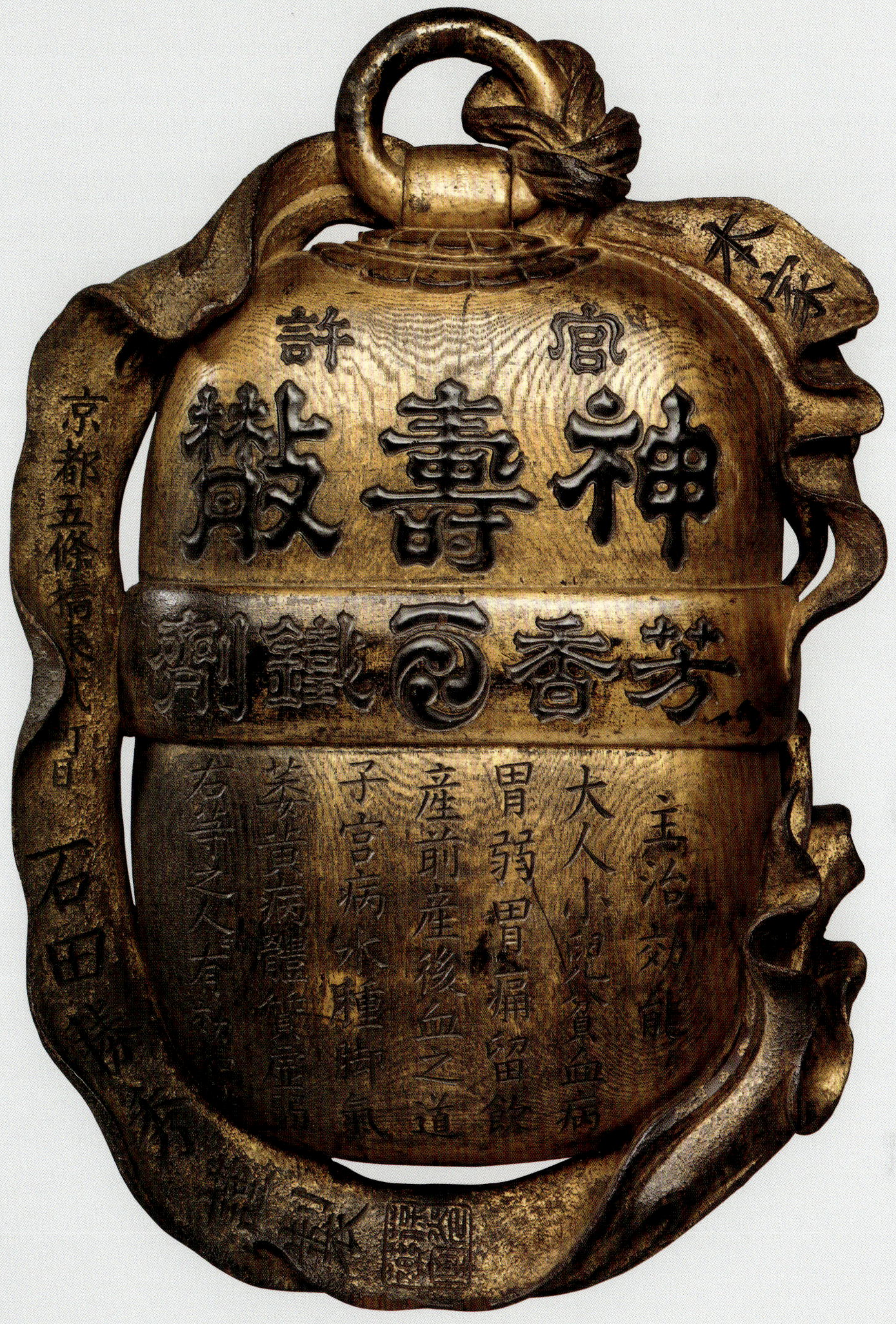

9

Shitta kanban for Shinjusan hôkô tetsuzai strength medicine, possibly made by Shimizu Kôjirô

Late nineteenth century

Wood, pigment, lacquer

25 × 16 in. (63 × 42.5 cm)

Peabody Essex Museum Purchase, R.C. Billings Fund, 1932, E20997

© Peabody Essex Museum, Salem, MA. Photograph by Kathy Tarantola

The craftsmen of kanban frequently interpreted nascent Japanese corporate "branding" in three-dimensional terms. The ribbon-adorned incense container for Shinjusan hôkô tetsuzai (Fragrant iron pills), for instance, became a well-known symbol of the Kyoto pharmacy of Ishida Katsuhide, appearing on many *hikifuda* (advertising flyers). This image was also used as a richly carved and embellished kanban to be suspended at the home shop on Gôjô Dôri in Kyoto as well as at the shops of regional distributors. The kanban-shi has used nearly every conceivable inch of space to communicate not only the name, trademark registration, and signifying crest of Katsuhide, but also, in the lower body of the sign, an exhaustive listing of all the ills Shinjusan was purported to address. Even the decorative ribbon is brought into service, with inscriptions listing Katsuhide's shop and its address. Other known examples of this sign include mother-of-pearl decoration. It is assumed that these were largely the work of Katsuhide's go-to sign maker, Shimizu Kôjirô.

or official permission, as required under the Meiji government's patent medicine regulations, in effect from 1870 to 1884. Along the top front is the medicine's name, "Shinjusan," engraved in a highly ornate style of kanji. The middle band bears the phrase "Hôkô tetsuzai," serving as a tagline or advertising catchphrase. The lower section holds a forty-six-character inscription listing the particular benefits ascribed to the pills. These include helping alleviate anemia in adults and children; facilitating digestion; overcoming stomach pains; soothing women's hysteria before and after childbirth; counteracting uterine diseases; and aiding in cases of dropsy, beriberi, and general weakness.[102] The two kanban are strikingly similar in execution, with subtle differences only in the ribbon pattern. One sign is in the PEM collection, while the other is in the Becton Dickinson corporate art collection. Both bear Katsuhide's ichi mitsudomoe mark. In the Peabody example, this is carved and inked in black. In the Becton Dickinson example, the mark is executed in mother-of-pearl, harkening back to the plum blossoms found on the sign made for Katsuhide by Shimizu Kôjirô for the Ume no yuki medicine described earlier. Though neither kanban is signed, the sophistication of the carving and the use of mother-of-pearl leads to the conjecture that these two signs were also the work of Shimizu Kôjirô.

Baiyaku Patent Medicines

The history of the patent medicine industry in Japan is generally traced to the medicine maker Bandai Jôkan of Katakami in Bizen. In 1682, Jôkan was called some distance to the aid of the ailing daimyô of Toyama, Maeda Seiho (b. 1649). Jôkan treated him with a baiyaku named Han-go-tan, and a remarkable recovery followed. Impressed with the effectiveness of Jôkan's "soul-reviving" medicine, Maeda formulated and initiated a distribution system, effectively shifting the center of patent medicine manufacturing to Toyama. By the early eighteenth century, a network of Han-go-tan medicine peddlers radiated out from Toyama. Each "band" of peddlers covered a specific district, making the long trek from Toyama across the mountains each year to service their clientele. What ultimately made Han-go-tan unique and exceptionally successful was its distribution practice: a consumer was given a supply anticipated to last for the coming year, with notations duly made of name, location, and quantity. When the peddler returned the following year, the customer only paid for what had been consumed, and the remainder was traded for a fresh supply.[103] The image of the Toyama medicine peddler with his green or blue cloth-wrapped box stenciled "Etchû Toyama," designating the place of origin, was a common one in Edo Japan.[104] Woodblock-print artists frequently captured these itinerant salesmen as they journeyed far distances (fig. 31). Kabuki, as we have seen, also capitalized on a certain exotic allure exercised by the medicine peddler. By the end of the Edo period, there were twenty-one recognized bands, ranging in size from 30 to 300, with a total of 2,600 peddlers offering Toyama's Han-go-tan.[105] By the early Meiji era, this number had jumped to 5,000 peddlers. By 1882 the number was as high as 9,000.[106] And by 1904 Toyama accounted for 25 percent of all the patent medicines manufactured in Japan.[107]

Like Uriô's Tonchinkô, discussed above, Han-go-tan was just one of many patent medicines available to the Edo and Meiji consumer. Hôtan, a specialty of Morita Jihei (1840–1912), was advertised as one of Japan's oldest patent medicines. The ninth-generation Morita, active in the early Meiji era, was a noted calligrapher, and his style became known as "Hôtan-style," with many kanban commissioned featuring his distinctive calligraphy.[108] A 1907 advertisement boasted that the tenth-generation Morita Jihei sold "up-to-date" medicine that enabled "its users to be proof against noxious exhalations and infectious diseases. . . . [It is] best for reinvigorating the drooping spirits. . . . Beware of imitations of which there

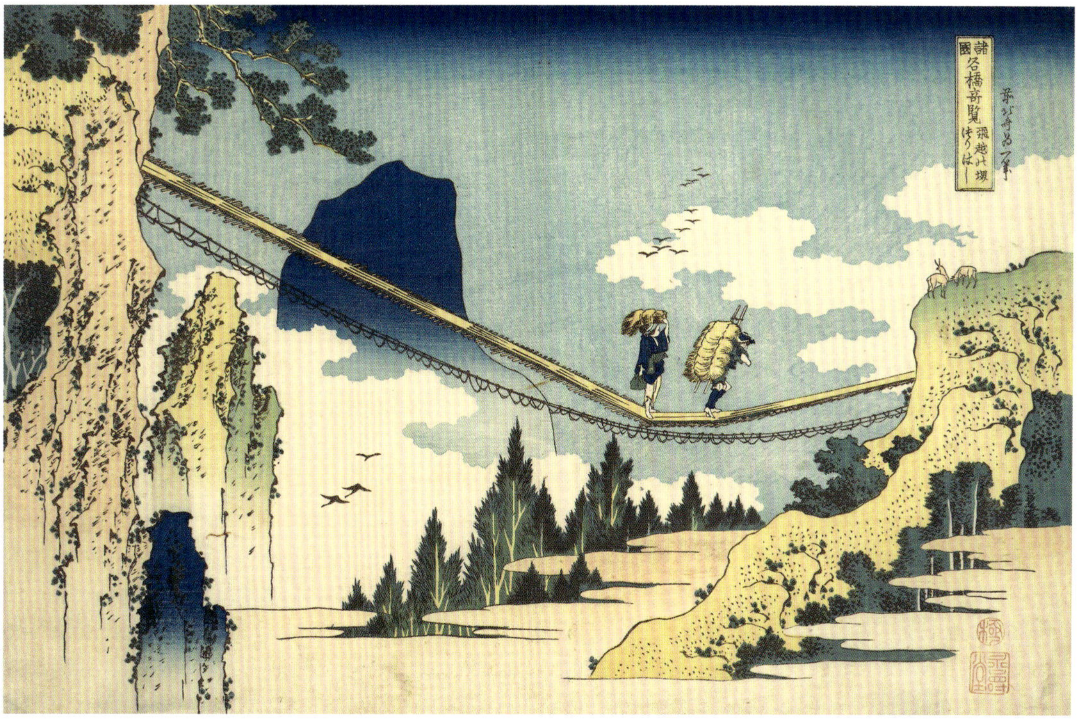

FIG. 31 *Hietsu no sakai tsuribashi* (The suspension bridge on the border of Hisa and Etchû Provinces), c. 1830, Katsushika Hokusai (1760–1849), from the series *Shokoku meikyô kiran* (Remarkable view of bridges in various provinces). Polychrome woodblock print, ink and color on paper, 10⅛ × 15⅛ in. (25.7 × 38.4 cm). Metropolitan Museum of Art, Henry L. Phillips Collection, Bequest of Henry L. Phillips, 1939, JP2944, www.metmuseum.org.

are several."[109] Morita X was also the king of the billboard. Taking full advantage of the modernization that had swept Japan in the late nineteenth century, Morita peppered the entire country with giant billboards, some lit up at night, in addition to advertising in the newly established newspapers and magazines that had flooded in on the heels of advanced printing techniques.[110] Rapidly fading into the past was the hand-carved kanban, and marketing in all its forms was taking on a decidedly modern aspect.

With the advent of the Meiji era and the subsequent abolishment of the samurai class, many in this suddenly disenfranchised segment of society gravitated toward the patent medicine business. Buddhist monks also engaged in the trade. In an 1899 article in the *Rikugô zasshi* medical magazine, Yamagata Tôkon reported that Buddhist magazines of the Meiji era were awash in patent medicine ads by specific monks and temples, counting seventy-eight separate medicines being offered.[111] Similarly, newly launched newspapers were inundated with patent medicine advertisements, helping to support their bottom lines. A survey of the Osaka-based *Asahi shimbun*, for example, revealed that in 1882 over 50 percent of the "newspace" was taken up by patent medicine advertisers.[112] On a national level, by 1896 there were 1,401 separately registered inventors of patent medicines, with 5,145 vendors.[113] Like the nostrums of nineteenth-century Britain or America, the names of these medicinal remedies were evocative in the extreme: Hyakudoku kudashi (Hundred poisons purgative), Bikkuri megusuri (Astonishing eye medicine), Tekimen-sui (Immediate effect water), and Seikisui (Purifying wonder water) or Seifuyu (Purifying women hot water).[114]

"Patent medicine" is a bit of a misnomer, in that there was no real "patent" for the product itself. Most of the medicines were herbal powders of various concoctions, and while the name and its associated designs and graphics may have

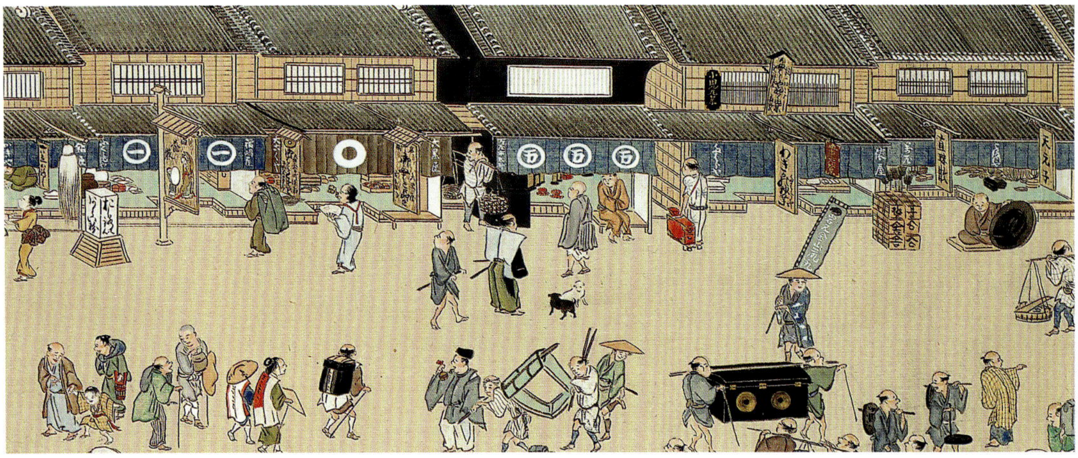

FIG. 32 Detail: Medicine shops along Nihonbashi, as depicted in the *Kidai shôran*. Museum of Asian Art, Berlin.

been registered, the actual recipe and ingredients were not patented. In 1870, the new Meiji government enacted a series of regulations regarding patent medicines in an attempt to capitalize on the success of this industry. These regulations functioned as part of a much broader national campaign to promote and advance the health of the citizenry, as Japan took its place among the nations of the world.[115] Initially this called for specific trademark nomenclature to be included in all advertisements, both kanban and print media. Prior to this, advertisements for patent medicines, in an effort to convey respectability, frequently included the phrase "*isshi-sôden*" (secretly handed down to posterity), "*shinju*" (divine gift), or "*kaden-hihô*" (medicine prepared from a family recipe). Or, in a nod to official sanction, the phrase "*gomen*" (registered) was used. However, with the new regulations, such vague terminology was replaced with the phrases "*kankyo*" (licensed) and "*naimushô-menkyo*" (licensed by the government). In 1884 new regulations were enacted mandating the term "*tôroku shôhyô*" (registered trademark). The vast majority of patent medicine kanban after this date bear these words adjacent to or flanking the shop's trademark.[116]

Shops and purveyors of patent medicines flourished in nearly every town. The *Edo kaimono hitori annai*, an early nineteenth-century consumer's guide to Edo compiled by Nakagawa Gorozaemon, lists 206 shops specifically dealing in *kusuri* (medicine). A similar guide for Osaka lists 178 shops.[117] The *Kidai shôran* handscroll, discussed above, depicts a number of these shops along Nihonbashi, including the drug seller and artificial tooth shop of Matsui, purveyor of Seiyôtan; the medicine and tobacco shop of Daikokuya Kichiemon; the face powder and medicine shop Kagi-ya; and the patent medicine wholesalers Hodoen, Fujiki, Konishi Rinbee, Manya, Tawaraya Morinoshi, Fukushima-ya, Echigoya, and Nishimura-ya (fig. 32). Most of these were clustered in the section just north of the important intersection with Suruga-chô, headquarters of the Echigoya dry goods store. This is the same section that is pictured in Berg's study of Nihonbashi, featuring the dramatic dragon-encrusted tate kanban and an apparent epicenter for the medicine trade in Edo.

Beginning in the Meiji era, it became common practice for *kusuri-ya* (pharmacies) to commission an extensive series of matching kanban that would be mounted on the upper floor of the shop exterior facing the street, announcing the medicines carried by the shop. Often embellished with gold-leaf or gold-lacquer grounds, these kanban conga lines created a beautiful visual array, easily

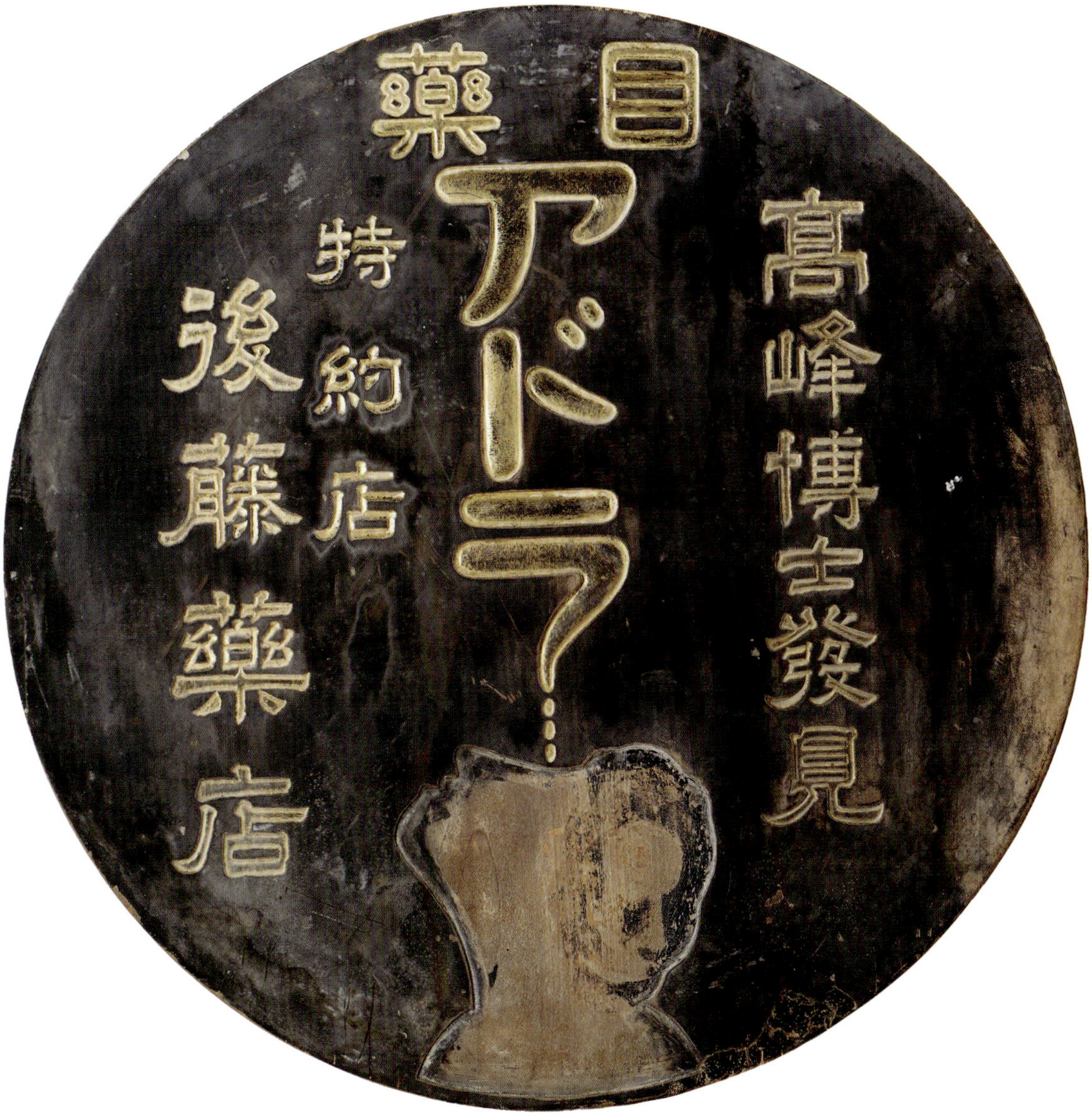

10

Circular shitta kanban for pharmacy selling Adora eye drops

Early twentieth century
Wood, gold leaf, pigment
24 in. (61 cm) in diameter
Private Collection

Meiji-era Japan was literally awash in eye medicines, as the Japanese attempted to use patent medicines and Western pharmaceuticals to address pervasive eye-related health issues. One of the more popular patent eye medicines was the Adora brand. Using katagana phonetic script, "Adora" was written so that the final syllable terminated in droplets falling into the eyes of a Western-style woman gazing expectantly upward toward the name. This shitta kanban, or double-sided kanban, is unusual in that it is executed as a circle. The supervising physician is listed as "Takamine Hakase."

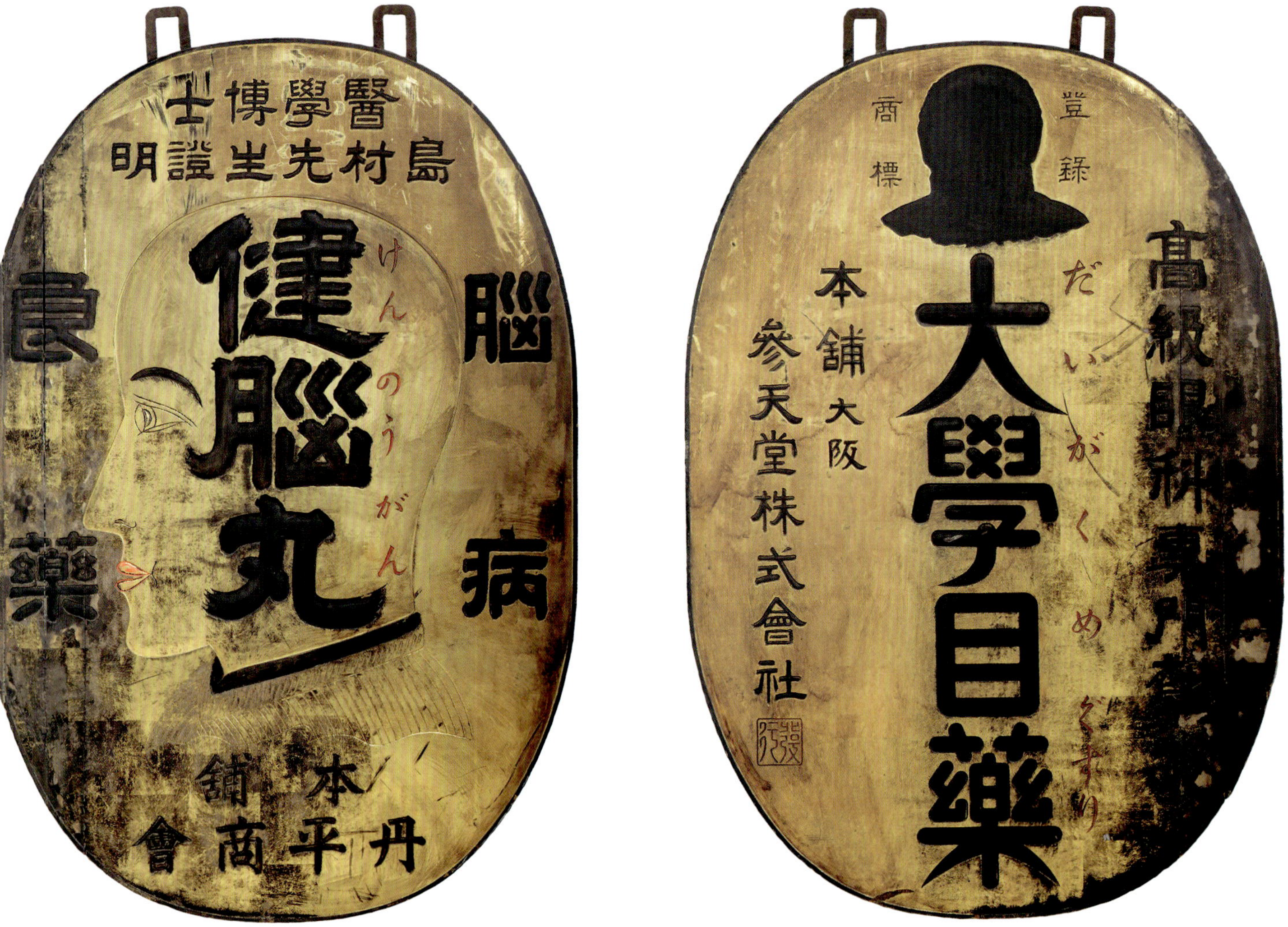

11

Shitta kanban for pharmacy selling Ken'nôgan, front and back views

Early twentieth century

Wood, gold leaf, pigment, ink, metal fittings

62 × 40 × 1¾ in. (157.5 × 101.6 × 4.4 cm)

Collection of John Joseph Schloss and Dieuwke Eijer

A cure for the mental stress and strain of modern-day life was promised in the patent medicine Ken'nôgan (Strengthening brain pills), taken for nervous disorders. Part of a gender-specific cluster of medicines designed to address "nervous exhaustion," "hysteria," and "neuritis," Ken'nôgan along with other "brain-strengthening" remedies such as Nôgan and Shinseieki catered to the modern Japanese male who was attempting to adjust to the accelerated pace of life. The popularity of Ken'nôgan was driven by an aggressive advertising campaign, attested to by the existence of many kanban for Ken'nôgan. This is a spectacular Ken'nôgan kanban of truly impressive scale; it is crafted from a number of pieces of wood carefully joined together, lacquered over, and then finally covered in gold leaf squares of a very high quality. The sign is notable for its unusual oval shape, with the iconic head in the center. The top reads, "*Igaku hakase Shimaura sensei shômei*" (Accredited by Dr. Shimaura). Along the right side are the characters "*nôbyô*"—referring to disorders affecting the brain and nervous system. Along the left are the characters "*ryôyaku*" or "effective medicine." The bottom lists the *honpo*, or main store, as Tanihira Shôkai. This is the primary format of the vast majority of Ken'nôgan signs, whether horizontal or vertical in orientation, with only small variations in design and nomenclature.

attracting the eye of the prospective buyer. Alternatively, a series of shitta (double-sided) kanban would be hung in rows just under the eaves of the shop's first floor; frequently the reverse advertised a different but related product, giving double duty to the sign. This widespread practice helps to account for the apparent consistency of certain kanban groupings. Some were horizontal, others vertical in orientation, but executed with matching frames and background treatments. The Naito Museum of Pharmaceutical Science and Industry has conserved numerous kanban sequences such as these from various historical kusuri-ya. A series of six kanban from the Yamagata Benkyôdo includes Morita Jihei's Hôtan cure-all, Ryûkakusan cough medicine, Jitsubosan women's medicine, Uzukyûmeigan children's medicine, Reiben sedative, and Adora eye drops (cat. 10).[118]

One of the more popular patent medicines of the Meiji era was Ken'nôgan (Strengthening brain pills). The distinctive image selected for this cure for nervous disorders was the profile of a man with a shaved head in gold, with "Ken-nô-gan" written in strong calligraphic characters in black down the middle, accompanied by lightly rendered hiragana phonetic script alongside (cats. 11, 12). The smooth-pated mascot can be read as a Buddhist monk, a student, or a Westerner. Kanban for Ken'nôgan uniformly feature this image, helping to create a very specific brand identity. Along with such medicines as Nôgan (Brain pills) and Shinseieki (Spirit-relaxing elixir), Ken'nôgan targeted mental health, countering the stresses and strains on the modern Japanese male's mental equilibrium.[119] To further suggest the integrity of the product, kanban for patent medicines of the Meiji era frequently appended the names of Western-style doctors, implying a trustworthy scientific grounding, eclipsing the concept of "secret family traditions" or "divine gifts" of the previous era. Doctor Shimaura was an Osaka-based doctor closely associated with the Ken'nôgan product, and his name appears on many kanban for Ken'nôgan, but nothing is known of Dr. Shimaura, his credentials, or even his veritable existence.

Ken'nôgan was made by the Osaka-based manufacturer Tanihira Shôkai. The Osaka aspect is important. Though there were a number of patent medicine manufacturers in nearly every city, particularly Kyoto and Edo/Tokyo, Osaka was the only true rival to Toyama in the patent medicine industry. In 1772, a group of 124 medicinal ingredient merchants in the Doshômachi area formed a *kabu nakama* (trade association) and were empowered by the government to collect taxes on the sale of medicinal ingredients across the country; similarly, they were granted a monopoly on the importation, trade, and distribution of components essential to or popular in many patent medicines.[120] Their focus historically had been on *kampo*, or traditional Chinese herbal medicines. However, with the advent of the Meiji era and the influx of Western approaches to medicine, Dôshomachi became the center of the developing pharmaceutical industry, eschewing tradition for science.

The Ken'nôgan kanban in the collection of John Joseph Schloss and Dieuwke Eijer is a shitta kanban, with the reverse advertising Daigakumegusuri (University eye drops). The name of the medicine, written in the center, is presided over by the darkened silhouette of a man's head incised into the sign. Unlike the Ken'nôgan profile, this image is a full frontal bust, executed in complete blackness, and it stands out somewhat ominously from the gold-leaf ground. An inspection of other signs for Daigakumegusuri in the Naito Museum of Pharmaceutical Science and Industry shows that this head would typically have been rendered in full color, depicting a bespectacled man with a balding head, mustache, and thick beard. Over the Meiji era, the face used in this advertisement drifted from one with a decidedly Western feel to Asian and back to Western again, as the eyes changed shape in various iterations.[121] In all of the signs, the tôroku shôhyô indications flank the bust of the figure,

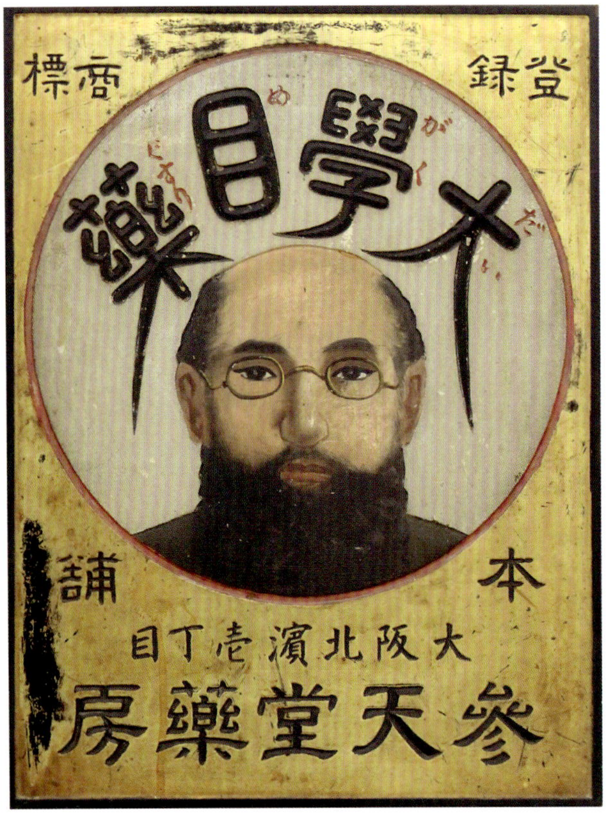

FIG. 33 Sage kanban for Daigakumegusuri (University eye drops), early twentieth century. 20 × 15 in. (51 × 39 cm). Naito Museum of Pharmaceutical Science and Industry.

clearly designating this as the medicine's registered image.

Who is this man? One theory is that this is the German doctor Erwin Bälz (1849–1913). Bälz initially taught medicine in Japan at the Tokyo Medical School in 1879. He would remain in Japan for twenty-seven years, ultimately marrying a Japanese woman and becoming private physician to the Meiji emperor in 1902. Bälz was arguably the most prominent Western doctor in Japan during the period, and perhaps it was thought that his distinctive bearded image would lend a sense of authority, if not indirect imperial sanction (fig. 33).

Other eye tinctures included Adora, Omearaigusuri, Fudômegusuri, Kokainsui, Hoshitorimegusuri, and Kuriru (Clear), but Daigakumegusuri, with its sage endorser, was by far the most successful. Daigakumegusuri was developed by the kusuri-ya Taguchi Santendô in the Kitahama section of Osaka in 1899. The company itself was started in 1890 by Kenkichi Taguchi, and its first product was a cold medication known as Heburin-gan. Interestingly, Daigakumegusuri is still sold today through Santen Pharmaceutical Co., making it the longest-selling eye drop medicine in Japan. The medicine still bears the image of a bespectacled man as its registered trademark.[122]

Tobacco Shops

Given the spectacular range of extant kanban and woodblock prints related to shops that sold tobacco leaves (*tabako*), tobacco pipes (*kiseru*), pipe cases (*kiseru-zutsu*), and tobacco pouches (*tabako-ire*), it appears that merchants in this commercial sector of Edo were almost as adept at advertising and self-promotion as their pharmaceutical counterparts. From all the evidence, it is certain that Big Tobacco was already an established phenomenon in Japan centuries before the Marlborough Man ever rode across an American billboard and into the cultural zeitgeist. Shoji screens studded with tobacco-leaf cutouts; diamond-shaped panels strung together, necklace-like, advertising the types of leaves available for purchase; mokei kanban featuring pipes and pipe cases of gargantuan proportions; shitta kanban embellished with relief carvings of pipes with copper fittings; noren emblazoned with yago and tobacco-leaf designs; hako kanban with images of pipes and details of the varieties of tobacco leaf handled; and an entire subculture of woodblock prints, fiction, and kabuki interlaced with tobacco shops, their proprietors, and fashionable smoking: all these bespeak a robust social and commercial culture centered on smoking and its paraphernalia.

The earliest recorded tobacco shop in Japan was not set in the bustling merchant center of Osaka, or amid the cultured enclave of Kyoto, or within the upstart vortex of Edo, or even in the early trade port of Nagasaki. Instead, in 1576 we find tax documents relating to a small tobacco shop operating in the coastal village of Izumozaki in remote Echigo province, south and west of

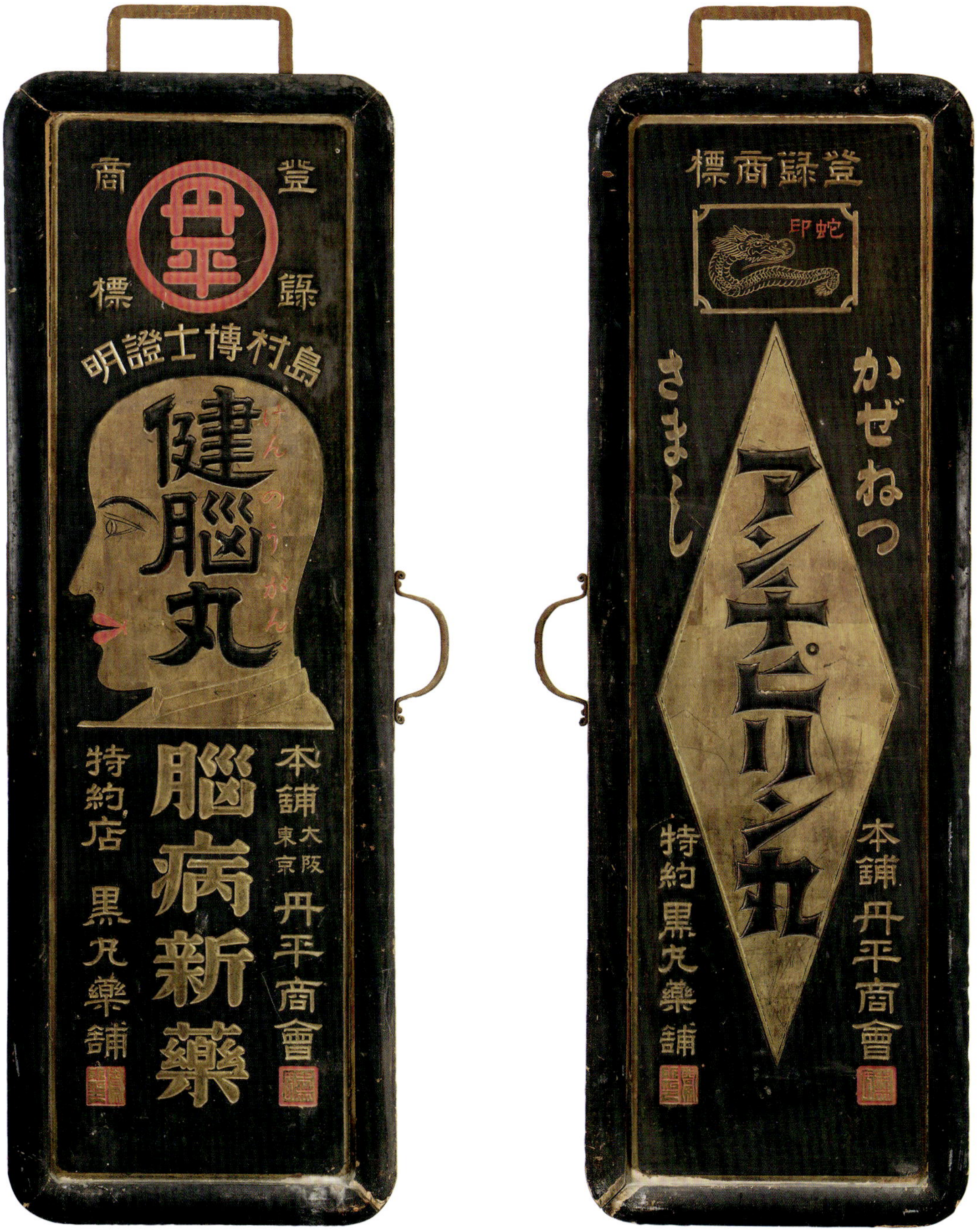

12

Shitta kanban for Ken'nôgan and Anchipirigan, front and back views

Early twentieth century
Wood, gold leaf, pigment, metal fittings
57 × 21 in. (144.8 × 53.3 cm)
Private Collection

As an advertising format, shitta kanban frequently did double duty, advertising one product on one side and a different product on the other. Here, a classic early twentieth-century shitta kanban with a side handle advertises Ken'nôgan on one face and the more obscure Anchipirigan on the other. Whereas the Ken'nôgan side bears the familiar profile of a stressed male in need of relief, the reverse features a large diamond covered in gold leaf, with the medicine's name, "Anchipirigan," written in hiragana. A cartouche immediately above bears the image of a dragon-like serpent of the *hebi jirushi* (snake brand). Further inscriptions indicate that this medicine was meant for easing colds and fevers. Both faces bear inscriptions indicating that this sign was used by the Kuroganyakuho pharmacy, an authorized distributor for Tanpei Shokai, which manufactured both medicines.

FIG. 34 Edo-period woodblock print depicting a tabako-ya with a diamond-shaped kanban advertising the varieties of tobacco sold. Reproduced from Tsuboi, *Kôshô gigei kanban kô,* 30.

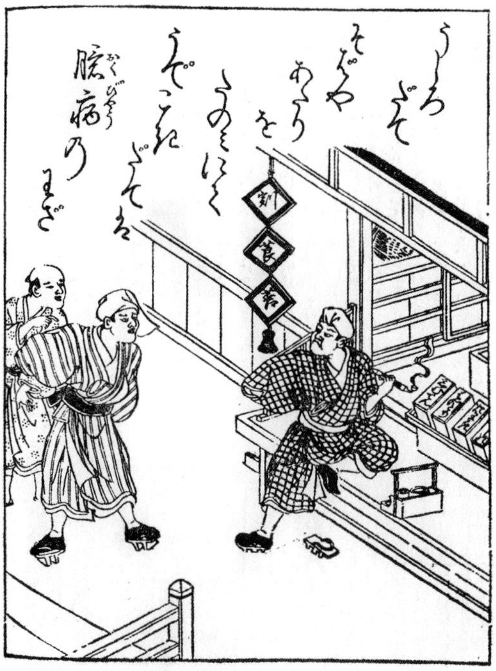

Niigata. Izumozaki had the good fortune to be the transit point for silver ingots mined on Sado Island. The silver was then transported to Nagasaki, where it was used in commerce with the Portuguese for Chinese silks and other commodities, making Izumozaki an unexpectedly important and affluent village. It is speculated that through Portuguese sailors, tobacco, in the form of rolled cigars, was being traded, and an outlet was established in Izumozaki, home to the wealthy Sado Island mine operators. This date indicates that tobacco was already making inroads into Japanese consumer culture even before it became a common item in Portugal and other European nations.[123] Barely forty years later, by 1612, Japanese farmers were so actively engaged in tobacco production that it was displacing staple food crops, and the government became forced to intervene. Nearly all of Japanese society, from samurai in the corridors of power, to Buddhist monks in mountain-fast temples, to merchants plying their wares on the streets of the urban metropolises, to courtesans in the pleasure districts, to farmers the length and breadth of the archipelago, had fully succumbed to the allure of smoking.[124]

Although much has been made of the restricted nature of Japan's foreign policy during the Edo period, Japan's earlier international trading efforts are less well known. Prior to 1635, when Japan initiated its formal "closed-country" (*sakoku*) policy, Japanese merchants operated a fleet of vessels known as *shuinsen* (red-seal ships) and maintained a network of seven trading outposts throughout southeast Asia, including Manila, Hoi An, Ayutthaya, Pattani, and Taiwan. It is speculated that Japanese fine-cut tobacco would have been an export item, filtering out to the world market through the shuinsen and trading outlets.[125] Far from simply being passive consumers for the West's nascent tobacco industry, from an early date, Japanese merchants were active players in the tobacco economy, on an international level as well as a domestic one.

Tabako-ya (Tobacco Leaf Shops)

Tobacco, of course, was not a native Japanese plant, but one introduced from the Americas through trade with the Portuguese. Tobacco arrived in Japan essentially at the same time as it did in European countries, initially as a medicinal plant, and soon thereafter for the pure, unadulterated pleasure of the puff. As a viable and rewarding cash crop, it spread rapidly. Regional differences in drying practices, soil conditions, fertilizers, and fermentation techniques soon led to the development of distinct varietals. Growing regions tended to supply the urban centers closest to them. For example, customers in Osaka and Kyoto tended to prefer Shinden, Hattori, and Yoshino "brands" of tobacco, while Edoites were likely to prefer Oyamada, Ishizu, and Tate varietals.[126] The most sought-after leaf, however, was referred to as "Kokubu" or "Kokufu," a product of Kagoshima Prefecture, far in the south, whose "pleasant taste and fragrant odour" made it the most popular (and expensive) of products (fig. 35).[127]

The word *tabako* itself was necessarily of foreign derivation, equivalent to the English word *tobacco*. This could be phonetically rendered in hiragana as *ta ba ko* or in kanji as "smoke" and "weed" or "varied leaf powder."[128] Shop signs

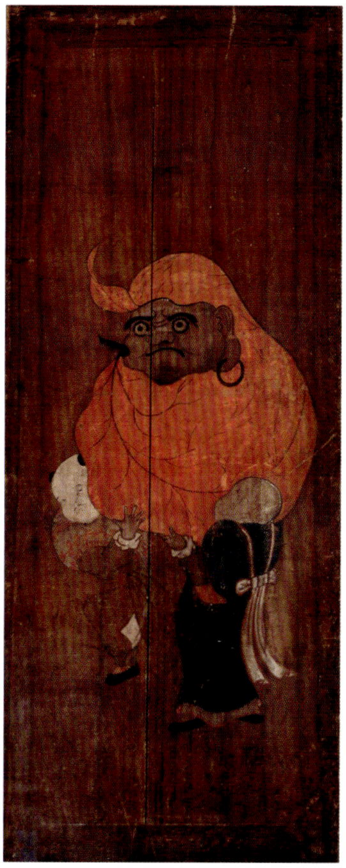

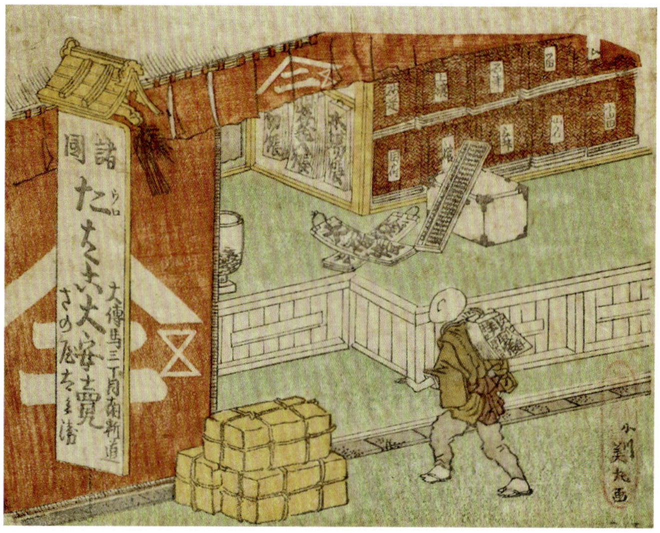

FIG. 35 Shitta kanban for a tabako-ya depicting two *karako* (Chinese-style children) carrying a large Daruma fashioned out of tobacco leaves, nineteenth century. 48 × 18 in. (121.2 × 46.3 cm). Tobacco and Salt Museum, Tokyo.

FIG. 36 Woodblock print depicting an Edo tabako-ya with its signature reddish-brown noren, Kitao Shigemasa II (1739–1820), Bunka era (1804–18). Tobacco and Salt Museum, Tokyo.

advertising tobacco leaves during the Edo period frequently featured a string of diamond-shaped panels inscribed with the hiragana characters *ta-ba-ko* or with characters indicating the types of leaves available.[129] These panels would be strung vertically, like a chain, or horizontally, each diamond bearing a small tassel at the bottom (fig. 34). In addition to the leaves themselves, the fineness of the cut was important. The Japanese favored an extremely thin cut called *hoso kizami*. This allowed for the bowl (*ganbuki*) of the pipe to be quite small. Tobacco cutting was an important industry in and of itself, and the skill of the cutter was a crucial selling point for a tabako-ya. Mokei kanban in the shape of tobacco leaves were another common form of signage. In Edo, a reddish-brown noren was the hallmark of a tobacco-leaf vendor, with additional designs of tobacco leaves done in a paste-resist stencil along with the shop's or proprietor's name and yago (fig. 36).

Unlike modern cigarettes or even the rolled cigar favored by early Portuguese sailors, pipes, particularly Japanese-style pipes, were equal parts delivery mechanism and paraphernalia. Smoking was as much a cultural endeavor as it was a recreational activity. Tobacco was paired with the tea ceremony early on, and as a result, the physical objects associated with smoking became exceptionally important, receiving both sophisticated artistic treatment as well as aggressive scrutiny.[130] The *kiseru* (pipe), the *kiseru-zutsu* (pipe case), the *tabako-ire* (tobacco pouch), and the *tabako-bon* (tobacco tray) were all important to the smoking experience and indicative of an individual's taste and sophistication. Shops with these individual specialties frequently clustered together but remained under separate management.

Kiseru-ya **(Pipe Shops)**

Unlike the Dutch, who favored short, white clay pipes of their own manufacture, the Japanese preferred Malay-style long-stemmed pipes. The long stem allowed for the smoke to cool a bit before it entered the lungs. By tipping the bowl end slightly upward while smoking, the smoker was also treated to periodic bursts of a coagulated nicotine drip.[131] The kiseru, the core object in the experience, received a variety of treatments. The earliest Japanese pipes, emulating other Asian styles, were made entirely of metal and known as *en-kiseru*. Generally they were of cupronickel, but other metals, precious and otherwise, were also employed. The term *kiseru* itself is a bit of a mystery and is thought to be of Dutch, Spanish, or even Cambodian origin.[132] The bowl (*ganbuki*, lit. "sparrow head") and the mouthpiece (*sui guchi*) were typically of metal, while the body (*rau*) could be executed in any number of materials, ranging from imported *shidan* (rosewood) and *kokutan* (ebony) to ivory, tortoiseshell, or silver.

The configuration of the pipe itself went through numerous phases. In its earliest stage, the Japanese pipe tended to be of exceptional length, with some pipes extending over a meter. Known as *date kiseru*, these pipes necessarily required larger bowls and were the epitome of conspicuous display; they had to be tucked into the belt like a sword. Early pipes made entirely of iron were known as *kenka kiseru*, or "fighting pipes," and doubled as small personal weapons.[133] Over the Edo period, pipes tended to become shorter, for convenience and more subtle individual expression. The Bunka-Bunsei-Tenpô eras, corresponding to 1804–44, are considered the golden age of the kiseru, with many pipes of exceptional quality being produced, coinciding with a general cultural efflorescence in many arenas (cat. 15).[134]

Owners of *kiseru-ya* overwhelmingly favored the mokei style of kanban (cat. 13). The pipe, enlarged and ornamented, was its own best advertisement. An exceptional and unusual kanban for the kiseru-ya Yamamasa, located along Nihonbashi in Edo and operated by Murata Shichiuemon, was a shitta kanban featuring a dramatic rendering of Mt. Fuji ringed by clouds, with the famous Miho pine grove below executed entirely of masterfully interlocked en-kiseru.[135] A woodblock-print image of this interesting kanban was included along with information on the Yamamasa shop in the *Edo kaimono hitori annai* buying guide, mentioned previously. Contemporary museum collections of kanban, including the PEM, Shôwa Neon Takamura Kanban Museum, Tobacco and Salt Museum, Japan Folk Crafts Museum, and Edo-Tokyo Museum, all contain excellent examples of kiseru-ya kanban, indicating not only their prominence but also their importance as traditional kanban.

Tabako-ire-ya (Tobacco Pouch Shops)

The quintessential accessory for the sophisticated Edo smoker was the pouch (*ire*) in which he carried his cut tobacco. These pouches were made of brocade, leather, waterproof crepe, or paper. Images of pipe and tobacco stores frequently include the indispensable ire-ya next door. In the *Kidai shôran*, the tabako-ire wholesaler Marukadoya is situated right next to the prosperous kiseru-ya Nakamuraya Genpachi, mentioned previously. The Marukadoya boasts a large roofed nikai kanban suspended over the street from the roof separating the first and second floors of the spacious shop, which is unquestionably larger than the Nakamuraya next door. The Marukadoya has also employed a large *hioke* awning with an eye-popping yago (a circle within a square) stenciled in white on the indigo blue textile.

However, undoubtedly the most famous of all ire-ya was the one owned and operated by the popular author and illustrator Santô Kyôden (Kitao Masanobu, 1761–1816). Kyôden, who was celebrated for his dry wit and works about life in the Yoshiwara pleasure quarters, opened a paper tabako-ire-ya in the Kyôbashi district of Edo in 1793, known as Kyôya. A favorite among the Edo cultural elite, his establishment featured mostly paper ire of Kyôden's own design, but also other related objects, ranging from kiseru to toothpick and handkerchief carriers. His shop became a cultural hub, appearing in novels and woodblock

13

Mokei kanban for pipe shop

Early twentieth century

Wood, pigment, metal

52½ × 9½ in. (133.4 × 24.1 cm)

Private Collection

Oversized kiseru pipes made for a natural form of mokei kanban. Extant examples, as well as woodblock prints dating from the Edo period, confirm that they were a particularly popular medium through which to advertise a tobacco pipe shop. The long stem of the pipe's *rau* (body) provided ample surface area for the name of the wholesaler (*ôroshi*) or retailer (*kouri*). A perfect example is this mokei kanban for the Kadaman kiseru-ya (pipe shop). The side-mounted handles allowed for this sign to be easily taken in and out of the shop or paraded through the streets as a form of moving advertisement. The rau is slightly notched and the kanban-shi has placed the shop's yago—a square frame (*kada*) with the character *man* (meaning 10,000)—for Kadaman. Flanking this is the tôroku shôhyô registration listing, and below are the characters "*Shiire dokoro*," indicating retail sales.

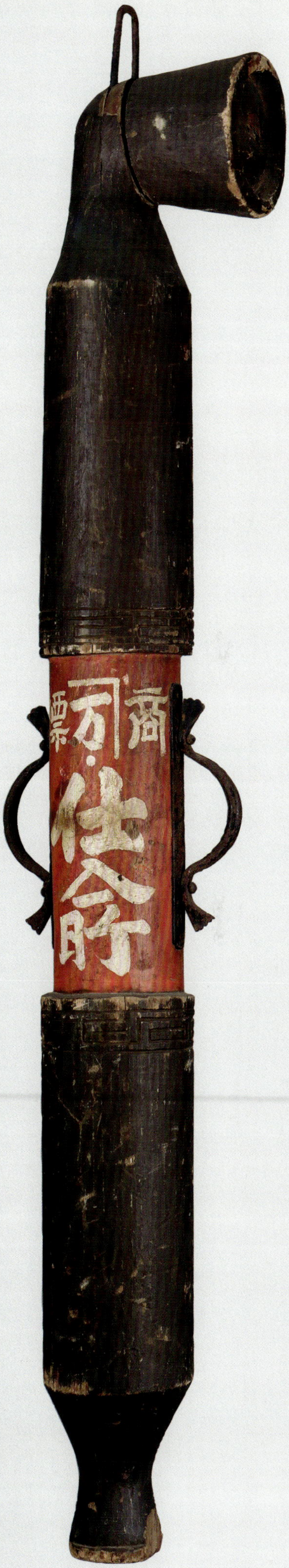

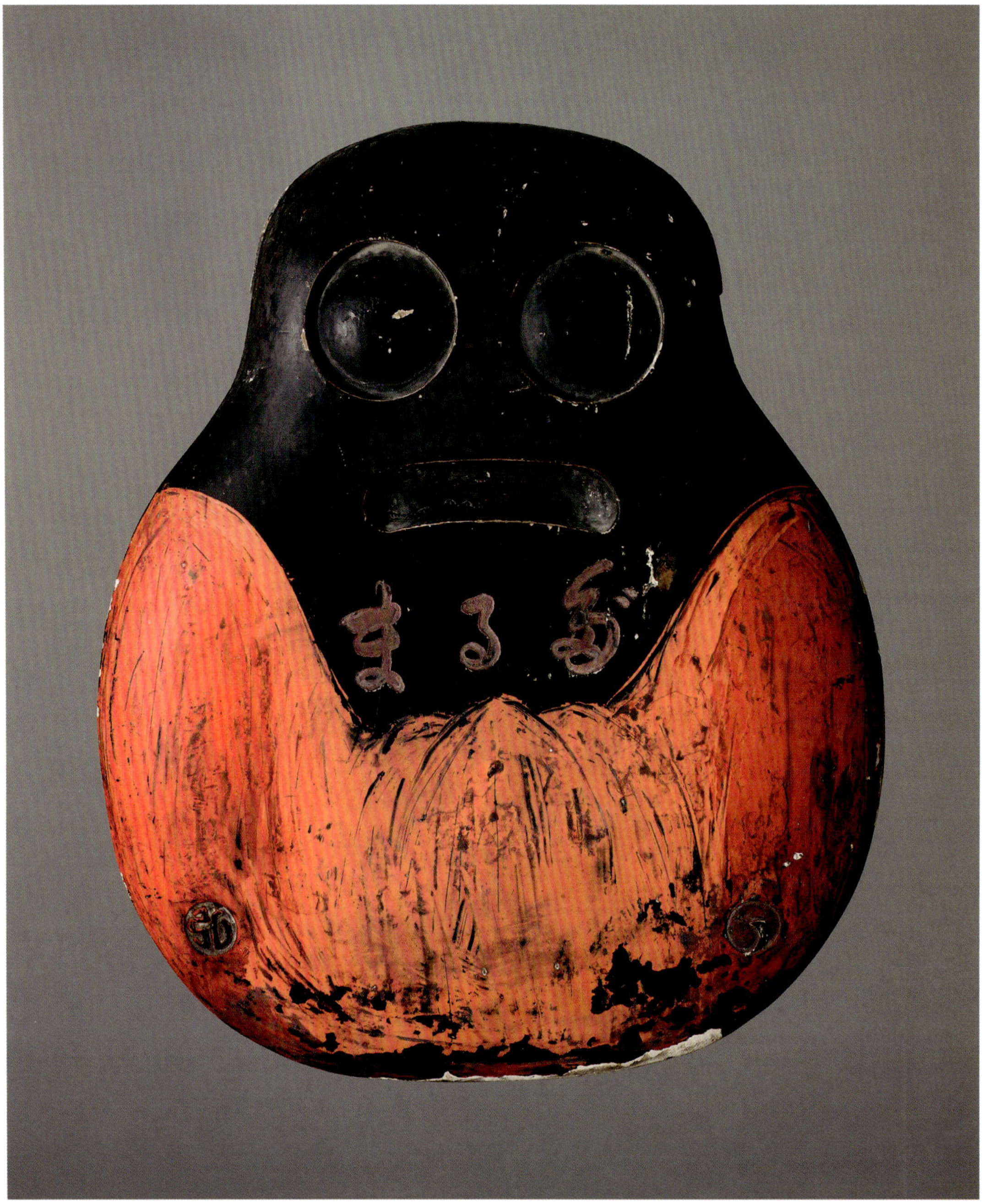

14

Mokei kanban for tobacco shop

Late nineteenth century

Wood, pigment, lacquer

20¼ × 15 in. (51.4 × 38.1 cm)

Private Collection

The myth of the Buddhist monk Daruma, or Bodhidharma, is that he rested in meditation for so long that his legs atrophied. Japanese depictions of him frequently interpret the founder of Zen Buddhism as a roly-poly, legless, hirsute monk swathed in red robes. Frankly ironic, if not sacrilegious, this iconic figure was exceptionally popular during the Edo period as an advertising image for a wide variety of products. The rounded image of the seated Daruma worked particularly well as a tabako-ire pouch filled with leaves, with the red of his robes echoing the red color of the dried tobacco leaves themselves. Here, a mokei kanban for a tabako-ya or a tabako-ire-ya is fashioned after a Daruma-shaped tobacco pouch, with the hiragana characters for "Da-ru-ma" inscribed across the front from right to left. The kanban is flat in back, with a hook-like ledge for hanging the sign flush against the wall.

15

Sage kanban for pipe shop

Late nineteenth century

Wood, gold leaf, pigment, lacquer

22½ × 5 × 2½ in. (57.2 × 12.7 × 6.4 cm)

Mingei International Museum Purchase, 2013-03-001

Far from being mere delivery mechanisms, pipes and their various accessories formed part of Japanese culture. Because sumptuary laws closely regulated the display of wealth, merchants and tradesmen found oblique ways to express their affluence, taste, and cultural sensibilities. In Edo Japan, this sense of sophistication and style was referred to as *iki* (chic and stylish, particularly with reference to objects) and *tsû* (sophistication, largely in reference to people and their comportment). Thus, a gentleman's or lady's pipe was frequently a marker of identity. Shop owners catering to this clientele had to find their own ways to speak to this sophisticated and taste-conscious market. Thus, kanban makers were enlisted to explore ways of communicating a shop's own iki and tsû. The kanban shown here conveys this admirably. A sage kanban designed to be mounted flush against the wall and viewed from one side only, it is given a thick lacquer treatment, with gold lacquer being used for much of the body and pipe bowl. In many pipe kanban, the narrow *rau* section of the body was used to communicate shop specifics, such as the shop's name and address, or perhaps its yago (logo). Here, however, are found the first three lines of a celebrated poem by the ninth-century courtier poet Ariwara-no-Narihira-ason (825–880). They read: "Chihayaburu / Kamiyomo kikazu / Tatsutagawa." The lower verse, not included, but implied, is "Karakurenai ni / Mizu kukurutowa." In translation, the poem essentially says: "Even the almighty gods of old never knew such beauty: on the river Tatsuta in autumn sunlight a brocade—reds flowing above blue water below." This poem was included in the classic poetry anthology known as the *Ogura hyakunin isshu* (One hundred poets, one poem each) compiled by Fujiwara no Teika (1162–1241) in the early thirteenth century. It would have been intimately familiar to those who prided themselves on tsû. A shop displaying this sign would have been advertising its cultural sophistication as much as its actual merchandise.

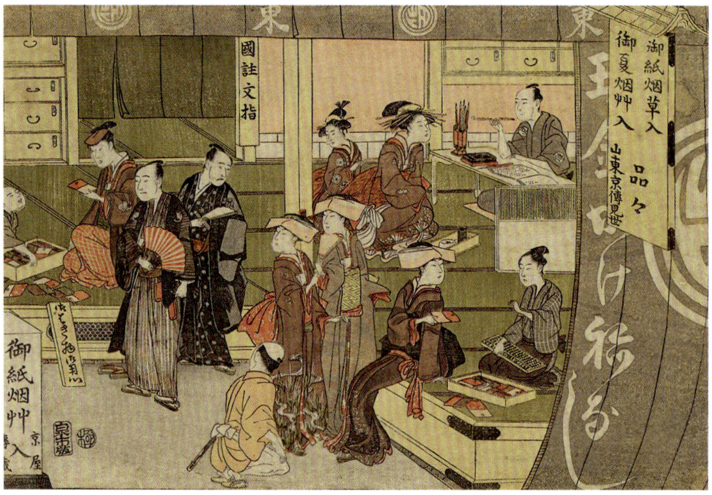

FIG. 37 *Santô Kyôden's Shop*, c. 1800, Kitao Masanobu (Santô Kyôden, 1761–1816). Polychrome woodblock print, ink and color on paper. Tokyo National Museum.

prints created by Kyôden and his friends. Takizawa Bakin, for example, published an entire love story based on the anthropomorphized life of a tabako-ire and kiseru sold separately from Santô Kyôden's shop, but happily reunited when their respective owners meet and fall in love.

Kyôden himself was shameless in working his shops into his popular novels, and he was equally comfortable with including himself as the proprietor. In the 1794 novel *Mikenjaku sannin namaei* (A winnow measure of three drunks), one of the characters quips: "My, what a large place! Why, this must be the new paper tobacco pouch shop of that fellow Santô Kyôden that everyone is talking about, where you can buy tobacco products at such low, low prices."[136] Such blatant plugs, the literary equivalent of the kabuki advertisements discussed earlier, were all part of the fun and the flavor of Edo fiction. On the artistic side, yet not one iota less brazen, Kyôden also famously produced a complex rebus filled with drawings and symbols that begged for decoding. The earnest reader who successfully interpreted this mélange of imagery was rewarded with the banal statement: "I hope this notice finds everyone well. Thanks to you, my shop is thriving. The shop will continue to offer modern, original paper tabako-ire this year. I gladly welcome your patronage." Kyôden's own kanban, as depicted in prints, included a hako kanban, a shitta kanban, and a billowing hioke awning emblazoned with the character "Kyô" (fig. 37).

Kanban for tabako-ire included all of the forms and styles we have encountered thus far. The ire also lent itself wonderfully to large-scale mokei kanban, with oversized paper or fabric bags emblazoned with the shop's name or yago. The bag, similar to a yôki or vessel kanban, was in itself sufficient to advertise the wares sold therein, particularly when paired with a massive *netsuke* (toggle). A stuffed tabako-ire, with its bulging fabric sides, could also easily resemble the squat figure of the seated Zen monk Daruma, the red of his priestly robes transmuted into tobacco leaves.[137] This popular figure became a mascot for many aspects of the tobacco market, appearing in painted images on shitta kanban, as well as serving as the model for mokei kanban for a number of tabako-ya and tabako-ire-ya (cat. 14).[138] The public service announcement "Hinoyôjin" (Careful of fire) was also frequently inked on the ire—a sage warning in traditional Japan, where urban density and wood construction frequently led to devastating conflagrations euphemistically known as the "flowers of Edo," not a few of which were likely caused by careless smokers.

Tobacco pouches were also frequently paired with pipe cases (*kiseru-zutsu*) to form a unified ensemble. Kanban for ire-ya relied on mokei kanban of the set, complete with an oversized netsuke, which was a *de rigueur* component (cat. 16). An unusual number of extant mokei kanban of this type feature the design of a bridge and bridge post with "Yodoyabashi" inscribed on the upright. As mentioned above, this bridge, a powerful symbol of the economic puissance of the Yodoya family of Osaka, was resurrected as an

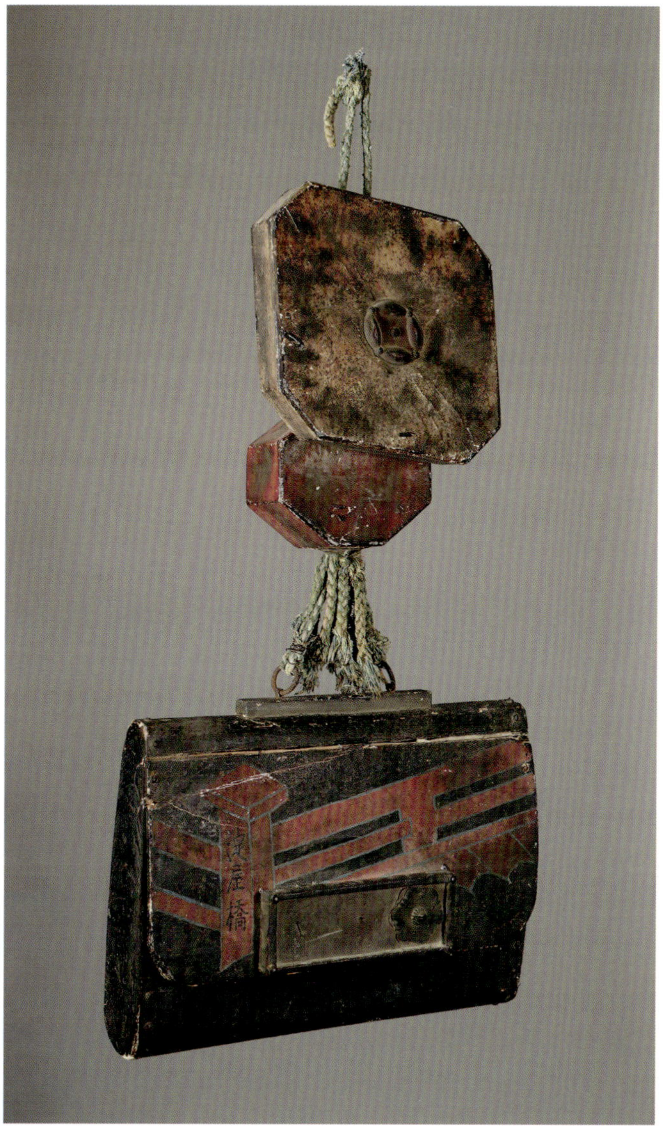

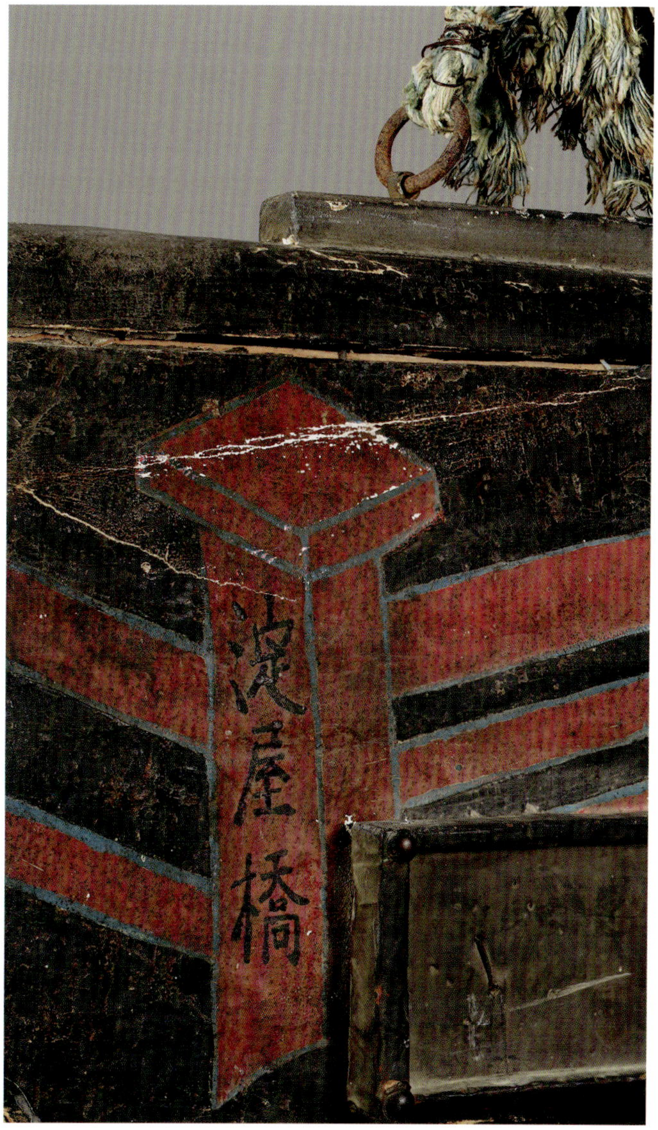

16

Mokei kanban for tobacco pouches

Nineteenth century

Wood, paper, lacquer, metal fittings, cotton cord

40 × 18 in. (101 × 46 cm)

Private Collection

Long before the phrase "Big Tobacco" was coined, alluding to the economic, social, and political power of contemporary tobacco companies, tobacco was already very big indeed in Edo Japan. For example, trade statistics for Osaka merchants in 1714 put tobacco in the top ten export items from this most important commercial hub, only slightly behind raw cotton in terms of value. As a result, tobacco merchants and those dealing in tobacco-related items could well afford to invest in glamorous and sophisticated advertising (like today). The gargantuan mokei kanban was one of the more popular media through which this was achieved, not only for stores that sold tobacco leaves and pipes but also those that sold tobacco pouches and carrying cases (an ensemble known as *kiseru soroi* or *mitsuzoroi*). The well-appointed citizen of Edo Japan would almost necessarily have carried his pipe, pipe case, and pouch on his person, suspended on his obi waist belt by a cord and secured by a netsuke toggle. The extraordinary popularity of netsuke centered largely on their application to lacquered *inrô* medicine boxes and kiseru soroi. Here, an exceptionally large ensemble is depicted and executed in wood and lacquered paper. The pouch itself features a functioning hinged lid with metal fittings. The front bears the red stanchion of the Yodoyabashi Bridge in central Osaka. The equally oversized, broad netsuke here is done in something akin to a *manju* style, which would have been in ivory or ivory inlaid with metal on an actual set.

Detail: Design element showing the stanchion for the Yodoyabashi Bridge in Osaka, a motif found on numerous tabako-ire (tobacco pouches).

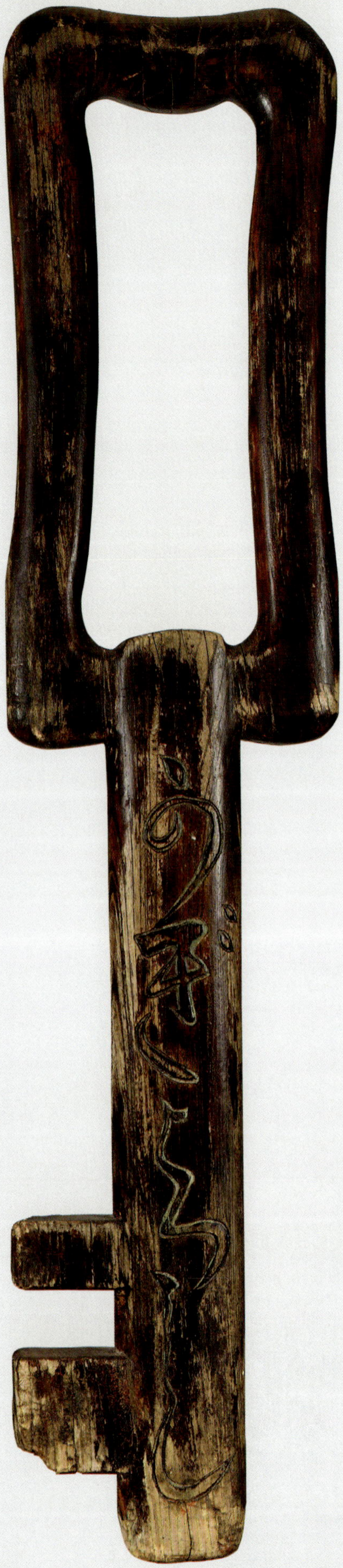

17

Mokei kanban for locksmith

Nineteenth century

Wood, lacquer

37½ × 8¼ in. (95.3 × 21 cm)

Private Collection

One of the more iconic categories of kanban is the mokei kanban, or model sign. These tended to be sculptural signs carved in three dimensions, depicting the object sold or indicating the service offered. Typically made of wood, these signs were not restricted to one category of shop, such as medicine or tobacco, but could be readily employed for an array of products and services. Here, a gigantic key carved out of a single piece of wood shows traces of lacquer bearing the inscription "*kagi naosu*" or "key repair," referring to both keys and locks (*jômae*). Japanese kagi tended to be made of metal and had a two-tooth design, frequently with the teeth slightly curved. Though not the most sophisticated or burglar-proof, the Japanese kagi was quite distinctive in shape, and any pedestrian strolling the streets of Edo Japan, especially one in search of a lock- or key-repair shop, would have easily spotted the familiar shape of a kagi. Some Edo-period mokei kanban depicted giant jômae instead, with the words "*kagi-ya*" inscribed, indicating a certain interchangeability of lock and key as a signifier. No specific shop name is recorded on this sign, which is somewhat typical for many mokei kanban of the Edo period.

18

Mokei kanban for brush shop
Nineteenth century
Wood, bamboo, pigment, cotton cord
43 × 7½ in. (109.2 × 19.1 cm)
Mingei International Museum, Gift of Jeaninne and Richard Helmstetter, 2000-04-003

The *fude,* or brush, has been integral to Japanese culture since the introduction of standardized writing systems from the continent of Asia in the fifth century. The brush developed in tandem with the evolution of Japanese writing systems from Chinese-derived characters (*kanji*) to the native syllabaries of *hiragana* and *katakana*. Deceptively simple in construction, the fude, with its hand grip and bristle head, allowed for writing as well as painterly expression, and its essential elements have not changed over the ensuing millennia. A *fude-shi* (brush maker) could set up shop wherever the requisite components could be found—wood or bamboo for the haft and animal hairs for the brush tip—as well as a customer base. Shops selling fude to government workers, businessmen, farmers, artists, craftsmen, and every other segment of literate society dotted the landscape from one end of the archipelago to the other as a truly indispensable component of Japanese culture. These *fude-ya* were among the first to use kanban as part of their customer outreach. Although simple images of brushes painted on wooden panels are the earliest-documented form of kanban, the design of the fude lent itself readily to the use of sculptural mokei kanban in affluent urban areas. Here, a spectacular mokei kanban for a fude-ya pairs a substantial section of *moso* timber bamboo with a head carved from *keyaki* (*Zelkova serrata*) elm to form a truly Brobdingnagian writing instrument. The head has been painted white overall, with the tip itself in black, simulating a brush dipped in ink. A simple loop of stout cord at the end allowed for the sign to be hung out of doors under the protective eaves of the building; it was likely brought inside at the close of each business day.

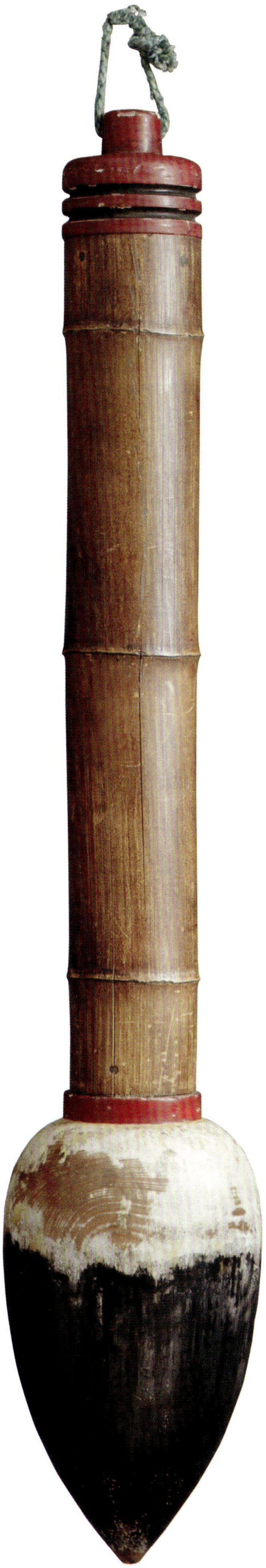

effective marketing tool for tobacco. No specific shop has yet emerged as directly connected with this sign, but significant examples in the PEM collection, the Tobacco and Salt Museum collection, as well as the one exhibited here from a private collection show that the Yodoya brand was an important as well as popular brand of tabako-ire and kiseru-zutsu.

Mokei Kanban: Shop Signs as Sculpture

An interesting and oft-noted subcategory of kanban is the mokei kanban, or sculptural sign. These three-dimensional forms typically rendered in an oversized format the article being sold, from radishes to footwear, or the services being offered, such as key repair, or *kagi naosu* (cat. 17). The word *mokei* itself refers to a model, maquette, or pattern. Mokei kanban were hung outside the shop as well as carried through the streets as a form of ambulatory advertising. The latter, of course, depended on the scale of the mokei kanban in question. Usually made of wood, mokei kanban frequently received exuberant treatment by the kanban-shi, and at times they were presented in significant scale. It is unlikely that a peddler would have hauled up and down the thoroughfares a mokei kanban of a comb, for example, that was four feet long. Although nearly any category of goods or shop could have availed itself of mokei kanban, certain types found them particularly effective. As we have seen, tabako-ya made frequent use of mokei kanban, but fan shops and brush shops appear to have been among the earliest to adopt this form.

Fude-ya **(Brush Shops)**

Fude-ya are generally considered to be the oldest category of shop to employ kanban as a consistent form of advertising.[139] Documents from the Muromachi period (1336–1573) onward illustrate a variety of kanban used by sellers of this all-important Japanese writing implement. Visual records indicate that ema-style kanban with images of a fude set on a wooden panel with a peaked roof dominated. Interestingly, the brushes are seldom rendered with any sense of actual proportion or verisimilitude, featuring instead squat, fat shafts and enormous bristles tipped in black—effective, but not very accurate. However, in Edo-period mokei kanban, oversized carvings of brushes became more common. These large kanban generally had wooden or bamboo shafts and well-shaped carved wooden heads, simulating white bristles dipped in ink (cat. 18). But brush shops regularly employed all of the kanban styles discussed here thus far, including hako kanban, noren, and tate kanban.

The oldest extant calligraphy brush, residing in the Shôsôin Repository in Nara, dates to the reign of Emperor Shômu (701–756). It is known as the Tempyô fude, referring to Shômu's reign period, Tempyô (729–749). Unfortunately, time and insects have eaten away the bristles of the brush, leaving only the *jikku* (shaft). As part of an advertising push, the stationery and office products company Tsubokawa attempted a full reconstruction of this famous brush in 2011, extrapolating what the bristle structure and arrangement might have been 1,200 years ago.[140] And appropriately, one of the oldest and most famous fude-ya in Japan is known as Tempyô Fude. Hayashi Yoshikazu includes an illustration of a mokei kanban from this illustrious shop in his *Edo kanban zufu*.[141] In a 2010 report by the Japanese databank Teikoku, the fude-ya Heisuke Fudefutsukodô (Fukkodô) of Fukuoka City is listed as being founded in 1501, earning it a spot on the list of the 100 oldest businesses in the world, of which Japan claims a strong majority.[142]

Brush shops went by a number of names besides fude-ya. They were also known as *o-fude-shi, o fude dokoro, o sumi fude dokoro*, and *o sumi fude suzuri dokoro*. These names reflect the fact that brush shops often sold ink (*sumi*) and

FIG. 38 Detail: Nakamura Chûbei's brush and ink stone shop on Nihonbashi, as depicted in the *Kidai shôran*. Museum of Asian Art, Berlin.

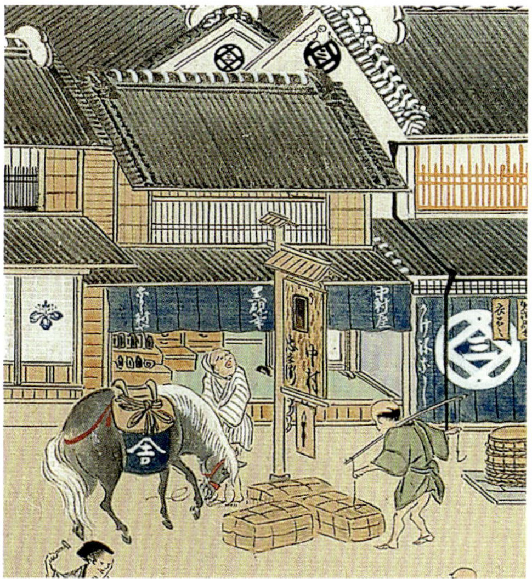

ink stones (*suzuri*). Paper shops, it appears, were generally a separate operation. Returning to the *Kidai shôran* scroll of prospering Nihonbashi, we find the brush and ink stone wholesaler Takashima Yosuke, whose shop features a hako kanban describing his wares. Nakamura Chûbei operated a brush and ink stone shop immediately next to the important Echigoya dry goods store. The Nakamura-ya boasted an impressive tate kanban featuring a large image of an ink stone, with a separate kanban appended featuring the painted image of a brush (fig. 38).

Imban-ya (Seal Shops)

The seal, an early adoption from China, has been a key element in official Japanese protocol through to the modern day. The most famous seal (*imban*) in Japan is unquestionably the Golden Seal of 57 CE, housed in the Fukuoka Art Museum. The subject of over 350 books and articles bisecting and trisecting every conceivable aspect to either verify or debunk its authenticity, the solid gold seal, weighing 4 ounces (108.729 grams) and topped by a snake-like handle, was discovered buried on Shikanoshima Island in 1789 by a farmer digging an irrigation ditch. The engraving reads in Chinese seal script, "Kan Wa Na Koku-O" (King of the State of Na in Wa under the Han Dynasty), and it is purported to have been given by the Chinese Han dynasty emperor Guangwu (5 BCE–57 CE) to petitioners from the state of Na in the Japanese archipelago. Listed as a National Treasure, the seal is used to help date the early foundations of a distinctly Japanese state.[143]

While the use of seals predominates today, signatures and abbreviated personal ciphers known as *kaô* were employed well into the Edo period. Kaô were typically stylized derivations of aspects of the characters used in personal names. In Buddhist circles, kaô frequently took on more abstracted elements. Essentially interpretive and artistic, they functioned as seals throughout much of the medieval period, when they were sometimes referred to as *kaki-han* (written seals).[144] For the illiterate, various signing methods evolved for official purposes, from the "finger measure" of the Nara period (whereby the "signer" to a document placed his forefinger on the paper and small horizontal lines were drawn next to the tip and base and at each joint, effectively measuring the finger) to the stem stamp (*fude jikuin*) method, in which the base end of a brush was dipped in ink and the signer merely pressed the blackened end to the paper. During the opening decades of the Edo period, the use of seals greatly expanded, largely displacing the use of signatures and ciphers. In 1694 the government mandated that all personal seals (*jitsuin*) had to be registered formally to serve as legal marks. In 1873 the Meiji government officially prohibited the use of all other forms of verification pertaining to legal documents and transactions, thereby investing all authority in the seal, or *imban*.[145] Just as the seal of Guangwu

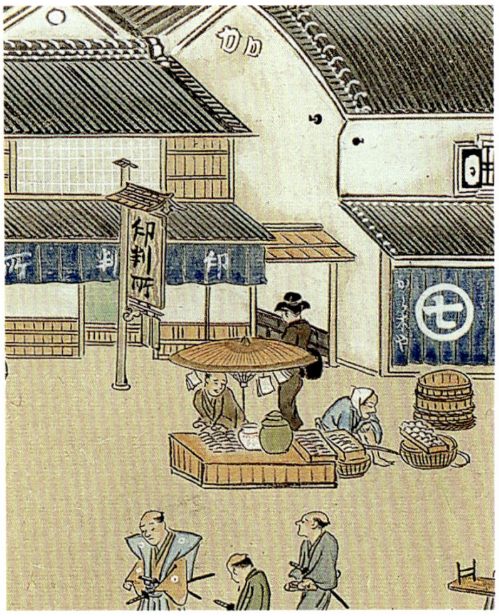

FIG. 39 Detail: An *imban dokoro* (seal shop) on Nihonbashi, as depicted in the *Kidai shôran*. Museum of Asian Art, Berlin.

served to legitimize a state, every transaction involving paperwork, be it commercial receipts, birth records, marriage licenses, or death records, involved the legitimizing use of an imban. And as such, the making of seals was an important if not sacred trade, a specialty craft much needed and valued in Edo society. Edo-period shopping guides (*kaimono annai*) from various cities around Japan frequently list the presence of seal carvers, speaking directly to their ubiquity in urban settings.

The creation of an individual's seal and the impression it made (*in'ei*, or "seal shadow") was a question of both daily necessity and individual expression. The seal as well as its impression were legal and personal statements. While the *hanko* of today tend to be simple cylinders crafted out of *hon tsuge* (boxwood) or *kuro suigyû* (black ox horn), historically imban took on a number of forms and were fashioned from a variety of substances, including quartz, ivory, and other prized materials. But most consisted of a contoured handle and a larger head bearing the reverse incised impression, with a shape not all that unlike that of a squat fude brush.

Kanban were an essential component of outreach to the consumer. Woodblock prints from the Edo period attest to a wide variety of kanban styles employed by imban-ya, from street-side hako kanban stenciled with the simple word "*in*," meaning "impression," to shitta and sage kanban ornamented with carved images of actual imban, to mokei kanban featuring three-dimensional renderings of seals (cat. 19). A seal shop depicted in the *Kidai shôran*, just a few noren up from the brush and ink stone wholesaler Takashima Yosuke, mentioned previously, has an impressive tate kanban with a tiled roof (fig. 39). The kanban simply reads, "Imbandokoro," with no accompanying drawings or visuals to enliven the subject. The term *dokoro* refers to a place where something is done, or in this case, made, and it was frequently used in the same way that the suffix "-ya" was used to indicate a shop or store.

The skill set needed to carve the intricate designs of these small seals, and rendering them in reverse, was quite particular. These were the same skills developed by artisans working in the woodblock-print industry, known as *hangi-shi*. As a result of this overlap, seal shops were also frequently known as *hangi-ya*. Like brush shops that also sold ink and ink wells, hangi-ya often sold ink pots with seal ink, typically in black, red, and blue.[146] Of course, seals also needed a pouch to be carried in (cat. 20), and specialized pouch shops for imban, or *imban-ire*, were a common sight on the streets of Edo Japan.

Ito-ya (Thread Shops)

Silk, along with cotton, tea, and sake, proved to be a key industry fueling Japan's transformation into a modern industrial society beginning in the late nineteenth century. An important cottage

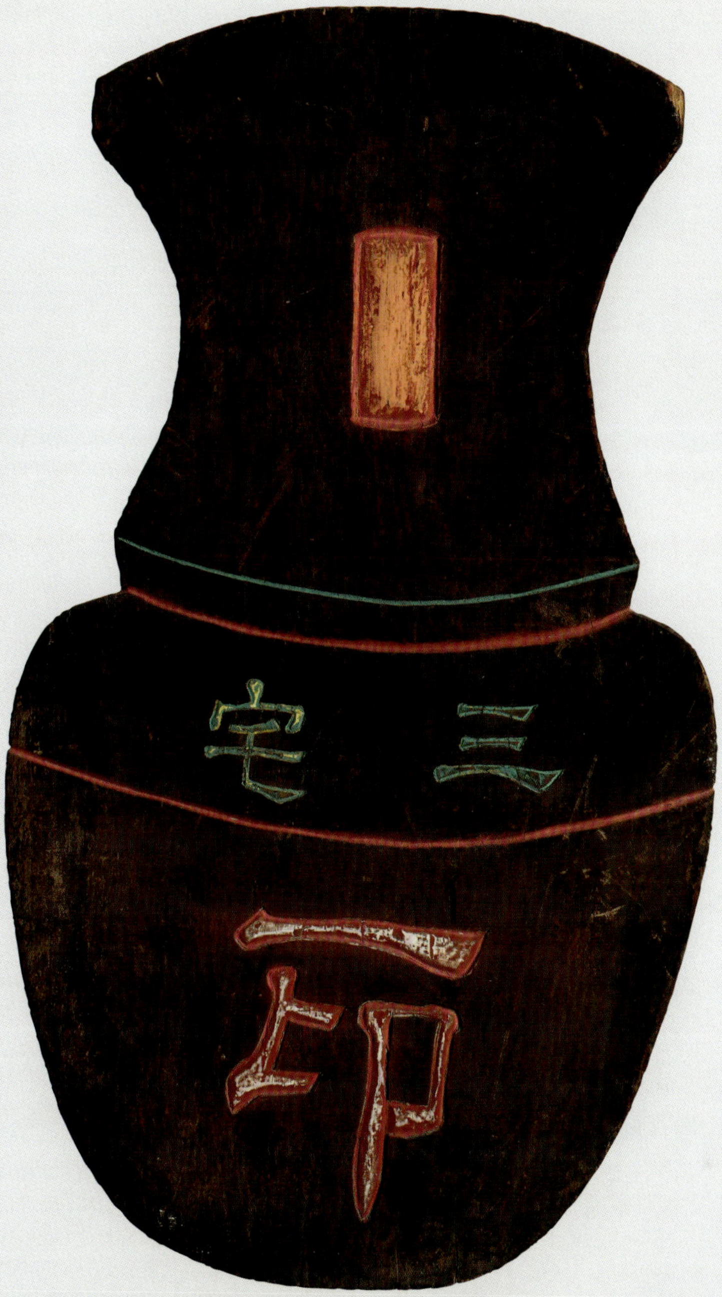

19

Shitta kanban for seal shop
Twentieth century
Wood, pigment
23¾ × 6¾ in. (60.3 × 17.1 cm)
Private Collection

The personal seal (*imban*), used in lieu of a signature to sign legal or personal documents, was an integral part of the well-dressed man's ensemble during the Edo and Meiji periods. It was particularly important among merchants for business transactions. During the Edo period, seals and their use became standard and even obligatory for many citizens, irrespective of economic status, and thus *imban-ya*, or seal shops, became another ubiquitous business encountered on the streets of Edo Japan. As with brushes, the shape of the imban itself was distinctive, and most imban-ya employed this image, either as a full mokei kanban or as a painted image on a shitta kanban. At times, examples of the craftsman's work would be included as part of the decorative design, and the face of the kanban would be studded with raised seals or their imprints.

Although many kanban made use of imagery that anyone could decipher based on its shape or their familiarity with the product, kanban for imban typically were designed for a more literate clientele. This shitta kanban for the Miyake imban-ya, crafted from a single piece of wood, depicts the familiar form of a fat-handled seal. The reddish cartouche at the top simulates the hole through which a cord would have been passed. The face is inscribed with the character "*in*" (impression), and the name of the shop is listed above, reading from right to left, "*Mi-yake*."

20

Mokei kanban for *inrô* shop

Mid-nineteenth century
Wood, pigment, lacquer, cotton, silk
46 × 15½ in. (116.8 × 39.4 cm)
Private Collection

A necessary accessory for seals (*imban*) was the seal basket, or *inrô*, used to carry them. This was typically suspended from the waist belt (obi) with a braided silk cord and secured with a fancifully carved toggle (netsuke). More than simply functional or convenient carrying devices, inrô (as well as netsuke) became the subject of much artistic focus and creativity. Owing to the vagaries and inconsistencies of Japanese sumptuary laws, from which inrô were surprisingly exempt, these simple cases surpassed their core function and were elevated to the level of fine art. Indeed, inrô became artistic vehicles for the top lacquer artists of the Edo period. Such artists as Ogawa Haritsu (Ritsuô, 1663–1747) developed specialized lacquer techniques specifically for inrô. And Ogata Kôrin (1658–1716), one of the most celebrated artists of his day, created inrô for select clientele. In addition to serving as seal cases, inrô were adapted to hold medicine and herbs. To fulfill this latter mandate, inrô morphed from single-chamber containers to a series of small stacked trays, each layer capable of holding a different medicinal necessity.

To keep the various trays held securely together, the suspension cord was passed through a round bead known as an *ojime*. Here, a mokei kanban depicting an oversized inrô bears the maker's yago of a circle divided by three lines, known as a *maru ni sanbiki*. The stout, silken cords pass through a large wooden ojime bead in direct imitation of a traditional inrô.

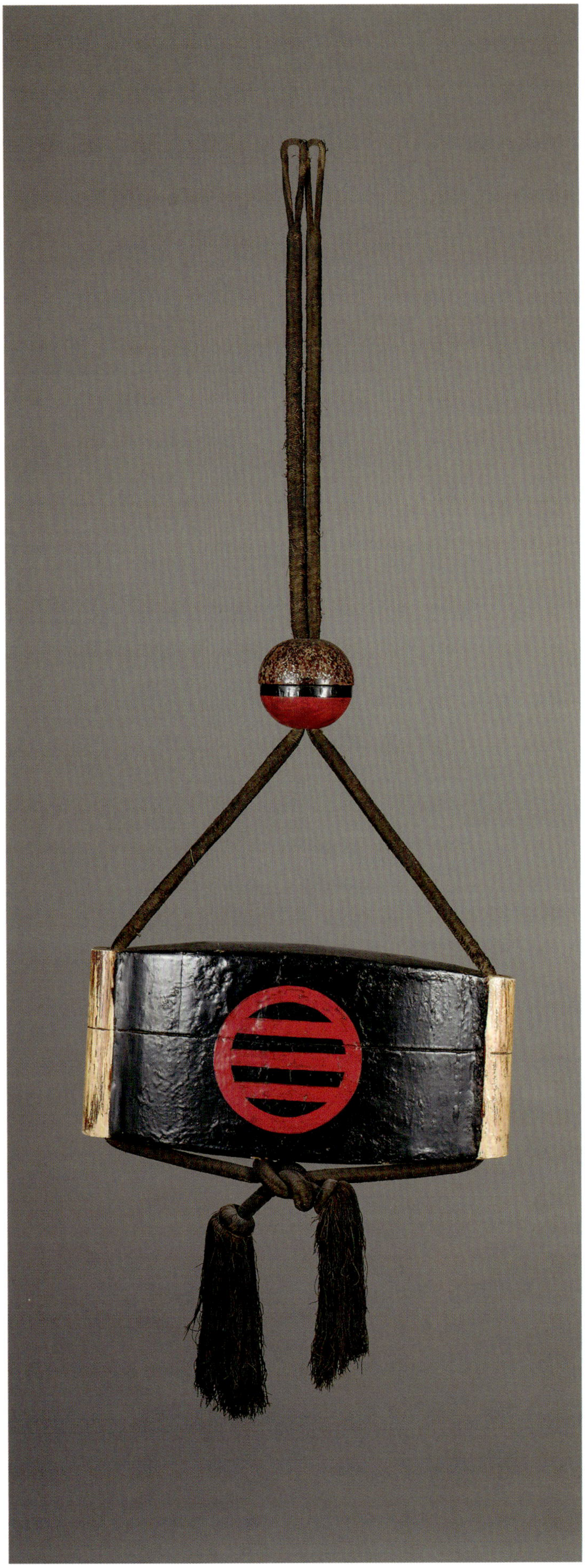

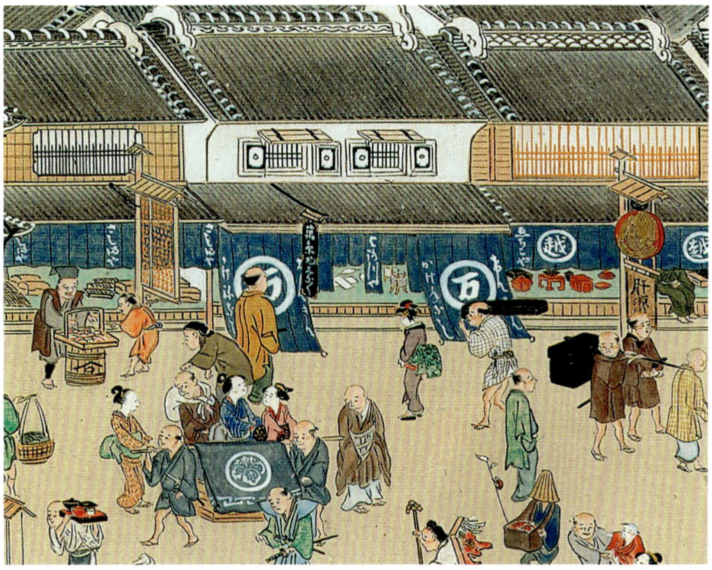

FIG. 40 Detail: The Man-ya ito-ya (thread shop) on Nihonbashi, as depicted in the *Kidai shôran*. Museum of Asian Art, Berlin.

industry during much of the Edo period, raw silk production increased through mechanized and automated processes to such a degree that by 1910, Japan had emerged as the largest exporter of raw silk in the world, nearly doubling the output of China. And by 1918 an impressive three-fifths of the world's raw silk came from Japan. Within the domestic economy, the skein was an iconic image symbolizing the entire silk industry, particularly *ito-ya* (thread shops), representing the way in which silk threads were wound, stored, shipped, and sold. In Japanese, the term for skein is *ito waku* (*ito* meaning "thread" and *waku* derived from the verb *maku,* meaning to wrap). A kanban of a colorful, thread-wrapped skein was the most common way of advertising one of these important shops, either as a jitsubutsu kanban, with the skeins themselves serving as effectively colorful advertisements, or as mokei and shitta kanban, with carved or painted depictions of ito waku displayed street-side (cats. 21, 22).[147] Kanji and hiragana inscriptions would declare the presence of an *itomono dokoro* (thread shop) and list some of the additional related products available. Sugiura's important early publication of his personal collection, entitled *Kazô kanban zufu* and described above, contains two photographs of kanban for ito-ya. One is a mokei kanban of a skein with five threads, and the second is a shitta kanban with an incised design of a skein very similar to the example shown here, but with an elongated panel that includes the name of the shop.[148]

Interestingly, the humble skein itself became an object of controversy as Japan emerged as a key exporter of silk during the Meiji era. Silk merchants occasionally engaged in the unscrupulous practice of weighing down silk skeins by embedding in their structure debris such as metal bits and small stones.[149] The 1690 *Jinrinkinmôzui* includes an entry for a *waku-shi*, or skein maker, helping to illustrate how each layer of the Edo economy was backed by practicing craftsmen and their respective trades.[150]

The *Kidai shôran* includes a depiction of an ito-ya known as Man-ya (fig. 40). Located between the abacus dealer Sashima-ya, with a mokei kanban of a giant functioning abacus, and the baiyaku drug wholesaler Echigoya, with an impressive tate kanban featuring a carp ascending a waterfall executed in gold lacquer, the Man-ya relied on noren and hioke awnings bearing the shop's logo, though a diminutive black-lacquer shitta moji kanban is suspended street-side. Between the curtains are skeins of raw white silk dotting the tatami mat, as well as some spindles of unwound thread and bolts of cloth. A fashionably attired lady with a plethora of *kanzashi* hairpins and a rich green brocade *obi* peers inside curiously.

Ito-ya served a number of functions within the Edo economy. Rather than simply selling thread,

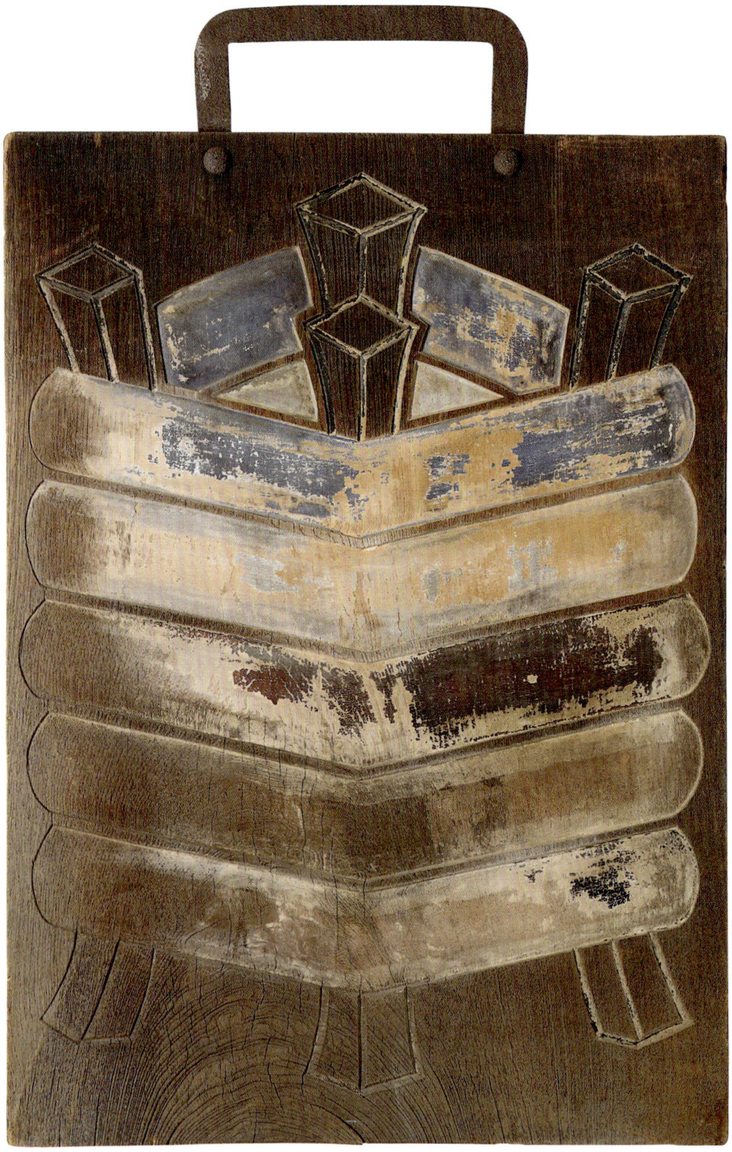

21

Shitta kanban for thread shop
Nineteenth century
Wood, pigment
24 × 15 in. (61 × 38 cm)
Private Collection

Whereas pharmaceutical kanban were frequently commissioned by organizations striving to create national brand identities with registered trademark imagery and memorable catchphrases, most kanban, particularly during the Edo period, sought to communicate simple offerings to a decidedly local clientele. These kanban tended to be more direct in presentation, even omitting the name of the shop and focusing instead on the most important matter at hand—the merchandise or service being offered within. The ito-ya, or thread shop, for instance, was a much-needed service in nearly every community. Whether of silk, cotton, or *asa* bast fiber, threads and textiles were essential to everyday life. Clothes, bedding, and a wide variety of fabric products invariably had to be made, mended, or altered on a regular basis, and the ito-ya provided an indispensable service for the farmer as well as the samurai. The almost universal symbol for an ito-ya was a thread-wrapped skein, or ito waku. Kanban for ito-ya almost universally employed this image as their representative symbol, whether as a simple painted image on a board, a more elaborately rendered panel with a painted and incised design, or a fully rendered mokei kanban depicting in three-dimensional form the skein itself. Here, a shitta kanban for an ito-ya uses a fine relief-carved rendering of a skein with five bands of thread thickly wound around the staves. Rather than a simple silhouette, the kanban-shi has created a slightly top-down view, exposing the back stave as well as a bit of the interior, dramatically enhancing the graphic. The skein fills the panel, leaving no room for additional text or explanation—none was needed. Originally treated with bright colors and shades of blue, white, red, yellow, and black, the thread colors have faded, with only the blue giving signs of its former intensity. A similar kanban with only three bands of thread and scalloped edges to the board is depicted in Matsumiya Saburô's *Edo no kanban*.

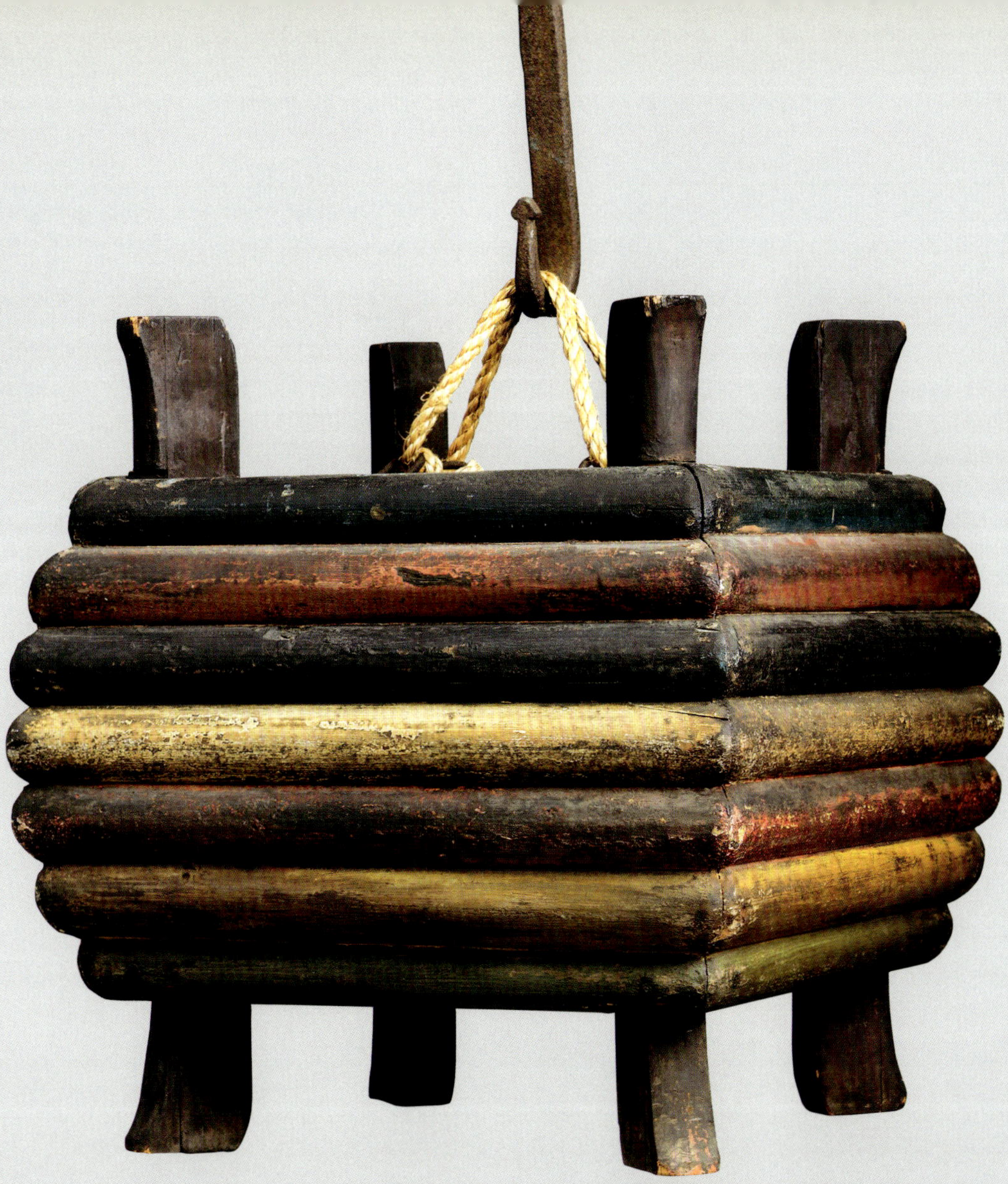

22

Mokei kanban for thread shop
Nineteenth century
Wood, pigment, metal fittings and hook
19 × 17¾ in. (48.3 × 45.1 cm)
Mingei International Museum Purchase, 2001-99-001

This large mokei kanban of an ito waku, or skein, for a thread shop is assembled from well-carved wooden segments, and it depicts an oversized skein with seven bands of thread in red, navy, black, yellow, and white. It is constructed as an actual skein with interior cross struts and slightly curving vertical arms to support the carved threads. The large metal hook would have allowed this exceptional kanban to be suspended either within the ito-ya or outside it, to catch the eyes of passersby. Typical of many of these earlier kanban, no specific shop name is indicated on the skein, but it is reported to have come from a shop in Shizuoka Prefecture.

FIG. 41 Oversized and iron-wrought geta donated to a subtemple at Daiyuzan Saijoji, near Odawara. Photo by Alan Scott Pate.

they also worked closely with dry goods stores selling clothing, braiding tassels, and cords for a wide variety of applications, including fans, netsuke, and inrô, as well as providing *sageo* (sword wrappings) and *tsukaito* (sword grip wrappings), which were an especially important service for the samurai.[151] A kanban for an ito-ya now in the PEM collection features a lightly carved and colored illustration of a skein and lists *ito hari* (sewing needles) and *shamisen ito* (samisen strings) as available products.[152]

Ito-ya were frequently pictured in the illustrations of craftsmen known as shokunin zukushi-e, discussed earlier, and the *Jinrinkinmôzui* includes an image of a thread shop, where it is referred to as a *nishiki-ya*, nishiki being a reference to silk brocade. Interestingly, the threads pictured in this early image are bundled in large braid-like formations without the structural skeins. A kanban featuring a similar simply interwoven thread bundle is found in the PEM collection; it was purchased from Yamanaka through the Billings Fund in 1914.[153]

Geta-ya (Clog Shops)

The wooden geta is perhaps the simplest and most ingenious form of footwear ever devised: a wooden base (*dai*) roughly approximating the size of the foot provides protection for the sole, with a minimal strap of cord (*hanao*) snuggled next to the big toe. Geta can have either flat bottoms or teeth (*ha*) that raise them to towering heights. From this basic concept emerges a plethora of forms and variations. *Okaku geta* feature single-block construction of both dai and ha, while *funageta* have separately rendered and attached teeth. *Tsumakawa geta* add a protective toe covering. Wooden geta were worn by all classes of society, and generally without the padding of tabi socks until the modern era. Worn-out and discarded geta were a common source of firewood among the urban poor.[154] *Sugi* (cedar) geta were considered the cheapest, while geta from *kiri* (paulownia) harvested in the north were especially prized. Regional variations abounded. Shellfish harvesters devised a tall, weighted

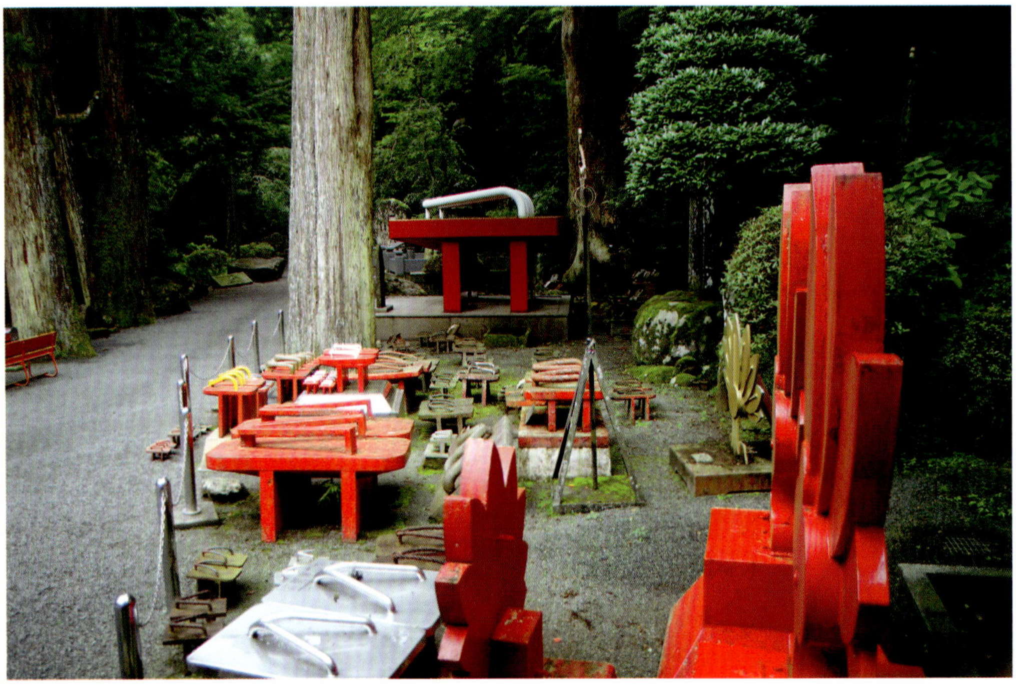

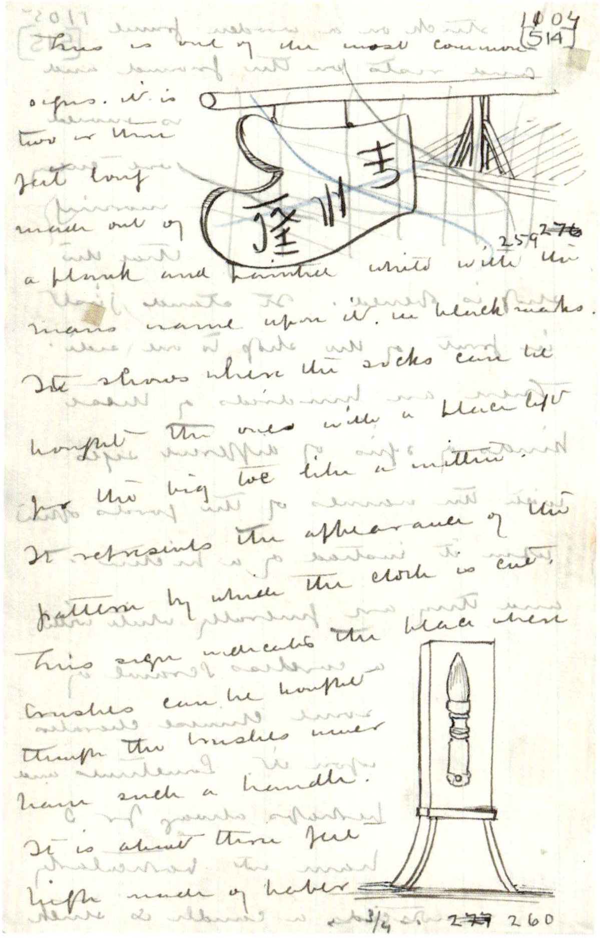

FIG. 42 Edward Morse's sketches of the kanban of a tabi maker and a brush shop. Peabody Essex Museum.

version of geta to allow them to roam the shallows in search of their product while keeping their feet dry. High-ranking courtesans known as *tayû* or *oiran* would wear tall, three-tine geta known as *mitsu-ashi koma geta* in their rounds to the pleasure houses, performing their balletic meandering *hachimonji* (figure-eight) step closely accompanied by attendants. Young girls were fitted with lacquered geta of thicker stock with bells embedded in a cavity below the toes, known as *pokkuri*, an onomatopoeic word imitating the sound these little wooden shoes made as the young girls approached the neighborhood shrine for presentation on the Shichi-Go-San holiday. A precarious, one-tine form of geta known as *ipponba* or *tengu geta* was believed to have been popular among the *tengu* (mountain goblins). A subtemple at Daiyuzan Saijoji, near Odawara and just southwest of Tokyo, is dedicated to the tengu and features a large collection of iron-wrought geta, with hundreds of pairs of these harsh clogs dotting the area adjacent to the temple (fig. 41). Dominating the scene, however, is a pair of clogs two meters tall. Tradition holds that if a pregnant woman walks through the upright *ha*, she will have an easy delivery. And a folk dance known as the *sô odori*, originating during the eighteenth century in Niigata Prefecture, featured three days of nonstop dancing wearing geta; this was intended to ward off calamities and poverty and ensure prosperity for the coming year.

Kanban for geta shops tended toward mokei and jitsubutsu kanban. It was a relatively simple affair for a geta maker to string up pairs of geta outside his shop to advertise his presence. However, some geta makers and wholesalers, already skilled at wood carving as an integral part of their work, created massive geta mokei kanban (cat. 23). The PEM and Shôwa Neon Takamura Kanban Museum collections both include cheery geta mokei kanban bearing the plump face of Okame, the goddess of mirth and merriment, with the hanao cleverly simulating the outlines of her hair.[155]

Tabi-ya (Sock Shops)

Edward Morse's sketchbook contains a delightful image of a kanban for a *tabi-ya*, or sock maker (fig. 42). Illustrating the distinctive separate large toe that is a hallmark of traditional Japanese tabi socks, Morse's interpretation looks like an oven mitt—exaggerated slightly, it would appear, for effect. Morse's image depicts a wooden mokei kanban suspended from a horizontal bamboo pole extending from the building. Its face is engraved with the phrase "*matahiki*," a slang expression that originally referred to Portuguese pantaloons but became associated with tabi during the Edo period.[156] The sewing skills required for tabi applied to other garments, such as *hanten* (short coats), *haragake* (aprons worn by children), *momohiki* (undergarments), and *patsuchi* (pants). As Japanese society transitioned from traditional to Western during the late nineteenth century, tabi-ya frequently served as the first tailor shops for clothing in the Western

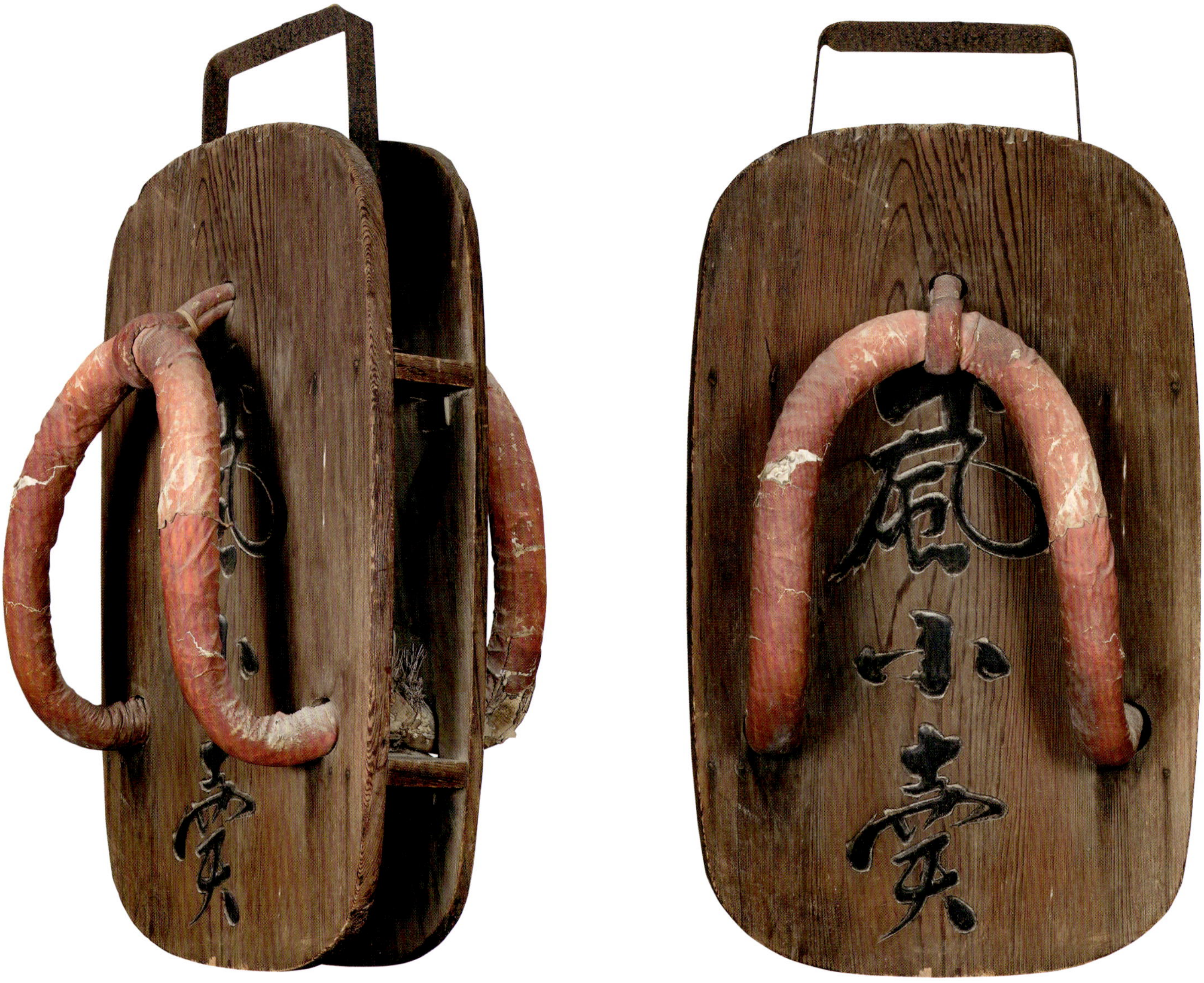

23

Mokei kanban for geta shop, front and side views
Nineteenth century
Wood, leather, iron
31 × 16 × 12½ in. (78 × 40 × 31.8 cm)
Private Collection

The mokei kanban is arguably the most dramatic of kanban forms. The kanban-shi, given license by the shop owner, had very few limitations in re-creating in oversized form the particular item offered for sale. Wood was the most natural choice of material, and the vast majority of extant mokei kanban from the Edo period are made of various woods, keyaki being the most durable. Comb makers, fan makers, parasol makers, brush makers, rosary makers, pipe shops, hair ornament shops, and locksmiths all took advantage of the mokei kanban as an effective form of advertisement. Here, an unnamed geta-ya announces its presence with a massive mokei kanban. The sign is double sided, with the ha (teeth) forming a bridge between the two faces. The hanao straps are of thickly padded red leather. Both faces bear an inscription; one face reads, "*geta kouri*" (retail), and the other face reads, "*shi-ire dokoro*" (place to make purchase). A similar example, minus the inscriptions, is included in Hayashi Yoshikazu's important work on Edo-period kanban, *Edo kanban zufu*.

mode.[157] Tabi were a popular personal clothing item, and so shops appeared in nearly every town and city. The signage in the *santô,* or three largest cities of Edo, Osaka, and Kyoto, was relatively consistent and in keeping with Morse's sketch. Other phrases that appeared with some frequency on tabi-ya kanban were "*ôjôbu,*" meaning strong and durable, a precursor to the modern-day expression "*daijôbu,*" meaning okay; and "*ashi agari,*" largely a Kyoto expression with a subtle hanji mono, or wordplay, relating to both putting on a tabi sock and hanging a tabi kanban. Another common format featured the use of the store's yago on the sign, with little additional information required—the shape of the sign said it all (cat. 24).

Prior to the Edo period, the vast majority of the population, including townsmen, craftsmen, farmers, and samurai, went barefoot indoors. Out of doors, they used straw sandals or geta without tabi socks. Indoors, tabi were generally reserved for the elderly, to keep their feet warm. Even councilors attending court had to receive special permission to wear them as part of their court attire. Until 1657, tabi as a rule were made of leather. However, after Edo's devastating Meireiki fire of that year, the cost of leather skyrocketed, and cotton was introduced as a substitute material for tabi. This dramatically increased affordability, and while leather tabi continued to be produced and used by certain segments of society, more and more people started using cotton tabi for comfort. Initially, a strap was wrapped around the ankle as a method of securing the tabi to the foot. But in the Genroku era (1688–1704), the use of a latch (*kobase*) along the back of the tabi became standard.[158] Tabi-ya were frequently included in the shokunin zukushi-e and the rakuchû rakugai zu screens discussed earlier, giving clear evidence of their importance and ubiquity in Japanese commercial culture.[159]

Juzu-ya (Buddhist Rosary Shops)

Visitors to Kyoto today are often drawn to the steep cobbled streets of Ninen-zaka and Sannen-zaka leading up the slopes of the Higashiyama district toward the towering pagoda connected to Kiyomizu-dera. This important temple complex has been visited by pilgrims and tourists for more than 1,200 years, since its founding in 778. Over time, the warren-like network of alleys and terraced streets near this Buddhist temple have become an important center for trades- and craftsmen. *Kiyomizu-yaki* pottery and *kiyomizu-ningyô* dolls made in the area have been particularly famous and popular *omiyage* (souvenirs) for visitors. Shops dating from the Edo period still dot these narrow streets, including *tôgarashi-ya* spice shops and *juzu-ya,* or Buddhist rosary shops.

Juzu-ya, supplying not only rosaries but also other objects associated with the personal practice of Buddhism, were a common sight on streets adjacent to Japanese temples large and small, from one end of the archipelago to the other. The historical capital of Kyoto, with its high concentration of Buddhist temples, has long been the center of Japanese juzu manufacture, and it is said to supply 90 percent of all Buddhist rosaries in Japan today. Many long-established juzu-ya are still in operation in Kyoto. On Kyoto's celebrated Teramachi Dôri (Temple Street), for example, the Yasuda Nenju Ten has been in operation since 1683. The entrance to the shop is marked by a mokei kanban featuring a massive thirty-six-bead juzu rosary protected by a small tiled roof (a holdover from the time before this section of Teramachi Street became a covered pedestrian mall). Further south down the street, the Nakano Isuke Shôten, which has been in operation since 1764, also features a mokei kanban, but with 108 wooden beads. And on the slopes of Kiyomizu, the Hokkaiya-Butsuguten fronts the street approaching the temple and boasts a massive thirty-six-bead juzu mokei kanban, its surface patinated by the passing of thousands of curious

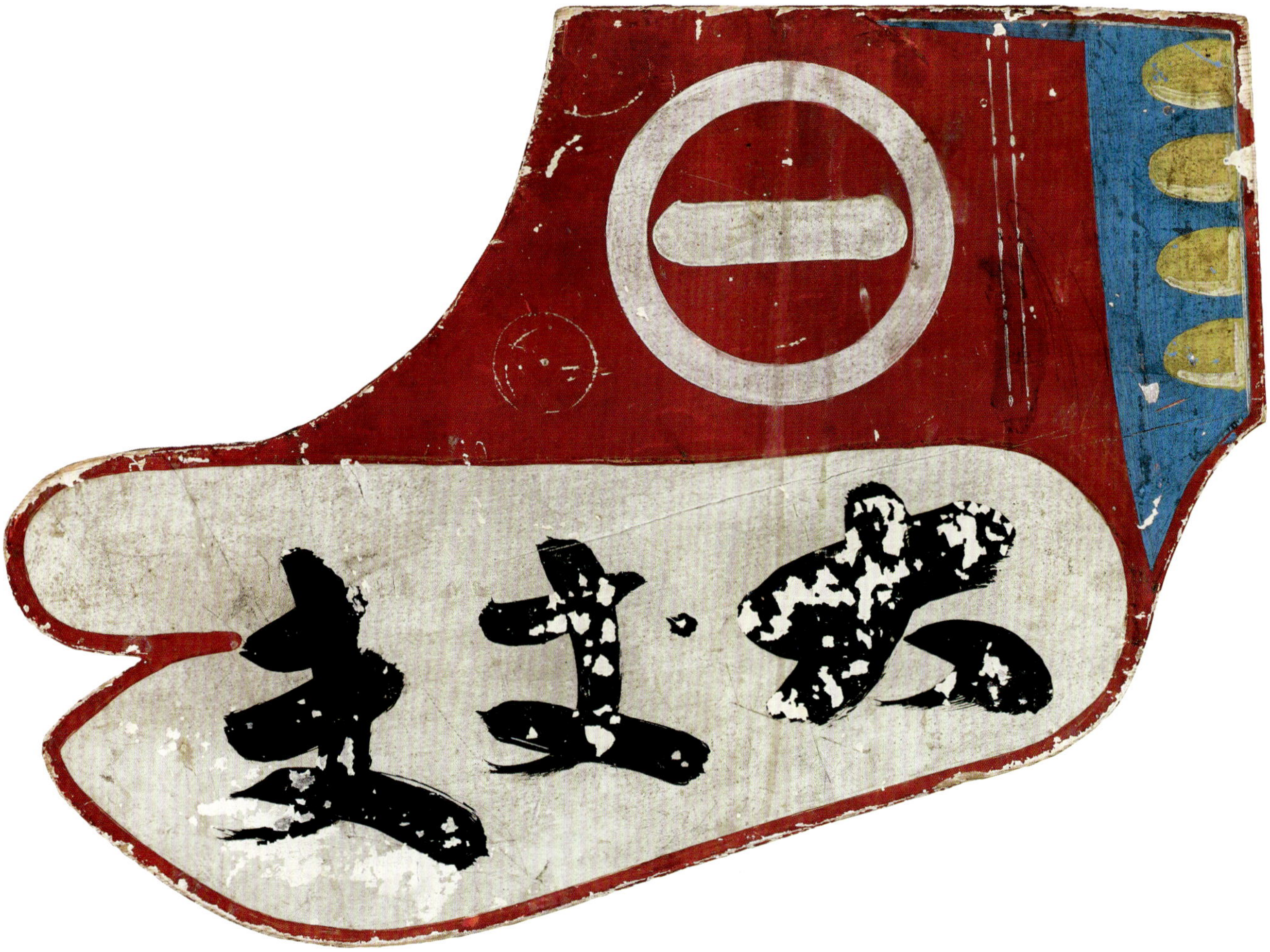

24

Mokei kanban for tabi shop

Early twentieth century

Wood, pigment

21 × 15 in. (53 × 39 cm)

Private Collection

Kanban for makers of tabi (split-toe socks) have remained relatively consistent in design over the centuries. Making use of the distinctive shape of the tabi, sellers had little need to augment their message with complicated particulars. This mokei kanban for a tabi maker is double-sided, bearing the phrase "*ôjôbu*," meaning durable, written right to left in the white sole area, with the upper section carrying the character for "*ichi*" (one) inside a circle, representing Maruichi or Ichimaru as the store's yago. The right edge of the sign depicts a series of *kobase* latches to secure the sock, a late seventeenth-century innovation.

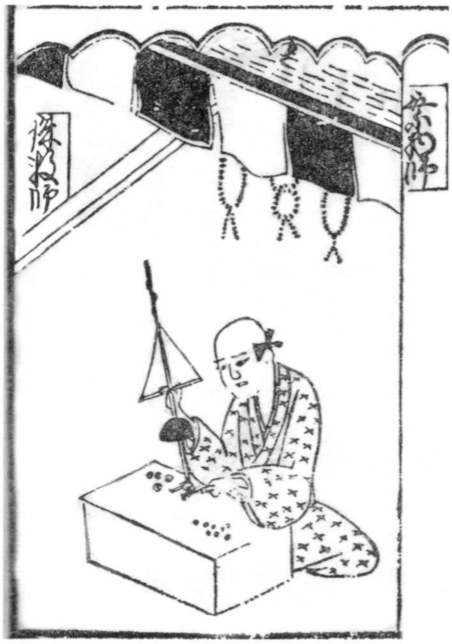

FIG. 43 Woodblock print of a juzu-shi (rosary maker) at work. Reproduced from *Jinrinkinmôzui* (1690), 204.

hands each day as tourists march up and down the hill of this popular destination.

Juzu composition can vary dramatically by sect in terms of the preferred materials, number of beads, and arrangement of larger counting beads, with additional variations depending upon whether one is a priest or a layperson. In terms of numbers, the most formal juzu consists of 108 beads. Each bead is said to represent one of the 108 *bonnô* (afflictions). By working one's way through the juzu faithfully, the individual's soul is purified and advances that much further toward nirvana. Frequently, there are two larger *guru* beads at the top and bottom of the strand, and four smaller beads inserted within the strand. Full 108-bead strands are long and quite cumbersome, so shorter, wrist-sized juzu are frequently used for personal practice; these consist typically of fifty-four, twenty-seven, or eighteen beads (all can be divided into 108). Certain sects also include supplementary tasseled strands radiating from the central loop as counting aids. In typical practice, the devotee holds the long strand in both hands or, with smaller versions, wraps the juzu strand around the hands pressed together in prayer while incanting the name of the Buddha in the *nembutsu* "Namu Amida Butsu." In certain more esoteric practices, exceptionally large juzu strands are used in a form of group prayer called the *hyakumanben juzu,* or 1 million nembutsu rosary. This rite developed in the first half of the twelfth century as a way for communities to ward off such disasters as famine, plague, or war. The hyakumanben juzu is said to have originated at Chion-ji in Kyoto, where the monks recited the nembutsu for seven days straight in order to stop an outbreak of disease. As early as the twelfth century, certain prominent monks encouraged rich and poor alike to engage in a hyakumanben juzu ceremony at least once a year for the betterment of the community.[160] In this practice, members of the assembled group sat in a circle, each holding the large juzu in both hands. As the group chanted the nembutsu, the juzu worked its way slowly around the circle. Although the most traditional juzu are made of wood, they have long been manufactured out of a variety of materials, including ivory, jade, glass, copper, gold, crystal, iron, amber, and ceramic.

Two skills were essential for *juzu-shi* (rosary makers): making smoothly rounded beads of uniform size and drilling holes so as to allow for straight alignment on the cordage. Irregularities in the shape of the beads or their alignment could interfere with the deep meditative practices associated with the juzu. Edo-period woodblock prints featuring juzu-shi at work typically show them seated at their workbenches with gimlets in hand, studiously augering holes into beads. The 1690 *Jinrinkinmôzui* includes such an image of a juzu-shi hard at work boring holes into beads in preparation for stringing. Above his head, hanging beneath his noren, are completed juzu strands (fig. 43).[161]

Juzu-ya were important shops, particularly in towns blessed with pilgrimage-worthy temples and temple complexes. Although it is believed that jitsubutsu kanban featuring a simple display of completed rosaries along the front of a shop were the earliest form of kanban for a juzu-ya, woodblock-print images indicate that juzu-ya also employed all of the standard kanban types at

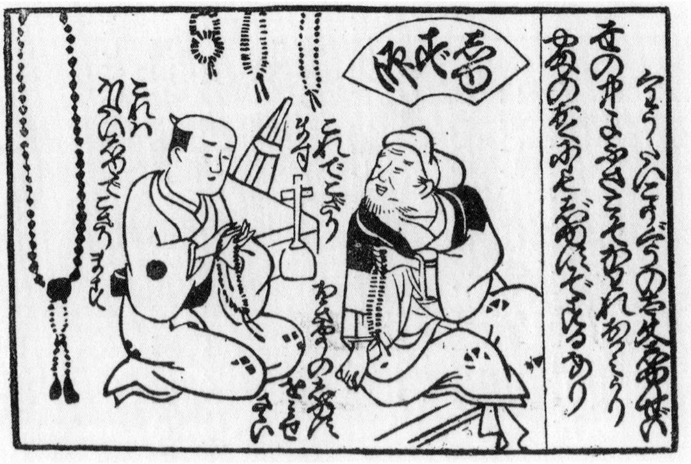

FIG. 44 A juzu-shi (rosary maker) and customer chatting, as depicted in the *Imayô shokunin-zukushi hyakunin isshu* by Kondô Kiyoharu, Kyôhô era, 1716–35. This woodblock print notably features both a large mokei kanban as well as a moji kanban in the shape of a fan placed overhead, reading, "Juzu-ya."

a shop's disposal, from simple ema-style shitta and sage kanban featuring painted images of juzu, to hako kanban with painted paper uppers with the characters for "juzu." The word *juzu* is typically written using the characters for bead (*ju*) and count (*zu*). The word can also be read as *zuzu,* and Edo renditions of the word frequently reversed the character order, as opposed to the modern-day reading.[162] Moji kanban with the words *zuzu* or *juzu* were also employed. However, during the Edo period, it became increasingly common for juzu-ya to employ oversized mokei kanban as advertisements (cat. 25). An interesting kanban in the PEM collection features a free-standing wooden frame with a large juzu hung inside, giving the impression of a tsuitate room divider, which may have been used within the juzu-ya or placed street-side and brought in each night for protection.[163] A frequently illustrated image from the *Imayô shokunin-zukushi hyakunin isshu,* published during the Kyôhô era (1716–35) by Kondô Kiyoharu, shows a juzu-shi seated with a customer (fig. 44). Above his head are actual strands of juzu, as in the *Jinrinkinmôzui*, but to the left is an oversized strand hanging at the shop's edge. A fan-shaped cartouche above reads, "Juzu-ya" in a combination of kanji and hiragana.[164]

Rôsoku-ya (Candle Shops)

Rôsoku is an exceptionally difficult word to write in Japanese. It is formed of two complex characters meaning "wax" and "light." Because Japanese candles have a distinctive tapered or hourglass shape, kanban makers spent little time trying to work out the intricacies of the kanji and focused on the shape of the rôsoku itself. For instance, they cut out paper silhouettes and pasted them to screens to make shoji kanban. In Toyama Prefecture, silhouettes were applied to wooden panels, creating easily identifiable double-sided shitta or sage kanban. Hako kanban were also effective signs for candles, with their box bases and paper uppers, which could be lit from within to show off drawings of rôsoku. Three-dimensional carvings of rôsoku, some truly massive in scale, were commonly used as mokei kanban. This predilection for using images over words is cleverly captured in an 1834 *kyôka* poem by Yama Imo that reads, "*Aramono ya ____ bakari mufude yomi,*" with the image of a candle drawn in place of the word. This means roughly, "That shop has a ______ so you can read it without words."[165] This poem was included in the 1834 edition of the popular comedic poem series *Yanagidaru* (The willow barrel).[166] It also wonderfully reflects the tongue-in-cheek quality of Edo humor. In essence, the poet is saying: "Why did the shop use only a drawing of a candle for its shop sign? Because no one can read the characters for candle!"

Some of the earliest recorded kanban are for rôsoku shops. A noted example from the Kyôhô era was done in an ema style, a simple board with a peaked frame top bearing the painted image of a rôsoku (fig. 45). Three-dimensional and oversized rôsoku kanban appear to have been a specialty in Osaka, the merchants' capital. A sketchbook and diary from a frequent visitor to Osaka from Edo describes in detail an exceptionally large rôsoku

25

Mokei kanban for rosary shop

Nineteenth century

Wood, cotton cord

110 in. (281 cm) long

Mingei International Museum Purchase, 2013-22-001

The earliest form of kanban for a juzu-ya, or rosary shop, appears to have simply been a jitsubutsu kanban, as the juzu-shi (rosary maker) suspended strands of his finished juzu street-side to attract customers. Over the Edo period, larger-scale mokei kanban featuring supersized beads on stout cord became popular, and they remain so to the present day. This mokei kanban for a juzu-ya consists of 108 beads of keyaki wood on a cotton cord, with larger counting beads.

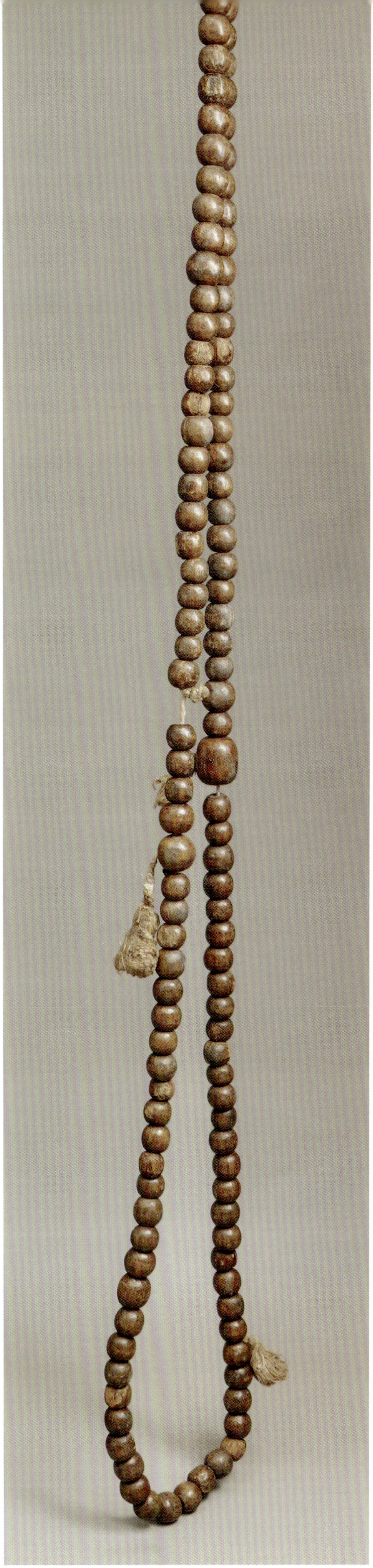

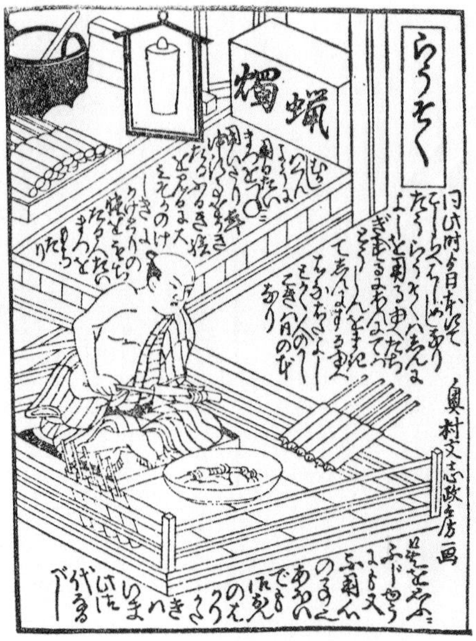

FIG. 45 Illustration of a rôsoku-shi (candle maker) at work in his shop with a simple ema-style kanban depicting a drawing of a rôsoku candle suspended overhead, from Okumura Masafusa's (1686–1764) *Toshidama himachi banashi*, c. 1747. Reproduced from Matsumiya, *Edo no kanban*.

kanban that was 8 feet (2.4 meters) high and 6 feet (1.8 meters) wide at the base. His commentary indicates that one would never find such a kanban in either Edo or Kyoto (cat. 26).[167]

Japanese rôsoku traditionally were made in either of two ways. *Tsutsukake* was a molded technique using whale oil and a central grass wick, whereas *kigake* was a rolled technique using wax derived from the *hasanoki* berry and a string core. In the latter technique, the size of the candle was determined by the number of rolled layers; a 100-layer candle, for example, was referred to as a *hyaku moko rôsoku* and was considered quite large. The kigake variety became essentially standard for shrine and votive use. The use of wax and paper string allowed for an easy overlap with other products, and rôsoku shops also frequently sold *moto yuki* (hair-tying cords) and *bin tsuke* (pomade).[168]

As a sideline, the famed Edo writer Takizawa Bakin (1767–1848) owned a rôsoku-ya and a medicine shop under his personal name, Takizawa Kiyouemon. In keeping with the brazenly self-promotional gestalt of the Edo period, some of his illustrated works depict his own shop and announce the superior quality of his products. In an illustration included in the *Edo kanban zufu*, Bakin's shop has a hako kanban out front, with a tall mokei kanban of a candle on top and the medicinal benefits of his other products outlined in script on the paper sides below.[169]

Kushi-ya (Comb Shops)

Is there a product more intimately connected with its user than the comb? The repeated use, the elixir of oils, the familiarity of the hand—all these create a unique bond between user and instrument. Combs factor into Japanese legend and are closely linked with the oldest and most sacred Shinto shrine, Ise Jingû.[170] This spiritual aspect is reflected in an older word for comb in Japanese: *kushibi* (lit. "working with spirits"). The more modern term, *kushi*, is a contraction of this ancient, meaning-laden term. Japanese lore ascribes mystical powers to combs, and popular culture held them as a locus of rejuvenation, fertility, and a robust sexuality.[171] Combs developed hand in hand with Japanese culture, ranging from the ritualistic to the utilitarian to the decorative.

During the Edo period, combs became closely associated in the popular imagination with the courtesans of the floating world, who used them not only for combing out their famously long tresses but also for their elaborate hair arrangements. A plethora of combs, pins (*kanzashi*), and other ornaments held these phantasmagorical creations in place. Woodblock-print imagery featuring celebrated beauties often included this constellation of accessories as a distinct feature of their occupation (fig. 46). Over the Edo period, partially as a result of the popularity of the courtesan, the use of combs for hair decoration became more common among "civilian" women as well. Although combs were fashioned of bamboo, *kiri* (paulownia), and *ume* (plum), as well as a variety of more local woods, combs made of boxwood (*tsuge*) became the standard, with tsuge from southern Kyûshû being especially prized.[172] The distinctive *chonmage* topknot, worn by men of the samurai class, also demanded the use of specialized combs. Most *kushi-ya* (comb shops) were concentrated in Edo, Osaka, and Kyoto. But regional comb production also spurred the

26

Mokei kanban for candle shop

Late nineteenth century

Wood, paper, pigment

36 × 11½ in. (91.5 × 29.2 cm)

Private Collection

The character set used for writing *rôsoku* (candle) is quite complex, and kanban makers typically relied on the distinctive shape of the candle itself to serve as an effective advertisement. The kanban for a candle shop could range from a simple silhouette to a fully rendered, massive mokei kanban suspended from or standing outside the entrance. This exceptionally large example is constructed using a thin wood veneer formed in the tapering shape of a rôsoku, with its exterior wrapped in paper and then painted. Red was the most common color for rôsoku, and here the outer red pigment has worn away to reveal the white undercoat.

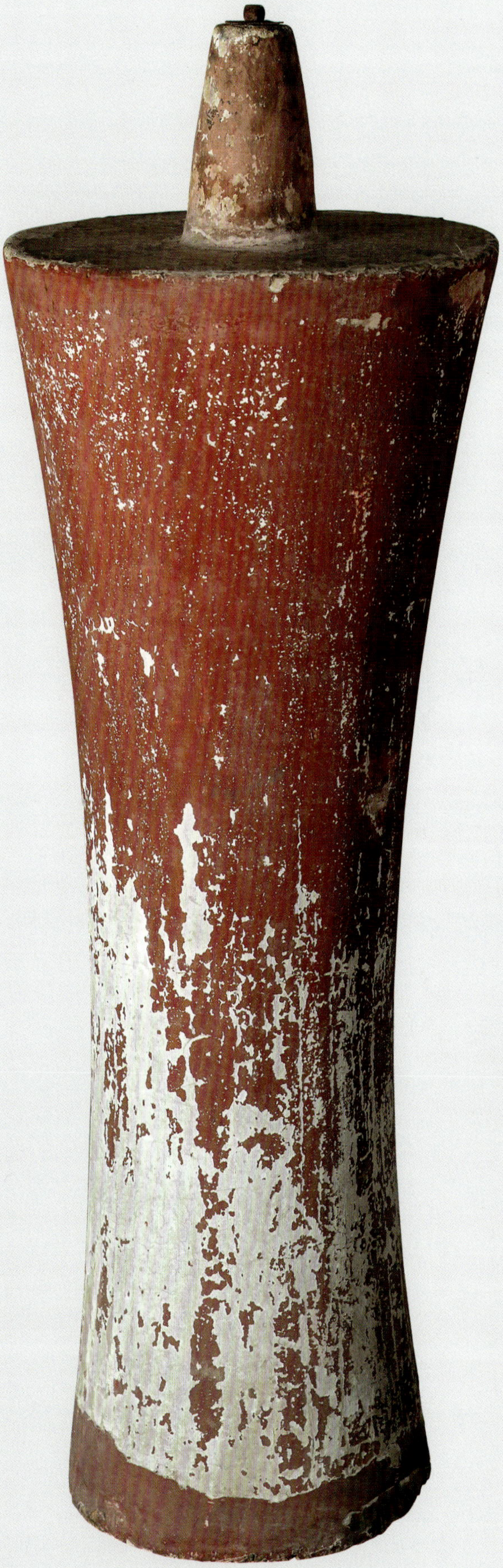

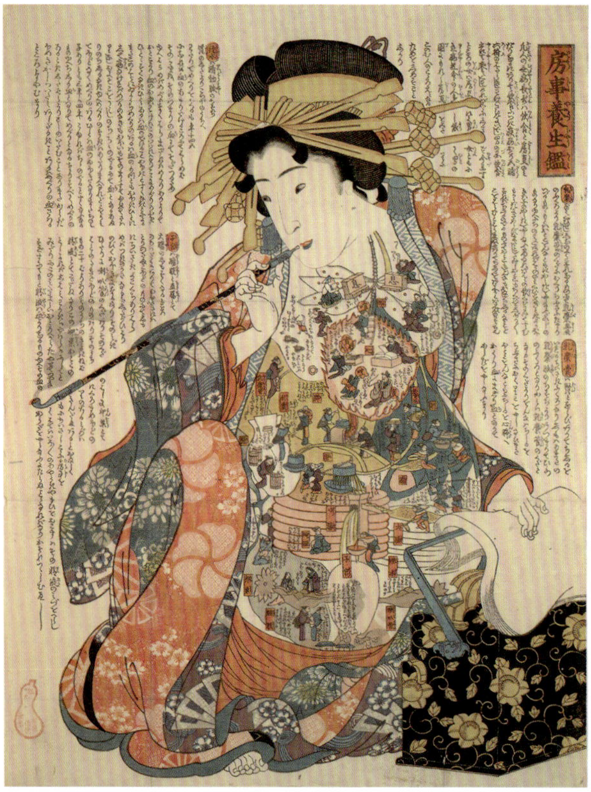

FIG. 46 This medical woodblock print depicts a courtesan with a long-stemmed kiseru pipe and a plethora of hair combs, both clearly indicative of her profession. The artist has portrayed the inner workings of her physiology through a series of humorous cartouches describing the various biological functions of the body. *Bôji yôjô kagami* (Rules of sexual life), Utagawa Kunisada (1786–1864), c. 1850. Reproduced by permission of the Nichibunken (International Research Center for Japanese Studies).

sale of combs as a popular tourist souvenir, such as the *oroku kushi* made of *minebali* wood from along the historic Nakasendô Highway in Nagano Prefecture.

It can be a decided marketing obstacle for a business to sell a product that calls to mind death, suffering, or ill-fortune (cats. 27, 28). Such was the dilemma facing makers of *kushi*, a homonym for suffering (*ku*) and death (*shi*). Fortunately, in the elastic wordplay that so often characterized Japanese kanban, there was an easy remedy: avoid the issue altogether and refer to the shop and product in another way. *Ku* can also be read as the number nine and *shi* can be read as the number four. Nine plus four is thirteen—hence the predilection for comb shops to use the name Jûsan-ya: *jû* (10) + *san* (3) = *jûsan* (13). A number of traditional Japanese comb shops still use the Jûsan-ya name, though they are not connected, and the name itself is not claimed in a proprietary way by any one shop. Generally, the characters are arranged from right to left—a hat-tipping gesture to tradition. The earliest-known shop bearing that name was established in Edo in 1736 in the city's Ueno-Ikenohata section. This area of Ueno, clustered around the Shinobazu Pond, was a popular district for traditional comb makers until the Great Kantô Earthquake of 1923.[173] The current owner, Tsutomo Takeuchi, is the fourteenth-generation proprietor, and the shop was designated by the Japanese government in 2003 as an Intangible Cultural Property. Another famous Jûsan-ya, located on Shijô in Kyoto, was founded in 1875. In 2013, the current head of the shop, fifth-generation proprietor Takeuchi Shinkichi, made the ritual combs enshrined during the rebuilding of Ise Jingu, which takes place every twenty years. Taking the name game a step further is Kyoto's Nijûsan-ya, or 23 Shop, specializing in bamboo combs. The shop combines the character for *to* (bamboo as well as the number 10) with the familiar *jû* and *san* (10 + 10 + 3 = 23).

***Katsura-ya* (Wig Shops)**

Kanban functioned as expressions of artistic creativity as well as commercial outreach. The extraordinary variety of kanban that exist for almost every trade bespeaks a truly fertile ground for the kanban-shi. However, sometimes there is a striking consistency among the kanban used for a given profession, which makes for interesting

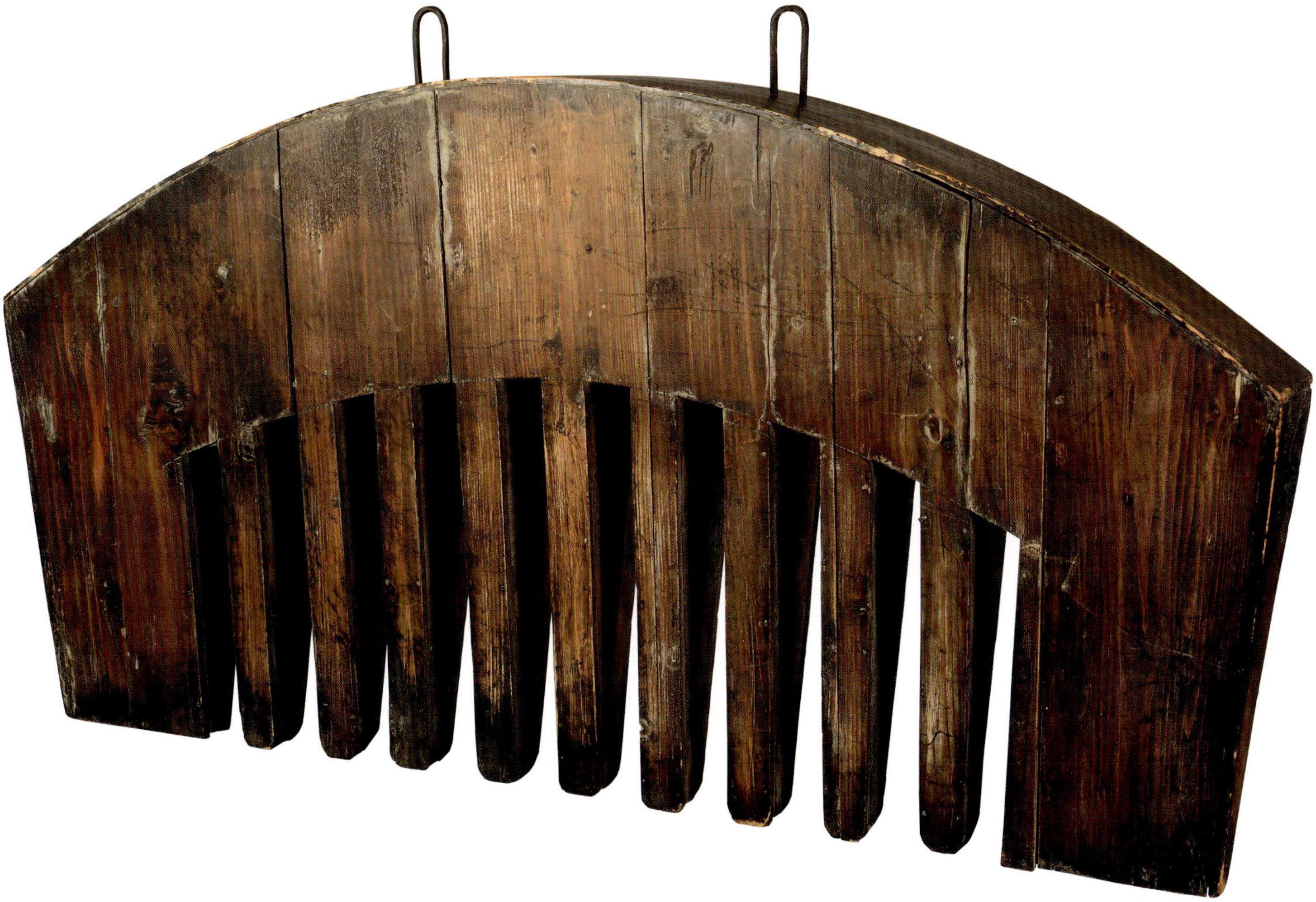

27

Mokei kanban for comb shop

Nineteenth century

Wood, metal fittings

24¼ × 45¼ in. (61.6 × 114.9 cm)

Private Collection

Kushi are distinctive in shape and construction. Although Japanese combs came in a wide variety of forms based on specific applications, a comb is a comb is a comb, and its handle and tines are immediately identifiable. Thus, kushi-ya (comb shops) frequently relied on mokei kanban to advertise their presence, with the flat space of the handle a convenient place to record the shop's yago.

The configuration of a comb made it ideal for hanging as an enlarged sculpture outside of a shop, easily functioning as a shitta kanban as well. This practice continues today. The impressive mokei kanban shown here is of truly Brobdingnagian proportions. The shape is curved and wedged just as a functional comb. A total of nineteen separate pieces of wood went into its execution. Because the sign is weather-worn, it is impossible to determine what may have been written across the handle or any particularities as to the location of the original shop. It stands as a wonderful tribute to the communicative power of kanban and the resourcefulness of the kanban-shi.

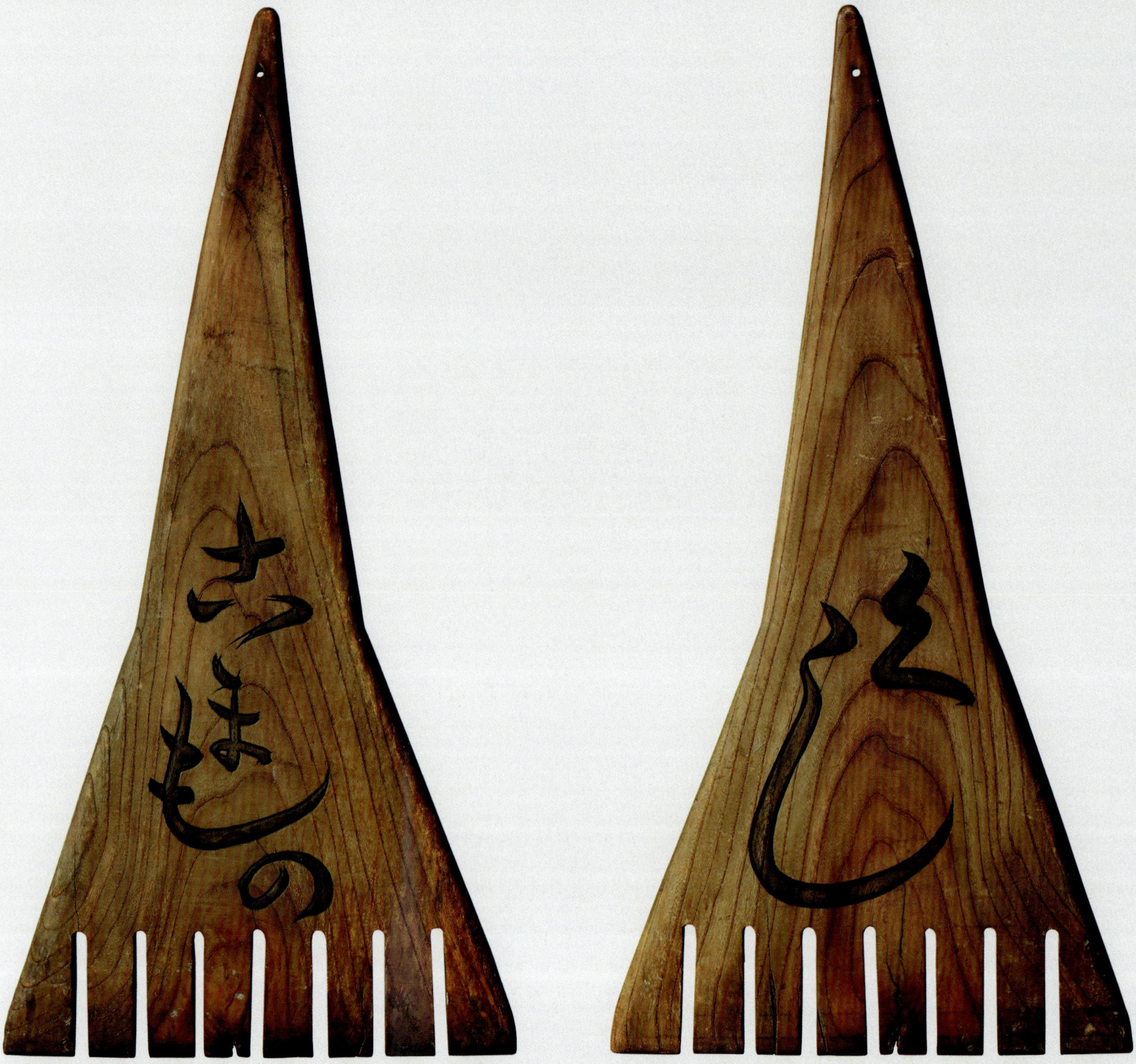

28

Mokei kanban for comb shop, front and back views
Nineteenth century
Wood, ink
33½ × 16½ in. (85 × 45 cm)
Shôwa Neon Takamura Kanban Museum

Traditional Japanese combs (kushi) were made out of a wide variety of materials and executed in an equally wide array of shapes, depending on their specific functions. Combs called *sukigushi* had exceptionally fine tines for cleaning hair and removing dandruff. Decorative combs were used to secure elaborate hairstyles. To aid in the dressing of hair, certain combs also featured long, pick-like ends. These latter, frequently made out of *tsuge* (boxwood), were an indispensable part of a woman's toiletry set. Here, a mokei kanban in the shape of a *suji-tate gushi*, used for combing and blocking hair during the arrangement process, bears the hiragana inscription "*kushi*" (comb) on one side and "*komamono*" (fancy goods) on the other, indicating that this shop also sold such objects as *kanzashi* (hairpins) and assorted accessories.

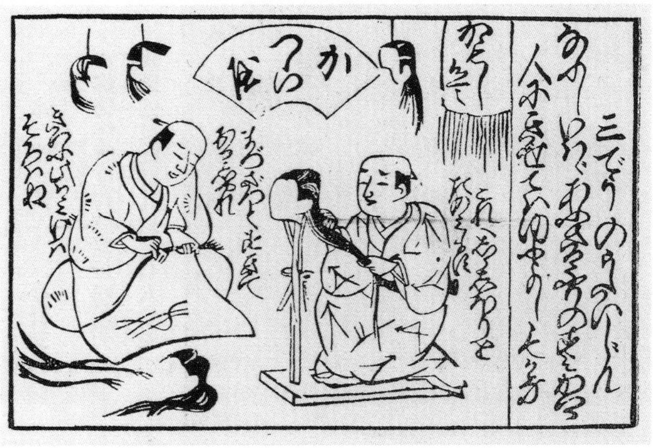

FIG. 47 Edo-period woodblock print of a katsura-ya, showing one attendant combing out the long queue of a wig while another worker prepares hair extensions. Suspended above are examples of finished wigs along with a fan-shaped kanban bearing the inscription "*Katsura-ya*" in hiragana. Depicted in the *Imayô shokunin-zukushi hyakunin isshu* by Kondô Kiyoharu, Kyôho era, 1716–35.

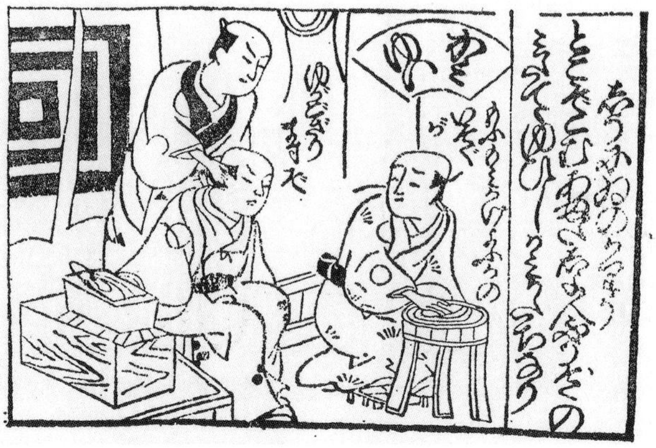

FIG. 48 Edo-period woodblock print of a kami yui dokoro, with a customer facing the street while a shop attendant helps to arrange his chonmage hairstyle. The noren in back bears the distinctive mi-masu crest associated with the Ichikawa Danjûrô lineage of kabuki actors, indicating a possible stage affiliation with the proprietor or a simple marketing ploy. Above in a fan-shaped kanban is the phrase "*Kami yui*" written in hiragana. Depicted in the *Imayô shokunin-zukushi hyakunin isshu* by Kondô Kiyoharu, Kyôho era, 1716–35.

study. Such is the case of the kanban for *katsura-ya*, or wig maker's shops (cat. 29). A faceless head featuring the shaved pate (*sakayaki*) and topknot of a samurai forms an almost iconic image for the wig maker, and nearly identical examples are found in a number of museums and private collections. The word *katsura* is inscribed in hiragana where the face would be. In Edo, this was generally pronounced *katsura*, and in Kyoto, *kazura*. Such shops, catering to men as well as women, also sold *kamoji,* or hair extensions, and other related products (fig. 47). Shops specializing in wigs for actors were known as *butai kazura-ya*, as they sold "wigs for show."[174]

Related shops included *kami yui dokoro*, or barbershops (fig. 48). We have already encountered one such shop at the base of the Gojô Bridge, as depicted in the Funaki screen. Prior to the Edo period, hairstyles as well as clothing styles were not so differentiated between men and women. When the sakayaki shaving practice became more standardized for men, shops providing this service proliferated, particularly in Edo. Under the governance of Tokugawa Ieyasu (1543–1616), special dispensation was given for those at the six principal guard stations for the newly established capital at Edo Castle; retainers and samurai were to have their pates shaved and their hair arranged in order to look presentable at court. Early kami yui dokoro were restricted to the samurai class alone. During successive eras, the practice spread and independent businesses emerged. By the middle of the eighteenth century, this sector of the service economy exploded, with over a thousand shops in Edo alone. So prevalent were start-up shops that the government intervened and established fairly strict rules and required a mandatory capital outlay in order to secure a permit to operate a kami yui-ya. Additionally, the government tried to regulate pricing in this area, and so, naturally, signs that read "*Oyoshishidai*" (Below market rate) also became common.[175]

So engrained a part of town culture had these shops become that by the early nineteenth century we find writers such as Kitagawa Morisada, author of the *Morisada mankô*, ranking the barbershops of the three principal cities. According to Morisada, Osaka had the best shops, which were decorated with potted flowers and offered amusements such as *go* games and books for waiting customers. Kyoto followed next. Edo barbers were seen as the worst, caring little for their customers and providing no comforts. In all three cities, customers generally sat on platforms street-side, not needing to actually enter the

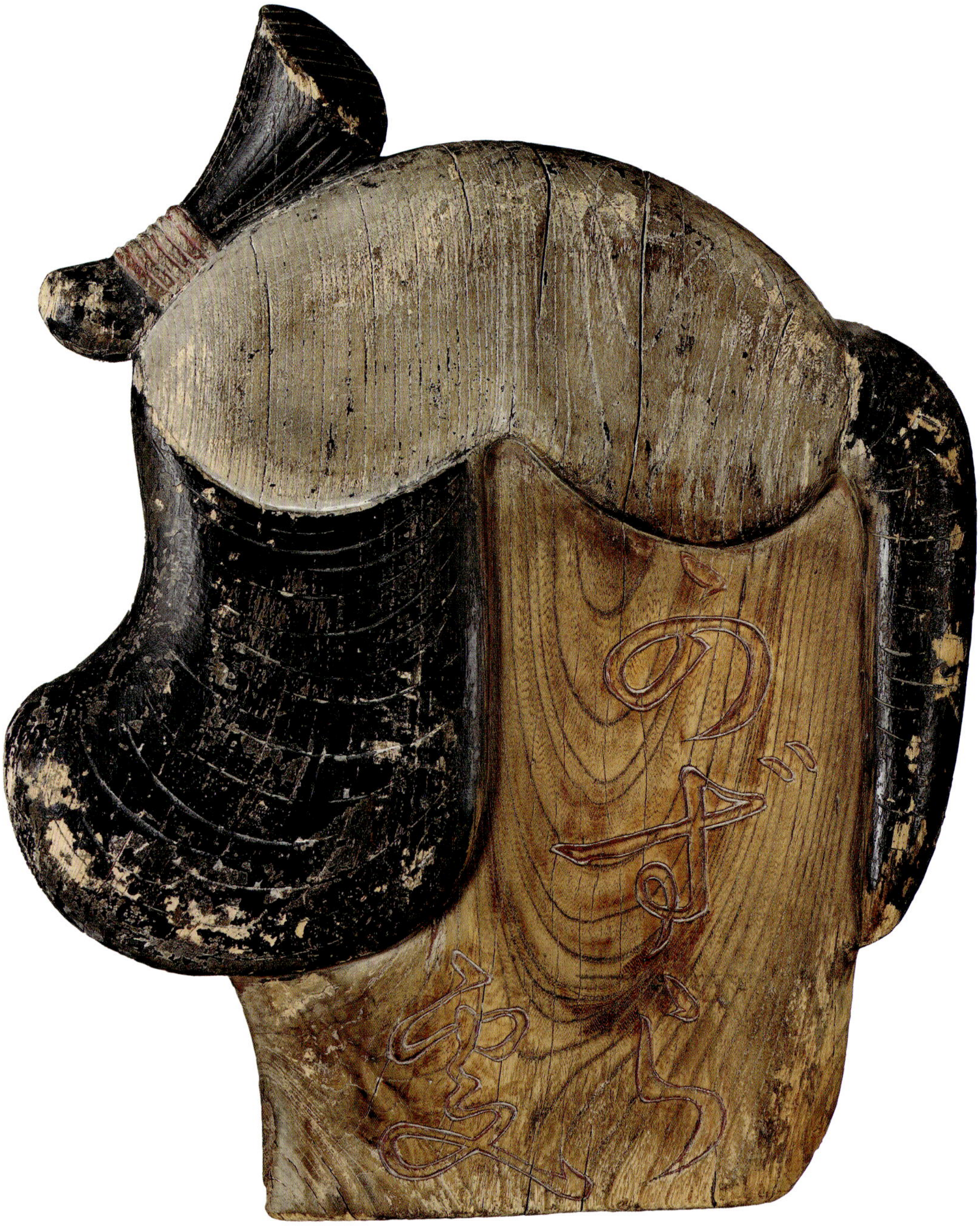

29

Mokei kanban for wig shop
Nineteenth century
Wood, pigment
17 × 13½ in. (43.2 × 34.3 cm)
Private Collection

Mokei kanban served as effective advertisements not only for specific products but also for various service industries. A curious category of mokei kanban is that used for wig makers. Rather than featuring the image of an elaborately coiffed woman, as one might expect, the signature kanban for this specialty trade showed the faceless head of a man with a shaved pate, with the simple phrase "*katsura dokoro*" or "*kazura-ya*" inscribed on the front. The uniformity of this type of sign is striking, with subtle variations in the length of the carved side-locks, the shape and height of the topknot rising from the back of the shaved area, and differences in writing styles. Closely related examples to this one are found in the National Museum of Japanese History, the Kenichi Higasa Collection, and the Shôwa Neon Takamura Kanban Museum.

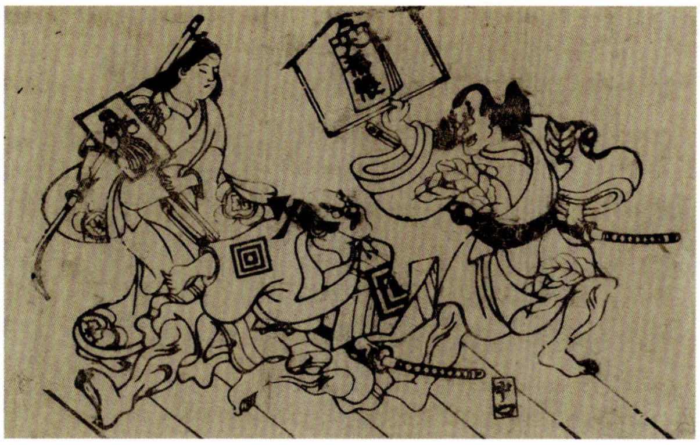

FIG. 49 The kabuki character Dazainojô holds up an ema bearing the image of a *daifukuchô* (ledger book) in a scene from *Daifukuchô Sankai Nagoya*, performed at the Nakamura Theater in Edo in 1697. Actors were Yamanaka Heikurô I as Dazainojô, Ichikawa Danjûrô I as Fuwa Banzaemon, and Sodeoka Masanosuke II as his wife Fujigae. Attributed to Torii Kiyonobu I (1664–1729), Edo period, 1697. Woodblock print, *sumizuri-e*, ink on paper, horizontal *chûban*, 6⅝ × 10⅛ in. (16.8 × 25.7 cm). Museum of Fine Arts, Boston, William Sturgis Bigelow Collection, 11.30349. Photograph © 2017 Museum of Fine Arts, Boston.

shops or even remove their geta. This created a very social aspect to the process, as clients remained free to interact with passersby while they were being groomed.[176]

The Funaki screen described above provides an image of a Kyoto kanban for a barber, featuring scissors and a comb. A similar kanban can be found on another pair of rakuchû rakugai zu screens in the Tokyo National Museum—indicating, again, a certain consistency in this particular sector of the economy. Early kanban for these shops also frequently employed images of actors, and some of the barbers had actually begun their careers in the theater, preparing wigs for performances. But intense loyalties could backfire on a proprietor who chose the wrong actor to use as a marquee element. A common hanji mono, or wordplay, kanban would use the character "*atari*" to advertise a kami yui-ya. On one level, atari means "big success" or "hit." But the verb *ataru* also means to shave the pate, as in a sakayaki. Woodblock-print images for the period depict shoji kanban with the atari character written in bold, black ink on the paper panels, serving de facto as the shop's name (Atari-ya) as well as advertising the service.[177]

Chômen-ya (Stationery Shops)

The signature item for a *chômen-ya* (stationery shop) was the *daifukuchô* (ledger book). Although the blank sheets of this thick book could be used as a travel diary, a personal record, or any number of other entry-based activities, its primary association was as a merchant's accounting ledger. The daifukuchô has played a unique role in Japanese cultural history. Aside from being a utilitarian tool, a book for a merchant to enter his daily accounts and notes, the daifukuchô (lit. "ledger of good fortune") also served as a symbol for merchant culture itself. In the 1692 play *Daifukuchô Asahina Hyaku Monogatari* (The great ledger book and Asahina's hundred stories), written by Ichikawa Danjûrô I, Asahina presents a chest of military secrets to the young samurai Ushiwaka-maru at his coming-of-age ceremony. When opened, it reveals, much to the chagrin of the virile warriors present, an abacus and a ledger. Asahina pronounces these "the sword and suit of armor of the merchant."[178] It was a line and a moment that captured the cultural zeitgeist, when there was a palpable recognition that the merchant was in the ascendant and the samurai in decline. In kabuki, the ledger book was worked into numerous performances as a central plot device. From that point on, many plays used the ledger book less as an accountant's tool than as a document containing secrets central to the identities of the characters in the play (fig. 49).[179] Daifukuchô also became synonymous with the summation critiques frequently written about Japanese cultural figures, from courtesans to actors.

Structurally, a Japanese daifukuchô was unique but quite simple. Typically, the long, vertically oriented pages were folded in half and then bundled together into a varying number of sets, depending upon the needs of the client. A thicker cover paper, sometimes lacquered, was attached to the top and bottom of the bundle as protection. Along the top, sewing holes were punched through the body, dividing the top edge roughly into thirds. One cord was passed through each hole, front and back, wrapped around the edges, creating a four-piece binding mechanism

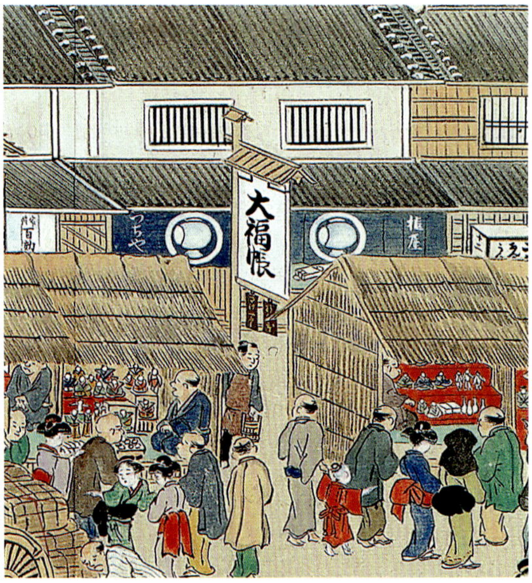

FIG. 50 Detail: The Tsuchi-ya Chômen-ya stationery shop on Nihonbashi, as depicted in the *Kidai shôran*. Museum of Asian Art, Berlin.

secured at the top, allowing the assembled daifukuchô to be suspended or carried easily. This tying system also created a distinct peaked outline of cord on the front and back faces of the daifukuchô, forming a specific "signature." From a technical standpoint, this is referred to as "stab binding." It was typical for the maker to write on the cover in bold calligraphic characters "Daifukuchô," as opposed to a business's name. New daifukuchô were traditionally started at the New Year, and the buying of a fresh ledger book was a seasonal rite attended to with an air of great festivity. Woodblock prints commemorating this event frequently depict daifukuchô suspended from freshly cut bamboo poles, with the leaves still abundantly present.

Kanban for chômen-ya frequently focused on the daifukuchô as the principal advertising image. The thick paper ledgers themselves could be used simply as jitsubutsu kanban, with the merchant stringing a series of ledgers along the front of the shop. The *Kidai shôran* illustrates the successful Tsuchi-ya Chômen-ya, which used an impressive tate kanban featuring a wooden sign all in white with the characters "Daifukuchô" at the center, with the outlines of the stab binding clearly seen (fig. 50). Attached below this large sign are two smaller ledgers. The Tsuchi-ya used a large mallet (*tsuchi*) within a circle as its yago, and the noren bears this symbol along with the name of the shop written in hiragana. Further down the street toward the Nihonbashi Bridge itself, located between the Kagi-ya face powder wholesaler and the Osaka-ya geta merchant, is another chômen-ya using an almost identical tate kanban. On the raised tatami floor of the interior is a partially bound daifukuchô; finished, blank ledgers hang from the wall, while packages of paper are stacked in the back. Edo-period chômen-ya also frequently used mokei kanban constructed of paper and stretched over a light bamboo frame in the shape of a daifukuchô.[180] An example of this latter type is in the PEM collection, a kanban for the Ameno Chôbo-ten (Heavenly Paper Store).[181]

A Meiji-era innovation was the creation of a freestanding wooden mokei kanban of a daifukuchô that could appear street-side in front of the shop. Created to look like a slightly flexing ledger with its pages flaring slightly at the bottom, this sign could read either the classic "Daifukuchô" or alternatively the name of the shop, with the shape of the kanban itself clearly reflecting the product being offered. In this format, the tied cords at the top were replaced by a metal handle for easy portage in and out of the shop each day (cat. 30).

Yôki Kanban: Container Shop Signs

A distinct and important subcategory of kanban is the *yôki kanban,* or a kanban that is fashioned after the shape of the container in which a specific product is sold. Edo Japan was awash in specialized products, with narrowly defined traditions and methods of production as well as practices for distribution and sales. We have already touched on the use of storage containers as jitsubutsu kanban, in the case of raw lacquer sellers who commonly strung up a series of straw-wrapped casks used to transport this important commodity. But a number of products were sold in containers whose mere outline was so distinctive and

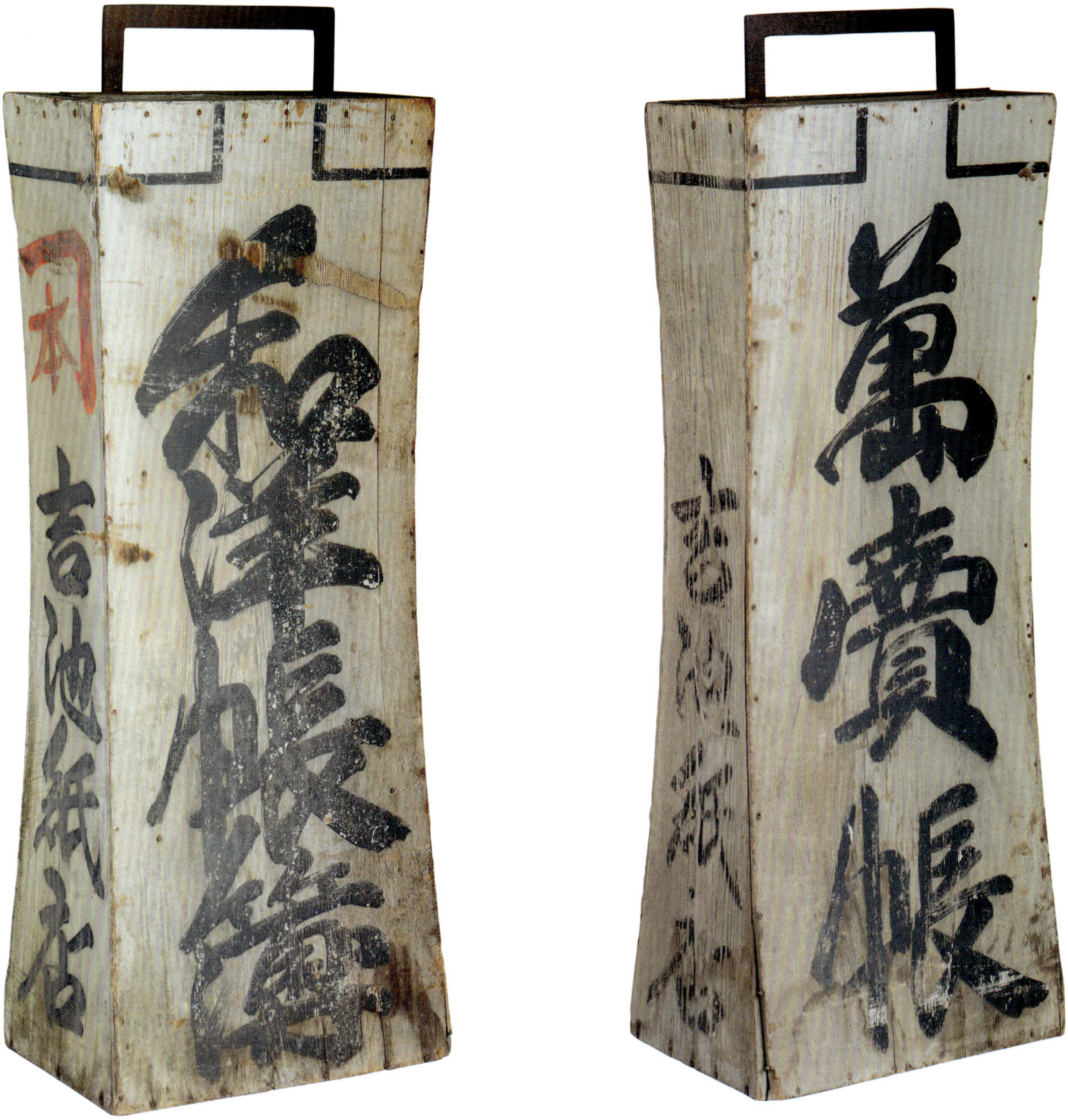

30

Mokei kanban for stationery shop, front and back views

Early twentieth century

Wood, pigment, metal fittings

33 × 12 × 8½ in. (83.8 × 30.5 × 21.6 cm)

Mingei International Museum Purchase, 2013-22-002

Despite the introduction of neon and the growing sophistication of digital marketing, kanban still play a significant role in Japanese commercial culture. Rather than reminders of a dead tradition, they have continued to evolve and develop alongside newer traditions from the Meiji era onward. Traditional shops have made room on their shelves for new iterations of older products or for entirely new commodities. Here, an early twentieth-century mokei kanban for the Yoshiike Kamiten chômen-ya, or stationery shop, takes the classic image of a daifukuchô (ledger book) and translates it into a freestanding sign with a carrying handle. Instead of the stock phrase "daifukuchô," used throughout the Edo period, the front reads "*yorozu uri chô*" (accounting books), and the back reads "*wayô-chôbo*," indicating that this shop offered both Japanese and Western-style paper. The name of the shop appears on the side, along with the shop's yago.

individual as to clearly announce the contents. The three most important of these were the *ha-cha-ya* (tea leaf shop), *shôyu-ya* (soy sauce shop), and *su-ya* (vinegar shop). Each of these popular consumables had its own distinct history and set of affiliated traditions.

***Ha-cha-ya* (Tea Leaf Shops)**

The 1,200-year history of tea in Japan is too well documented to merit a full recounting here. But a brief review would note that records in the Shôsoin Repository dating to 739 mention tea being used for its medicinal properties. Domestic production began soon after 805, when the Buddhist priest Saichô (Dengyô Daishi, 767–822) brought seeds back from China. In 1191, the priest Myôan Eisai (1141–1215) began using powdered tea as part of a Zen Buddhist tea ritual. And in 1271, the Buddhist monk Kôken planted camellias in the Uji area outside of Kyoto, which would become and remains today one of the most important tea-growing regions in Japan.[182] The prevalence of tea consumption in Edo Japan was preceded by the familiar trickle-down effect in which manners and customs engaged in by the cultural elite slowly expanded and penetrated various social strata. Early manufacture and distribution of Japan's celebrated green tea was exceptionally limited, and commoners were largely restricted to a humbler brown tea known as *bancha* or *hôjicha*. The wider appeal and consumption of Japan's *matcha* (green tea) is attributed to the particular genius of Sohen Nagatani (1681–1778) of Uji, who developed a process by which green tea could be produced in large quantities. By the advent of the Edo period, tea shops for consuming tea and shops specializing in the sale of tea leaves were a familiar part of the cultural topography, and the *cha-tsubo* (tea jar) or simply *tsubo*, used to store tea leaves, was a singular and iconic image (cat. 31).

Cha-tsubo were of a very particular shape, with design details that made them ideally suited for storing green tea leaves until they were ready to be ground into powder. The ability of tsubo to keep the leaves fresh until needed made them indispensable. The tall neck allowed for a long, fitted wooden stopper to be inserted, in order to keep out air and humidity. The broad shoulders were augmented with four lugs, through which cords were passed to help secure the lid. Over this, a paper wrapping was applied and then secured with a cord around the neck, providing additional temperature and humidity control. For more ceremonial containers, a secondary wrapping cloth of silk brocade (*kuchiôi*) was sometimes used. This outer wrapping could be quite large, cascading over the shoulders of the tsubo and, combined with the tasseled cord (*kuchio*), giving the vessel a decidedly festive air (cat. 32).

Ceramic and stoneware tsubo of varied sizes were used, whether for short-term or long-term storage, business use or domestic consumption, ceremonial or personal use. Various kilns were appreciated for the beauty of their tea-related wares. Shigaraki, Hagi, Bizen, Tamba, and Tokoname were all popular for their utilitarian and artistic tsubo. Within the tea ceremony, the tsubo itself became an object of special focus. Over time, certain tsubo became celebrated cultural artifacts, making the transition from workaday tea jars to heralded art objects. The mid-thirteenth- to-mid-fourteenth-century cha-tsubo known as "Chigusa" (meaning "Thousand grasses" or "Myriad things") is a stoneware tea storage jar with a mottled amber iron glaze; it was originally made in China but has been revered in Japan for over seven hundred years for its fine shape (fig. 51). The bottom bears the fifteenth- and sixteenth-century inscriptions of a succession of high-powered owners, all practitioners of the art of the tea ceremony. Illustrious tea masters made notes in their personal diaries whenever Chigusa made an "appearance" at a tea ceremony. Chigusa has shared tea with the likes of the military warlord Toyotomi Hideyoshi (1536–1598) and Sen no Rikyû (1522–1591), the ultimate arbiter of taste within the context of the

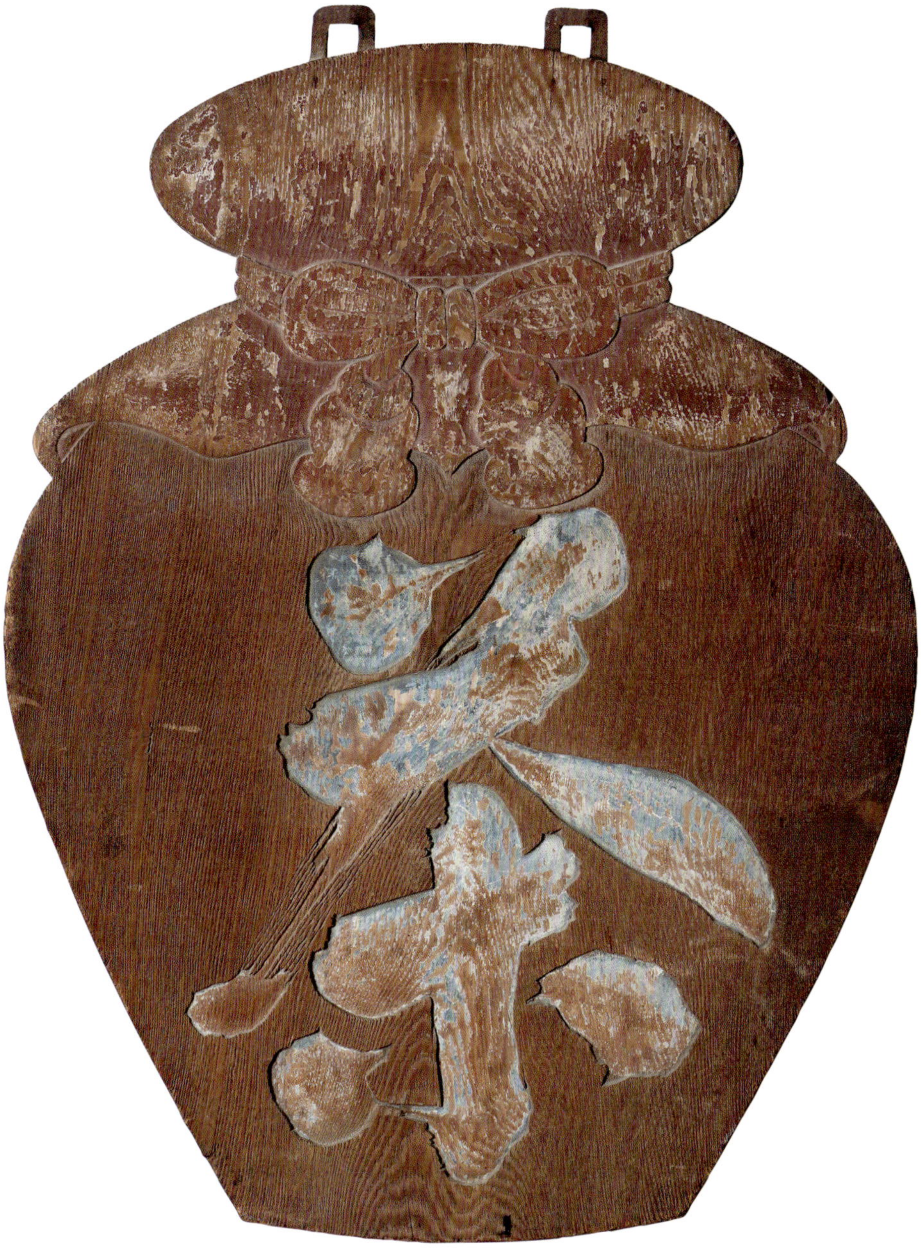

31

Yôki kanban for tea leaf shop

Late nineteenth century

Wood, pigment, metal fittings

24½ × 18½ in. (62.2 × 47 cm)

Private Collection

Yôki kanban represented the overall shape of the container in which a particular consumable was shipped, sold, and stored. Certain vessel designs were shorthand for the product itself, and a simple flattened shape or silhouette of the container functioned as clear and precise advertising. The tea leaf jar, or cha-tsubo, was one of the more important categories of yôki kanban, as tea merchants relied heavily on this form of advertising well into the modern era. Indeed, even today one finds neon renditions of the cha-tsubo, its contours outlined in pulsing light. Of course, on traditional wooden kanban, the flattened surface of the panel also allowed for the communication of specific details or a simple redundant statement of the product sold: "tea." Hung perpendicular to the street, shitta kanban communicated to passersby in both directions. Here, a yôki kanban does double duty as a shitta kanban, with both faces inscribed with the characters "*ô-cha*." The lid, wrapping cloth, and decorative tasseled tie cords receive additional detail and treatment, elevating this sign far above the simple outline of a cha-tsubo.

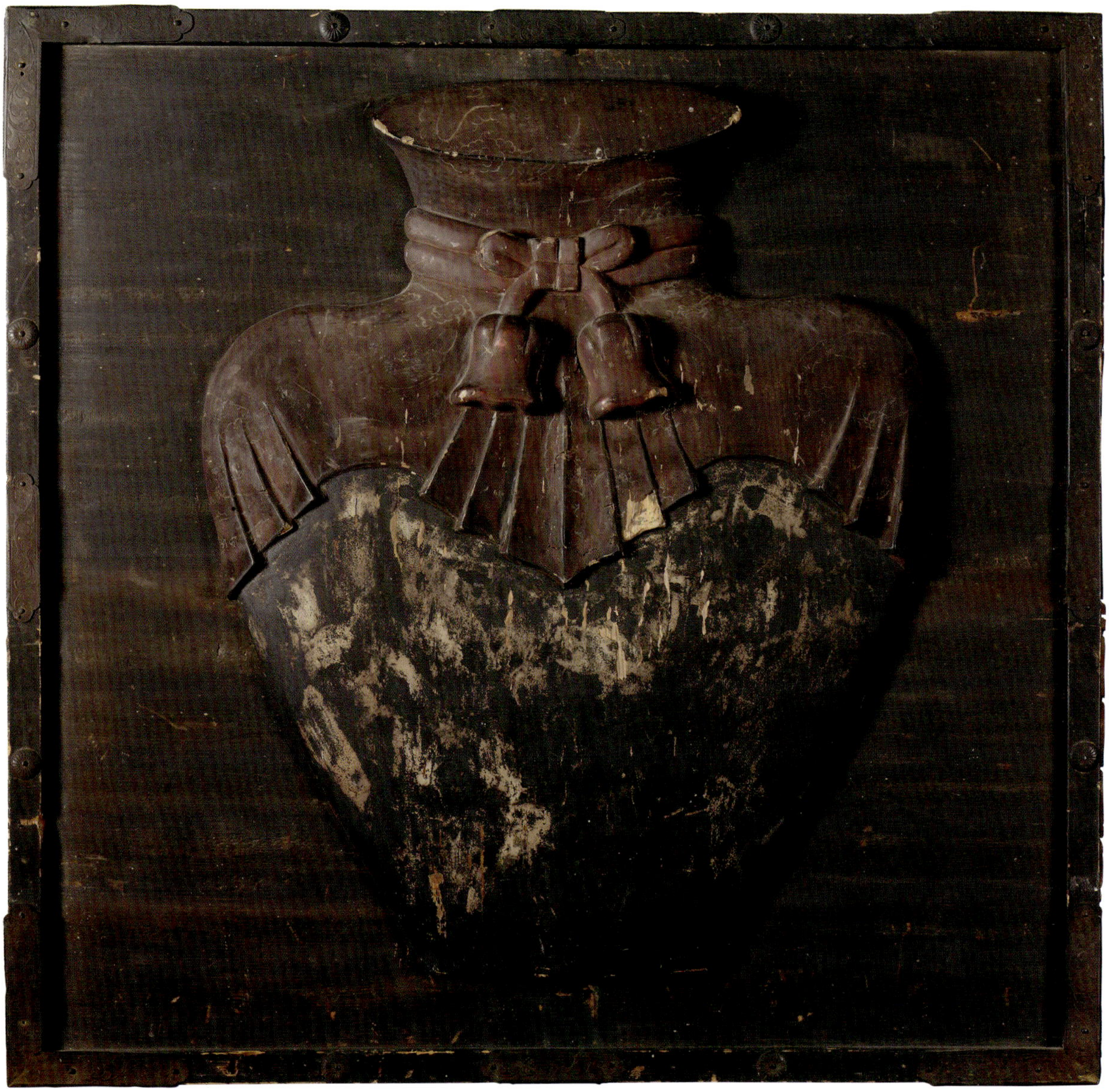

32

Sage kanban for tea leaf shop

Nineteenth century

Wood, pigment, lacquer, metal

Frame: 25 × 24 in. (63.5 × 62 cm); jar: 20 in. (52 cm) tall

Private Collection

Although street-side yôki kanban predominated as the preferred form of signage for ha-cha-ya (tea leaf shops), occasionally we find other forms of kanban used, ranging from tate to hako kanban. One-sided signs that hung flush with the wall were known as sage kanban or *kattamen kanban*. Here, a one-sided sage kanban depicts a deeply carved appliqué of a cha-tsubo. The two-board backing panel is framed with incised metal fittings. The jar itself features a very tall neck and a princely *kuchiôi* (wrapping cloth) in lacquered red that drapes luxuriously over the broad shoulders of the jar and covers the entire upper third of the vessel with deeply contoured folds. The *kuchio* (securing cords) form a tight knot at the neck, and the decorative tassels form a double punctuation mark just below.

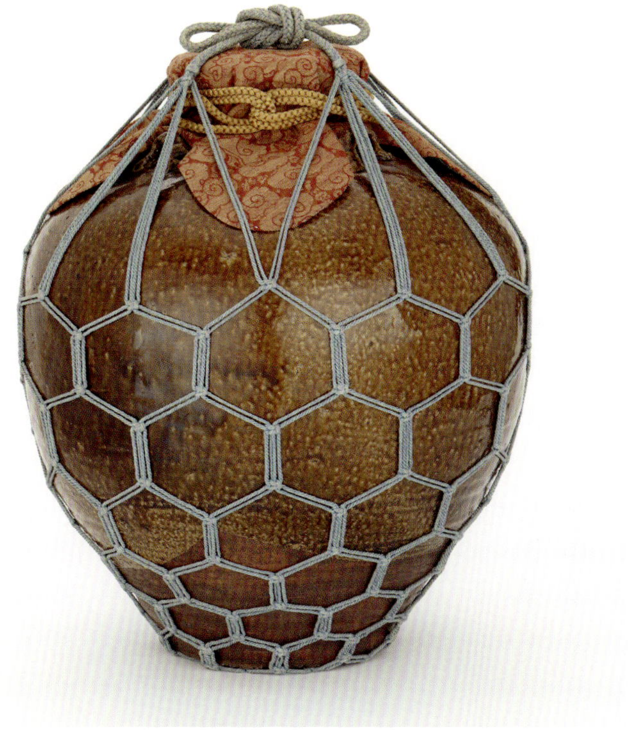

FIG. 51 Perhaps the most famous of all tea leaf storage jars is the cha-tsubo named "Chigusa." China, Guangdong or Fujian province, Southern Song or Yuan dynasty, mid-thirteenth to mid-fourteenth century. Stoneware with iron glaze, 16⅜ × 14⁷⁄₁₆ in. (41.6 × 36.6 cm). Freer Gallery of Art, Smithsonian Institution, Washington, D.C.: Purchase—Charles Lang Freer Endowment, FSC-P-6964.1.

Japanese tea ceremony—evidently, Chigusa was not found wanting. During the Edo period, Chigusa shuttled back and forth among various members of the Tokugawa clan, offered as a gift of special importance and cultural magnitude.[183] In 2009, Chigusa was purchased by the Smithsonian's Freer Gallery of Art at a Christie's auction held in New York for $662,500. The silhouette of Chigusa, replete with its lid and splendid fifteenth-century Chinese silk brocade kuchiôi wrapping cloth at the top, presents the perfect and classic image of a cha-tsubo, and it could easily have served as a model for the innumerable yôki kanban made for ha-cha-ya the length and breadth of Japan.

Shôyu-ya (Soy Sauce Shops)

The American consumer might consider *shôyu*, or soy sauce, to be quintessentially Japanese, even though this salty soybean-derived condiment originated in China, with commercial production in that country dating from at least 160 CE. Soy sauce is also a popular taste enhancer used historically in Korea, Vietnam, the Philippines, and elsewhere within the greater Chinese orbit, each country with its own traditions, manufacturers, and brands. But when Americans reach for soy sauce in grocery store aisles or on the tables of Chinese restaurants, frequently it is Japanese soy sauce. And more often than not, it is the soy sauce made by Kikkoman, a three-hundred-year-old company that commands 60 percent of the soy sauce market in the United States.[184]

Somewhat apocryphally, Japanese shôyu is said to have been developed by the Buddhist monk Shinchi Kakushin (1207–1298) in 1254. Following his trip to the Zen temple complex Kinzanji in China to study meditation techniques, Kakushin settled in the Yuasa area of what is now Wakayama Prefecture. He brought back with him a particular style of miso favored by the monks at Kinzanji. It is said that, while the miso fermented, he discovered the usefulness of the liquid that pooled at the bottom. By 1288, this "pooling liquid" was being produced commercially in Yuasa; to this day, Yuasa remains an important center for traditional shôyu in Japan.

The Japanese term *shôyu* is of relatively recent vintage. It comprises the characters meaning, simply enough, "soy" and "sauce," but using the most archaic Chinese form of the terms. This rendering came into popular use in the mid-sixteenth century, and this largely as a deft

FIG. 52 Detail: The Ota-ya miso shop on Nihonbashi, as depicted in the *Kidai shôran*. Museum of Asian Art, Berlin.

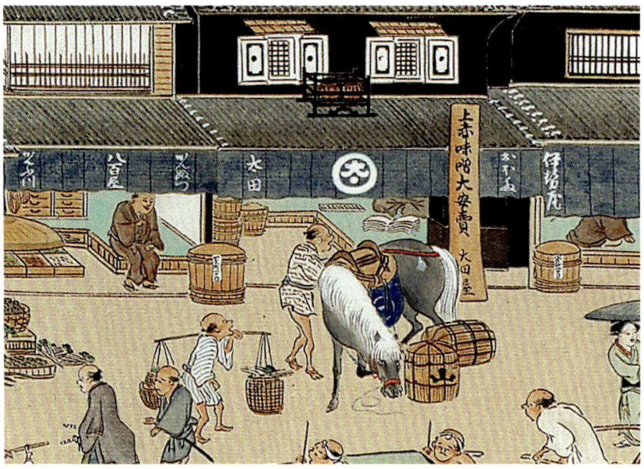

marketing tool by merchants and manufacturers to draw attention to the latest improvements on this miso by-product. "Shôyu" could in many ways be considered an early brand name, rather than a generic name for the product itself. Prior to this, soy sauce was called *tamari*, based on the verb *tamaru*, meaning "to pool" or "to accumulate"—which graphically described the manner in which this flavorful condiment was created during the miso fermentation process. The Dutch initiated the export of soy sauce through the port of Nagasaki in 1737, referring to it variously as *soije, sooje, zoihe,* and *soijo*, and the English word *soy* appears to be a catchall derivative of these various Dutch interpretations of the Japanese *shôyu*.[185]

Kanban for shôyu tended to be yôki kanban, created in the shape of an urn with a flared mouth, with the characters "*ta-ma-ri*" in the center. Alternatively, the word *shôyu* was used, but in a combination of both kanji and hiragana, the archaic characters for *shôyu* being a challenge for some Japanese consumers (cat. 33).[186] As a rule, the shape of the container tended to be more exaggerated than its refined cha-tsubo counterpart. Similarly, the tsubo for shôyu lacked the decorative flourishes of wrappings and tassels that helped make the cha-tsubo so distinctive. On an artisanal level, essentially the same kilns that manufactured tea tsubo would have been employed to make containers for shôyu. But not benefiting from the elevating influence of the tea ceremony, these more utilitarian containers used for storing and shipping shôyu remained just that, utilitarian, with none of the aesthetic overlay enjoyed by the cha-tsubo. There is no Chigusa equivalent for a vessel for soy sauce.

Miso-ya (Miso Shops)

Given the close connection between miso and shôyu, it is not surprising that many shops sold both products. But rather than focusing on storage containers, kanban for miso shops tended to be mokei-style kanban, employing the *setsukai* paddle or *shamoji* spatula (cat. 34) as iconic images.[187] The paddle itself, traditionally made of sugi (cedar), was used to scrape the edges of the fermentation vats (*shikomi oke*) where salt and *kôji* agents were added to the soy mash. This paddle was designed with a long handle to reach into a large vat. Its head had a flat top with a relatively square edge and a rounded bottom portion that fit the contours of the vat. At times, actual paddles were mounted to the eaves or support posts of a store after the manner of a jitsubutsu kanban. The *Kidai shôran*, however, illustrates the important Edo miso shop Ota-ya with two miso cauldrons (*kama*) mounted on the roof as jitsubutsu kanban, while the shop's noren is emblazoned with the Ota-ya yago, an encircled character reading "O" (fig. 52). Many shops had combinations of paddles and shôyu yôki kanban, indicating that both products were being offered for retail or wholesale.[188] Typical of this is an illustration included in the 1688 *Nippon eitai gura* series of short stories of successful merchants by Ihara Saikaku (1642–1693). In the image, a pair of shitta kanban hang from the roof side by side (fig. 53). The kanban closest to the building depicts the blade of a setsukai paddle with the hiragana for "miso" inscribed. Furthest out is a yôki kanban for shôyu. Both signs bear the smaller side inscription "*ôroshi*" (wholesale).

The oldest continuously operating miso manufacturer in Japan is Maruya Hatchô Miso in Okazaki City, east of Nagoya. Founded in 1337,

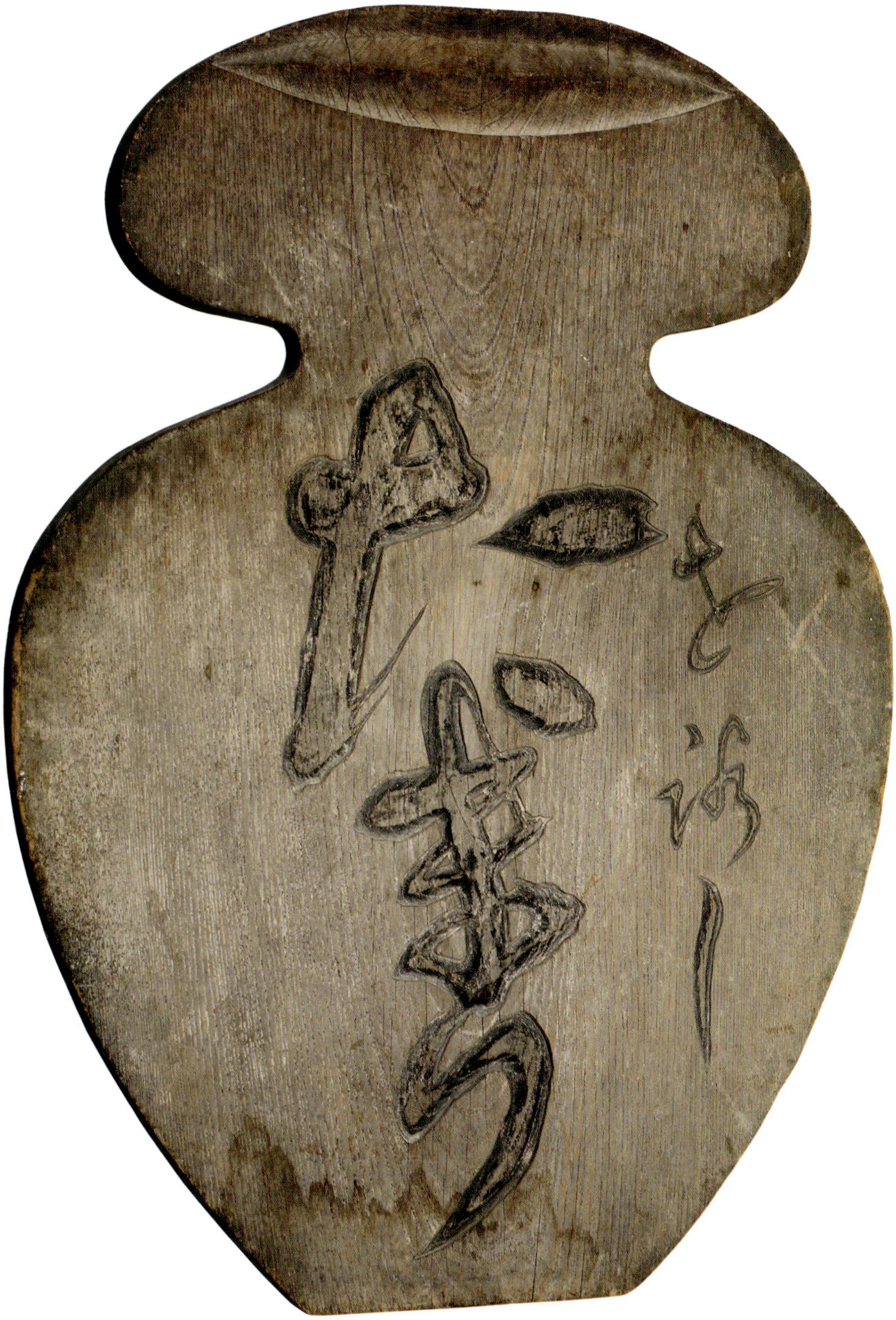

33

Yôki kanban for soy sauce shop

Nineteenth century

Wood, pigment

24½ × 17½ in. (66.2 × 44.5 cm)

Private Collection

Contrasted with the elegant and sophisticated yôki kanban for tea leaf shops, this very simple yôki kanban for a shôyu-ya (soy sauce shop) has an almost cartoon-like character to it, with its exaggerated lip and slightly asymmetrical execution. The artist has fashioned this sign from a single piece of keyaki (zelkova elm) and has given the jar a small contoured detail at the top to simulate an open mouth. A double-sided shitta kanban, it bears the inscription of the more colloquial term, "*tamari*," in hiragana on one side and the more formal term, "*shôyu*," in kanji on the reverse. Both faces bear an additional small side inscription reading "*ôroshi*" (wholesale).

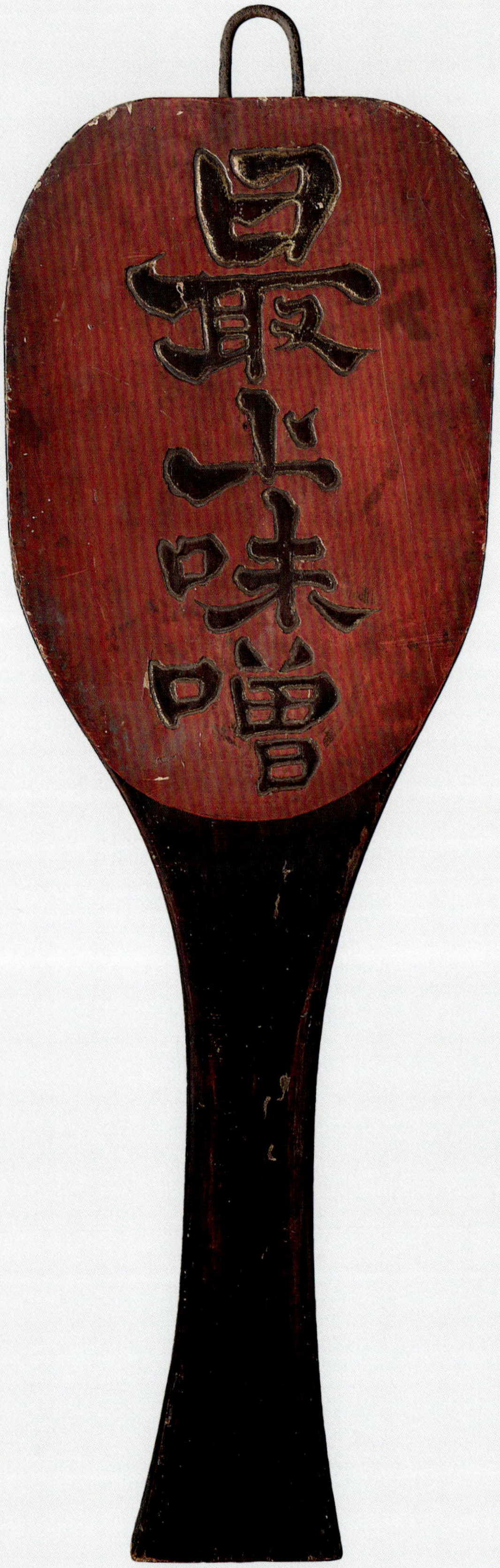

34

Mokei kanban for miso shop

Early twentieth century

Wood, pigment, lacquer, metal fitting

24¼ × 12 in. (61.6 × 30.5 cm)

Private Collection

One type of mokei kanban used for miso shops was shaped like the shamoji (spatula) used to dispense miso paste to the customer. Unlike the setsukai paddle, used to stir miso, the shamoji has rounded edges on both sides, with only a slightly flattened top and a slightly concave bowl. These spatulas were traditionally made out of bamboo or lacquered wood, and would have been nearly as iconic and identifiable to the Edo consumer as the setsukai. Kanban employing oversized shamoji frequently made use of the bowl area to indicate the shop's name. As a general rule, these would not have been wholesale establishments, but retail only. Here a mokei kanban advertises the presence of the Mogami miso shop, with its name in artfully rendered kanji on the red concave face of the shamoji. Carved from a single piece of wood, the spatula is treated in a black lacquer overall, with a dramatic red lacquer for the face. The characters were once covered in gold gilding, but now only traces remain around the edges, giving them a slightly highlighted aspect.

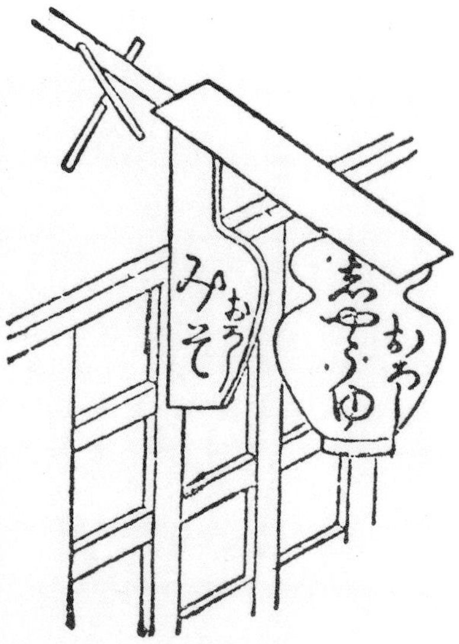

FIG. 53 A pairing of kanban for a miso-ya and a shôyu-ya, as depicted in Ihara Saikaku (1642–1693), *Nippon eitai gura* (The Japanese family storehouse) (1688).

Maruya fronted the legendary Tôkaidô Highway, and it was conveniently located only eight blocks from the castle seat of the Tokugawa family. The shop was founded by Ota Yajiuemon, hence the "ya" in Maruya. Unusually, Maruya has functioned under a hereditary management system, rather than a hereditary ownership system. The current manager is the twenty-sixth generation of the Okamoto family to serve as *banto* (head clerk), and the shop continues to employ traditional production methods.[189] One of the most interesting aspects of traditional miso production is the use of river rocks as a compression method. Once the miso has been mixed and the cedar vat sealed, a total of 3 metric tons of river rocks are placed on each lid. Approximately six hundred pieces of stone are arranged in a pyramid atop the lid to achieve an even distribution of weight, which compresses the miso and allows for the release of most of the water used in the mixing process. Each vat contains up to 4 tons of miso and remains sealed for three years.

The yago for Maruya Miso, the encircled hiragana character "ya," is still used as the corporate logo today. Beginning in the Meiji era, companies like Maruya and its rival upstart, Hatchô Miso, founded in 1645, adopted kanban very similar to those used by patent medicine manufacturers. Rather than yôki or mokei styles, these lacquered rectangular panels, referred to as moji kanban (written signs), featured the company's yago and simply listed the shop's particulars in a combination of hiragana and kanji. In the case of Hatchô, the logo of the character "eight" was set in a square and superimposed on an image of straw-wrapped shipping casks. Interestingly, on a kanban for Kikkoman soy sauce in the PEM collection, the same type of image is used. In this case, a mokei kanban of two conjoined wrapped shipping casks bears a hexagon with the "*man*" (10,000) character, which has been the logo for the Takanashi family since 1820.[190]

_Su-ya_ (Vinegar Shops)

Three distinct kanban forms were traditionally used for shops that sold vinegar, or *su*: a simple silhouette of a vinegar jar; a yôki kanban featuring this shape, embellished with the hiragana character "su" (cat. 35); and a wordplay kanban featuring a missed archery target, discussed above (page 62).[191] Like the container for shôyu, the vinegar jar was not very glamorous, but it was innately functional and recognizable as a shop sign—so much so that its mere outline was a clear indicator of the shop's wares. Excellent examples of kanban of the second type are included in the PEM and Shôwa Neon Takamura Kanban Museum collections. The other two kanban styles are known through woodblock-print images from the period. One particularly interesting image from the 1690 *Jinrinkinmôzui* shows an aged shopkeeper kneeling on his tatami mat floor in a room opening directly onto the street. A large jar of rice vinegar rests at his side. Stains from past usage encircle the rim and cascade down the sides. A young customer holds out a small jar to be filled with vinegar. In the upper right-hand corner of the print is a silhouetted yôki kanban (fig. 54). Although there is no text on the kanban itself, a glyph provided by the artist reads, "Su-ya." The accompanying explanatory text reads:

> The vinegar of Waizumi is well known. In one book, it says that even the Buddhist

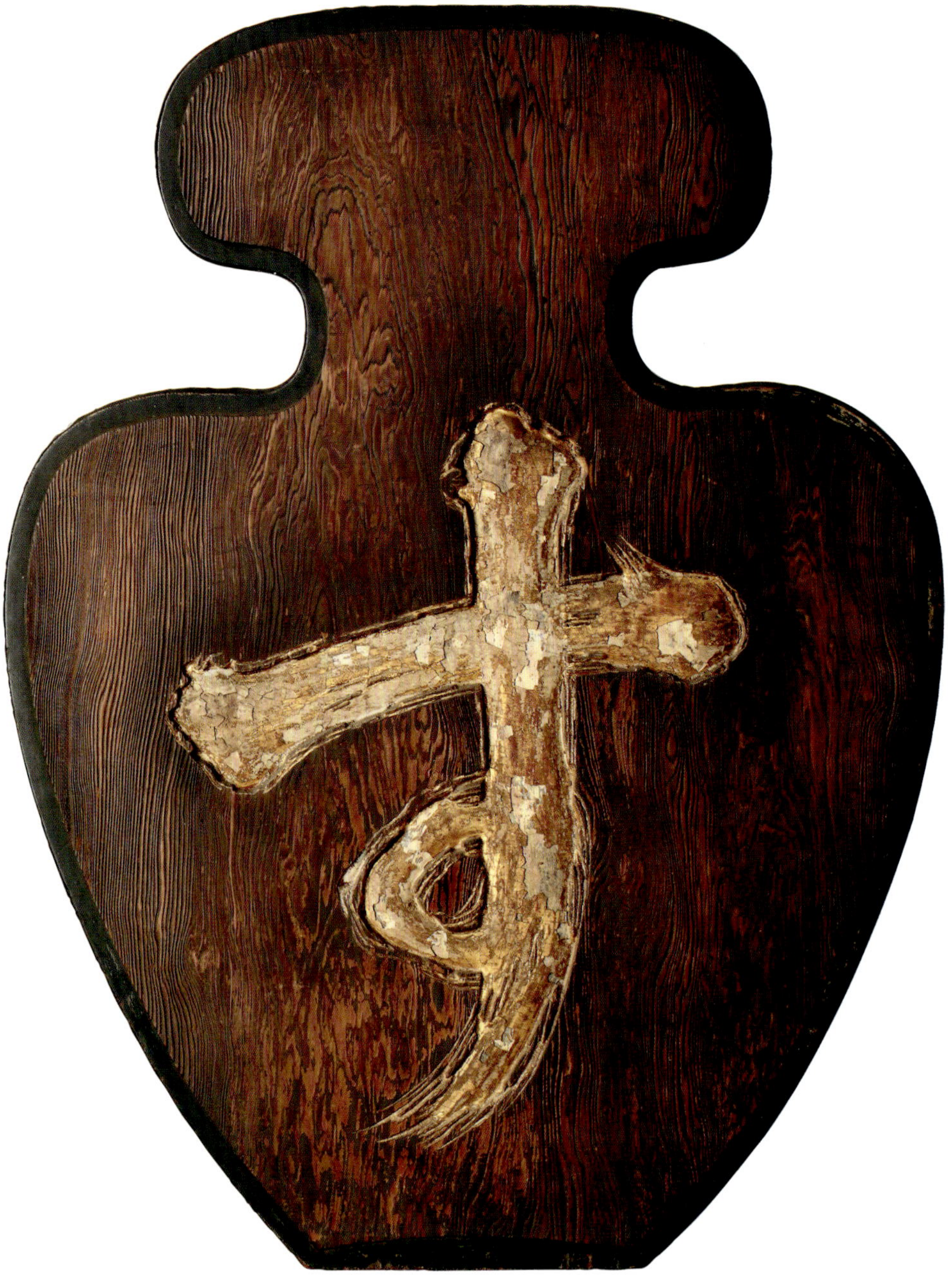

35

Yôki kanban for vinegar shop

Nineteenth century

Wood, pigment

38 × 28 in. (96 × 71 cm)

Shôwa Neon Takamura Kanban Museum

A yôki kanban for a su-ya (vinegar shop) reveals a shape not unlike those used for soy sauce shops. To help differentiate between the two, a bold hiragana character reading "*su*" commands the face of this Edo-period example. The contoured edges of the vessel are nicely rounded, giving it an almost three-dimensional, mokei-kanban feel. The incised character is painted gold, creating a bold and readily visible graphic. Measuring 38 by 28 inches (96 by 71 cm), the kanban is also quite impressive in size.

FIG. 54 Woodblock print of a su-ya (vinegar shop). Reproduced from *Jinrinkinmôzui* (1690), 143.

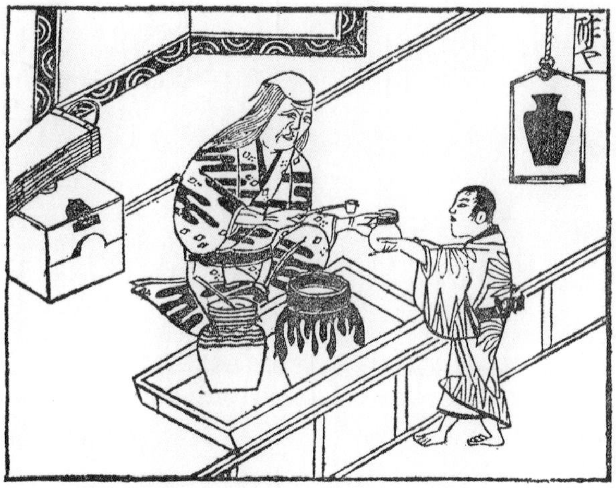

> saints like vinegar. Also in Taoist scripture it says: "Open your eyes by drinking vinegar." Lao-tzu asks for vinegar by pointing west. Shaka and the Buddha also liked vinegar very much. Therefore they called themselves "Su-sui" [Vinegar Suckers]. We call a vinegar pot that has pictures of Lao-tze, Shaka, and Buddha "San-sui" [Three Suckers] or "Su-sui."[192]

Although rice-based vinegar (*komezu*) in Japan has long been used as a preserving agent and has been an important ingredient in many sushi dishes since the Edo period, vinegar was also traditionally viewed as a healthful energy drink—truly an elixir of the gods, from the above quotation. The Waizumi-ya was a famous su-ya at the base of the Nihonbashi Bridge, conveniently situated next to the thriving fish and produce markets that dominated this end of Nihonbashi. Mentioned in 1690, the Waizumi-ya was depicted in the 1805 *Kidai shôran* as well, indicative of the great longevity of some of these shops and their products.

Consumer Goods: Kanban and Daily Necessities

Yao-ya (Greengrocers)

In the *Kidai shôran,* Nihonbashi is busy from one end to the other, with buyers and sellers and pedestrians, porters, mendicant monks, dogs, horses, oxen, and movement of all kinds, but the section nearest the Nihonbashi Bridge is by far the most active. In fact, it is downright chaotic, with shoppers and vendors literally choking the main and side streets. This is where the highest concentration of food stalls, called *yao-ya* (greengrocers),[193] and, of course, the celebrated Uo'ichiba fish market were located. This locus of activity reflects the truism that the busiest shops are the ones that cater to the everyday needs of the populace. And while kabuki actors may have touted the latest patterns offered at Echigoya, or a spectacular, eye-arresting tate kanban might have marked the entrance to a medicine shop, those vendors who sold daily consumables—the vendors of fresh and dried fish, the mushroom sellers, the wheat purveyors, the daikon radish dealers—were always going to be the busiest. Many of these vendors operated simple stalls that were set up and broken down each busy day. But other shops were essentially permanent, and in this short section of the *Kidai shôran* are the shops of Man-ya and Kanô-ya, yao-ya providing food staples of various kinds (fig. 55).

Although one now thinks of rice as a staple of the Japanese, for portions of the Edo period, government edicts limited what commoners could consume. Rice grown in villages was largely reserved for tax payments, not for consumption. *Soba* (buckwheat noodles) or *udon* (wheat noodles) were also controlled. The brewing of sake was likewise proscribed for commoners. These rules were frequently ignored, or at least not enforced uniformly or with strict severity. The general diet centered on fish (when it could be afforded), tofu, *mugi* (wheat), *kibi* (millet), *hie* (Deccan grass), and *daikon* (giant white radish).[194] Overall improvements in agricultural productivity toward the end of the Edo period also ensured a secure supply of *mizuna* (mustard greens), burdock, taro, sweet potato, eggplant, and corn. This was in addition to such fruits as plums, apricots, peaches, Japanese pears, persimmons, loquats, and figs[195]—all of which would have been available through various yao-ya (fig. 56).

Daikon was in many ways the Japanese equivalent of the Irish potato. Grown in many regions, it sustained the vast majority of the populace. Its highest concentration of cultivation was in the Kantô plain around Edo, and this city, with its 1 million inhabitants, was important as both an outlet for sales and a source of fertilizer, both animal and human, for the crop. Woodblock prints and paintings show the human waste collectors who would walk the streets, pay for this precious commodity, and then cart it out into the area's fields to enrich the soil.[196] As the plant was sensitive to soil conditions and easily modified, regional daikon varieties abounded and even increased during the Edo period. A survey of agricultural products conducted by the botanist Niwa Shohaku (1691–1756) from 1735 to 1738 revealed 164 names for daikon in 34 growing regions.[197] Daikon is written using the characters *dai* (long) and *kon* (root). The *moriguchizuke* daikon lived up to its etymology; it was famous for its extreme length (up to 6 feet, or 2 meters) and was historically favored in Kyoto tea circles. It was considered an auspicious gift among the nobility. The Shôgoin daikon, by contrast, developed as an area oddity in Owari, with a squat, rounded shape. The Kameido daikon was noted for its delicate size and soft white coloring. Around Edo, the most famous daikon was the Nerima daikon. Today, Nerima Daikon Brothers is the name of an über-popular anime series, but during the late Edo period, the Nerima daikon, developed in the rich loam of volcanic ash soil from Mt. Fuji, was considered the premier daikon, and it was even accepted as tax payment to the Tokugawa government. As a consequence, the daikon was the go-to symbol for many yao-ya (cats. 36, 37).

In many respects, kanban for yao-ya were not strictly necessary. The display of assorted consumables street-side made a shop's focus evident. But at times, merchants wanted to advertise specialty products or simply state the superiority of their offerings through the display of well-wrought kanban.

FIG. 55 Detail: Yao-ya (greengrocers) located near the foot of the Nihonbashi Bridge, as depicted in the *Kidai shôran*. Museum of Asian Art, Berlin.

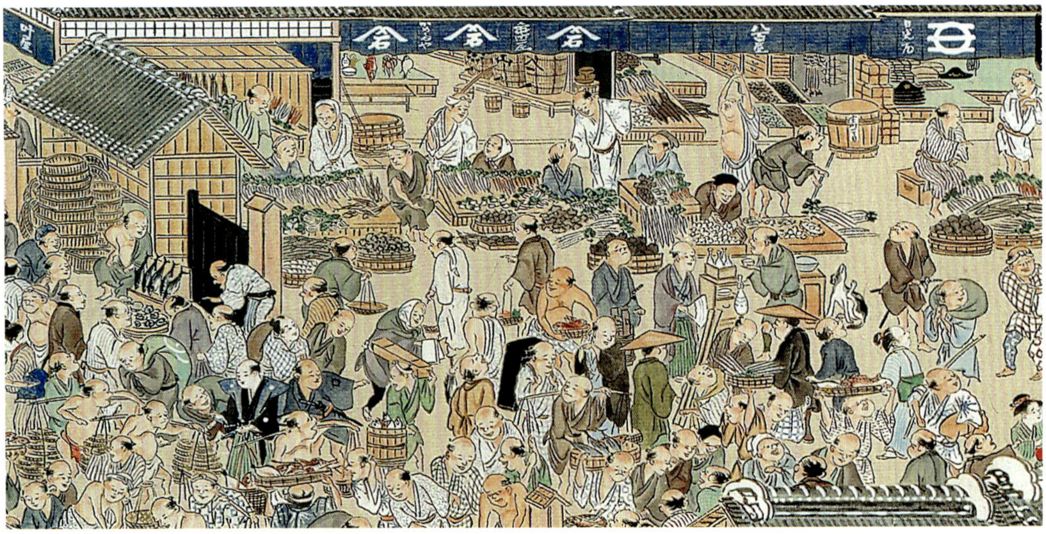

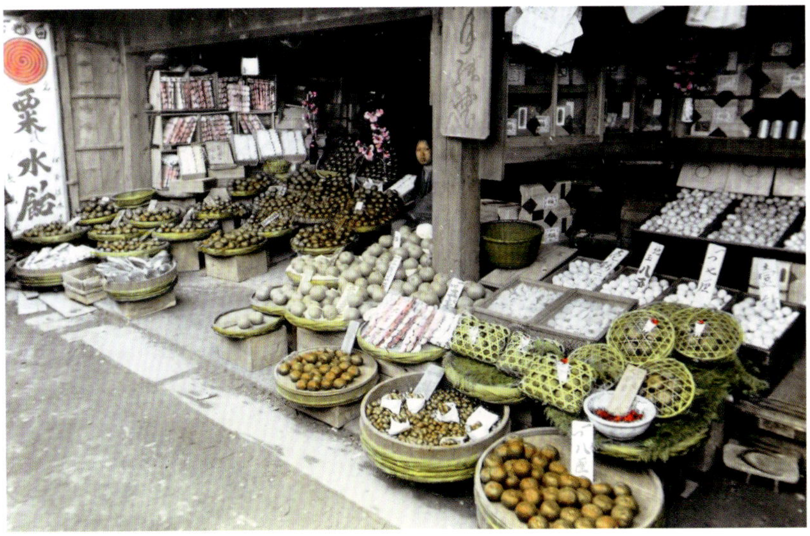

FIG. 56 Fruit store. Archival photograph. Peabody Essex Museum.

Nori Tsukudani Shops (Preserved Seaweed Paste Shops)

Absolutely anything can seem fascinating when looked at closely enough and from the right angle. This includes preserved seaweed paste, or *nori tsukudani*.[198]

The present city of Tokyo originated as a provincial fishing village near the confluence of the Sumida River and Edo Bay. Although he was originally from Aichi Prefecture far to the southwest, the military overlord Tokugawa Ieyasu chose the sleepy hamlet of Edo as his seat of power in 1590. Once Ieyasu assumed the mantle of Sei-i Taishôgun in 1603, effectively becoming ruler of the country, Edo suddenly became the epicenter of the Japanese world. In planning his castle at Edo, and in anticipation of its role to come, Ieyasu expended much time, thought, and capital in developing Edo's infrastructure of roadways, canals, and bridges. He drained swamps and filled in land. Ieyasu also thought ahead to provisioning his new capital. Edo Bay was rich in fisheries, and Ieyasu granted a noted fisherman from the village of Tsukuda in the Osaka area, Mori Magoemon, an allotment of land in the Nihonbashi area, as well as exclusive rights to use a broad sandbar in the Sumida River delta as a base for his operation, provided that he supplied the castle and Tokugawa family with fish and other seafood. This sandbar or small island became the base of operations for Mori and thirty-two fishermen from Tsukuda. The island in the river was ultimately named Tsukuda-jima.

Tsukuda-jima became the center of operations supplying fresh fish and seafood not only to the Tokugawa government but also to the bourgeoning metropolis of Edo. Mori's son took advantage of the land allotment at the base of the Nihonbashi Bridge to establish a fish market, which evolved into the famous Nihonbashi Uo'ichiba depicted in the *Kidai shôran* and described earlier. Over the years, Tsukuda-jima itself expanded, with the government granting license to fill in adjacent areas, ultimately creating a multiple-island community centered on the fishing industry but also including residential areas for both samurai and townspeople. The wives of the Tsukuda-jima fishermen, as a way to augment their diet and provide a durable food for the days their husbands spent at sea, developed a method of simmering down (*nikiru*) bits of seafood mixed with salt, shôyu, and *mirin* (sake) until all the moisture was extricated, leaving a relatively nonperishable paste. Rich in nutrition and easy to carry, this long-lasting *tsukudani*, as it was termed, became popular among not only the fishermen but also the townsmen and daimyô living in Edo as part of their mandatory service to the Tokugawa. The popularity of tsukudani spread throughout the country, and it ultimately became a recognized specialty product (*meibutsu*) of Edo.

The popularity of Edo-made tsukudani increased during the Meiji era. The government saw the benefits of this nonperishable food, and it supplied its armies with tsukudani, first during the Satsuma Rebellion of 1877 and then during both the Sino-Japanese War and the Russo-Japanese War. Its popularity and use as a side dish expanded as soldiers returned to their home regions.

Tourists visiting Tokyo today can go to the Tsukuda-jima area where three Edo-period

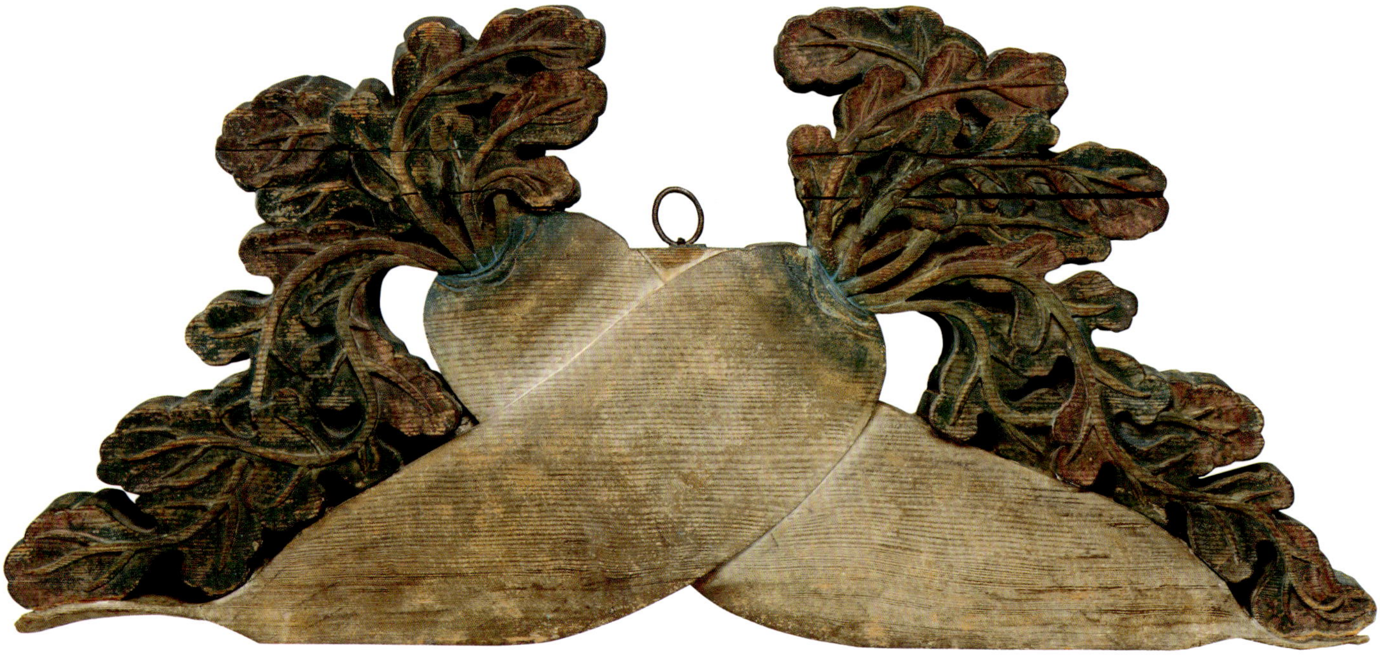

36

Mokei kanban for greengrocer

Nineteenth century

Wood, pigment, metal fitting

$16\frac{9}{16} \times 35\frac{13}{16}$ in. (42.1 × 91 cm)

Peabody Essex Museum, Gift of Dr. Charles Goddard Weld, 1909, E12465

A significant mokei kanban for a yao-ya (greengrocer) in the PEM collection features this bold carving of two crossed daikon, their green tops cascading down the sides and the whole forming a graceful pyramidal shape. The sign, measuring an impressive 36 by 16½ inches (91 by 42 cm), was a gift of Dr. Charles Goddard Weld in April 1909, making it one of the earlier kanban acquisitions for the Peabody Essex Museum. There is no inscription on the sign providing details of its original location or shop name; it would have been at home in any number of yao-ya in the Edo period, no matter whether daikon was an exclusive specialty.

37

Shitta kanban for greengrocer, front and back views

Late nineteenth century

Wood, pigment, lacquer, metal fittings

$41\frac{1}{4} \times 14\frac{1}{4} \times 1\frac{1}{4}$ in. (104.8 × 36.2 × 3.2 cm)

Mingei International Museum Purchase, 2012-24-001

In modern-day advertising parlance, a shitta kanban is known as a "blade sign" and is trumpeted as an effective way to attract pedestrian customers. This concept was nothing new to the shopkeepers and kanban makers of Edo and Meiji Japan. A surprisingly elegant shitta kanban for the Uzen Yachi Tamiya Shôten in Yamagata Prefecture, dating from the Meiji era, features a large daikon as its primary advertising image. One side pictures a large daikon paired with a carrot, suggesting that a variety of produce was offered, while the other side features a large daikon paired with a squat Owari Shôgoin daikon. The Tamiya Shôten also used the kanban to indicate that they specifically offered Nerima daikon and Nerima carrots (another Nerima-area specialty) from the Tokyo area as well as *miyashige* daikon from Owari. Interestingly, the sign bears none of the mandatory verbiage listing trademark registration, indicating a decidedly local outlook for the Tamiya Shôten, appealing to customers in the neighborhood. The yago for the shop is a corner frame with three dots. The seal reads "Daihanbai jyûsho," which likely represents the shop owner's seal, but could conceivably be that of the kanban-shi.

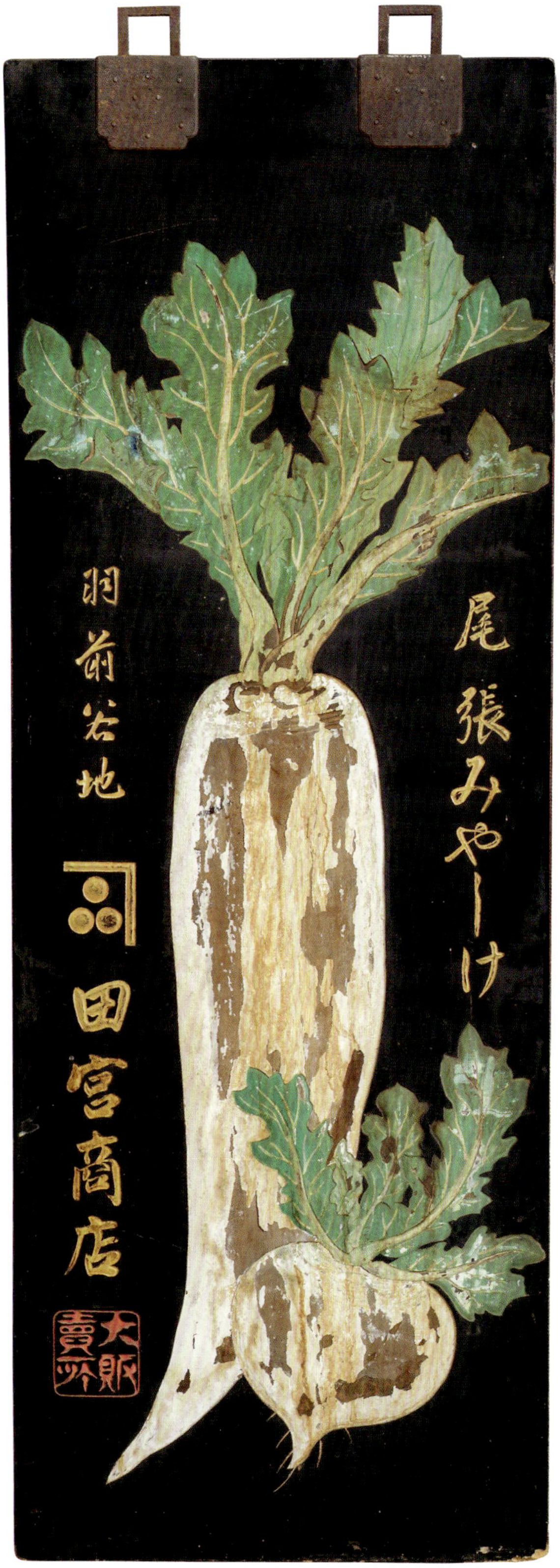
尾張みやーけ
羽前谷地
田宮商店

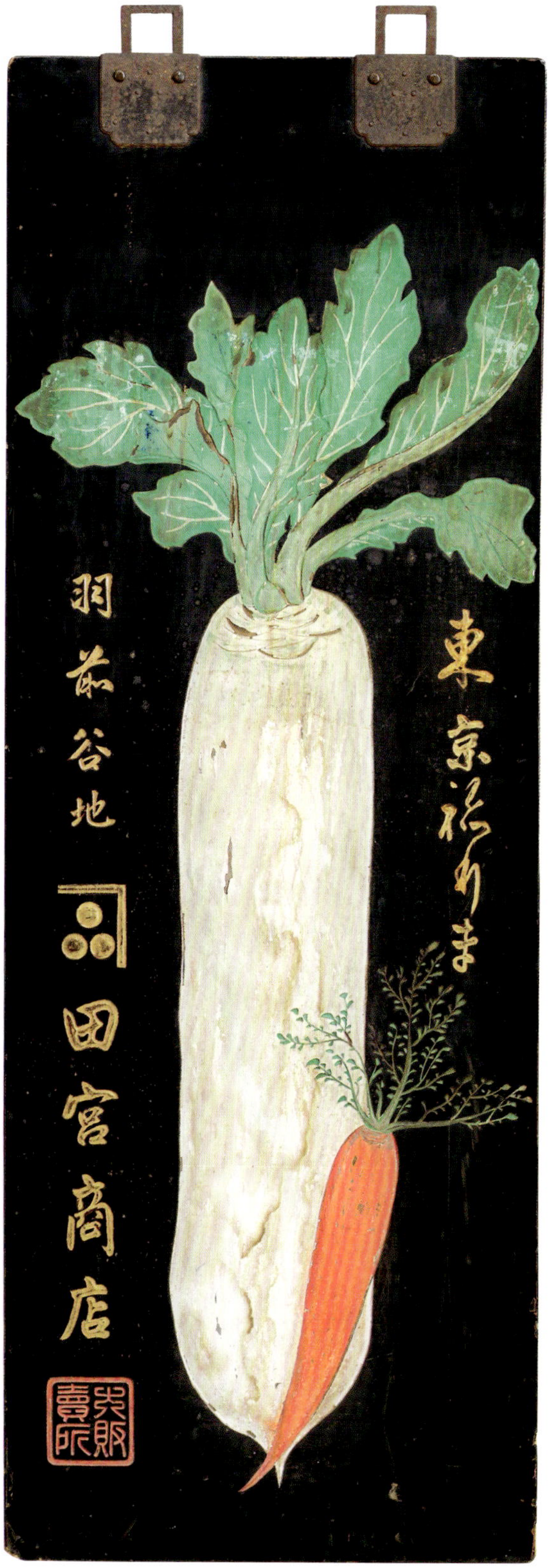
東京ねりま
羽前谷地
田宮商店

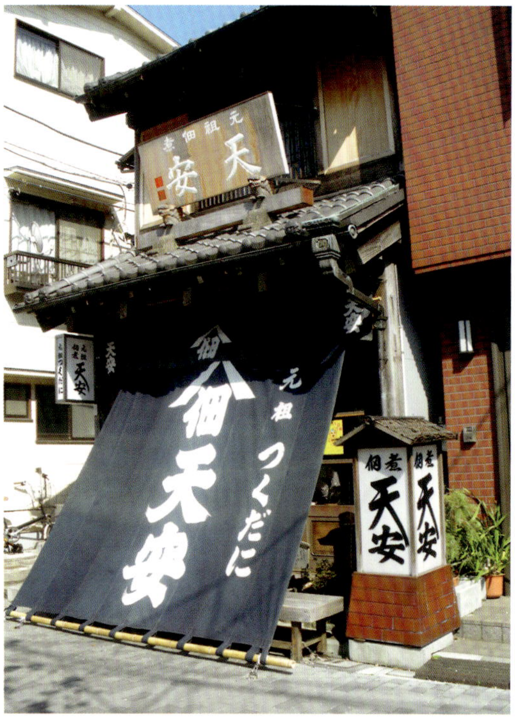

FIG. 57 The Tenyasu tsukudani shop in Tsukuda-jima, Tokyo, as it appears today. Kamemaru2000.

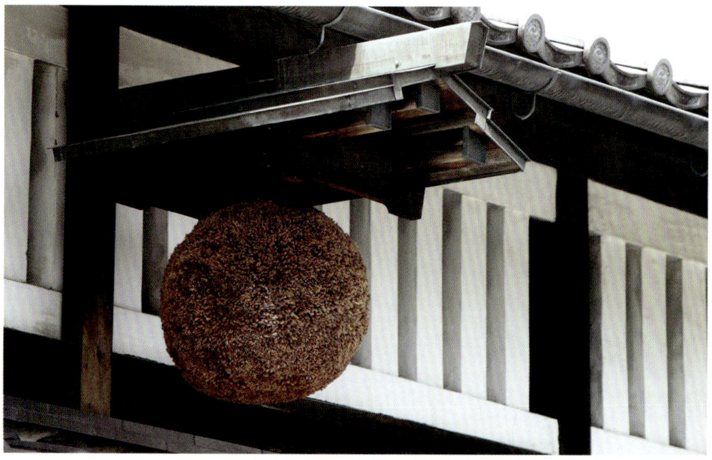

FIG. 58 A sakabayashi cedar ball hanging in front of a sake shop in Hagi. Stock Photo: 205700335. Copyright KPG_Payless.

tsukudani shops still operate, including Tenyasu, the first commercial shop specializing in tsukudani, founded in 1837; Tanakaya, founded in 1843; and Marukyu, established in 1859. The kanban for Tenyasu is a large wooden gaku moji kanban with the name inscribed in bold characters, in addition to a noren emblazoned with the shop's yago (fig. 57). On particularly sunny days, the shop extends a large hioke awning that angles down to the street and is weighted down by a stout bamboo pole.[199] This Edo-period building, with its dark-blue noren and street-fronting sliding doors, tiled roof, and large wooden kanban, is frequently photographed, and it perfectly captures the essence of the small-scale businesses and craftsmen that were the hallmark of Edo commercial culture.

Edo-period kanban for *nori* (seaweed) were disks mimicking the shape of the hiragana character *no,* with a diminutive *ri* within the circle. Examples of kanban of this type are found in the PEM, the Shôwa Neon Takamura Kanban Museum (cat. 38), as well as the Edo-Tokyo Museum collection.[200] There are apparently few extant kanban for shops specifically selling tsukudani. The famous shops of Tsukuda-jima focused on their noren and shop names, relying on cachet to announce their product. However, beginning in the Meiji era, as mass production was brought to bear on this traditional food supplement, moji kanban began to dominate the sector (cat. 39).

Saka-ya (Sake Shops)

One of the more intriguing kanban forms ever devised is the *sakabayashi* ball of sugi (cedar) twigs used by brewers of sake (rice wine). More than just a sign, the ball is a timepiece and fermentation barometer of sorts (fig. 58). Since the mid-seventeenth century, sake brewing has historically been a winter activity, begun soon after the fall rice harvest and known as *kanzukuri*.[201] When a new batch of sake has been started, a ball is fashioned out of fresh cedar boughs and hung under the eaves at the entrance to the building. The floating green sakabayashi ball can seem almost jewel-like—hence its alternate name, *sugitama* (cedar jewel). As the sakabayashi ages, the leaves turn from lustrous green to brown and then to dark brown, ultimately dropping off and leaving only the twigs. When the ball is at its darkest brown, usually by March, the sake is said to be ready. Soon, only the hoop from inside the sakabayashi remains. This empty ring from the sakabayashi in many ways parallels the empty ring used by vinegar shops as a

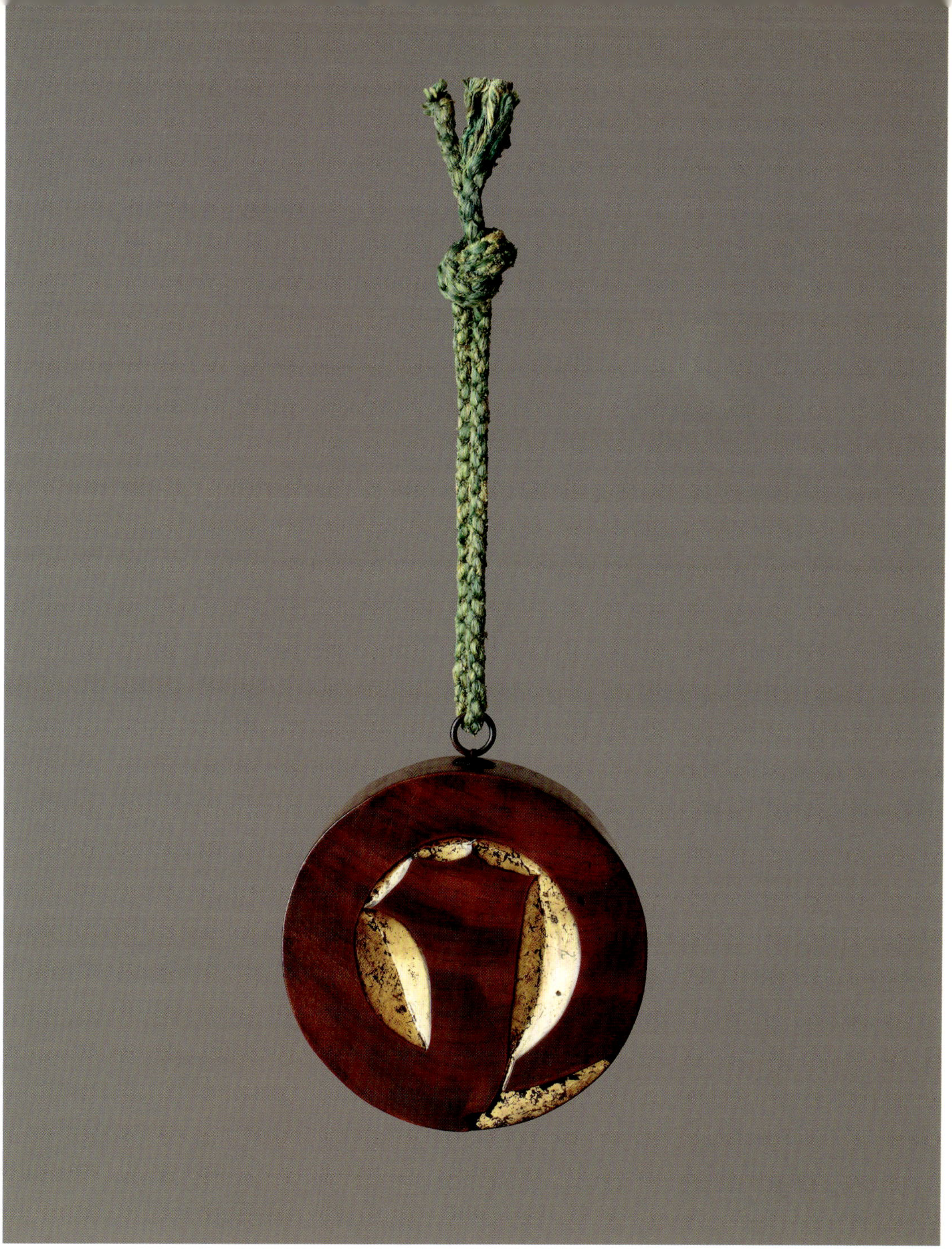

38

Shitta kanban for seaweed shop

Nineteenth century
Wood, pigment, metal fitting, cotton cord
8 × 8 in. (21 × 21 cm)
Shôwa Neon Takamura Kanban Museum

Hanji mono or wordplay kanban were a specialty of the Edo period. These signs mixed wit with insider knowledge and deft creativity to form effective and memorable advertising for a variety of shops, products, and services. At times, however, a word itself was brought to bear as both sign and symbol. We have seen how the character *"su"* for vinegar was frequently emblazoned on yôki kanban to help identify the product available within. Kanban for nori-ya (dried seaweed shops) were often carved with the hiragana character *"no,"* announcing the presence of a nori-ya. At times, an additional hiragana glyph for *"ri"* was written in sumi ink within the broad down stroke of the character *"no."* But, generally, the pleasingly round shape of the character *"no"* was all that was required. Here, a thickly carved wood roundel is fashioned into a calligraphic *"no,"* with its deeply incised contours highlighted in gold. Double-sided in its execution, this simply elegant and effective sign is reminiscent of the *dai-sho* kanban used by moneylenders for indicating the long and short months, discussed below (page 146).

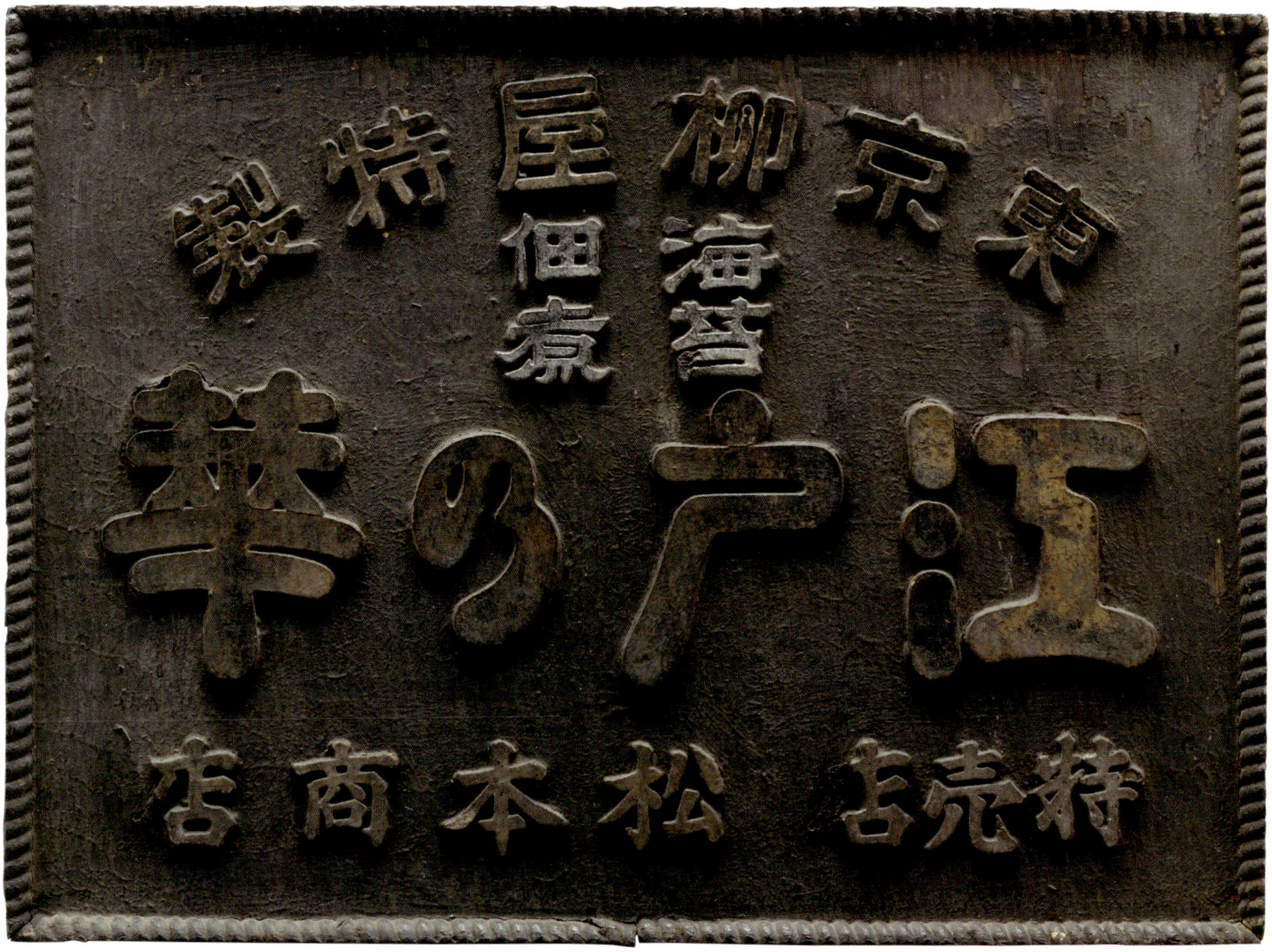

39

Moji kanban for preserved seaweed paste shop

Early twentieth century

Wood, pigment, lacquer

17¾ × 23¾ × 1½ in. (45.1 × 60.3 × 3.8 cm)

Mingei International Museum Purchase, 2014-05-001

This rare kanban specifically for nori tsukudani advertises the Edo no Hana (Flowers of Edo) brand, made by the Yanagiya of Tokyo. This moji kanban features individually carved characters mounted to a simple framed board. The characters, read right to left, indicate that this preserved seaweed paste was distributed exclusively through the Matsumoto Company.

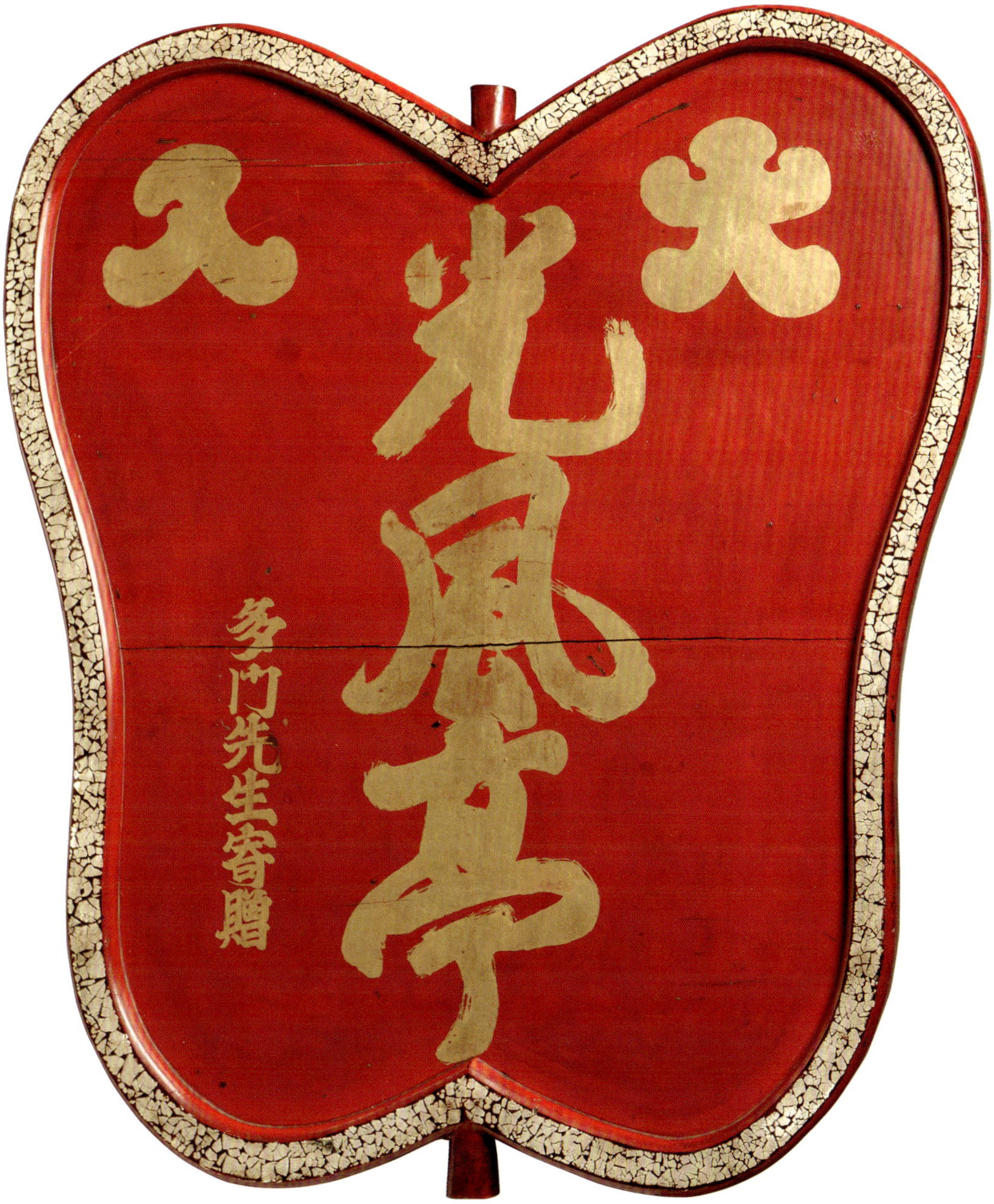

40

Mokei kanban for restaurant

Twentieth century

Wood, pigment, lacquer

41 × 37½ × 2¾ in. (104.1 × 95.3 × 7 cm)

Mingei International Museum Purchase, 2014-08-001

Symbols have a tendency to migrate. This is particularly true for positive symbolism that has found lodgment in popular culture. Here, the Kôfûtei restaurant has appropriated two symbols that are closely associated with sumo wrestling. The first is found in the overall shape of the sign, that of a *gunbai* fan. First employed by the military as a signaling device, the gunbai was later adopted by sumo referees (*gyôji*), with the gunbai itself becoming a symbol for sumo tournaments. The second aspect of this sign that was employed by sumo tournaments as well as theaters is the expression "*ôiri,*" meaning essentially "great crowd" or "full house." Though literally referring to the lack of availability of seats within a stadium or theater, the term also came to symbolize the success of almost any type of commercial endeavor. Kanban bearing the ôiri character set were often given as gifts to new enterprises as wishes for success and good fortune. Here, the large, red-lacquered gunbai fan bears the name of the restaurant in gold lettering vertically in the center; the ôiri characters flank the spine of the central handle. In smaller characters is the name of the shop's proprietor: "Tanmon sensei kizô."

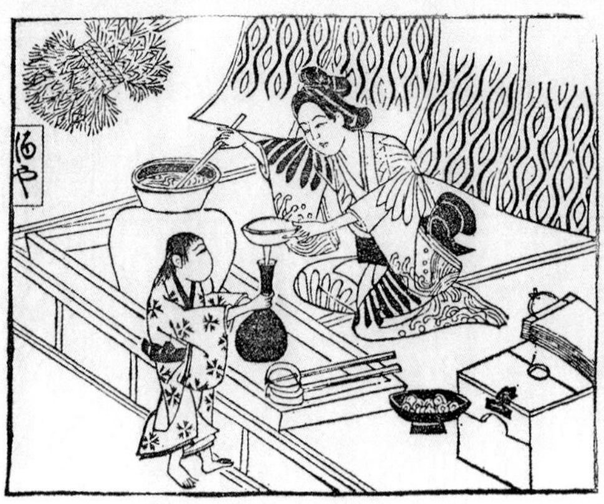

FIG. 59 Woodblock print of a saka-ya using a sakabayashi cedar ball as a kanban. Reproduced from *Jinrinkinmôzui* (1690), 142.

wordplay kanban, discussed earlier. Though not actually intended as a kanban per se, sakabayashi came to symbolize sake brewers and effectively doubled as kanban. In the *Jinrinkinmôzui*'s depiction of a saka-ya, a merchant dispenses sake from a large jar, passing the liquid through a bowl-like funnel into the client's awaiting smaller jar. In the upper left corner of the image, a sakabayashi strapped to a pole serves as the shop's kanban (fig. 59).[202] Tsuboi Shôgorô, in his 1887 *Kôshô gigei kanban kô,* illustrated and described a number of sakabayashi variations.[203] Due to their inherent fragility, sakabayashi kanban are a rarity. The PEM collection contains one sakabayashi kanban that was purchased through Yamanaka in 1916.[204]

Historically, sake has been stored and transported in cedar barrels known as *taru* or *sakadaru*. Composed of rectangular planks held together with bamboo hoops and fitted with round lids with stopper holes, taru of this type have been used for storing sake, as well as shôyu and lacquer, for centuries. Once the sake is poured into the taru and the lid opening is sealed, the whole barrel is wrapped in a straw mat called a *komo*. The komo itself is decorated with the name or symbol of the specific sake brand. Beginning in the late Meiji era, the decoration also included various stamps for awards and commendations given to the sake brewer over the years. The encased taru is then set on a woven mat base for protection, which is tightly secured with stout rope and knotted in a decorative fashion on the top. It has been estimated that during the Edo period there were over five hundred *sakadaru-shi* (makers of taru for sake). Smaller sake barrels for domestic use, called *tsunodaru* (horned barrels), are tapered in shape and feature two vertical gripping handles that give the form its name. The PEM collection contains a jitsubutsu kanban for a *tsunodaru-shi* inscribed with the shop name "Ichi Tani."[205]

The original word for sake in Japanese is *miki*, meaning "wine for the gods," indicating how important sake has been as a part of Shinto rituals. Historically, local and national sake brewers have generally provided the *o-miki* required for numerous Shinto ceremonies. Empty, decorative sakadaru, known as *kazaridaru,* are common offerings to shrines, and it is not unusual on festival days to find hundreds of kazaridaru carefully arranged in stacked rows, all donated by sake brewers who have provided o-miki as an offering to help ensure their prosperity in the coming year (figs. 60, 61). A far more secular tradition, one popular on YouTube videos, is the *kagami-biraki,* or the ceremonial breaking open of a sake cask using a wooden mallet.

The sakadaru has long been emblematic of the sake industry as a whole. In illustration we can look to a series of woodblock prints from around 1794 entitled *Natori zake rokkasen* (The Peers of Sake Likened to Denizens of Six Houses) by Kitagawa Utamaro (1753?–1806), comparing courtesans with famous sake brands. Utamaro uses floating images of sakadaru emblazoned with the trademarks of highly respected sake brands and pairs these with specific, coveted courtesans from Edo's Yoshiwara pleasure district (fig. 62).[206] Nanatsu-ume sake, signified by its bold, seven-dot plum design, for example, is paired with the celebrated courtesan Asaiju of the Daimonjiya. Sakagami's Kenbishi sake, originating in 1505 and marked by an abstract diamond pattern, is paired with Hanazuma of the Hyôgoya. The courtesan Shiratsuyu of the Wakanaya brothel is paired with Otokoyama sake. Marked by name in kanji, and founded in the Kanbun era (1661–73), it enjoyed a high reputation among the samurai elite. It is worth noting that all

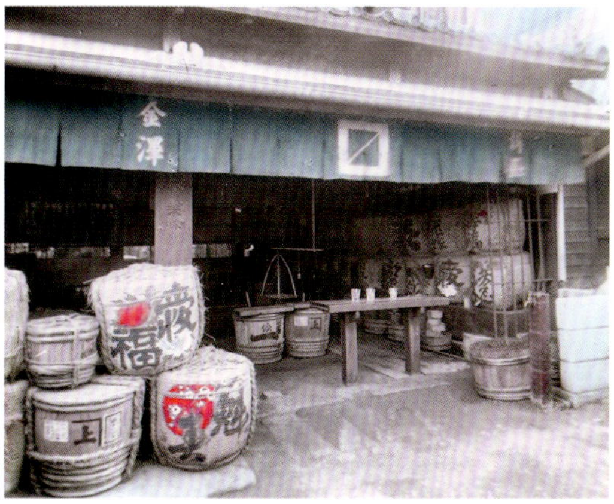

FIG. 60 Sake store. Archival photograph. Peabody Essex Museum.

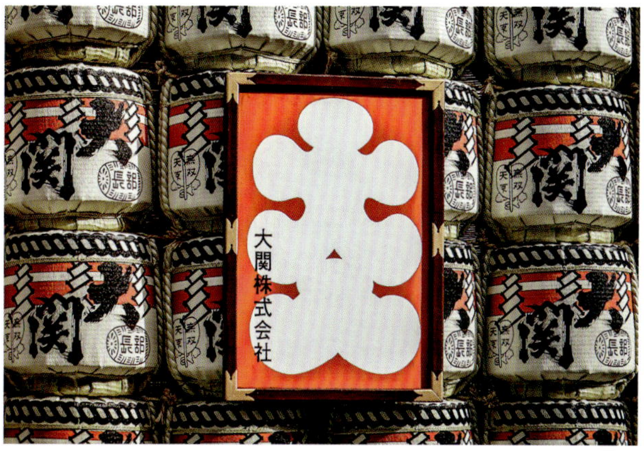

FIG. 61 A large stack of dedicatory *sakadaru* (*sake* casks) and a felicitation sign bearing the characters "*ôiri*" outside of the Kabuki-za in the Ginza section of Tokyo. Photo by Starcevic.

six of the brands illustrated by Utamaro are still popular today.

The bold graphics for these noted sake brands, whether symbol- or character-based in design, would have been immediately recognizable to Edo consumers and are a clear indication of what would today be termed "brand awareness." Utamaro and other artists included sakadaru and their familiar labels in a number of woodblock-print series. This practice can be seen as the sake corollary to the flaunting of baiyaku patent medicine kanban in the kabuki setting, and perfectly illustrates how the popular medium of the woodblock print was in many ways an open avenue of commercial advertising exploited by important sake brewers during the Edo period.

It is unclear when kanban depicting sakadaru became standard for sake retailers and brewers alike. No Edo examples seem to exist. For example, the Shôwa Neon Takamura Kanban Museum collection has four wonderful sakadaru kanban, but all are Meiji in date.[207] The PEM collection contains only three kanban for saka-ya, none of which are in the sakadaru style. One is a straightforward yôki kanban in the shape of a ceramic sake jar, which is almost indistinguishable from a vinegar jar. It bears an incised design of a sake cup on one side with the phrase "*gokinjô*" (superior quality), and a design of *sasa* bamboo leaves on the other with "*ari*" (we have) just below, written in hiragana. Inscribed on the neck is the phrase "*dai gokinjô*" (best quality). Sasa or bamboo leaf is an Edo-period term for sake, so "Sasa ari" simply means that the store carries sake.[208] A second kanban is a finely painted shôkei display kanban for interior use depicting a scene of travelers on the slopes of Mt. Fuji, advertising the Shiraito brand of sake.[209] And a third is a moji kanban for a sake distributor bearing raised characters over a carved peony.[210] Edo-period woodblock prints of sake brewers or saka-ya almost invariably depict the sakabayashi cedar bough as the indicative kanban. Thus, it was likely only during the rapid growth and commercialization of the sake industry during the opening decades of the Meiji period, when government taxation policies forced breweries into increasingly large-scale production and distribution, that sakadaru kanban came into vogue.[211]

Sakadaru kanban are essentially yôki kanban, depicting the signature container, rather than the product—similar to yôki kanban used for tea, vinegar, and shôyu. Sakadaru kanban are carved of wood in deep relief and very closely mimic the actual cask, replete with securing rope tied at the top and a protective mat at the bottom, though not fully three-dimensional (cat. 41). Most are lacquered over, frequently in gold with a black lacquer undercoat. At times, actual cordage is adhered to the wood carving, adding greatly to its verisimilitude. Much detail is accorded the various awards that have been received by a

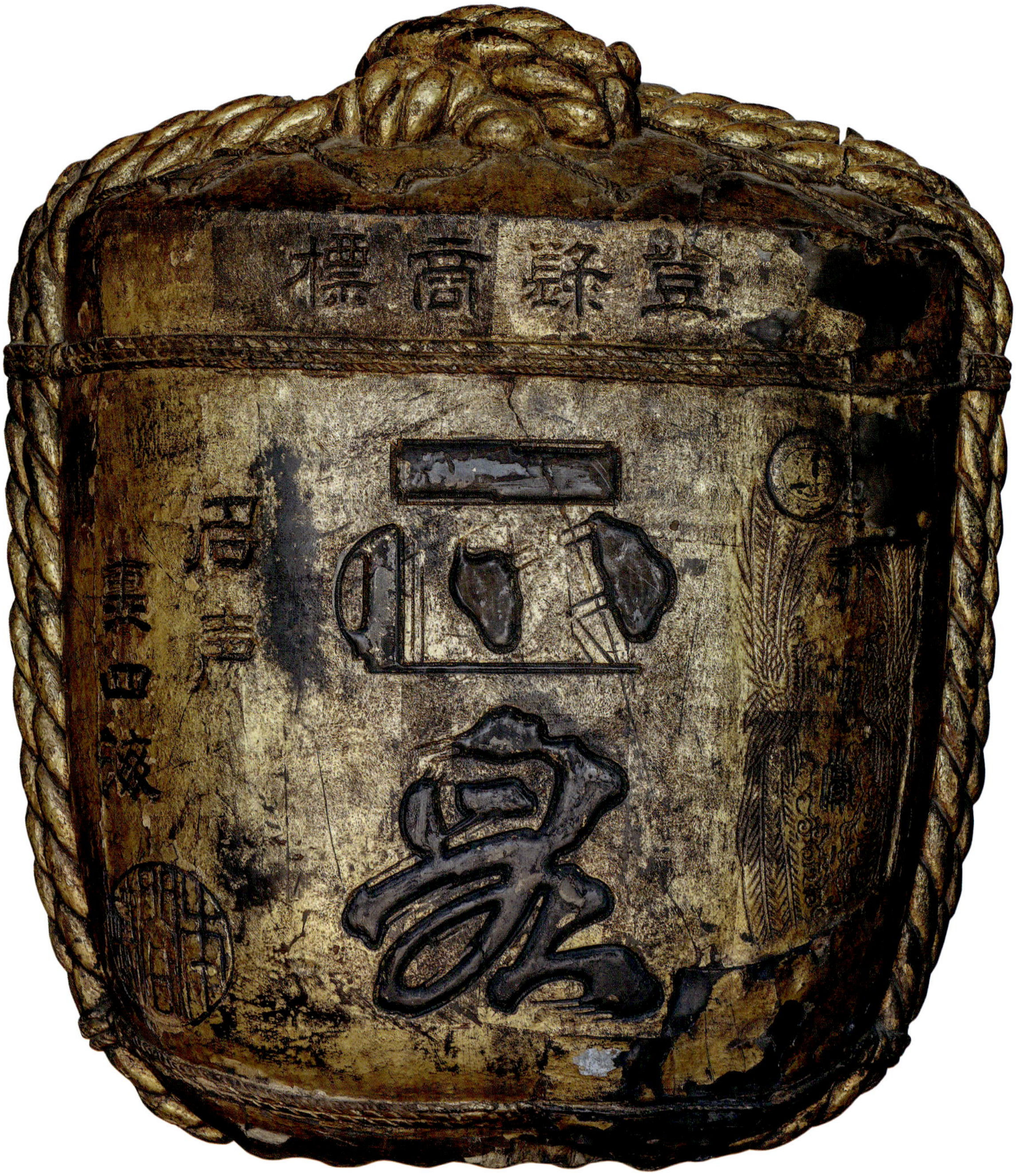

41

Yôki kanban for sake shop

Early twentieth century

Wood, pigment

33 × 29 in. (84 × 73.7 cm)

Private Collection

This classic late Meiji-era kanban for a sake maker makes use of a carved rendition of the sakadaru cedar barrel used for storing and shipping sake. These kanban usually simulated the woven komo (straw mat) protective layer, emblazoned with the name of the sake brand in addition to whatever awards it might have received. Here, the Masa Izumi brand of sake is presented. The kanban-shi has included woven rope tied in a decorative knot to add to the verisimilitude of the carving. Covered overall in gold lacquer, the kanban replicates in decorative detail the particularities of a commercial sakadaru. The top bears the official "tôroku shôhyô" designation. A number of now-illegible award seals and markings appear on the right side, and the manufacturer's name is inscribed on the left as "Mesei Urashikai"; below, the brewer is listed simply as "Honma."

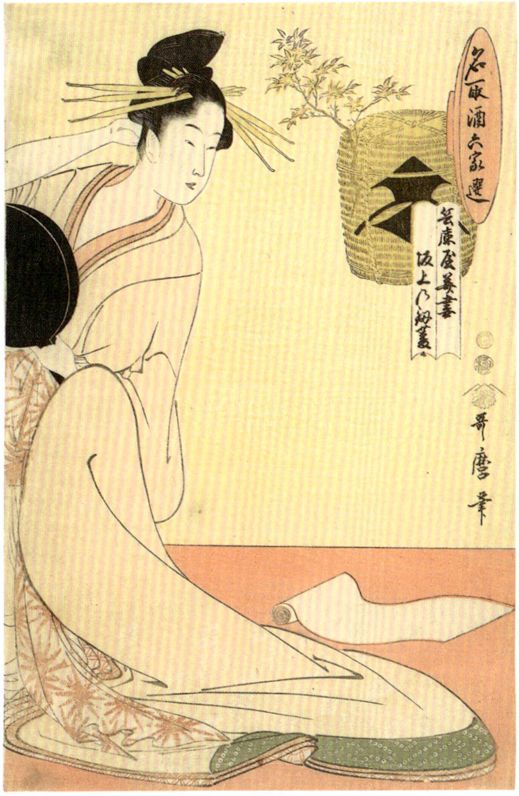

FIG. 62 *Hanazuma of Hyôgoya, Kenbishi of Sakagami (Hyôga Hanazuma, Sakagami no Kenbishi)*, from the series *Natori zake rokkasen* (The Peers of Sake Likened to Select Denizens of Six Houses) by Kitagawa Utamaro (1753?–1806), Edo period, c. 1794. Polychrome woodblock print, ink and color on paper, 14¾ × 9½ in. (37.5 × 24.1 cm). Metropolitan Museum of Art, Rogers Fund, 1925, JP1461, www.metmuseum.org.

particular sake brand, as expressed in incised depictions of medals and first-place ribbons, playing off of koma decorations found on actual sakadaru. The prestigious Zenkoku Shinshu Kanpyo-kai (National New Sake Awards) began in 1911, near the very close of the Meiji era, and are sponsored by the National Research Institute of Brewing, which itself was not founded until 1904.[212] Prior to this, the nationwide association of brewers and brewing experts had been issuing awards at sake tasting meets since the early 1890s.[213] As with many kanban from the Meiji era, following government registration policies, the top band usually included the phrase "tôroku shôhyô," "zenkei tôroku," or occasionally, "shôhyô yûken." Although this latter nomenclature dates from the Edo period, it appears to have been somewhat grandfathered into the sakadaru kanban form. A clear example of this is seen in the much-published sakadaru kanban for the sake brand Fukumusume in the Shôwa Neon Takamura Kanban Museum.[214] Though bearing the Edo "shôhyô yûken" inscription, it is festooned with twelve Meiji-era medals.

Kanban and Specialty Trades

Megane-ya (Eyeglass Shops)

Not unlike the blue eyes and yellow-rimmed glasses of Dr. T. J. Eckleburg presiding over the Valley of Ashes in F. Scott Fitzgerald's *The Great Gatsby*, the commercial thoroughfares of Edo Japan had their own version of the all-seeing eyeglass shop sign. *Megane-ya*, or eyeglass shops, were a relatively common sight in the three principal cities. Japanese glasses were generally used as a minor vision-enhancing tool for special tasks and, particularly, as reading glasses for the elderly.[215] They were not worn continually and were considered more of an accessory than a health-related item.[216] Eye medicines (*megusuri*) were also quite popular, but the kanban for these products, as discussed above, were quite different in style and focus.

Glasses were first introduced to Japan in 1551 by Jesuit missionaries, and the earliest Japanese manufacture of eyeglasses used technology acquired from the Dutch in Nagasaki. The earliest Japanese term for eyeglasses is *aitai*, a complex character combination meaning roughly, "clouds that move yet stay." Some of the earliest Japanese-made forms were devised with a handle, somewhat like opera glasses, and were called *te-megane* (hand glasses). During the Edo period, a pince-nez form was developed that perched on the bridge of the nose, freeing the hands. These were known as *tengu-megane*, referring to the long-nosed goblins (tengu) of popular lore. Distinctive to this form was a downward-extending support strut underneath the bridge between the two

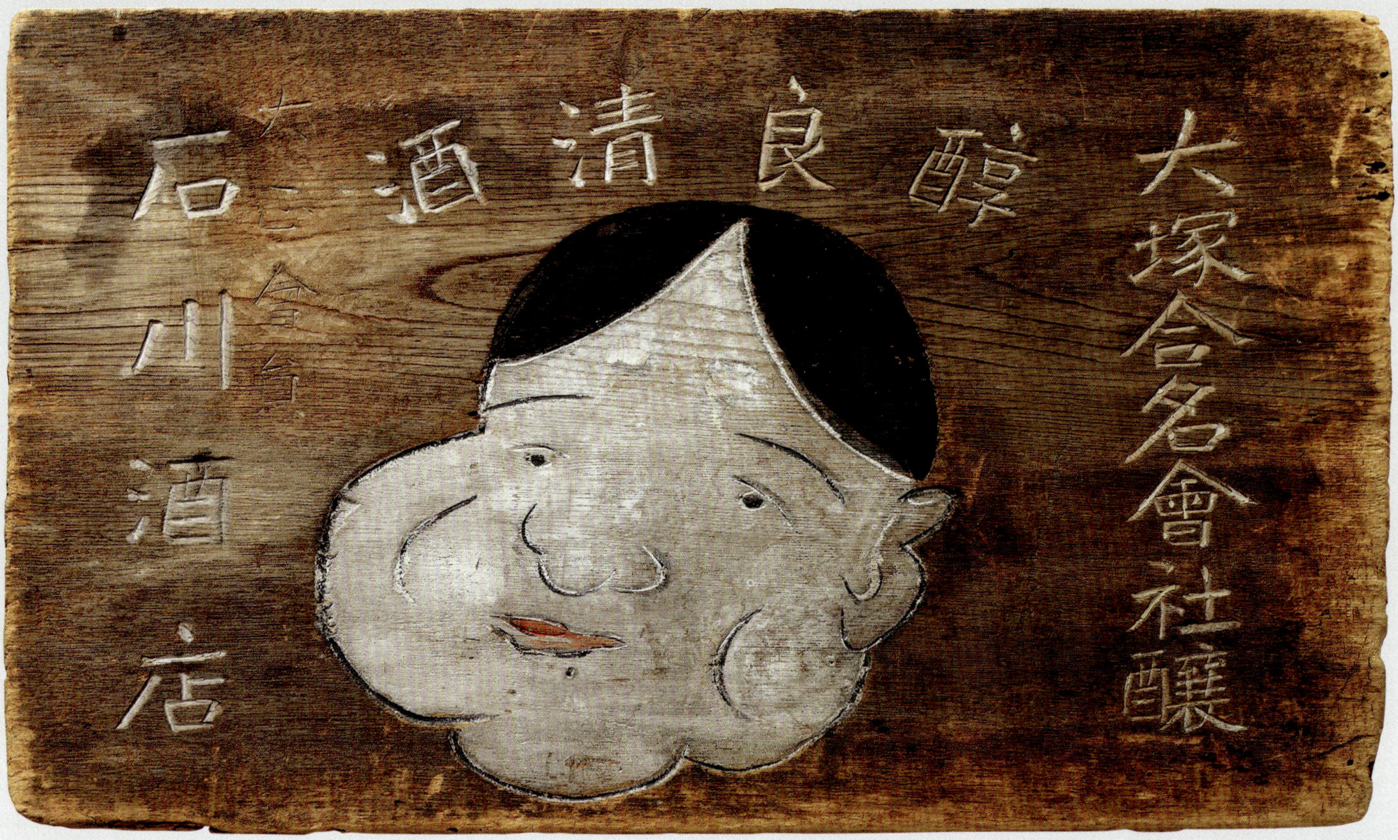

42

Kattamen kanban for sake brewer

Nineteenth century

Wood, pigment

16¼ × 23¾ × 2 in. (41.3 × 60.3 × 5.1 cm)

Mingei International Museum, Gift of Maurice M. Kawashima, 2010-06-001

Prior to the formalization of copyright and licensing, many Japanese shops, merchants, craftsmen, and artisans adopted images from legend, lore, and religious tradition to become the literal "faces" of their brands and products. Here the plump-cheeked, mirthful face of the goddess Okame serves as a logo for the Ishikawa sake brewer. The inscription above reads, "*Jôryoseishu*" (Good-quality clear brew), while the right-hand inscription lists the distributor as Otsuka Somei Kaisha Jô. This Edo-period sign, crafted before trademark registration requirements went into effect, represents a pre-modern approach to kanban and branding. Okame, or Otafuku, as she was popularly known, had an especially frisky aspect to her personality that was eminently suitable as a symbol for a sake brewer.

lens frames that aided in the correct positioning of the glasses and has been held to be a Japanese innovation. Occasionally cords were attached that wrapped around the ears to allow for longer viewing times. Frames were typically made out of *bekko* (tortoiseshell) or *tsume* (horse or buffalo hoof), with brass frames becoming more popular toward the end of the Edo period. Occasionally, ivory frames were made as well. The lenses themselves were generally made of rock crystal ground smooth, although some lenses were made from melted glass trade beads imported from Korea, called *bidoro*. Shops known as *bidoro-ya* also specialized in small-scale glass production, offering small vases, bottles, and beads.[217] Because of the skill set required in making lenses, the majority of megane-ya were also jewelry stores (*tama-ya*) that dealt in *ojime* (cord fasteners associated with netsuke and inrô) and juzu rosary beads.[218]

Woodblock prints from the Edo period featuring megane-ya often depict artisans at work polishing the crystal lenses on large whetting stones set in low tubs of water. This process was evidently quite labor-intensive and strenuous, and the craftsmen are generally depicted shirtless, intently bent over their task. These prints show that kanban for megane-ya came in all the forms we have come to expect, including hako kanban, noren, shitta kanban, and mokei kanban. The most distinctive aspect of some mokei and shitta kanban is the inclusion of actual lenses, enlarged to fit the sign itself, creating a very Eckleburg-like effect. In these instances, the glasses depicted are almost always of the tengu-megane (pince-nez) type (cat. 43). Hayashi Yoshikazu includes in his *Edo kanban zufu* three photographic illustrations of kanban from megane-ya taken from Sugiura's *Kazô kanban zufu*; one is a true mokei kanban with rock crystal lenses 6 inches (15 cm) wide. Another is a shitta kanban measuring 22 by 13 inches (55 by 34 cm) that is very similar to the example from a private collection, published here for the first time, but lacking the rock crystal lenses.[219]

Kinpaku-ya (Gold Leaf Shops)

Few cultures have prized gold leaf or used it with such dexterity as the Japanese. Generally known as *haku* or, more specifically, *kinpaku*, gold leaf has been applied with tremendous skill to myriad objects. In the religious realm, gold has been seen as symbolic of the Buddha, life-affirming, and a counter to death and impurities. As a result, gold leaf has been used with liberality in many elements of Buddhist art, including sculpture, metalwork, lacquer, ceramics, textiles, and even architecture.[220] Consider Kinkaku-ji, the Golden Pavilion, built between 1397 and 1407, with its top two stories covered in gold leaf on lacquer. In the secular realm, gold has been prized naturally enough for its allure and its ability to reflect light. In interior decoration, gold and silver leaf has helped to reflect and amplify light. It has also been put to exquisite effect on lacquerwork, painted handscrolls, folding screens, ceramics, the repair of ceramics, textiles, metalwork, and kanban. As noted above, a kanban in the PEM collection is for the shop of Hakoshô, a goldsmith who did repair work (*senshûfuku*) to the gold leaf on kanban, as well as to Buddhist home altars (*butsudan*), clearly indicating the popularity of gold leaf as applied to the surface of kanban.[221] The popularity of butsudan during the Meiji era led to a sharp increase in demand for both the production of raw gold leaf as well as its application in these home altars. As a consequence, goldsmiths and artisans working in gold (and silver) leaf have been in high demand to the present day.

Edo-period woodblock prints depicting kinpaku-ya (gold leaf shops) typically focus on two aspects of the work. One is the systematic pounding of the gold leaf into ever thinner and finer sheets (fig. 63). The second is the application of small squares of gold leaf onto paper for storage and resale. Thus, a small square of gold leaf became the de facto symbol for the haku industry as a whole, both gold and silver leaf. Kanban for kinpaku-ya tended toward the ema style: a generally rectangular form with a slightly peaked top, with two incised or raised squares highlighted in gold. Unlike ema, which had quite thin boards, kinpaku-ya kanban were generally fashioned from relatively thick slabs of wood. The face of either side featured two squares, both covered in gold leaf (cat. 44). Or, alternatively, one was covered in gold leaf, and the other in silver leaf (*ginpaku*). The background was generally black lacquer to help accentuate the gold or silver.[222]

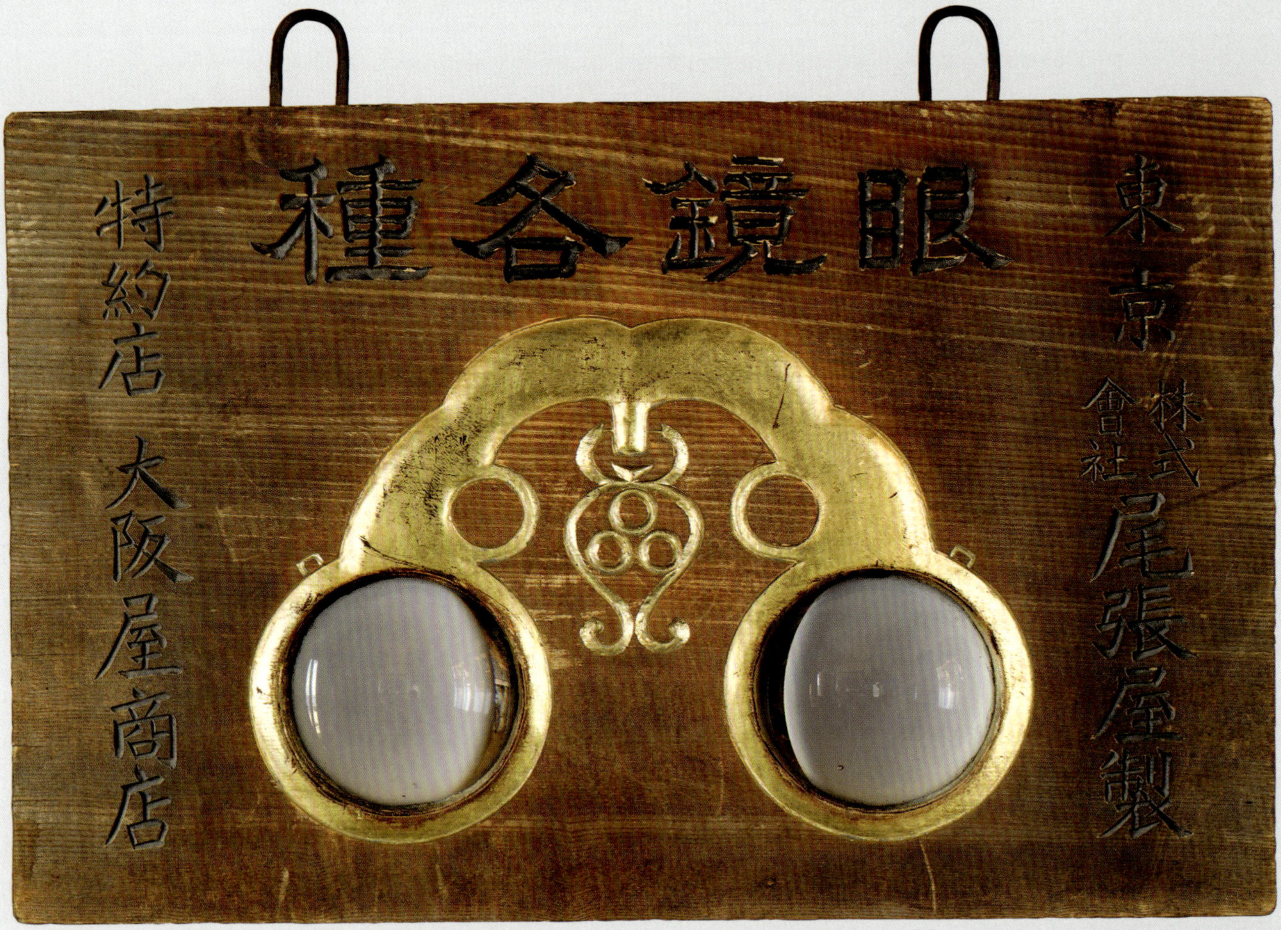

43

Shitta kanban for eyeglass shop

Early twentieth century

Wood, pigment, lacquer, metal fittings, glass

14 × 21½ in. (35.5 × 54.6 cm)

Private Collection

Although mokei kanban featuring enlarged eyeglasses, typically of the tengu type, are documented in numerous publications, the more common kanban for a megane-ya (eyeglass shop) was a shitta kanban. This was composed of a very large single slab of wood with the incised design of the frames for tengu megane (pince-nez) in the center, often highlighted with gold lacquer. The signature aspect of this type of sign was the frequent, though not universal, inclusion of actual rock crystal lenses within the board, passing through to the other side, making them visible from both directions when hung perpendicular to the street. When no actual lenses were included, the artisan typically depicted them as two large inscribed circles. Here, a shitta kanban for the Osakaya Shoten advertises that it is an authorized distributor (*tokuyakuten*) for the Owariya Shoten and that it carries a wide variety of eyeglasses (*gankyo kakushyu*), all manufactured by this Tokyo-based company. The sign sports an ornate incised carving of tengu megane highlighted in gold lacquer, with actual rock crystal lenses that are convex on both sides. Interestingly, a trade journal for 1917 lists the Owariya Shoten in the Nihonbashi area of Tokyo as being a manufacturer and exporter of "all sorts of optical goods, purses, pocket books, hand bags and hosieries." The top of the print ad shows a tengu megane–style pair of glasses.

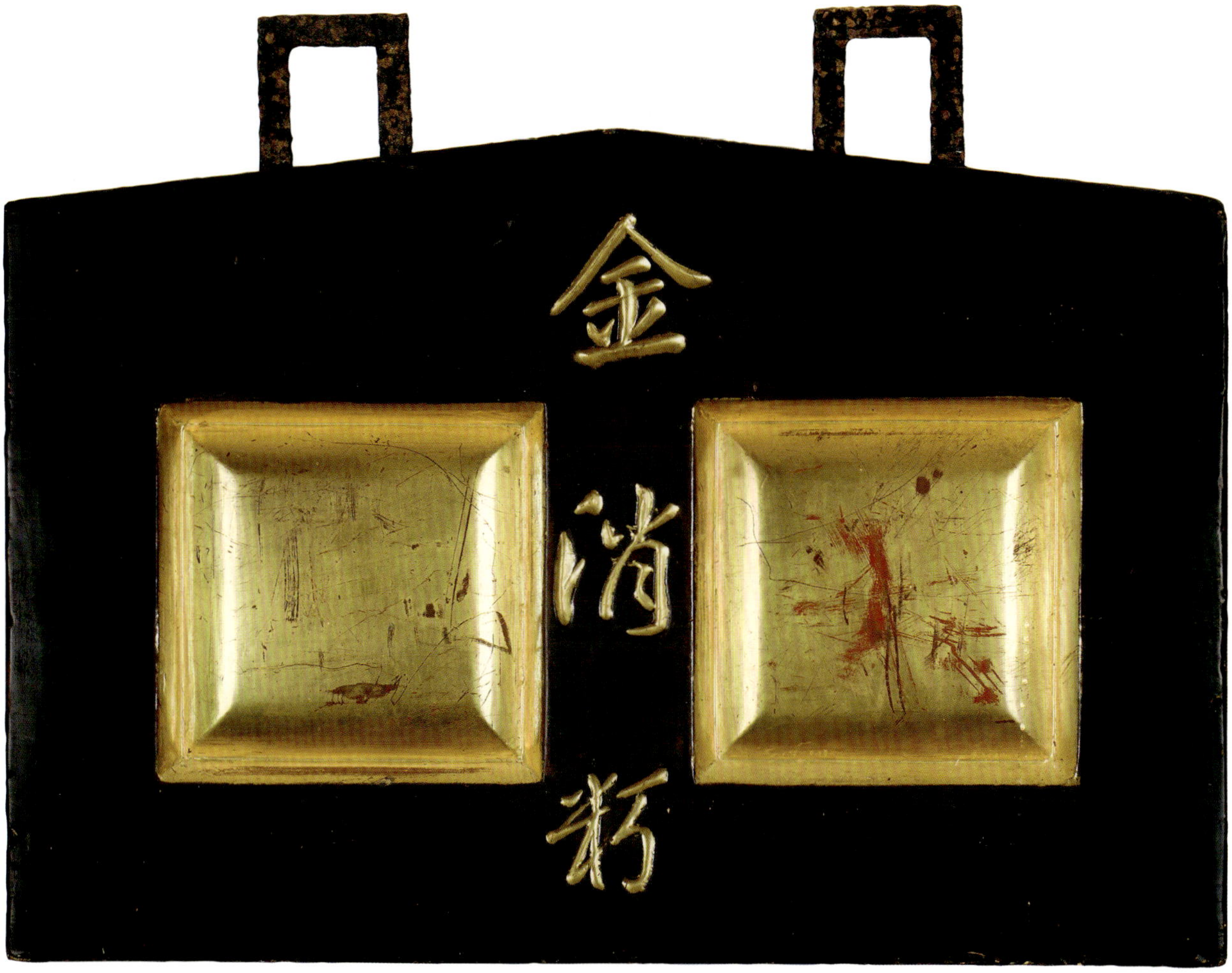

44

Shitta kanban for gold leaf shop
Late nineteenth century
Wood, pigment, lacquer, metal fittings
13¾ × 20 in. (34.9 × 50.8 cm)
Private Collection

In addition to selling sheets of gold leaf, kinpaku-ya sold other gold leaf–derived products, such as *keshihun*, a powdered gold leaf flake used in high-quality decorative *maki-e* treatments on lacquer. This simple but elegant shitta kanban for a kinpaku-ya is crafted from a thick slab of wood and has a slightly peaked, ema-style shape, covered overall in black lacquer. The two faceted squares are covered in gold lacquer. Where the gold has rubbed away, there are traces of a red lacquer undercoat, which was often applied to give an added richness to the outer gold layer. On this double-sided sign are identical double gold leaf squares, front and back. Rather than promoting the shop's specific name, one side bears the highlighted gold-inscribed phrase "*kin keshihun*"; likewise, the reverse announces "*yake keshihun*," the shop's specialty.

FIG. 63 An Edo-period woodblock print of a *haku-ya*, showing two workers pounding out the gold leaf while another presses small squares of gold leaf onto paper. A fan-shaped cartouche above reads, "*Haku-ya*," and an ema-style kanban featuring two squares of gold leaf set against a black ground is seen hanging in the upper left corner. Depicted in the *Imayô shokunin-zukushi hyakunin isshu* by Kondô Kiyoharu, Kyôhô era, 1716–35.

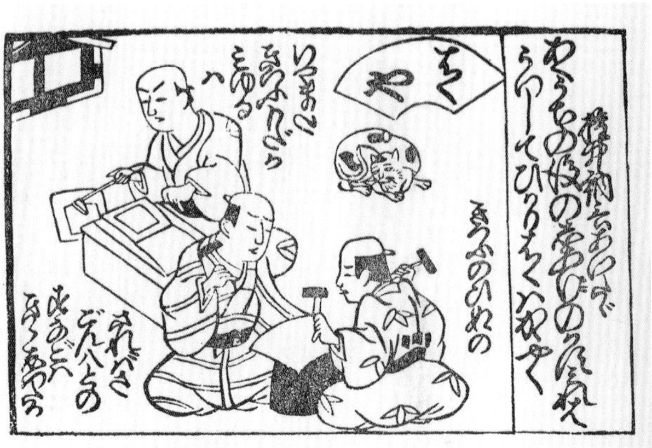

The *Morisada mankô* compendium of many things "Edo," mentioned above, lists a number of shops dealing in both kin- and ginpaku. The Suzuki Shoten in the Azabu Ikura district of Edo was a particularly famous kinpaku-ya.[223] Sugiura's *Kazô kanban zufu* contains a wonderful shitta kanban for a kinpaku-ya operated by Ishida Naoshichi in the Kansai area (Kyoto-Osaka). Sugiura's example is 58 inches (148 cm) long and has two suspension loops at the top as well as two side portage handles. The haku squares at the top are relatively small compared to the bold calligraphic inscription that reads, "*Kin gin paku bun rui dokoro*."[224]

Ryôgae-ya (Money Changers)

Of course, gold and silver were valued for more than just their decorative applications and pleasing allure. These two metals, as well as copper, served as the currency of Japan. The historical topography of Japanese coinage is a numismatic nightmare, with official government-minted currency in circulation alongside a plethora of regional coins of varying weights, purity, shapes, and sizes, in addition to Chinese-minted coins that were in common use until the early seventeenth century. Tracking these coins and their relative and constantly shifting values was one of the principal roles of a *ryôgae* (money changer). Officially, a ryôgae belonged to a specially licensed guild. Research shows that by the end of the seventeenth century, there were more than a thousand practicing ryôgae, divided into some twenty-two areas of specialization.[225] But in actuality, anyone with money could lend it and thereby serve as an unofficial ryôgae. Nobility, priests, samurai, farmers, and of course merchants, when possessed of a certain amount of liquidity, frequently engaged in the highly profitable practice of money lending. And while this free flow of coin helped to finance significant industrial and economic progress for Edo Japan as a whole, the more usurious side, the aspect of greed and unimaginable profit to be gained from money lending, was a common lament. Nobility and members of the samurai classes not infrequently sold the right to use their family crests to ryôgae, providing a gloss of legitimacy and security and permitting the lender to charge even higher interest rates.[226]

Kanban for ryôgae-ya varied greatly, depending upon the size of the operation, and to some extent the region or locality. The largest ryôgae-ya were naturally found in the *santô*, or three largest cities: Edo, Osaka, and Kyoto. Practices even among these three cities varied. The *Morisada mankô* explains that the ryôgae system was the most advanced in Osaka, where merchants and even private households frequently stored their money with a ryôgae-ya rather than leaving it in the shop or at home, and in this respect, a ryôgae-ya functioned much like a bank. These larger ryôgae-ya, also known as *hon-ryôgae,* often used only a plain blue noren as a shop sign. In Edo, hon-ryôgae tended to use *tenbin* (scales) as jitsubutsu kanban, placing these essential instruments near the shop's open doorway, discreetly advertising their services. Playing off of the tenbin theme, *fundo* weights also became emblematic of ryôgae-ya, and oversized fundo of lacquered wood functioned as mokei kanban, while incised designs of this distinctive

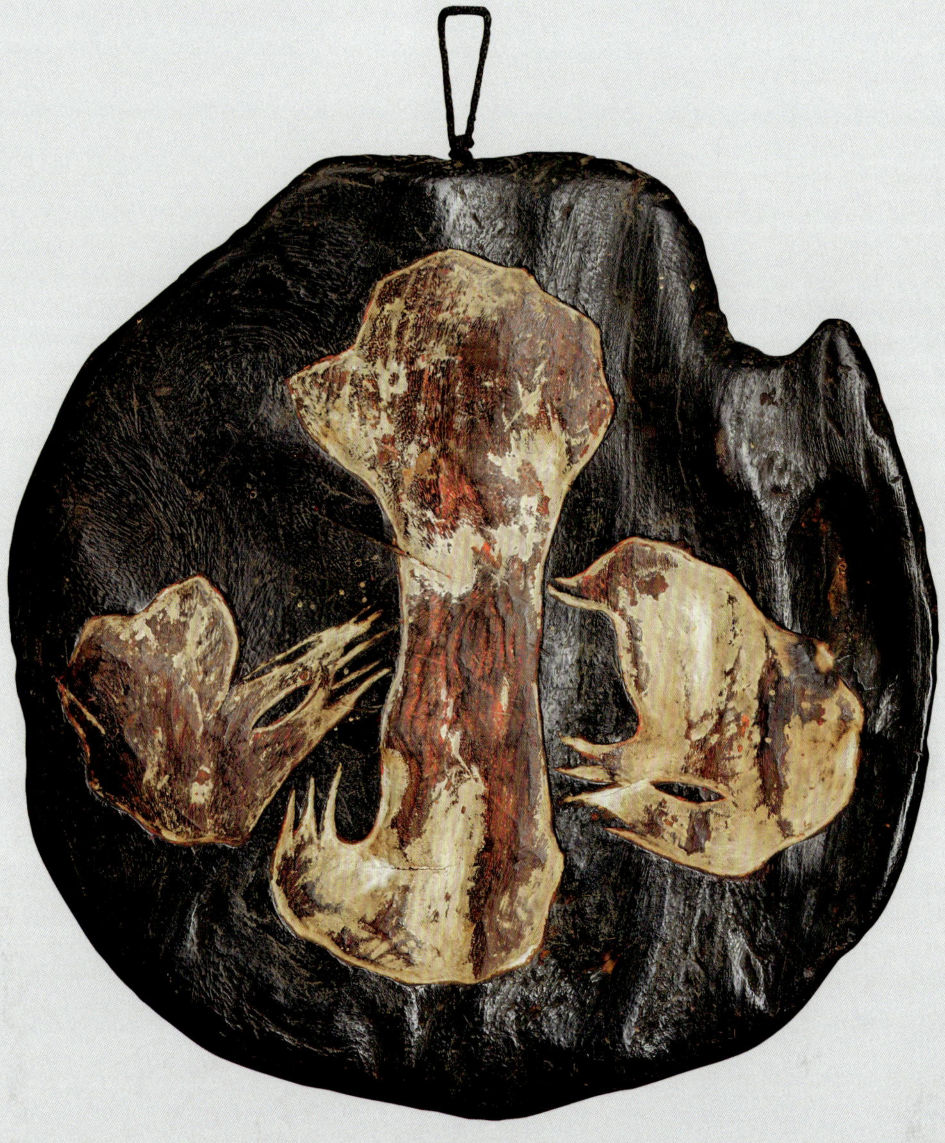

45

Circular kanban for money changer
Nineteenth century
Wood, pigment
10 × 10 in. (25.4 × 25.4 cm)
Collection of David M. Kahn

Kanban featuring the characters *dai* (long) on one side and *sho* (short) on the other were unique to *ryôgae,* or money changers. These two characters referred to long and short months (or years) in Japan's lunar-solar calendar. These affected the interest rates being charged for loans. Signs ranged from rudimentary disks with hastily brushed characters to highly polished and refined panels of expensive keyaki wood with the *dai* and *sho* characters etched deeply into the surface, with additional gilt treatments. This latter type of sign could be found hanging from the doorways of ryôgae merchants or appended to the entrances of seemingly unrelated businesses that offered money-lending services on the side. Here, a deeply weathered roundel of keyaki features the *sho* character executed in a highly expressive style and painted white. The pronounced grain pattern, rich patina, and overall organic shape of the wood lends this sign a decidedly mingei sensibility.

shape ornamented shitta kanban. The *Morisada mankô* also cites the very common practice of retailers and wholesalers of other trades and commodities offering ryôgae services.[227] These unlicensed businesses used a variety of kanban to advertise this side trade, known as *zeni kouri* (small money exchange), to their customers: hako kanban, jitsubutsu kanban, mokei kanban, shitta kanban, noren, hatta, and hioke were all viable options to businesses offering zeni kouri.

An unusual kanban style associated with ryôgae-ya consisted of a simple wooden plaque that was round, square, or even faceted (cat. 45). One face bore the character *dai* (long) or the character *sho* (short). These *dai-sho* kanban served two purposes: first, their presence indicated that the establishment (whether hon-ryôgae or zeni kouri) offered money-lending services; and second, they helped the potential borrower know whether the current month was a long or short one, which affected the interest rate. Prior to Japan's official adoption of the solar Gregorian calendar on January 1, 1873, it relied on a lunar-solar calendar. Known as the *Taiin taiyô reiki*, this calendar was introduced in 602 by the Korean Buddhist priest Kanroku (Korean: Kwaljik). The lunar-solar calendar needed frequent adjustments to maintain its accuracy, and this resulted in a system of long and short months, with the additional insertion of intercalary months (*urû*) every three years on average, which added yet another level of complexity by creating some years with double months. For example, for the year 1805, closely associated with the *Kidai shôran* illustrated in this volume, the long months were 2, 4, 8, 9, 10, and 11, while the short months were 1, 3, 5, 6, 7, and 12. In addition, there was a short intercalary eighth month, resulting in thirteen official months for that year.[228] Keeping track of this shifting terrain was complicated, and charts were devised to help nonastrologers stay accurate. This was exceptionally important for scheduling religious holidays and festivals, as well as for borrowing and lending money.

Dôgu-ya (Tool Shops)

The Japanese are celebrated the world over for their exceptional love of wood and skill in the use of it. For millennia, wood has been used for shrines, temples, palaces, commercial buildings, homes, huts, and lean-tos, as well as for utilitarian and artistic objects used in both everyday life and special rituals. Japanese construction and fabrication techniques that use sophisticated and precise joinery—without the need for nails, bolts, screws, or even glue—are universally admired. Wood was once also the primary source of fuel: in the home, for heating and cooking, and in industry, for tasks such as firing pottery and smelting iron. Forest products such as leaves, bark, and twigs have also historically been the source of much of Japan's agricultural fertilizer, and a significant industry developed around the collection and transportation of these essential elements for Japanese food production.[229] The tools needed for harvesting, shaping, and refining wood for all its myriad applications have also enjoyed a long history. Axes, saws, chisels, planes, hammers, gimlets, pincers, awls, drills, taps, levels, squares, chalk lines, and scissors (cat. 46) of seemingly infinite gradations of fineness and specificity all hold unique positions in Japanese artisanal and commercial history. Tools were needed throughout society, from the mother trimming the hair of her child or dicing daikon for the evening meal, to the farmer hoeing or raking his crop, to the Buddhist sculptor employing a wide range of chisels and saws, to the master carpenter building a temple or rebuilding a portion of an entire city after a fire. Even the kanban-shi himself would have needed a set of woodworking tools to create his product. And where there was a need for a tool, there was also a toolmaker and a tool seller (cat. 47).

Dôgu-ya, or tool and hardware shops, made frequent and effective use of kanban. The term *dôgu* is quite elastic and can embrace anything from a crude handsaw used to limb trees, to

46

Shitta kanban for scissors shop

Nineteenth century

Wood, pigment, metal fitting

48 × 11 in. (122 × 29 cm)

Private Collection

The domestic uses of Japanese blades might best be illustrated by an image of a pair of scissors (*nigiri-basami*). Whereas Western-style scissors usually have finger loops and a central pivot point, classic Japanese nigiri-basami are shaped more like clippers; the blades are open in the resting position, and the user cuts by applying pressure just behind them. Here, a shop advertising "myriad forged blades" (*yorozu uchi hamono*) uses a tall shitta kanban with the painted image of nigiri-basami scissors. The cutting edge of the blade is lighter in shade than the body, emphasizing its sharpness. The sign is fashioned from a single block of wood; time and the elements have abraded the sumi ink and caused the wood grain to become more pronounced. Traces of the shop's name, "*Naka*," can be discerned along the lower left edge of the sign. A metal suspension hook would have supported the sign as it was brought in and out of the shop at the beginning and close of each business day.

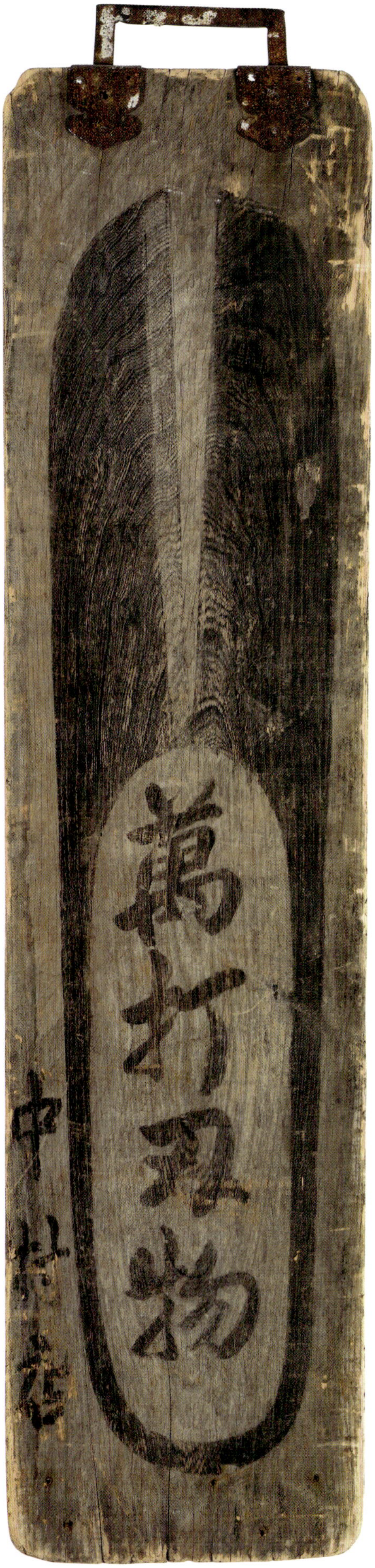

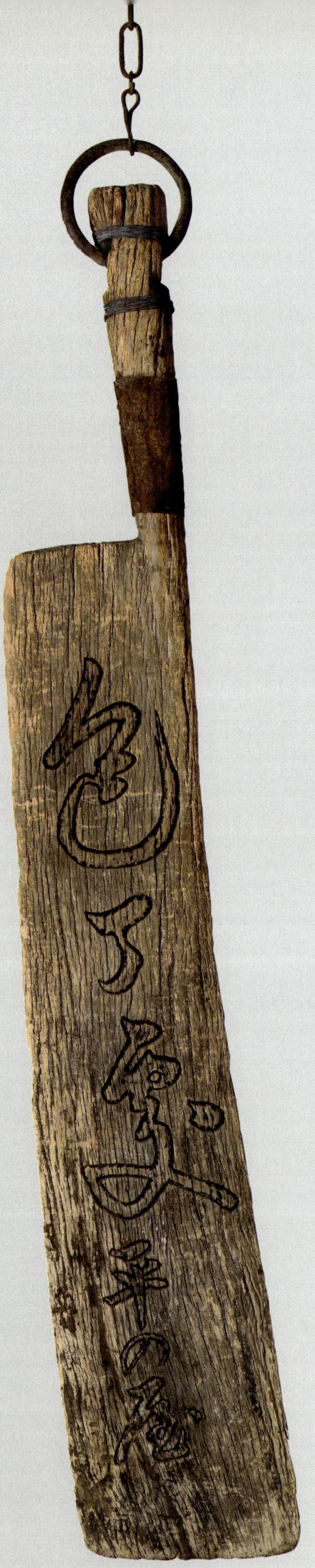

47

Mokei kanban for saw-sharpening shop

Nineteenth century

Wood, pigment, metal fittings

50 × 7½ in. (127 ×19.1 cm)

Private Collection

Japanese saws come in a wide range of formats, each designed for a specific use and application. While the general term for saw is *nokogiri*, an entire universe of more specific terms are used, depending on whether the teeth are set on one side (*kataha*) or both sides (*ryoba*). A precision, fine-bladed saw is called a *dôzuki*, and a blade for cutting curvilinear shapes a *hikimawashi*. The list is endless. However, all blades eventually need to be sharpened, no matter their intended use or specific design, making a *matate-ya*, or saw-sharpening shop, arguably as essential a link in the tool chain as the dôgu-ya that first made the blade. Here, a saw-sharpening shop advertises its presence with an oversized wood-crafted saw serving as a double-sided mokei kanban. The head of the blade bears the simple inscription "*metate-ya*" (blade sharpening/filing shop) on both faces. The kanban-shi has gone to great lengths to create an accurate interpretation of a working kataha hand saw, including the simulation of rattan wrapping where the "blade" joins the long wooden handle.

pierced work and incised hardware employed on traditional Japanese *tansu* furniture, to the refined lacquer accessories that are displayed alongside the dolls used in annual Hina-matsuri celebrations. But as a general term, dôgu is essentially synonymous with the English word *tool* (cat. 48). And dôgu-ya kanban ran the full range, from noren with artistically stenciled designs to mokei kanban featuring giant planes (cat. 49), saws, and axes.

Hamono, or hand-forged blades, play a distinct role in Japanese history. Japanese *hocho* knives, used in nearly surgical culinary maneuvers, remain coveted today (cat. 50). Many of the specialty hamono shops operating in Japan can trace their origins to smithing traditions associated with the long and short swords used by the military classes from deep antiquity. Samurai blades (*katana*), so sharp as to cut neatly through a floating sheet of paper or strong enough to hew a bamboo stalk, are iconic elements in Japanese art as well as military history, and much research has been given over to the study of blade masters since the earliest times. Edo-period depictions from a number of shokunin zukushi-e, discussed above, illustrate sword polishers as well as sword blade forgers. The Kita-in example shows two sword polishers (*tôgi-shi*) hard at work. A whetstone is before them. But unlike the images of other craftsmen using whetstones to polish glass or metal objects, in which the men are typically bare chested, here the tôgi-shi are depicted in formal *hakama* trousers with court caps set on their heads, indicating an intense formality to the process. A young female attendant passes a sword to the tôgi-shi, her eyes averted and shielded with a cloth, speaking to the reverence with which all aspects of sword making were treated. A young samurai approaches the studio, his attendant carrying a wooden sword box on his back, undoubtedly bringing more blades to the tôgi-shi for polishing.

The annals of Japanese sword craft are filled with the names of noted makers, with innumerable forging traditions (*den*), schools (*ha*), and lineages (*mon*), all recorded in sword smith directories extending back to the Nara period. The most celebrated sword maker in Japanese history, however, is unquestionably Masamune (Gorô Nyûdô, c. 1264–1343), of the Soshu-den of blade making. His most famous sword, Honjô Masamune, named after one of its early owners, Honjô Shigenaga (1540–1614), is the stuff of legend. Considered to be perhaps the finest sword ever created, it disappeared during the U.S. military occupation of Japan following World War II. In December 1945, Prince Tokugawa Iemasa (1884–1963) brought Honjo Masamune along with thirteen other prized heirloom swords to the Mejiro district police station in Tokyo, in compliance with U.S. orders to surrender all privately held weaponry. These swords, including Honjo Masamune, were, in turn, purported to have been dutifully turned over to an official from the Foreign Liquidation Commission in January 1946. From there, the sword disappeared into oblivion, the subject of scores of Internet chat rooms and conspiracy theories, constituting perhaps the ultimate treasure hunt.

The Masamune lineage continued making swords of repute through the end of the Edo period. However, beginning with the Meiji era and the Japanese government's promulgation of strong measures to reshape Japanese society along Western lines, a series of edicts were issued that essentially stripped the samurai of their identifying symbols, effectively eviscerating them as a distinct class. In 1871 the Dampatsurei edict forced all samurai to cut off their topknots, a traditional source of identity and pride. And in 1876 the Hatôrei prohibited the public wearing of swords, relegating them to ceremonial use only. With a stroke of the administrative brush, centuries of craftsmanship and tradition were rendered virtually obsolete, and many sword makers were forced to turn to making Western-style military swords, or, alternatively, dôgu, as a means of economic survival. A generation of

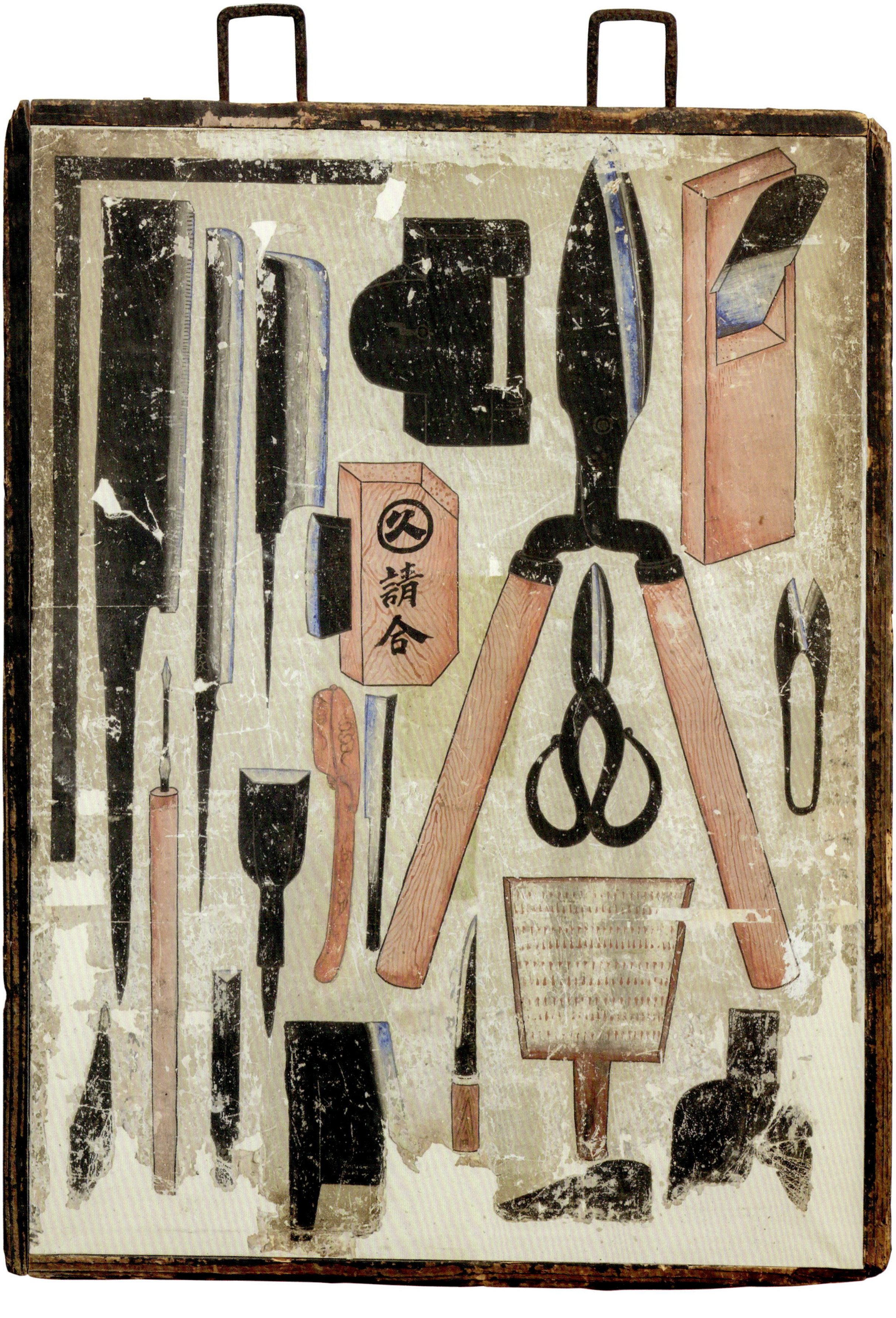
㊇
請合

48

Shitta kanban for blade shop, front and back views

Late nineteenth century

Wood, paper, pigment, metal fittings

33¾ × 23¾ × ¾ in. (85.7 × 60.3 × 1.9 cm)

Mingei International Museum Purchase, 2009-48-001

A particularly rare and unusual sign for a dôgu-ya, exhibited here for the first time, is part of Mingei International Museum's permanent collection. It is a shitta kanban, featuring designs on both sides, and it is exceptionally fashioned out of thick paper set in a wooden frame. This kanban presents finely painted and detailed images of approximately forty various tool types available from the toolmaker. A *hiuchi gane* (flint) resting on its side features the shop's yago and the promise "*ukeai*" (quality guaranteed). Aside from saw blades, chisels, and planers of various sizes, the selection includes a metal square and a lock, indicating that this shop was a metal fabricator or specialist. The reverse of the sign continues the display of various tools and blades. Some blades carry further inscribed assurances, such as "*daigokujô*" (good-quality blade). And, borrowing a historic gloss of superior craftsmanship, one blade bears the inscribed name of Kinkazan Kiyonaga, a reference to the celebrated Genroku-era (1688–1704) blade master Kinkazan Fujiwara Kiyonaga of Gifu Prefecture. Interestingly, one of the blades also has an inscription bearing the name of the famous metalsmith and saw maker Nakaya Kyûsaku (1839–c. 1908). The fifteenth-generation Kyûsaku was active in the Meiji era, when this kanban was likely produced.

It is exceptionally rare to have biographical information regarding the artisans for the shops for which there are extant kanban. In the case of Nakaya Kyûsaku, a noted blade maker during his day, we know a surprising amount of personal detail. Kyûsaku's real name was Morimura Kyûsaku. He was born in 1839, son of the fourteenth-generation Nakaya Kyûsaku. He began his apprenticeship in 1851, when he was twelve years old. When his father died in 1874, Kyûsaku took on the mantle as the fifteenth head of the family of metalsmiths. In Meiji 12 (1879), Kyûsaku was forty years old and living and working at 15, Kitamaki, Kyôbashi-ku. At the time, he had two *deshi* (apprentices) and four blade makers working at his shop. By Meiji 27 (1894), Kyûsaku had expanded to an additional location at 19, Kitamaki (which today corresponds to 1-1-1 Kyôbashi, Chûô ku, near the Yaesu, central exit, at Tokyo Station). His shop's name at that time was noted as Nokogiri Kaji Nakaya Kyûsaku (Saw Blade Maker Nakaya Kyûsaku). While his shop name is known, the specific yago employed by the shop has yet to be documented (Hoshino and Funabiki, "Nokogiri kaji: Nakaya Kyusaku").

The kanban shown here gives the shop's yago on front as "Marukyû," presenting us with the strong possibility that this was a kanban made specifically for Kyûsaku's shop, which would make it quite significant. Alternatively, it could have been for a shop specializing in blades, including those by this famous maker.

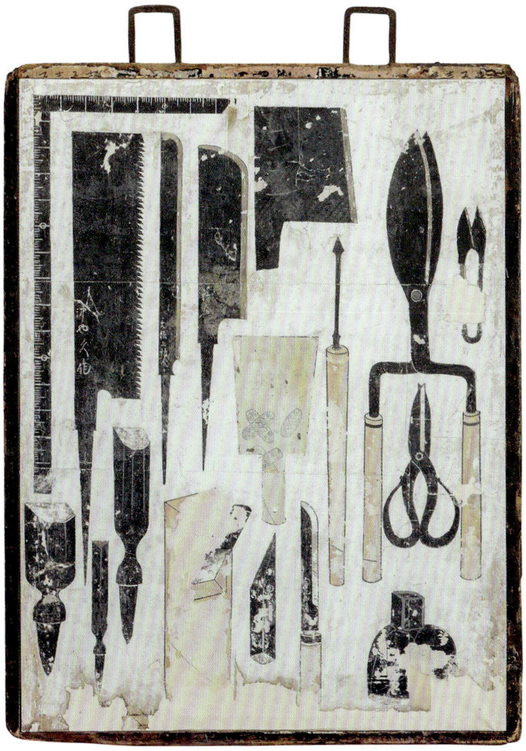

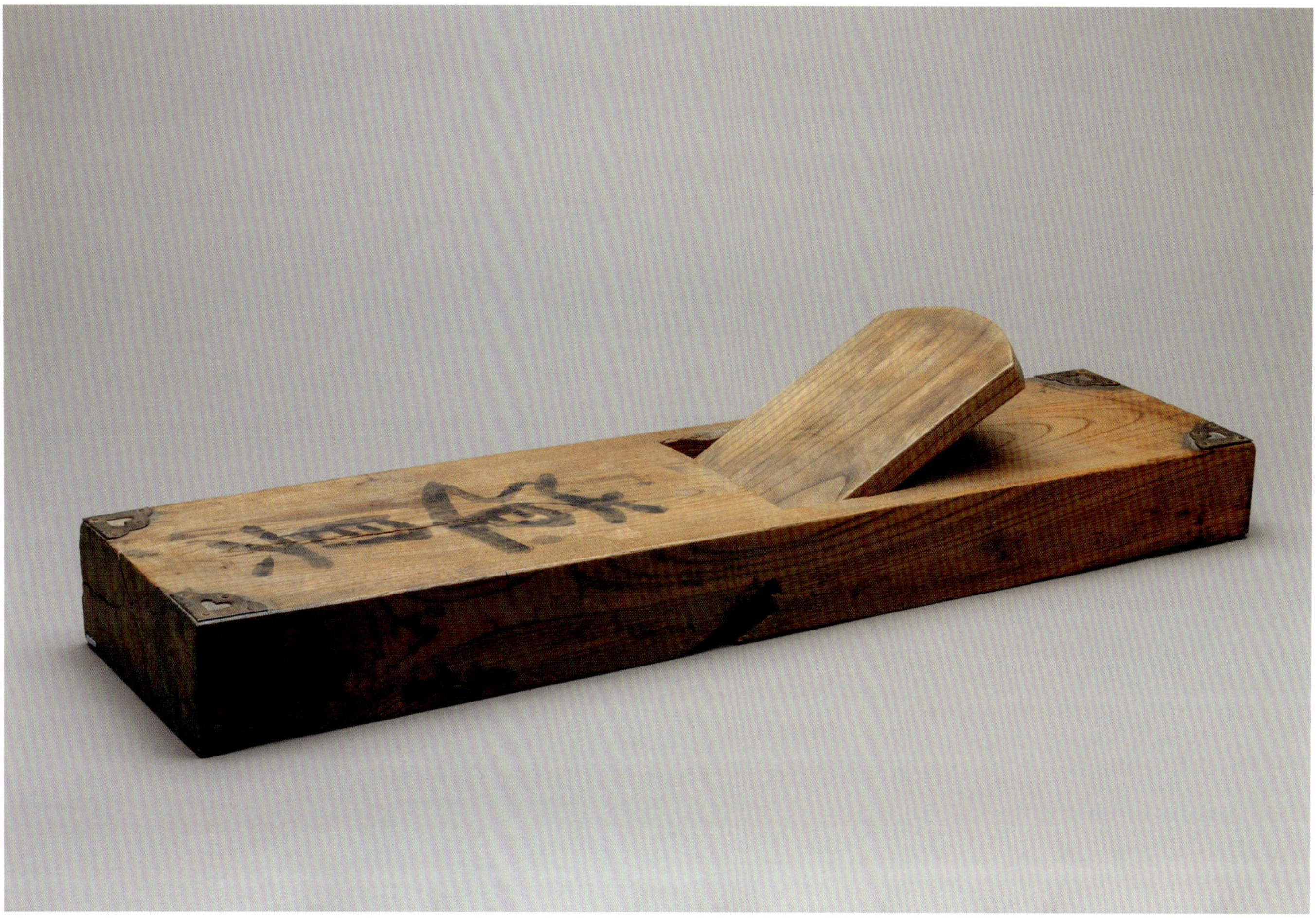

49

Mokei kanban for tool shop

Early twentieth century

Wood, pigment, metal

27½ × 7 × 2½ in. (69.9 × 17.8 × 6.4 cm)

Mingei International Museum, Gift of Ted Cohen, 2016-18-001

Japanese carpenter's planes are referred to as *kanna*. These varied, depending on size and application, but they were essential tools for the smoothing and planing of wood for any number of applications, whether building a temple or making a *tansu* clothing chest. Here, a mokei kanban of a kanna is inscribed "*dôgu*," or tool. Formed from a large slab of wood, it is constructed true to a large plane, or *hira-kanna*: the corners are mounted with metal fittings, and the central "blade" for planing is removable. The inscription in sumi ink stands out against the natural color of the wood, with the grain pattern adding to the overall beauty of the sign. The reverse bears the inscription "Kanamono-ya," either the shop's name or a straightforward indication of what it was: a metal tool shop.

50

Mokei kanban for knife shop

Nineteenth century

Wood, pigment

38 × 7¾ in. (96.5 × 19.7 cm)

Private Collection

The Sakai area of Osaka is famous for its *hocho*, or knife-forging guilds. It is held that blade forgers were initially attracted there during the excavation and construction of some of the early giant tombs that have dotted this area of Japan since the Kofun period (250–538 CE). They supplied blades for the hoes, picks, adzes, and numerous other tools required for these ambitious projects. Sakai's position as an important center of blade production was secured during the Edo period, when knives designed specifically to aid in the cutting of tobacco leaves were developed by the area's craftsmen. As a result of their acknowledged quality and superiority, Sakai *hamono* blades produced by members of the local trade guild association (*kumiai*) were given special recognition by the Edo government in 1761. Blades from this area were given a particular mark reading "*Sakai kiwame*," or Sakai exclusive. Sakai-area blade companies such as the Narita Corporation still command much respect in the international world of cutlery. Here, a knife shop advertises its presence with a mokei kanban rendered as an inverted hocho. The face of the knife bears the inscription "*hocho dokoro*" (knife shop), with the shop's name listed in smaller characters as "Hiranoya." It is impossible to tell where this shop was originally located, but it would have been one of the many shops across the country selling knives for domestic as well as commercial use, from the paring of fruits and vegetables to the gutting of fish.

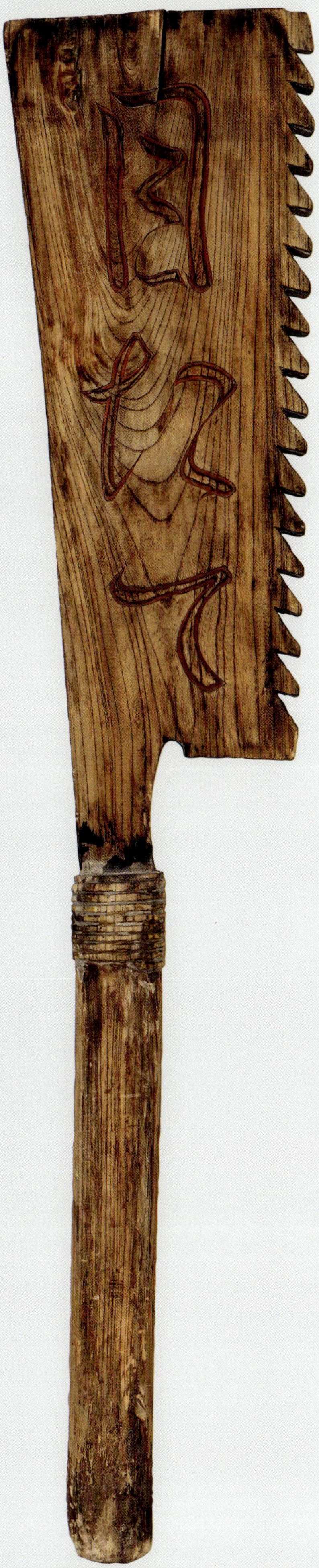

artisans had to rapidly shift into new lines of manufacture and production. The twenty-second-generation Masamune, who was practicing at that time, turned to making farm implements, literally turning swords into ploughshares, before expanding into domestic and commercial cutlery. The current Masamune, Yamamura Hirotsuna (Masamune XXIV), is head of the Masamune Bijutsu Kogeisho (Masamune Sword and Blade) in Kamakura, which still specializes in swords and cutlery.

Kanban for sword makers and their shops are exceptionally rare. Three signs in the PEM collection relate to craftsmen specializing in swords and sword mountings. The shitta kanban for the Katana-ya Zenbeye features a forged arrow in the *karimata* (forked or "wild goose") style, set within a cartouche. The sign's inscription indicates that Zenbeye was a *kobu-gôyo*, a designated supplier to daimyô and samurai.[230] A fine wooden shitta kanban for the Katana-ya Tahei advertises a specialization in *tôkenrui* (swords) and *kodôgurui* (sword accessories) and includes a jitsubutsu wrapped sword hilt, set within a contoured aperture at the top.[231] And an exquisite jitsubutsu kanban for a scabbard maker (*saya-shi*) presents fifteen sections of saya in varying materials, ranging from sharkskin to bamboo, ornate lacquer, and inlaid mother-of-pearl.

Yoroi-ya (Armorers)

By the late Edo period, armor for the samurai fulfilled a much different function than it did during Japan's feudal period. Nearly three hundred years of Pax Tokugawa had largely removed bloodletting combat from the samurai's official résumé and career arc. *Yoroi* (armor), *kabuto* (helmets), *katana* (swords), *saya* (scabbards), *tsuba* (sword guards), and the dizzying array of costuming and mechanical elements that went into a samurai's fighting regalia had largely shifted from intensely functional and battlefield pragmatic to ceremonial and flashy (cat. 51). As a result, the artistic and artisanal qualities of each of these aspects of a warrior's wardrobe and arsenal reached new heights during the Edo period. The traditions associated with the manufacturing processes of these elements remained deeply entrenched in Japanese economic culture, but with a much more liberalized and artistic expression. Shops producing, repairing, and maintaining samurai armor and related accoutrements remained important throughout the Edo period but abruptly found themselves without customers after the advent of a civil government under the Meiji Restoration of 1868.

Kanban and Pastimes

Drinking (*nomu*), gambling (*utsu*), and whoring (*kau*) were known as the "three depravities." Drinking is obvious, and whoring is a topic for another book, so this discussion will focus on gambling. Soon after the arrival of the Portuguese in the sixteenth century, the Japanese became infatuated with *karuta* (Portuguese: *carta*; English: cards). This pastime, introduced by foreign sailors, typically featured a forty-eight-card deck in four suits: batons, coins, cups, and swords—with European symbols and imagery. The Japanese quickly adopted the game and gradually transformed these European suits to match native sensibilities. The first Japanese variation is thought to be the style known as Tenshôkaruta.[232] The cards' portability made them popular among the warring classes, who could easily carry them on campaigns and while away many hours of waiting. Gambling, however, was the focus from the beginning, and as various iterations seeped into Edo society, the government stepped in to suppress karuta, but this only served to spawn new game formats designed to confound the authorities. Popular tradition holds that the term *Yakuza* (Japanese mafia) derives from the karuta game of *zanmai*,

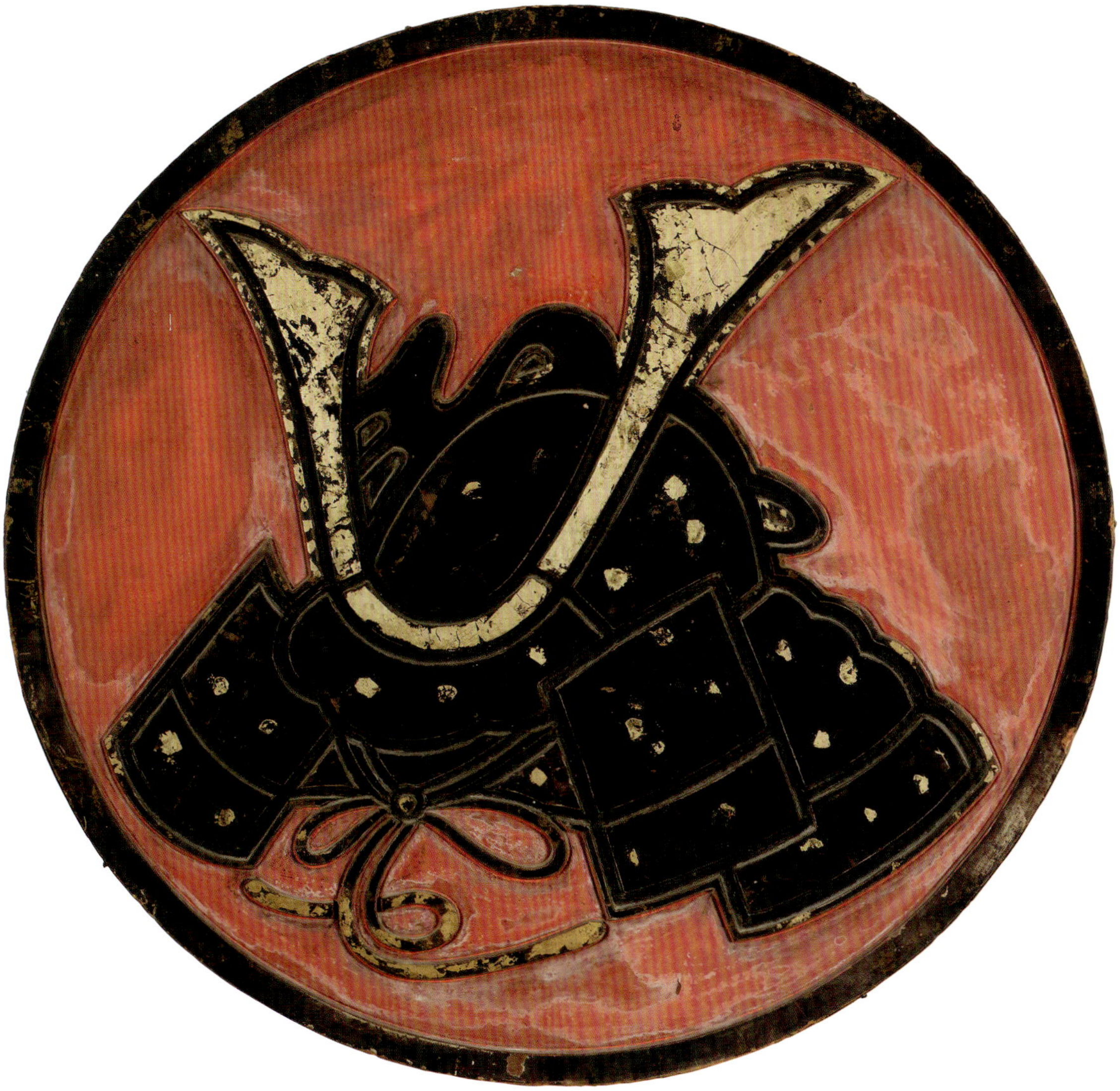

51

Circular sage kanban for armorer
Dated Bunsei 2 (1819)
Wood, gold leaf, pigment, lacquer
23 in. (58.5 cm) in diameter
Private Collection

Beginning in the Edo period, commercial advertisers frequently co-opted iconic images of figures drawn from legend, lore, or actual military history as registered trademarks or brands. Much as an American insurance company might use the visage of Benjamin Franklin to convey a sense of history and integrity, a Japanese manufacturer of medical tooth powder, for example, would use an image of the fierce warrior Katô Kiyomasa (1562–1611) subduing a tiger to convey a sense of the product's strength and effectiveness. To claim a product's popularity with or use by famous individuals was also a common feature of early advertising. This graphically bold and unusual circular kanban advertising the services of a yoroi-ya, or armorer, from Echizen (now Kanazawa) features the stark rendering of a *kabuto* (helmet) in black with flecks of gold leaf, set against a red lacquer ground. The reverse bears an inscription dated Bunsei 2 (1819) that reads "*Minamoto asson senjôzaijô*." "Minamoto asson" refers to the great founder of the Kamakura shogunate, Minamoto Yoritomo (1147–1199). "Senjôzaijô," roughly interpreted, means "always carried this into battle," conveying a sense that Yoritomo himself used this armorer for his military regalia. No shop name is listed, but the kanban-shi is noted as "Kyokuriki." Though potentially spurious in his claims, akin to the real estate cliché "George Washington slept here," this Echizen armorer was, in effect, asserting a pedigree and lineage extending back over 650 years, with direct patronage by one of the greatest military leaders in Japanese history.

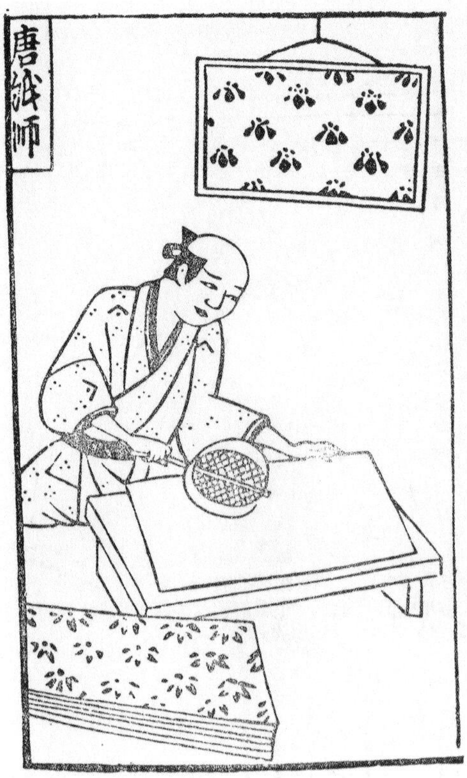

FIG. 64 Woodblock print of a *karukami-shi* making paper for karuta playing cards. Reproduced from *Jinrinkinmôzui* (1690), 217.

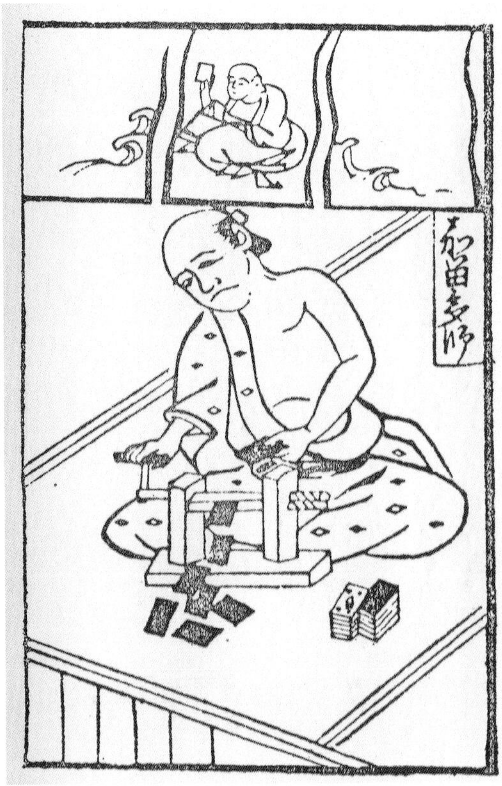

FIG. 65 Woodblock print of a *karuta-shi* cutting the final cards after the sheets of paper have all been pressed together. Reproduced from *Jinrinkinmôzui* (1690), 189.

preferred by professional gamblers (*bakuto*) during the Edo period. Similar to blackjack, the object was to accumulate a hand of three numbered cards totaling nineteen. The combination of eight (*yatsu*), nine (*ku*), and three (*san*) equaled twenty, and thus a bust or a bad hand. It is maintained that *yatsu-ku-san* was an expression employed by gamblers to disarm their marks into thinking that they were losers or bad players, and that the victim had a good shot at winning. Yatsu-ku-san was eventually contracted into *yakuza*.

Over time, variations on the basic card game and its designs proliferated, but generally headed in one of two directions. One remained true to the Portuguese concept of suits, with utsu (gambling) as a primary focus. The other married karuta forms to an earlier pastime known as *kai awase* (shell matching). This second diversion, frequently referred to as *uta karuta*, was an innocent, though competitive, amusement. Perhaps the most popular version of uta karuta was known as *hanafuda* (flower cards), consisting of forty-eight cards divided into the twelve months, four images related to each month; it remains a particularly popular version today. Other variations were phonetically based and known as *iroha garuta*. But the inherent flexibility of karuta itself led to an untold number of variations, including *yôkai karuta*, which was based on ghost stories. In many of these latter versions, imagery became key and therefore was an important component in the manufacturing process.

Karuta manufacturing consisted largely of adhering layers of paper of varying thickness, with the topmost layer bearing the desired image. This was usually accomplished through woodblock-printing techniques, with all of the card images printed on a single sheet and then cut out, to be applied to the base stock. Interestingly, the *Jinrinkinmôzui* shows two craftsmen associated with the production of karuta. One is a *karukami-shi*, specializing in printed paper for karuta (fig. 64).[233] The other is a *karuta-shi*, depicted in the process of cutting the individual finished cards to exact size. To his side is a stack of cards with just a suggestion of surface designs (fig. 65).[234] In the commercially competitive world of Edo Japan, illustrations became increasingly important, and producers of karuta would engage popular woodblock-print artists of the day, such as Katsushika Hokusai and Andô Hiroshige (1797–1858), to create eye-catching visuals.[235] The town of Miike in Fukuoka Prefecture became an early and important center of karuta manufacture, and the Miike Karuta History Museum in Omuta, Fukuoka, preserves the history of Japanese karuta.

Kanban for *karuta-ya*, or playing card shops, tended to be in the shitta style, double-sided signs that relied on a combination of text and imagery. A woodblock print from 1733 shows a large sage kanban with two crossed Western-style épée swords (Japanese: *isu*; Portuguese: *espada*) from a Tenshôkaruta deck, with the phrase "*iro ari*" (we have assorted) written in hiragana below. As a foreign-derived word, *karuta* was most frequently written in hiragana, or occasionally in *ateji* (phonetic kanji). It was generally placed at the center of an elongated panel, with painted images of cards from various suits arranged according to an artistic sensibility (cat. 52). As mentioned above, hanafuda, perhaps the most popular karuta form, can also be written with the character *hana*, meaning nose, as a homonym for *hana* (flower); the ubiquitous long-nosed tengu goblin was an early and much-used mascot for the karuta-ya. A shop sign for a Kyoto karuta-ya in the Shôwa Neon Takamura Kanban Museum features a tasseled mask of a tengu at the top, surmounted by the tôroku-shôhyô registered trademark indicator.[236] Three hanafuda cards cascade down the sign: the topmost is *matsu* (pine) for January, featuring a crane and pine boughs; the middle card is *sakura* (cherry blossoms) for March, featuring a blossoming cherry tree glimpsed behind a field curtain; and finally, the August card shows a full moon with a red sky and is part of the *susuki* (grass) series (fig. 66).

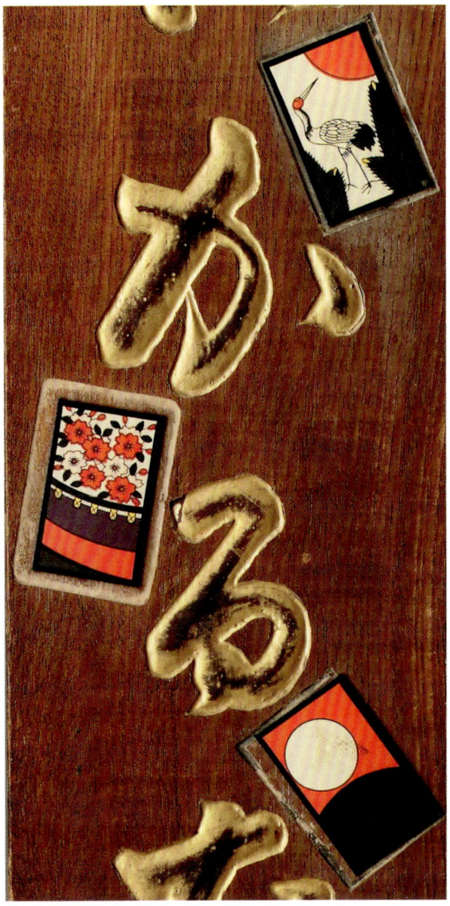

FIG. 66 Detail of cat. 2 showing the hanafuda cards for matsu (pine), sakura (cherry blossoms), and susuki (grass) from a sage kanban for the Oishi Tengudo playing card shop. Shôwa Neon Takamura Kanban Museum.

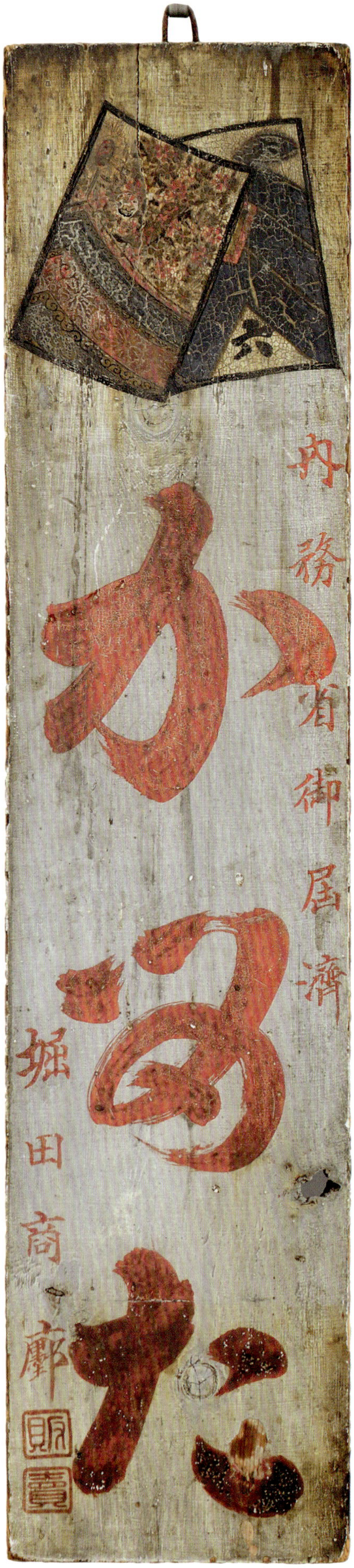

52

Sage kanban for playing card shop

Twentieth century

Wood, pigment, metal fitting

37¾ × 8⅝ × ¾ in. (95.9 × 21.9 × 1.9 cm)

Mingei International Museum, Gift of Dane Owen, 2014-45-001

This shitta kanban for the Hotta Shoro karuta-ya (playing card shop) is executed on a painted board, with *"ka-ru-ta"* written down the center. The top features two playing cards: the topmost card is the *sakura* curtain card for March from a hanafuda deck, as found on the Shôwa Neon Takamura Kanban Museum example, and the other is the *roppô*, or number six card, taken from a *kabufuda* gambling deck.

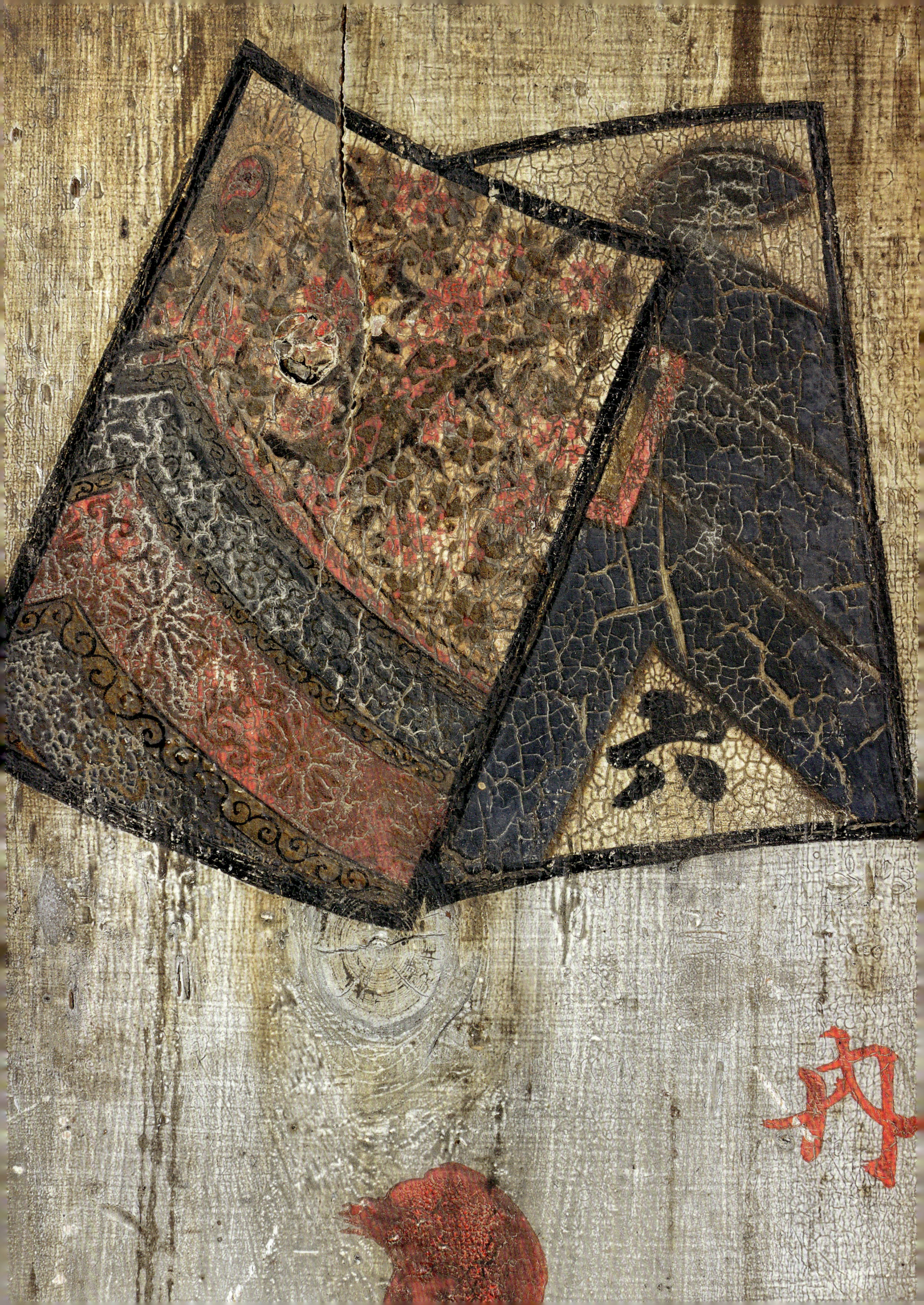
六
内

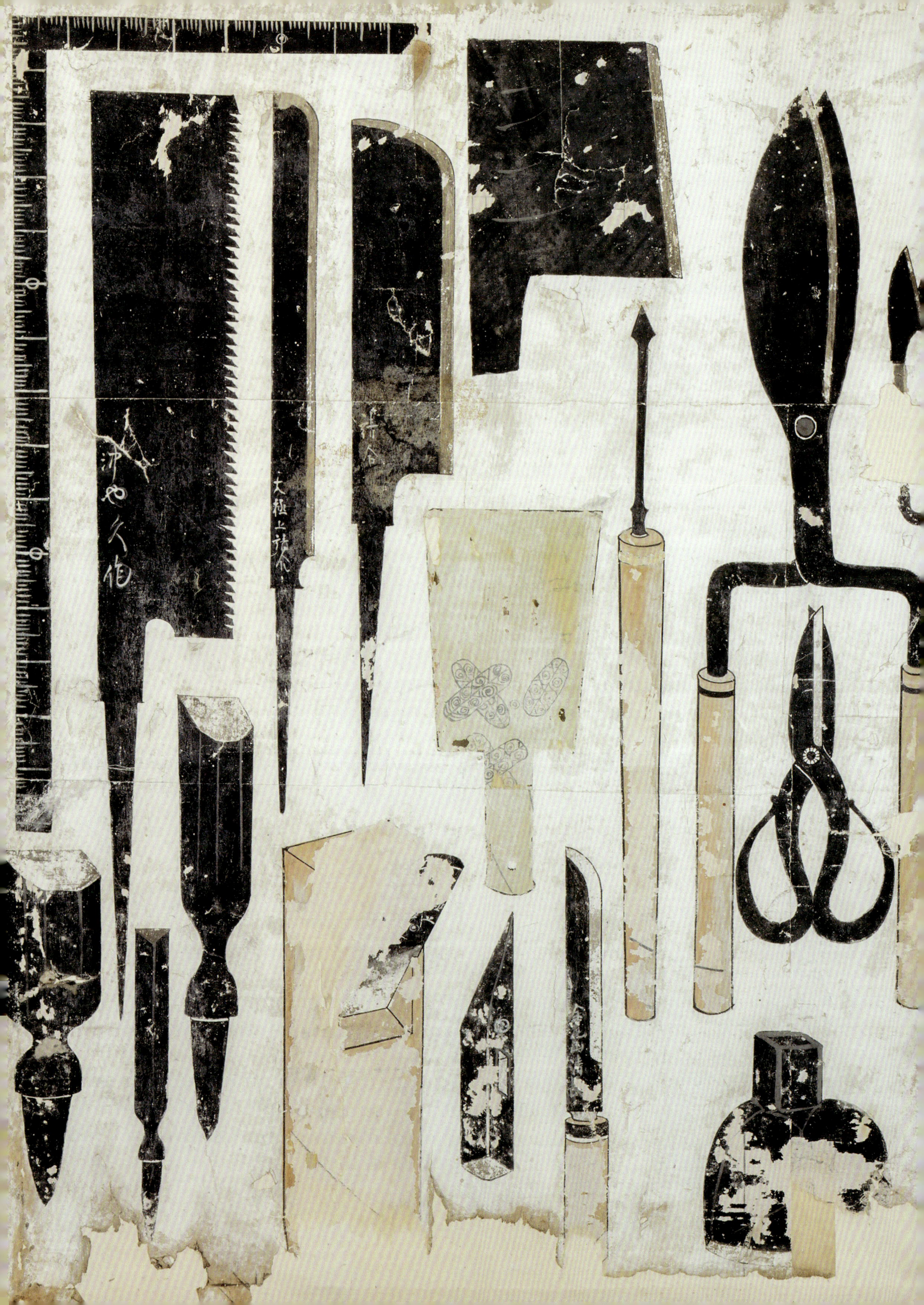

NOTES

1. Catherine Sallant, "Pair Sheds New Light on L.A.'s Claim to Neon Fame," *Los Angeles Times*, December 3, 2013.

2. Wang Shucun, *Shop Signs of Imperial China*, trans. Li Xin (Beijing: Foreign Language Press, 2006), 6.

3. Matsumiya Saburô, *Edo no kanban* (Tokyo: Tôhô Shoin, 1959), 28.

4. Matsumiya, *Edo no kanban*, 26; a stricter translation, by Michelle Osterfeld Li, is: "I went alone to the western market / The silk I bought on my own / without carefully examining / was really a poor choice."

5. William Wayne Farris, "Trade, Money, and Merchants in Nara Japan," *Monumenta Nipponica* 53, no. 3 (1998): 304.

6. Matsumiya, *Edo no kanban*, 168.

7. Oka Hideyuki, "*Kanban no kataji to moji*," in *Bakumatsu, Meiji kanbanten* (Tokyo: Nihon Terebi Hôsômô, 1984), 16.

8. Matsumiya, *Edo no kanban*, 168.

9. Shôwa Neon, *Jidai o utsusu kanban* (Tokyo: Shôwa Neon Takamura Kanban Museum, 2010), 15.

10. Shibusawa Keizô, *Japanese Life and Culture in the Meiji Era* (Tokyo: Ôbunsha, 1958), 66.

11. Hayashi Yoshikazu, *Edo kanban zufu* (Tokyo: Miki Shobô, 1977), 134.

12. Matsumiya, *Edo no kanban*, 168.

13. Tanabe Satoru, "*Kanban no sekai—sono rekishi mizokuteki sokumen*," in *Bakumatsu*, 10.

14. Hayashi, *Edo kanban zufu*, 81; Matsumiya, *Edo no kanban*, 101.

15. Translation by Robert Mangold.

16. Peabody Essex Museum, E15749. Notes in the card catalog at the Peabody Essex interpret this sign as belonging to an incense shop, as opposed to a pharmacy or patent medicine dealer, reading "*jako sei*" as thyme rather than deer musk.

17. Naito Museum of Pharmaceutical Science and Industry, *Kusuri kanban* (Kawashima: Naito Museum of Pharmaceutical Science and Industry, 1986), 21.

18. Naito Museum of Pharmaceutical Science and Industry, *Kusuri kanban*, 23.

19. Peabody Essex Museum, E15749.

20. Peabody Essex Museum, E16552.

21. Peabody Essex Museum, E15924.

22. Peabody Essex Museum, E16467.

23. Peabody Essex Museum, E16510.

24. Peabody Essex Museum, E16555.

25. Peabody Essex Museum, E16568.

26. Peabody Essex Museum, E19203.

27. *Jinrinkinmôzui* (1690; reprint, Tokyo: Kodansha, 1990), 204.

28. *Jinrinkinmôzui*, 191.

29. *Jinrinkinmôzui*, 188.

30. *Jinrinkinmôzui*, 176.

31. Matthew Philip McKelway, *Capitalscapes: Folding Screens and Political Imagination in Late Medieval Kyoto* (Honolulu: University of Hawai'i Press, 2006), 152.

32. McKelway, *Capitalscapes*, 163.

33. Kazuko Kameda-Madar, "Shokunin Zukushi-e, 'Pictures of People of Various Occupations in Their Workshops' in Early Modern Japan," *Kaikodo Journal* 31 (2015): 30–31; Dôshin Satô, *Modern Japanese Art and the Meiji State: The Politics of Beauty*, trans. Hiroshi Nara (Los Angeles: Getty Research Institute, 2011), 73.

34. Hayashi, *Edo kanban zufu*, 60.

35. Matsumiya, *Edo no kanban*, 266.

36. Matsumiya, *Edo no kanban*, 266.

37. McKelway, *Capitalscapes*, 10.

38. McKelway, *Capitalscapes*, 46.

39. Hayashi, *Edo kanban zufu*, 339.

40. Matsumiya, *Edo no kanban*, 83.

41. Naito Museum of Pharmaceutical Science and Industry, *Kusuri kanban*, 8.

42. Naito Museum of Pharmaceutical Science and Industry, *Kusuri kôkoku* (Kawashima: Naito Museum of Pharmaceutical Science and Industry, 1995), 82.

43. Naito Museum of Pharmaceutical Science and Industry, *Kusuri kôkoku*, 12, 82.

44. Sebastian Dobson, "Split Visions: Wilhelm Heine and Albert Berg in Japan," in *Under Eagle Eyes: Lithographs, Drawings & Photographs from the Prussian Expedition to Japan, 1860–61*, ed. Sebastian Dobson and Sven Saaler (Munich: Iudicium Verlag, 2011), 141.

45. Quoted in Dobson, *Under Eagle Eyes*, 228.

46. Quoted in Dobson, *Under Eagle Eyes*, 198.

47. Hayashi, *Edo kanban zufu*, 29–30.

48. Quoted in Beatrice M. Bodart-Bailey, *Kaempfer's Japan: Tokugawa Culture Observed* (Honolulu: University of Hawai'i Press, 1999), 349.

49. Kobayashi Junichi, *ŌEdo happyaku-yachô* (Tokyo: Edo-Tokyo Museum, 2003).

50. James L. McClain, *Japan, a Modern History* (New York: Norton, 2002), 49.

51. *Lust, Commerce, and Corruption: An Account of What I Have Seen and Heard, by an Edo Samurai*, ed. Mark Teeuwen and Kate Wildman Nakai (New York: Columbia University Press, 2014), 232.

52. Charles D. Sheldon, "Merchants and Society in Tokugawa Japan," *Modern Asian Studies* 17, no. 3 (1983): 479.

53. E. Herbert Norman, *Japan's Emergence as a Modern State: Political and Economic Problems of the Meiji Period* (1940; reprint, Vancouver: University of British Columbia Press, 2011), 107n8. Various purported inventory lists sampling the goods confiscated have been in circulation since the 1705 event, and an oft-quoted list includes "50 pairs of gold screens, 3 toy ships made of jewelry, 373 carpets, 10,050 *kin* of liquid gold, 273 large precious stones and numberless small stones, 2 chests of gold, 3,000 large gold coins, 120,000 *ryô* of *koban*, 85,000 *kwamme* of silver, 75,000 *kwan* of copper money, 150 boats, 730 storehouses, 17 storehouses for jewelry, 80 granaries, 80 storehouses for beans, 28 houses in Osaka, 64 houses in other places, a rice stipend for one *daimyô* amounting to 332 *koku* and 150 *chobu* of cypress forest."

54. *Lust, Commerce, and Corruption*, ed. Teeuwen and Nakai, 265n36.

55. J. Mark Ramseyer, "Thrift and Diligence: House Codes of Tokugawa Merchant Families," *Monumenta Nipponica* 34, no. 2 (1979): 217.

56. Yoshimura Norihisa and Hidekazu Sone, "Observations of Kongô Gumi's Corporate Creed: Research on the Corporate

Creed Observed in the Living Company in Japan," *The Annals of the Economic Society, Wakayama University* 10 (2006): 143–52.

57. *Sources of Japanese Tradition*, vol. 2, *1600 to 2000*, ed. William Theodore de Bary (New York: Columbia University Press, 2006), 267.

58. Ramseyer, "Thrift and Diligence," 217.

59. Matao Miyamoyo, "The Management Systems of Edo Period Merchant Houses," *Japanese Yearbook on Business History* 13 (1996): 11.

60. I am indebted to Robert Mangold for his translation of this inscription.

61. David Pollack, "Marketing Desire: Advertising and Sexuality in Edo Literature, Drama, and Art," in *Gender and Power in the Japanese Visual Field*, ed. Joshua Mostow, Norman Bryson, and Maribeth Graybill (Honolulu: University of Hawai'i Press. 2003), 81.

62. Donald Shively, "The Social Environment of Tokugawa Kabuki," in *Japanese Aesthetics and Culture: A Reader*, ed. Nancy G. Hume (Albany: State University of New York Press, 1995), 225.

63. Pollack, "Marketing Desire," 82.

64. David Pollack, "A Note on Advertising and the Arts of the Edo Period," *Oboegaki* 5, no. 1 (1995): 6.

65. Pollack, "Marketing Desire," 83.

66. Ichikawa Danjûrô XII, "*Kanban yomoyama banashi*," in Shôwa Neon, *Jidai o utsusu kanban*, 114.

67. Pollack, "Marketing Desire," 85.

68. Shôwa Neon, *Jidai o utsusu kanban*, 122.

69. Danjûrô XII, "*Kanban yomoyama banashi*," 122; Hayashi, *Edo kanban zufu*, 299.

70. Hayashi, *Edo kanban zufu*, 299.

71. "The Medicine Peddler: *Uriô uri*," trans. Laurence Kominz, in *Kabuki Plays on Stage*, vol. 1, *Brilliance and Bravado, 1697–1766*, ed. James R. Brandon and Samuel L. Leiter (Honolulu: University of Hawai'i Press, 2002), 98.

72. "The Medicine Peddler: *Uriô uri*," 96.

73. *Kôkoku wa kataru: Ado myûjiamu tôkyô shûzô sakuhinshû* (Tokyo: Advertising Museum of Tokyo, Yoshida Hideo Memorial Foundation, 2005), 28.

74. Shively, "Social Environment," 209.

75. Rebecca Salter, *Japanese Popular Prints: From Votive Slips to Playing Cards* (Honolulu: University of Hawai'i Press, 2006), 183.

76. Pollack, "A Note on Advertising," 6.

77. Alan Scott Pate, *Japanese Dolls: The Fascinating World of Ningyô* (North Clarendon, Vt.: Tuttle, 2008), 25.

78. Takao Sofue, "Anthropology in Japan: Historical Review and Modern Trends," *Biennial Review of Anthropology* 2 (1961): 173.

79. Tsuboi, *Kôshô gigei kanban kô*, 40.

80. Hayashi, *Edo kanban zufu*, 128.

81. Tsuboi, *Kôshô gigei kanban kô*, 34.

82. *Jinrinkinmôzui*, 212.

83. Tsuboi, *Kôshô gigei kanban kô*, 17.

84. The following profile is derived largely from Hayashi, *Edo kanban zufu*, 333.

85. Hayashi, *Edo kanban zufu*, 333.

86. Shuko Koyama, "History of the Morse Collection," in *Soul of Meiji: Edward Sylvester Morse, His Day to Day with Kindhearted People*, ed. Junichi Kobayashi and Shuko Koyama (Kyoto: Seigensha, 2013), 36.

87. Noah Y. McCormack, *Japan's Outcaste Abolition: The Struggle for National Inclusion and the Making of the Modern State* (New York: Routledge, 2012), 101.

88. *Documents Printed by Order of the House of Representatives of the Commonwealth of Massachusetts during the Session of the General Court of 1915*, Act No. 867, January 1915; the Peabody Essex Museum name was adopted in 1992 as a result of the formal merger with the Essex Institute.

89. Koyama, "History of the Morse Collection," 33.

90. Koyama, "History of the Morse Collection," 33.

91. Peabody Essex Museum, E4718.

92. Peabody Essex Museum, E4168.

93. Takamura Gorô, "*Kanban yomoyama banashi*," in Shôwa Neon, *Jidai o utsusu kanban*, 113.

94. *Kanban: The Art of the Japanese Shop Sign*, photography and design by Dana Levy and commentaries by Lea Sneider (San Francisco: Chronicle Books, 1983), 39.

95. Wang, *Shop Signs of Imperial China*, 14.

96. Tanabe, "*Kanban no sekai*," 10.

97. *Kanban: The Art of the Japanese Shop Sign*, 131–63.

98. Salter, *Japanese Popular Prints*, 73.

99. Naito Museum of Pharmaceutical Science and Industry, *Kusuri kôkoku*, 72.

100. See for example, Waseda University Library Collection, #10 08001 20; http://www.wul.waseda.ac.jp/kosho/bunko10/b10_8001_20/.

101. Waseda University Library Collection, #10 08001 0017; http://www.wul.waseda.ac.jp/kotenseki/html/bunko10/bunko10_08001_0017/index.html.

102. *Kanban: The Art of the Japanese Shop Sign*, 153.

103. Ernest W. Clement, "Japanese Medical Folk-lore, *Transactions of the Asiatic Society of Japan* 35 (1907): 17; "Patent Medicines in Japan," *British Medical Journal* 1, no. 2455 (January 18, 1908): 162.

104. Nishiyama Matsunosuke, *Edo Culture: Daily Life and Diversions in Urban Japan, 1600–1868*, trans. and ed. Gerald Groemer (Honolulu: University of Hawai'i Press, 1997), 141.

105. "Patent Medicines in Japan," 162; W. M. Royds, "Japanese Patent Medicines," *Transactions of the Asiatic Society of Japan* 35 (1907): 4.

106. Michael Lewis, *Becoming Apart: National Power and Local Politics in Toyama, 1868–1945* (Cambridge, Mass.: Harvard University Asia Center, 2000), 56.

107. "Patent Medicines in Japan," 162.

108. Naito Museum of Pharmaceutical Science and Industry, *Kusuri kôkoku*, 33.

109. Clement, "Japanese Medical Folk-lore," 18.

110. Susan L. Burns, "Marketing Health and the Modern Body: Patent Medicine Advertisements in Meiji-Taishô Japan," in *Looking Modern: East Asian Visual Culture from Treaty Ports to World War II*, ed. Jennifer Purtle and Hans Bjarne Thomsen (Chicago: Center for the Art of East Asia, 2009), 183.

111. Clement, "Japanese Medical Folk-lore," 16.

112. Burns, "Marketing Health and the Modern Body," 183.

113. Clement, "Japanese Medical Folk-lore," 16; Royds, "Japanese Patent Medicines," 55.

114. For a list of remedies and their names, see Clement, "Japanese Medical Folk-lore," 17–23.

115. Burns, "Marketing Health and the Modern Body," 184.

116. Naito Museum of Pharmaceutical Science and Industry, *Kusuri kôkoku*, 8.

117. Burns, "Marketing Health and the Modern Body," 174.

118. Naito Museum of Pharmaceutical Science and Industry, *Kusuri kôkoku*, 76.

119. Burns, "Marketing Health and the Modern Body," 192.

120. James L. McClain, "Space, Power, Wealth, and Status in Seventeenth-Century Osaka," in *Osaka, the Merchant's Capital of Early Modern Japan*, ed. James L. McClain and Wakita Osamu (Ithaca, N.Y.: Cornell University Press, 1999), 65.

121. Naito Museum of Pharmaceutical Science and Industry, *Kusuri kôkoku*, 81.

122. Santen Pharmaceutical Company history and profile, http://www.santen.com/en/about/outline/history.jsp.

123. Barnabas Tatsuya Suzuki, "Tobacco Culture in Japan," in *Smoke: A Global History of Smoking*, ed. Sander L. Gilman and Zhou Xun (London: Reaktion Books, 2004), 77.

124. Timon Screech, "Tobacco in Edo Period Japan," in *Smoke*, ed. Gilman and Xun, 92.

125. Suzuki, "Tobacco Culture," 78.

126. Tobacco and Salt Museum of Tokyo didactic panels.

127. Nôshômushô, *A Descriptive Catalogue of the Agricultural Products Exhibited in the World's Columbian Exhibition* (Tokyo: Seishibun-sha, 1893), 94.

128. Hayashi, *Edo kanban zufu*, 222.

129. Tsuboi, *Kôshô gigei kanban kô*, 27–30; Hayashi, *Edo kanban zufu*, 217–18.

130. Suzuki, "Tobacco Culture," 79.

131. Screech, "Tobacco in Edo," 94.

132. Hayashi, *Edo kanban zufu*, 134.

133. Tobacco and Salt Museum of Tokyo didactic panels.

134. Hayashi, *Edo kanban zufu*, 124.

135. Hayashi, *Edo kanban zufu*, 124.

136. Pollack, "Marketing Desire," 77.

137. *Kanban* (Tokyo: Tobacco and Salt Museum of Tokyo, 2001), 10, 26, 55.

138. *Kanban: The Art of the Japanese Shop Sign*, 138.

139. Hayashi, *Edo kanban zufu*, 269.

140. Reed Exhibitions press release, June 21, 2011, http://www.bk-w.jp/RXJP/RXJP_ISOT/documents/2011/en/Press-Release_vol5_takumi.pdf.

141. Hayashi, *Edo kanban zufu*, 270.

142. Teikoku Databank, http://www.tdb.co.jp/report/watching/press/pdf/s100901_80.pdf.

143. Joshua A. Fogel, "The Discovery of the Gold Seal in 1784 and the Waves of Historiography Ever Since," *Journal of Cultural Interaction in East Asia* 2 (2011): 15–32.

144. Richard Rubinger, *Popular Literacy in Early Modern Japan* (Honolulu: University of Hawai'i Press, 2007), 42.

145. Rubinger, *Popular Literacy in Early Modern Japan*, 45.

146. Hayashi, *Edo kanban zufu*, 65.

147. Hayashi, *Edo kanban zufu*, 60.

148. Hayashi, *Edo kanban zufu*, 60.

149. Yuki Allyson Honjo, *Japan's Early Experience of Contract Management in the Treaty Ports* (London: Routledge, 2013), 118.

150. *Jinrinkinmôzui*, 220.

151. Hayashi, *Edo kanban zufu*, 60.

152. Peabody Essex Museum, E16451.

153. Peabody Essex Museum, E15901.

154. Saga, "From the Traditional City to the Modern City," 50.

155. Peabody Essex Museum, E16458; Shôwa Neon, *Jidai o utsusu kanban*, 25.

156. Matsumiya, *Edo no kanban*, 107.

157. Hayashi, *Edo kanban zufu*, 225.

158. Hayashi, *Edo kanban zufu*, 224.

159. One modern version of the tabi is the *jika-tabi* with durable rubber soles, typically worn by construction workers, farmers, and pullers of jinrickshaw. The invention of these durable and thoroughly modern tabi is accredited to Ishibashi Shôjirô (1889–1976), founder of the Bridgestone Tire Company.

160. Ikumi Kaminishi, *Explaining Pictures: Buddhist Propaganda and Etoki Storytelling in Japan* (Honolulu: University of Hawai'i Press, 2006), 77.

161. *Jinrinkinmôzui*, 204.

162. Hayashi, *Edo kanban zufu*, 194; Matsumiya, *Edo no kanban*, 102.

163. Peabody Essex Museum, E15930.

164. Hayashi, *Edo kanban zufu*, 194; Matsumiya, *Edo no kanban*, 102.

165. Matsumiya, *Edo no kanban*, 109; Hayashi, *Edo kanban zufu*, 325.

166. Haruo Shirane, *Early Modern Japanese Literature: An Anthology, 1600–1900* (New York: Columbia University Press, 2004), 522.

167. Hayashi, *Edo kanban zufu*, 326.

168. Hayashi, *Edo kanban zufu*, 325.

169. Hayashi, *Edo kanban zufu*, 326, Illust. #874.

170. Robert S. Ellwood, "The Saigû: Princess and Priestess," *History of Religions* 7, no. 1 (1967): 35.

171. Gary L. Ebersole, "'Long Black Hair Like a Seat Cushion': Hair Symbolism in Japanese Popular Religion," in *Hair: Its Power and Meaning in Asian Cultures*, ed. Alf Hiltebeitel and Barbara D. Miller (Albany, N.Y.: State University of New York Press, 1998), 91–92.

172. Hayashi, *Edo kanban zufu*, 139.

173. Kazuko Ide, "Combing through Antiquity for Quality," *Japan Times*, April 24, 1999.

174. Hayashi, *Edo kanban zufu*, 117.

175. Hayashi, *Edo kanban zufu*, 122.

176. Hayashi, *Edo kanban zufu*, 123.

177. Hayashi, *Edo kanban zufu*, 124.

178. Faubion Bowers, *Japanese Theatre* (Rutland, Vt.: Tuttle Publishing, 1974), 61–62; Brandon, *Kabuki Plays on Stage: Brilliance and Bravado, 1697–1776*, 45.

179. Brandon, *Kabuki Plays on Stage: Brilliance and Bravado, 1697–1776*, 45.

180. Hayashi, *Edo kanban zufu*, 231.

181. Peabody Essex Museum, E16465.

182. Matsumiya, *Edo no kanban*, 126.

183. "The Freer Gallery of Art Acquires Renowned Object of Japanese Tea Culture," press release, Freer Gallery of Art and Arthur M. Sackler Gallery website, https://www.asia.si.edu/press/past/prTea.htm.

184. "Kikkoman's U.S. HQ Turns 50," *San Francisco Examiner*, June 5, 2007.

185. William Shurtleff and Akiko Aoyagi, *History of Soy Sauce (160 CE to 2012)*, Soyinfo Center website, 2012, http://www.soyinfocenter.com/books/153.

186. Matsumiya, *Edo no kanban*, 127.

187. Matsumiya, *Edo no kanban*, 127.

188. Tsuboi, *Kôshô gigei kanban kô*, 40.

189. Haruo Funabashi, *Timeless Ventures: 32 Japanese Companies That Imbibed 8 Principles of Longevity* (New Delhi: Tata McGraw-Hill Education, 2009), 48.

190. Peabody Essex Museum, E15920. The kanban itself was acquired from Yamanaka for the PEM through the Billings Fund in 1914.

191. Matsumiya, *Edo no kanban*, 131; Hayashi, *Edo kanban zufu*, 203.

192. *Jinrinkinmôzui*, 143. "Shaka" is the name used to refer to the historical Buddha (Gautama), while "the Buddha" could refer to any of the other four principal Buddhas: Dainichi, the central, cosmic Buddha; Amida, Lord of the Western Paradise; Miroku, the Buddha who is yet to come; and Yakushi, Lord of the Eastern Paradise. Lao-tzu's pointing west was likely a reference to the Amida Buddha. Together Dainichi, Amida, Shaka, Miroku, and Yakushi represent the five principal Buddhas, especially in the Shingon sect of Buddhism.

193. The term *yao-ya* is written with the kanji for "800" and "shop," simply indicating that the store sold many things, but it is essentially the same as a greengrocer.

194. Nishiyama, *Edo Culture*, 159.

195. Ayako Ehara, "Vegetables and Meals of *Daimyo* Living in Edo," Kikkoman website, http://www.kikkoman.co.jp/kiifc/foodculture/pdf_18/e_002_008.pdf.

196. McKelway, *Capitalscapes*, 156.

197. Ehara, "Vegetables and Meals."

198. Finding published information on the detailed history of niche food items is largely a task for the Internet. The most interesting and fun read regarding tsukudani is from Marky Star's *Japan This!* series: https://markystar.wordpress.com/tag/tsukudani/.

199. Numerous articles about hidden by-ways in Tokyo as well as articles related to traditional Japanese cuisine discuss Tsukudajima and tsukudani. See, for example, Kit Nagamura, "Casting around in Tsukudajima," *Japan Times*, May 29, 2011, http://www.japantimes.co.jp/life/2011/05/29/travel/casting-around-in-tsukudajima/#.Vn25NZOANBd.

200. Peabody Essex Museum, E16464; Shôwa Neon, *Jidai o utsusu kanban*, 47.

201. Tatiana Bouzdine-Chameeva and Mari Ninomiya, "A Japanese Sake Brewery Making Decisions," *Supply Chain Forum* 10, no. 1 (2009): 108–16.

202. *Jinrinkinmôzui*, 142.

203. Tsuboi, *Kôshô gigei kanban ko*, 11.

204. Peabody Essex Museum, E16441.

205. Peabody Essex Museum, E15917.

206. Edmond de Goncourt, *Utamaro* (New York: Parkstone, 2012), 119.

207. Shôwa Neon, *Jidai o utsusu kanban*, 78–80.

208. Peabody Essex Museum, E16534.

209. Peabody Essex Museum, E15931; *Kanban: The Art of the Japanese Shop Sign*, 132.

210. Peabody Essex Museum, E15546.

211. Edward E. Pratt, *Japan's Proto-Industrial Elite: The Economic Foundations of the Gônô* (Cambridge, Mass.: Harvard University Asia Center, 1999), 174.

212. National Research Institute of Brewing, "The Story of Sake," http://www.nrib.go.jp/English/sake/pdf/SakeNo01_en.pdf.

213. Victoria Lee, "Mold Cultures: Traditional Industry and Microbial Studies in Early Twentieth-Century Japan," in *New Perspectives on the History of Life Sciences and Agriculture*, ed. Denise Phillips and Sharon Kingsland (Cham: Springer, 2015), 236.

214. *Kanban: The Art of the Japanese Shop Sign*, 132; Shôwa Neon, *Jidai o utsusu kanban*, 78.

215. Timon Screech, *The Lens within the Heart: The Western Scientific Gaze and Popular Imagery in Later Edo Japan* (Honolulu: University of Hawai'i Press, 2002), 185; Hayashi, *Edo kanban zufu*, 297.

216. Screech, *The Lens within the Heart*, 189.

217. Hayashi, *Edo kanban zufu*, 264.

218. Hayashi, *Edo kanban zufu*, 298.

219. Hayashi, *Edo kanban zufu*, 297–98.

220. Karen M. Gerhart, *The Material Culture of Death in Medieval Japan* (Honolulu: University of Hawai'i Press, 2009), 93–94.

221. Peabody Essex Museum, E15924.

222. Matsumiya, *Edo no kanban*, 99.

223. Matsumiya, *Edo no kanban*, 99.

224. Hayashi, *Edo kanban zufu*, 257.

225. McClain, "Space, Power, Wealth, and Status in Seventeenth-Century Osaka," 64.

226. *Lust, Commerce, and Corruption*, ed. Teeuwen and Nakai, 10.

227. Hayashi, *Edo kanban zufu*, 320.

228. For an exceptionally thorough presentation of Japan's lunar-solar calendar and all its complexities, see J. Noel Chiappa, "The Japanese Lunar-Solar Calendar," http://mercury.lcs.mit.edu/~jnc/prints/calendar.html, which provides the long and short months, along with intercalary months, for every year from 1688 to 1872.

229. Jared Diamond, *Collapse: How Societies Choose to Fail or Succeed* (New York: Penguin, 2014), 297.

230. Peabody Essex Museum, E16484, Yamanaka, January 1916.

231. Peabody Essex Museum, E20988, Billings Fund, 1932.

232. Salter, *Japanese Popular Prints*, 183; a very helpful explanation of the early origins and derivations of karuta is found on the website http://cards.old.no/japan/.

233. *Jinrinkinmôzui*, 217.

234. *Jinrinkinmôzui*, 189.

235. Salter, *Japanese Popular Prints*, 183.

236. Shôwa Neon, *Jidai o utsusu kanban*, 15.

GLOSSARY

Andon kanban—
An *andon* is a traditional Japanese lantern with a fixed, as opposed to collapsible, framework. An *andon kanban* was a display lantern with the shop's name, or *yago* symbol, printed on the paper surround; this was particularly effective as nighttime advertising, especially for restaurants, teahouses, and houses of assignation. Also known as *mise saki andon*.

Baiyaku—
Patent medicine. Although patent-style medicines were popular throughout the Edo period, beginning in the Meiji era, large-scale manufacturers of *baiyaku* invested heavily in advertising, both print media and kanban, to help establish what today would be referred to as "brand identity." The majority of extant kanban from the Meiji era are for *kusuri-ya* (pharmacies) advertising baiyaku.

Chochin kanban—
A *chochin* is a traditional Japanese paper lantern that is designed to collapse and extend in an accordion-like manner. *Chochin kanban* functioned similarly to *andon kanban* but were collapsible. As with andon kanban, the shop's name or *yago* would have been printed on the paper covering. Also known as *mise saki chochin*.

Chôkoku-shi—
A carver of wooden kanban.

Chônin—
A townsman or merchant.

-dokoro—
Suffix used to indicate a shop or maker of a particular type of item. Similar to the suffix *-ya*.

Ema—
"Horse picture": a painted wooden votive plaque donated to a Shinto shrine to make a wish or show gratitude for good fortune. Typically structured as a rectangular panel with slightly peaked rooflines, *ema*-shaped kanban for a variety of trades were popular in the Edo period and comprise a particularly early form of kanban.

Gaku—
A carved name sign, usually used for a temple, shrine, or gate and consisting of a flat wooden panel mounted in a large, frequently elaborate frame.

Gaku hori—
A carver of wooden kanban or *gaku* that typically consisted of inscribed characters as opposed to imagery.

Gomen—
A general term in use throughout the Edo period meaning "permission," *gomen* was applied to kanban beginning in the Meiji era to indicate that a given business mark, or *yago*, had been registered with the government. This terminology was mandated to be included on kanban for nationally distributed products, particularly *baiyaku* (patent medicines), in the early Meiji era, from roughly 1870 to 1884.

Goro awase—
"Word battle": *goro awase* refers to a kanban employing a subtle play on words to communicate the product sold or service offered.

Hako kanban—
"Box sign": a kanban constructed of a simple wooden box bottom that rested directly on the ground, usually immediately in front of the shop. It also featured a stretched paper upper section (similar to an *andon kanban*) that bore images of the product sold, a description, and the shop's name and *yago*. *Hako kanban*, like many kanban forms, were usually brought into the shop each night for protection. The inherent fragility of the paper necessitated frequent repair work.

Hangi-gaki—
An artisan entrusted with sketching out the lettering to be carved into kanban and *gaku*.

Hanji mono—
Nearly synonymous with *goro awase*, the term *hanji mono* speaks to creative wordplay or puns in the imagery of the kanban, such as associative meanings or homonyms (or near homonyms).

Hanshida-gaki—
A craftsman responsible for writing out the characters to be carved into a kanban or *gaku*. Synonymous with *hangi-gaki*.

Hatta—
A flag flown above a shop, frequently decorated with the shop's *yago*.

Hikifuda—
A printed advertising flyer that was cheap to manufacture and widely distributed, particularly popular in the *baiyaku* (patent medicine) industry.

Hioke—
An awning that helped to shield a shop from the sun and elements. Frequently emblazoned with the shop's name or *yago*, the *hioke* functioned as an advertisement, much like the noren shop curtain.

Hiragana—
Native Japanese phonetically based script, as opposed to the Chinese-derived *kanji* ideographs.

Jitsubutsu kanban—
"Actual object sign": *jitsubutsu kanban* originally referred to the practice of hanging or displaying actual examples of the products sold, from textiles to palanquins to footwear. During the Edo period, jitsubutsu kanban also included shop signs that appended examples of products to the signboards, frequently accompanied by carved or painted inscriptions.

Ka-mon—
A family crest. This early form of heraldry prefigured the use of *yago* to represent shops.

Kanban—
The general term for a shop sign or signboard used in advertising is composed of two characters: "*kan,*" meaning "to see," and "*ban,*" meaning "board." It is unclear when the term itself entered the Japanese language, but its use has been recorded as early as the Nara period in regulations involving the *tôzai ichi* monthly markets. Prior to this, the term *mokkan* was used, referring to written announcements on boards. The Engishiki compilation of rules governing commerce, compiled in 905–927, mandated that every shop had to display a kanban for its specific product.

Kanban-gaki—
An itinerant craftsman who specialized in the creation and repair of *shoji, hako, andon,* and *chochin kanban*, all of which used stretched paper as the advertising surface. Easily damaged and in frequent need of repair, these kanban forms created an entire subindustry based on their maintenance.

Kanban-shi—
A general term for a craftsman who made kanban of all forms.

Kanji—
Ideograph-based characters derived from the Chinese writing system.

Kankyo—
The term *kankyo* (government permission) was created by the Meiji government as part of its censorship regulations for print media. Kankyo was also appended to *moji kanban* related to patent medicines and other nationally distributed products, such as certain brands of sake. The mandated use of the term kankyo, or alternatively *gomen* (permission) and *naimushô menkyo* (licensed by the Home Ministry), was generally in effect from 1870 to 1884. After 1884, the universal phrase *tôroku shôhyô* (registered trademark) was required.

Kansei—
An alternative term for a *kanban-shi*, or sign maker.

Kattamen kanban—
A one-sided kanban that was frequently mounted flush with the wall.

Kobu gôyo—
A phrase included on a kanban to indicate that the shop was an authorized supplier to the samurai and noble classes.

Mitate—
A term roughly equivalent to "parody," *mitate* speaks to the depiction of a well-recognized figure from history, religion, or popular lore but used in an unusual or unorthodox way. Mitate was a device employed by many craftsmen, from classically trained painters to doll makers to the makers of kanban.

Moji kanban—
"Letter sign": a kanban that relied on the written word rather than imagery to communicate a shop's message. Writing styles varied from phonetic hiragana to ideographic kanji. This style of kanban became increasingly popular beginning in the Meiji era with the increase in general literacy among the populace, and they were employed to great effect by shops selling patent medicines.

Mokei kanban—
"Model sign": a style of kanban that employed carved reproductions of the items sold or used three-dimensional carvings to represent a service rendered. *Mokei kanban* can refer to standalone sculpture or to sculptural elements applied to a board with verbiage.

Mono-gaki—
An alternative term for a *kanban-gaki*.

Naimushô-menkyo—
Beginning in the Meiji era, the government began to tighten regulations on the advertising of certain products, particularly *baiyaku* (patent medicines), as part of a modernized taxation system. *Naimushô-menkyo*, which means "licensed by the Home Ministry," was an early form of product licensing. Along with the phrase *gomen* (permission), it was generally mandated from 1870 to 1884. After 1884, the universal phrase *tôroku shôhyô* (registered trademark) was stipulated instead.

Nazo kanban—
A *nazo*, or "hidden meaning," kanban was a sign that used indirect imagery to advertise a marginal or culturally sensitive product or service. Meat such as boar, horse, or deer, for instance, was advertised discreetly with playing cards, owing to the Buddhist prohibition against consuming these items.

Nikai kanban—
"Second-story sign": nearly synonymous with *yane kanban* (roof kanban), this refers to a permanent, roof-mounted kanban, usually placed under the eaves between the first and second stories of a shop. Such a kanban tended to have its own tiled roof structure as protection from the elements.

Noki kanban—
A general overarching term for both *shitta kanban* and *sage kanban*, *noki kanban* refers to a kanban that was suspended street-side in front of the shop, frequently underneath the overhanging eaves (*noki*) of the roofline as protection from the weather. It is also referred to as a *nokizuri kanban*. When double sided and hung perpendicular to the street, it is called a *shitta kanban*. When single sided and hung flush with the wall, it is known as a *sage kanban* or *kattamen kanban*.

Noren—
Cotton or *asa* (hemp) curtains suspended horizontally along shop fronts and typically dyed a dark indigo blue, frequently stenciled with the shop's *yago* or name.

Oki kanban—
A freestanding screen also known as a *tsuitate kanban*, an *oki kanban* was usually placed on the tatami mat floor in the interior of the shop, but was still visible from the street. Oki kanban also served as room dividers and privacy screens, depending on scale and placement.

Rakuchû rakugai zu—
"Scenes in and around the capital": *rakuchû rakugai zu* depicted a slightly aerial view of the capital (Kyoto), illustrating its streets, bridges, temples, theaters, rivers, and other places of interest. Though this genre of painting originated as depictions of Kyoto to help document its reconstruction and growing prosperity in the opening decades of the Edo period, rakuchû rakugai zu were also created for Osaka, Edo, and other urban centers. Their generally accurate depictions of shops and merchant culture make them an invaluable resource for the study of kanban.

Sage kanban—
"Hanging kanban": a kanban typically stored indoors at night and displayed outside during the day. *Sage kanban* typically featured iron suspension loops at the top that allowed for simple installation. Sage and *shitta kanban* also frequently had side handles to help not only with carrying the sign in and out of the shop each day but also with toting it through the streets.

Shinôkôshô—
This term, referring to nobility (*shin*)—farmer (*nô*)—craftsman (*kô*)—merchant (*shô*), encapsulates the rigid Confucian-based hierarchy, which placed the merchant at the bottom tier of society.

Shitta kanban—
A double-sided kanban typically hung perpendicular to the street so that both faces could be viewed by passersby. Though employed by many product makers and service industries, *shitta kanban* were particularly popular among *kusuri-ya* (medicine shops), which advertised two medicines on the same sign.

Shoji kanban—
A sign that featured painted lettering or designs on the paper panels of shoji, which frequently served as sliding doors for shops, teahouses, and restaurants—a particularly popular and inexpensive form of advertising.

Shôkei kanban—
A highly ornamented kanban that was typically designed for interior display rather than street-side advertising. *Shôkei kanban* tended to feature refined and elegant components, inlaid materials, extensive use of gold leaf and gold lacquer, and a high level of artistry.

Shokunin zukushi-e—
An early Edo-period genre of painting that focuses on craftsmen (*shokunin*), and therefore an important source of information on trade and craft practices.

Tate kanban—
A sign mounted on a tall, freestanding post or pillar installed in the roadway just in front of a shop, frequently involving elaborate construction techniques, a sheltering tiled roof, and decorative carvings, in addition to the main kanban element itself. *Tate kanban* were most common in Edo, where the roads were wide enough to accommodate these elaborate structures.

Tôroku shôhyô—
On June 7, 1884, the Meiji government initiated the Shôhyô Jôrei (Trade Name Registration Law), which, among other things, mandated the inclusion of the phrase *tôroku shôhyô* (registered trademark) on kanban created for nationally distributed items, particularly *baiyaku* (patent medicines) and certain brands of sake. The trademark registration applied largely to the business *yago*, or crest.

Tsuitate kanban—
A freestanding kanban executed in the manner of a *tsuitate*, or room divider. These kanban varied dramatically in size, from a small screen that might be placed on top of a low table, to a truly massive one that literally formed a wall or room divider. Tsuitate kanban were rarely designed to be displayed out of doors, and many received quite elaborate and luxurious treatments, such as mother-of-pearl inlay or gold-lacquer embellishments, which qualified them as *shôkei kanban* as well. Tsuitate kanban are also referred to as *shôritsu kanban*, alluding to this decorative element.

-ya—
Suffix indicating a house or shop. For example, a *geta-ya* was a shop selling *geta* clogs. Similarly, a shop using the image of the god of daily wealth (Daikoku) as its symbol would have been known as the Daikoku-ya.

Yago—
A *yago* or *shônoin yago* was a crest adopted by a merchant to identify his shop. Clearly deriving from the *ka-mon*, or heraldic symbol, used by the noble and samurai classes, business yago were often images that helped to identify the shop's name but not necessarily convey a sense of the specific product sold or service offered; they are the direct precursors to modern-day corporate logos.

Yane kanban—
"Roof-mounted kanban": a permanently installed sign that usually required the construction of a small tiled roof to protect it from the elements.

Yôki kanban—
A kanban in the shape of the container in which a given product was sold, sometimes with an inscription as well. The most common forms of *yôki kanban* were *tsubo* jars used for the storing of tea leaves, vinegar (*su*), and soy sauce (*tamari*).

BIBLIOGRAPHY

Japanese-Language Sources

Hayashi Yoshikazu. *Edo kanban zufu*. Tokyo: Miki Shobô, 1977.

Hoshino Kinya and Funabiki Etsuko. "Nokogiri kaji: Nakaya Kyusaku." *Takenaka Dôgu Hakubutsukan zasshi* 20 (2010).

Ichikawa Danjûrô XII. "*Kanban yomoyama banasahi*." In Shôwa Neon, *Jidai o utsusu kanban*.

Kobayashi Junichi. *ŌEdo happyaku-yachô*. Tokyo: Edo-Tokyo Museum, 2003.

Matsumiya Saburô. *Edo no kanban*. Tokyo: Tôhô Shoin, 1959.

Naito Museum of Pharmaceutical Science and Industry. *Kusuri kanban*. Kawashima: Naito Museum of Pharmaceutical Science and Industry, 1986.

——. *Kusuri kôkoku*. Kawashima: Naito Museum of Pharmaceutical Science and Industry, 1995.

Oka Hideyuki. "*Kanban no kataji to moji*." In *Bakumatsu, Meiji kanbanten*. Tokyo: Nihon Terebi Hôsômô, 1984.

Ritto History Museum. *Edo no kanban: Moji no messêji*. Ritto: Ritto History Museum, 1992.

Shôwa Neon. *Jidai o utsusu kanban*. Tokyo: Shôwa Neon Takamura Kanban Museum, 2010.

Takamura Gorô. "*Kanban yomoyama banasahi*." In Shôwa Neon, *Jidai o utsusu kanban*, 112–29.

Tanabe Satoru. "*Kanban no sekai—sono rekishi mizokuteki sokumen*." In *Bakumatsu, Meiji kanbanten*, 9–14. Tokyo: Nihon Terebi Hôsômô, 1984.

Tani Minezô. *Nihon okugai kôkokushi*. Tokyo: Iwasaki Bijutsusha, 1989.

Tsuboi Shôgorô. *Kôshô gigei kanban kô*. Tokyo: Tetsugaku Shoin, 1887.

Western-Language Sources

Aoki, Michiko Y., and Margaret B. Dardess. "The Popularization of Samurai Values: A Sermon by Hoshoi Heishû." *Monumenta Nipponica* 31, no. 4 (1976): 393–413.

Bodart-Bradley, Beatrice M. *Kaempfer's Japan: Tokugawa Culture Observed*. Honolulu: University of Hawai'i Press, 1999.

Bowers, Faubion. *Japanese Theatre*. Rutland, Vt.: Tuttle Publishing, 1974.

Burns, Susan L. "Marketing Health and the Modern Body: Patent Medicine Advertisements in Meiji-Taishô Japan." In *Looking Modern: East Asian Visual Culture from Treaty Ports to World War II*, ed. Jennifer Purtle and Hans Bjarne Thomsen, 173–96. Chicago: Center for the Art of East Asia, University of Chicago, 2009.

Clement, Ernest W. "Japanese Medical Folk-lore." *Transactions of the Asiatic Society of Japan* 35 (1907): 15–32.

de Goncourt, Edmond. *Utamaro*. New York: Parkstone International, 2012.

Diamond, Jared. *Collapse: How Societies Choose to Fail or Succeed*. New York: Penguin, 2014.

Dobson, Sebastian. "Split Visions: Wilhelm Heine and Albert Berg in Japan." In Dobson and Saaler, eds., *Under Eagle Eyes*, 125–91.

Dobson, Sebastian, and Sven Saaler, eds. *Under Eagle Eyes: Lithographs, Drawings & Photographs from the Prussian Expedition to Japan, 1860–61*. Munich: Iudicium Verlag, 2011.

Dunn, Charles J. *Everyday Life in Imperial Japan*. New York: Dorset Press, 1969.

Ebersole, Gary L. "'Long Black Hair Like a Seat Cushion': Hair Symbolism in Popular Japanese Religion." In *Hair: Its Power and Meaning in Asian Cultures*, ed. Alf Hiltebeitel and Barbara D. Miller, 75–104. Albany, N.Y.: State University of New York Press, 1998.

Ellwood, Robert S. "The Saigû: Princess and Priestess." *History of Religions* 7, no. 1 (1967): 35–60.

Farris, William Wayne. "Trade, Money, and Merchants in Nara Japan." *Monumenta Nipponica* 53, no. 3 (1998): 303–34.

Fleishman, David A. "Spectacles in Japan." Antique Spectacles website, http://www.antiquespectacles.com/topics/japanese/japanese_influence.htm.

Fogel, Joshua A. "The Discovery of the Gold Seal in 1784 and the Waves of Historiography Ever Since." *Journal of Cultural Interconnection in East Asia* 2 (2011): 15–32.

"The Freer Gallery of Art Acquires Renowned Object of Japanese Tea Culture," press release, Freer Gallery of Art and Arthur M. Sackler Gallery website, https://www.asia.si.edu/press/past/prTea.htm.

Fujioka, Rika. "The Development of Japanese Department Stores in the Early 20th Century—The Process of Western Adaptation." Osaka University of Economics. http://www.gla.ac.uk/media/media_167604_en.pdf.

Fukami, Giichi. "Japanese Department Stores." *Journal of Marketing* 18, no. 1 (1953): 41–49.

Funabashi, Haruo. *Timeless Ventures: 32 Japanese Companies That Imbibed 8 Principles of Longevity*. New Delhi: Tata McGraw-Hill Education, 2009.

Gerhart, Karen M. *The Material Culture of Death in Medieval Japan*. Honolulu: University of Hawai'i Press, 2009.

Gibney, Frank B. "The Marks of a Japanese Merchant." In *Kanban: The Art of the Japanese Shop Sign*, photography and design by Dana Levy and commentaries by Lea Sneider, 7–29. San Francisco: Chronicle Books, 1983.

Grimmer-Solem, Erik. "German Social Science, Meiji Conservatism, and the Peculiarities of Japanese History." *Journal of World History* 16, no. 2 (2005): 187–222.

Honjo, Yuki Allyson. *Japan's Early Experience of Contract Management in the Treaty Ports*. London: Routledge, 2013.

Ide, Kazuko. "Combing through Antiquity for Quality." *Japan Times*, April 24, 1999.

"Japanese Folk Medicines." *British Medical Journal* 2, no. 2429 (July 20, 1907): 165.

Kameda-Madar, Kazuko. "Shokunin Zukushi-e, 'Pictures of People of Various Occupations in Their Workshops' in Early Modern Japan." *Kaikodo Journal* 31 (2015): 238–46.

Kaminishi, Ikumi. *Explaining Pictures: Buddhist Propaganda and Etoki Storytelling in Japan*. Honolulu: University of Hawai'i Press, 2006.

Kominz, Laurence R., trans. "The Medicine Peddler: *Uriô uri*." In *Kabuki Plays on Stage*, vol. 1, *Brilliance and Bravado, 1697–1766*, edited by James R. Brandon and Samuel L. Leiter, 96ff. Honolulu: University of Hawai'i Press, 2002.

Koop, Albert J. *Guide to the Japanese Textiles: Part II, Costume*. London: Victoria and Albert Museum, 1920.

Koyama, Shuko. "History of the Morse Collection." In *Soul of Meiji: Edward Sylvester Morse, His Day to Day with Kindhearted People*, edited by Junichi Kobayashi and Shuko Koyama. Kyoto: Seigensha, 2013.

Lee, Victoria. "Mold Cultures: Traditional Industry and Microbial Studies in Early Twentieth-Century Japan." In *New Perspectives on the History of Life Sciences and Agriculture*, edited by Denise Phillips and Sharon Kingsland, 231–52. Cham: Springer, 2015.

Lewis, Michael. *Becoming Apart: National Power and Local Politics in Toyama, 1868–1945.* Cambridge, Mass.: Harvard University Asia Center, 2000.

McClain, James L. *Japan, a Modern History.* New York: Norton, 2002.

——. "Space, Power, Wealth, and Status in Seventeenth-Century Osaka." In *Osaka, the Merchant's Capital of Early Modern Japan*, edited by James L. McClain and Wakitu Osamu, 44–79. Ithaca, N.Y.: Cornell University Press, 1999.

McKelway, Matthew Philip. *Capitalscapes: Folding Screens and Political Imagination in Late Medieval Kyoto*. Honolulu: University of Hawai'i Press, 2006.

Miyamoyo, Matao. "The Management Systems of Edo Period Merchant Houses." *Japanese Yearbook on Business History* 13 (1997): 131–32.

National Bank of Commerce in New York. "Raw Silk." *Commerce Monthly* 1, no. 9 (1920): 23–30.

Nishiyama Matsunosuke. *Edo Culture: Daily Life and Diversions in Urban Japan, 1600–1868*, translated and edited by Gerald Groemer. Honolulu: University of Hawai'i Press, 1997.

Norman, Herbert E. *Japan's Emergence as a Modern State: Political and Economic Problems of the Meiji Period.* 1940; reprint, Vancouver: University of British Columbia Press, 2011.

Nôshômushô [Ministry of Agriculture and Commerce]. *A Descriptive Catalogue of the Agricultural Products Exhibited in the World's Columbian Exhibition.* Tokyo: Seishibun-sha, 1893.

Otori, Ranzaburo. "The Acceptance of Western Medicine in Japan." *Monumenta Nipponica* 19, nos. 3–4 (1964): 254–74.

Pate, Alan Scott. *Ningyô: The Art of the Japanese Doll*. Boston: Tuttle, 2005.

——. *Japanese Dolls: The Fascinating World of Ningyô*. North Clarendon, Vt.: Tuttle, 2008.

"Patent Medicines in Japan." *British Medical Journal* 1, no. 2455 (January 18, 1908): 161–63.

"Playing Cards from Japan." *Science* 17, no. 435 (June 5, 1891): 316.

Pollack, David. "Marketing Desire: Advertising and Sexuality in Edo Literature, Drama, and Art." In *Gender and Power in the Japanese Visual Field*, edited by Joshua Mostow, Norman Bryson, and Maribeth Graybill, 71–88. Honolulu: University of Hawai'i Press, 2003.

——. "A Note on Advertising and the Arts of the Edo Period." *Oboegaki* 5, no. 1 (1995): 6–8.

Pratt, Edward E. *Japan's Proto-industrial Elite: The Economic Foundations of the Gônô*. Cambridge, Mass.: Harvard University Asia Center, 1999.

Ramseyer, J. Mark. "Thrift and Diligence: House Codes of Tokugawa Merchant Families." *Monumenta Nipponica* 34, no. 2 (1979): 209–30.

Royds, W. M. "Japanese Patent Medicines." *Transactions of the Asiatic Society of Japan* 35 (1907): 1–14.

Saga, Ashita. "From the Traditional City to the Modern City: Based on Studies of Urban Regional Societies in 19th Century Osaka." *UrbanScope: e-Journal of the Urban-Culture Research Center* 3 (2012): 34–54.

Sallant, Catherine. "Pair Sheds New Light on L.A.'s Claim to Neon Fame." *Los Angeles Times*, December 3, 2013.

Salter, Rebecca. *Japanese Popular Prints: From Votive Slips to Playing Cards.* Honolulu: University of Hawai'i Press, 2006.

Satô, Dôshin. *Modern Japanese Art and the Meiji State: The Politics of Beauty*. Translated by Hiroshi Nara. Los Angeles: Getty Research Institute, 2011.

Schoelwer, Susan P. "Rediscovering the Public Art of Early American Inn Signs." In *Lions & Eagles & Bulls: Early American Tavern & Inn Signs from the Connecticut Historical Society*, edited by Susan P. Schoelwer, 2–13. Hartford, Conn.: Connecticut Historical Society in association with Princeton University Press, 2000.

Screech, Timon. *The Lens within the Heart: The Western Scientific Gaze and Popular Imagery in Later Edo Japan.* Honolulu: University of Hawai'i Press, 2002.

——. "Tobacco in Edo Period Japan." In *Smoke: A Global History of Smoking*, edited by Sander L. Gilman and Zhou Xun, 92–99. London: Reaktion Books, 2004.

Sheldon, Charles D. "Merchants and Society in Tokugawa Japan." *Modern Asian Studies* 17, no. 3 (1983): 477–88.

Shibusawa, Keizô. *Japanese Life and Culture in the Meiji Era.* Tokyo: Ôbunsha, 1958.

Shirane, Haruo. *Early Modern Japanese Literature: An Anthology, 1600–1900*. New York: Columbia University Press, 2004.

Shively, Donald H. "The Social Environment of Tokugawa Kabuki." In *Japanese Aesthetics and Culture: A Reader*, edited by Nancy G. Hume, 193–244. Albany: State University of New York Press, 1995.

Shurtleff, William, and Akiko Aoyagi. *History of Soy Sauce (160 CE to 2012)*. Soyinfo Center website, 2012, http://www.soyinfocenter.com/books/153.

"A Skein of Silk: How It Is Manufactured in Japan." *Wanganui Chronicle* 47, no. 1218 (April 4, 1904): 2.

Sofue, Takao. "Anthropology in Japan: Historical Review and Modern Trends." *Biennial Review of Anthropology* 2 (1961): 173–214.

Suzuki, Barnabas Tatsuya. "Tobacco Culture in Japan." In *Smoke: A Global History of Smoking*, edited by Sander L. Gilman and Zhou Xun, 76–83. London: Reaktion Books, 2004.

Teeuwen, Mark, and Kate Wildman Nakai, eds. *Lust, Commerce, and Corruption: An Account of What I Have Seen and Heard, by an Edo Samurai*. New York: Columbia University Press, 2014.

Teruoka, Yasutaka. "The Pleasure Quarters and Tokugawa Culture." In *18th Century Japan: Culture and Society*, edited by C. Andrew Gerstle, 3–32. New York: Routledge, 1989.

Toi, Satoshi. "'Karuta' Card Store Still Going Strong 90 Years On." *Japan Times*, September 4, 2013.

Tonomura, Hitomi. "Forging the Past: Medieval Counterfeit Documents." *Monumenta Nipponica* 40, no. 1 (1985): 69–96.

Umemura, Maki. "Reviving Tradition: Patients and the Shaping of Japan's Traditional Medicines Industry." In *The Historical Consumer: Consumption and Everyday Life in Japan, 1850–2000*, edited by Penelope Francks and Janet Hunter, 176–206. New York: Palgrave Macmillan, 2012.

Vaporis, Constantine Nomikos. *Tour of Duty: Samurai, Military Service in Edo, and the Culture of Early Modern Japan*. Honolulu: University of Hawai'i Press, 2008.

——. *Voices of Early Modern Japan: Contemporary Accounts of Daily Life during the Age of the Shoguns*. Boulder, Colo.: Westview Press, 2014.

Vincent, Margaret C. "'Some suitable Signe . . . for the direction of Strangers': Signboards and the Enterprise of Innkeeping in Connecticut." In *Lions & Eagles & Bulls: Early American Tavern & Inn Signs from the Connecticut Historical Society*, edited by Susan P. Schoelwer, 36–55. Hartford, Conn.: Connecticut Historical Society in association with Princeton University Press, 2000.

Wang Shucun. *Shop Signs of Imperial China*. Translated by Li Xin. Beijing: Foreign Language Press, 2006.

Wolf, Bryan J. "Signs of the Times: A Brief Cultural History of Sign Painting." In *Lions & Eagles & Bulls: Early American Tavern & Inn Signs from the Connecticut Historical Society*, edited by Susan P. Schoelwer, 14–21. Hartford, Conn.: Connecticut Historical Society in association with Princeton University Press, 2000.

Yi, Feng. "Shop Signs and Visual Culture in Republican Beijing." *European Journal of East Asian Studies* 6, no. 1 (2007): 103–28.

Yoshimura, Norihisa, and Hidekazu Sone. "Observations of Kongô Gumi's Corporate Creed: Research on the Corporate Creed Observed in the Living Company in Japan." *The Annals of the Economic Society, Wakayama University* 10 (2006): 143–52.

Zeng, Kangmin. *Dragon Gate: Competitive Examinations and Their Consequences*. London: Cassell, 1999.

MINGEI INTERNATIONAL MUSEUM

ANCESTORS TO THE FUTURE

Providing for the Museum in their estate plans

Barbara C. Adachi*
Jane M. Ahring*
Claire Anderson
Anonymous
Norm Applebaum, AIA
Jan Bart
Maurine B. Beinbrink
Angelina Boaz
Robyn Bottomley
Patricia C. Dwinnell Butler*
Carmela Caldera Bowen
J. Dallas and Mary H. Clark*
Theodore Cohen
Kathleen and Joel Cook
Roger Cornell, M.D.
Florence B. Covell
Kathryn Crane
Katy and Mike Dessent
Alice and Doug Diamond
DeWitt Drury
James and Madeleine Kemp-Eisen
Michele Fergoda
Fran and John Ferris
Walter Fitch, III*
Audrey S. Geisel
Mrs. Milton D. Goldberg*
Jean Hahn and John I.* Hardy
Carol F. Hinrichs
Jerry and Linda Hirshberg
Marilee Hong
Steve and Nancy Howard
Frances Hunter*
Robert Bruce Inverarity*
Gladys Lucille Johnstone*
Wayne S. Julien
Charmaine and Maurice Kaplan*
Louisa S. Kassler*
Maurice M. Kawashima
Maureen Pecht King
Rita Krieger
Daina A. Krigens and Hugh Lawrence
Greg La Chapelle*
Theresa F. Lai
Clara and L. Curtis* Larson
Charlotte G. and Don B. Leiffer*
Theodora F. Lewis
Robin J. Lipman
Martha Longenecker*
Josephine R. MacConnell
The Mayers Family Trust
Christa McReynolds
Elaine and Lane McVey
Juanita H. Dahlstrom Miller*
Nancy L. Nenow
Carolyn and Tom Owen-Towle
Gwendolyn E. Peacher*
Sydney Martin Roth*
Dr. Beverly H. Sheiffer*
Curt Sherman
Ron Shore In Memory of Patrice Lekas
Rob Sidner
Nancy E. Snyder
Dorothy Day Stewart*
Leona Mercer Vennard*
Dorothy Vogler

Joanne C. and Frank R.* Warren
Bert Waxler
Therese T. Whitcomb
Thomas A. White
Terri Peterson Zimdars

*deceased

FOUNDER'S CIRCLE

Leading growth of the Museum's collection and permanent endowment

Carol and Martin Dickinson, Chairs

Marcy Carsey and Susan Baerwald
Myron Eichen Memorial Fund at The San Diego Foundation
Audrey Geisel, the Dr. Seuss Fund at The San Diego Foundation
Ingrid B. Hibben and Victor La Magna
Joan and Irwin Jacobs
Maureen and Charles King
Courtenay McGowen
Audrey S. Ratner
Pat and John Seiber
Rob Sidner
Brinley Thomas
Hope Turney
Jo and Howard Weiner

CONNOISSEURS

Dedicated to building the Museum's collection

Jan Bart, Chair

Norman Blachford and Peter Cooper
Carmela Caldera Bowen
Ann Craig
Maurice M. Kawashima
Christa McReynolds
Carolyn and Tom Owen-Towle
Mary and Ron Taylor
Frances Hamilton White
Al and Armi Williams

CORPORATE, FOUNDATION AND GOVERNMENT SUPPORTERS

Akaloa Resource Foundation
Allison and Robert Price Family Foundation
Anne Ray Charitable Trust
Anonymous
Azuki Sushi
Bead Society of San Diego County
Bettina Hahn Events
Bloomingdale's
Buddhist Temple of San Diego
California Arts Council
City of San Diego Commission for Arts and Culture
The County of San Diego and Supervisor Ron Roberts
David C. Copley Foundation
The Donald C. and Elizabeth M. Dickinson Foundation
Richard and Beverly Fink Family Foundation
French Masserini Funds
KPBS
Las Patronas
Modern San Diego
Muzita Abyssinian Bistro
Neyenesch Printers
Patrons of the Prado
Qualcomm Foundation
ResMed Foundation
Rising Arts Leaders San Diego
Royal Little Family Foundation
Stone Brewing Co.
Takeda Pharmaceuticals
Televisa Channel 12
U.S. Bank
UBS Financial Services
Union Bank Foundation
Warren Family Foundation
Waters Fine Foods & Catering
Wells Fargo Foundation
Westlake Private Wealth Management
Walter J. and Betty C. Zable Foundation
Zephyr Partners

THE DIRECTOR'S CIRCLE

Furnishing core support for the Museum's exhibitions

Patricia Alvarez de los Cobos and
Stephen Saunderson
Anonymous
Norm Applebaum, AIA and Barbara Roper
Cia and Larry J. Barron
Darlene Bates
Maurine B. Beinbrink and James Algert
LaDean Berry and Lauren Murphy
Barry and Seonaid McArthur Bielinski
April Blankfort
Mr. and Mrs. Robert A. Bowden
Molly and Charles Brazell
Norman Bricker and Bonnie Anderson
Althea Brimm
Gordon Brodfuehrer
Terri Bryson
Louisa Campagna
Roger Cornell, M.D.
Kathryn Crane
Carlos Cristiani
Elisabeth Crouch
Patricia Cué
Alison Cummings and Phil Pryde
Jim and Mary Dawe
Katy and Mike Dessent
Alice and Doug Diamond
Mary Dilligan
Clive E. and Olivia E. Dorman
Lorrain and John Duffy
Drs. Steve Eilenberg and Marie Tartar
Connie K. Golden
Mr. and Mrs. Michael E. Hallor
Susan Hayes
Richard C. Helmstetter
Thomas and Alison Henry
Lawrence and Suzanne Hess
Carol F. Hinrichs
Jerry and Linda Hirshberg
Steve and Nancy Howard
Dr. Sheila Johnson
Gary Jugum
Mr. and Mrs. Frederick Kleinbub
Bonnie Knoke
Theresa F. Lai
Drs. Eli Shefter and Elizabeth Lancaster
Robin J. Lipman
Carroll Long
Jennifer Luce
Bosco and Debbie Luján
Beverly Maloof
Ernie Meadows
Ellen Merewether
Carol Miller
Rena Minisi and Rich Paul
Nessa Moll
Marian Moses In Memory of My Daughter Deb
Rebecca and David Mrachek
Lyn Nelson
Thomas and Patricia Nickols
Alexis and Amber O'Banion
Lawrence Paull and Marcy Bolotin
Susan and Tom Polakiewicz
The Honorable Anne-Imelda Radice, PhD
Mary M. Rathbun
Joan Reilly and Satinder Raina
John and Dannie Sue Reis
Jan and Doug Rightmer
Dr. and Mrs. Alan Robbins
T. Wayne and Christine Rounsavell
Mrs. William C. Ruzich
Robert and Lora Sandroni
Gail Schneider and David Matlin
Curt Sherman
Virginia and Lawrence Sherwood
Jack C. and Bonnie Sipe
Walter Smoyer
Nancy E. Snyder
Joel and Dotti Sollender
Jeanette Stevens
Bonnie and Ray Stewart
Gwen Stoughton
J. L. Tanzer
Molly Thornton
Susan and Richard Ulevitch
Robert Wallace
Nell Waltz
Joanne C. Warren
Mary Kay Waters
Abby and Ray Weiss
Therese T. Whitcomb
Carolyn Yorston-Wellcome and Bard Wellcome
Terri Peterson Zimdars

As of July 15, 2016

INDEX

Page numbers in italics refer to illustrated material.

armorers (*yoroi-ya*), 25, 154–55, *155*

barbershops (*kami yui dokoro*), 31, *31*, 113, *113*, 115
  See also wig shops (*katsura-ya*)
bathhouses, 15–16, *15*
Berg, Albert (1825–1884), 38–41, *38*, *40*, 76
blade shops. *See* tool shops (*dôgu-ya*)
Bodhidharma (Daruma), *83*, 86, *86*, 88
brush shops (*fude-ya*), *1*, 13, 42, 91–94, *91*, *93*, *101*

candle shops (*rôsoku-ya*), 42, 64, 106, 108, *108–9*
Chigusa (famous tea storage jar), 118, 121, *121*
clog shops (*geta-ya*), 20, *20*, 100–101, *100*, *102*, 116
comb shops (*kushi-ya*), 59, 110–12, *111–12*
cork companies, 66, *66*, 67

Daruma, *83*, 86, *86*, 88
doll (*ningyô*) shops, 25, 42, *50*, 103, 149
druggists. *See* pharmacies
dry goods stores, *45*, 100
  Ebisu-ya, 29, *29*
  Echigoya, 43, *44*, 56, 76, 93, 97, 127
  Enoguya, 50

Ebisu (god of daily provision), 29, *29*
eyeglass shops (*megane-ya*), 139, 141–42, *142*

fan makers (*ôgi-shi*), 28, 30–31, 39–40, *49*, 63, 92

gold leaf shops (*kinpaku-ya*), 64, 141, 143–44, *143–44*
greengrocers (*yao-ya*), 127–28, *128–31*, 130

Hayakawa, Naokichi, 35, 39

Ichikawa, Danjûrô I (1660–1704), 56, *113*, 115, *115*
Ichikawa, Danjûrô II (1688–1758), 56–57, *56–57*
Ichikawa, Danjûrô VII (1791–1859), 58, *58*, 64
Ichikawa, Danjûrô XII (1946–2013), 67
Ichimura, Uzaemon (1699–1762), *58*, 59
Ishida, Katsuhide, 21, 23–24, 70, 72–74
Iwai, Murasakiwaka, 58, *58*
Iwasa, Matabei (1578–1650), *30–31*, 31

jewelry stores (*tama-ya*), 141

kabuki, 55–59
  barbershops and, *113*
  comb shops and, *58*
  cosmetics and, 56, 58, *58*
  dry goods stores and, 56, 127
  medicine peddlers and, *57*, 74
  moxa shops and, 56–57, *56*
  stationery shops and, 115, *115*
  tobacco shops and, 80
  See also specific actors
kanban calligraphers (*kanban-gaki*), 19, 32, *32*
kanban carvers (*kanban-shi*)
  as sculptors, 92, 102, 148
  seals and signatures of, 21–24, 130
  tools of, 146
  visual strategies of, 19, 73, 98, 138
  See also Hayakawa, Naokichi; Kyokuriki; Shimizu, Kôjirô (act. late Meiji era)
Katsukawa, Shunshô (1726–1792), *57*
Katsushika, Hokusai (1760–1849), 32, *33*, *75*, 157
Kidai shôran (An excellent view of our prospering age), 41–44, *42–44*, 76, *76*, 84, 93–94, *93–94*, 97, *97*, 116, *116*, 122, *122*, 127–29, *128*
Kitagawa, Utamaro (1753?–1806), *139*
Kitao, Masanobu (1761–1816), 87–88, *88*
Kitao, Shigemasa II (1739–1820), *83*
knife shops (*hocho dokoro*), 149, 153, *153*
Kondô, Kiyoharu, 106, *106*, *113*, *144*
Kyokuriki, 155

lacquer shops (*urushi-ya*), 20, 116, 136
locksmiths, 67, 90, *90*, 102

mallet makers (*shumakushi*), 25, *25*
malt syrup (*mizuame*) shops, 42, *43*

medicine peddlers, 51, 56–57, *57–58*, 74, *75*
See also pharmacies
miso shops (*miso-ya*), 42, *54*, 62, 122–25, *122*, *124–25*
money changers (*ryôgae-ya*), 144–46, *145*
moxa shops, 56–57, *56*

Okumura, Masafusa (1686–1764), *56*, *108*
Okumura, Toshinobu (act. c. 1725–50), *58*, 59

pharmacies
advertising prints for, 34, *34–35*, 70, 72, *72–73*
along Nihonbashi, *76*
selling Adora eye drops, 3, *77*, *77*, 79, 80
selling Anchipirigan, 81, *81*
selling Daigakumegusuri eye drops, 79–80, *80*
selling ground turtle shell, 23–24, *24*, *36*
selling Ken'nôgan, *46*, 78–79, *78*, 81, *81*
selling Kenpien, 14, *14*, 97
selling Shinjusan, 72–74, *72–73*
selling Tsurigan laxative, *68*, 70–71, *71*
selling Ume no yuki, *18*, 21–23, *22*, 74
See also Ishida, Katsuhide; medicine peddlers; moxa shops
pipe shops (*kiseru-ya*), 80, 83–85, *85*, *87*
See also tobacco shops (*tabako-ya*)
playing card shops (*karuta-ya*), 17, *17*, 25, 70, 154, 156–58, *156–59*

restaurants, 15, 56, 64, 135, *135*
rice cake shops (*mochi-ya*), 62–63, *63*
rosary bead shops (*juzu-ya*), 25, *60*, 63, 103, 105–6, *105–7*

sake shops (*saka-ya*), 132, *132*, 136–39, *136–38*, *140*
samurai class. *See* armorers (*yoroi-ya*)
Santô, Kyôden (1761–1816), 87–88, *88*
saw-sharpening shops (*metate-ya*), 148, *148*
See also tool shops (*dôgu-ya*)
scissors shops, 147, *147*
See also tool shops (*dôgu-ya*)
seal basket (*inrô*) shops, 96, *96*
seal shops (*imban-ya*), 93–95, *94–95*
seaweed paste (*tsukudani*) shops, 129, 132, *132*, 134, *134*
seaweed shops (*nori-ya*), 133, *133*
Shibuya Crossing, Tokyo, *8*, 9–11, *10*, 13, 25
Shimizu, Kôjirô (act. late Meiji era), 21–24, *24*, 70, 73–74, *73*
shoe shops. *See* clog shops (*geta-ya*)
sign carvers (*gaku hori*), 25–26, *26*
sock shops (*tabi-ya*), *30*, 31, 63, 101, *101*, 103–4, *104*
Sodeoka, Masanosuke II, *115*
soy sauce shops (*shôyu-ya*), 121–23, *123*, *125*
stationery shops (*chômen-ya*), 115–17, *116–17*

tea leaf shops (*ha-cha-ya*), 28, 52, *52*, 118–21, *119–20*
thread shops (*ito-ya*), 94, 97–100, *97–99*
See also yarn makers (*ito-shi*)
tobacco pouch shops (*tabako-ire-ya*), 49, 80, 84, 86, 88–89, *88–89*, 92
tobacco shops (*tabako-ya*), 70, 82–83, *82–83*, 86, *86*, 88, 92
See also pipe shops (*kiseru-ya*)
tool shops (*dôgu-ya*), 6, 146–54, *150–52*, *160*
Torii, Kiyonobu I (1664–1729), *115*
toy shops, 39, 40, 42, *65*
Tsuboi, Shôgorô, *15*, 61–64, *62–63*, 69, *82*, 136

Utagawa, Kunisada (1786–1864), *110*
Utagawa, Sadahide (1807–1878/9), 12, *12*
Utagawa, Toyohiro (1773–1828), *29*
Utagawa, Toyokuni II (1777–1835), 58, *58*

vinegar shops (*su-ya*), 15, 28, 62, *62*, 125–27, *126–27*, 132–33

wig shops (*katsura-ya*), 110, 113–15, *113–14*
See also barbershops (*kami yui dokoro*)

Yamanaka, Heikurô I, *115*
Yamanaka & Co., 21, 64, 100, 136
yarn makers (*ito-shi*), 27, *28*
See also thread shops (*ito-ya*)

This book is published in conjunction with the exhibition *Kanban: Traditional Shop Signs of Japan*, presented at Mingei International Museum from April 15 to October 15, 2017.

Library of Congress Cataloging-in-Publication Data
Names: Pate, Alan Scott, author.
Title: Kanban : traditional shop signs of Japan / Alan Scott Pate.
Description: San Diego, CA : Princeton University Press, 2017. | Includes bibliographical references.
Identifiers: LCCN 2016043615 | ISBN 9780691176475 (hardback)
Subjects: LCSH: Signs and signboards—Japan. | Commercial art—Japan. | Shop signs. | Art, Japanese. | BISAC: ART / History / General.
Classification: LCC GT3911.77 .P38 2017 | DDC 302.23—dc23
LC record available at https://lccn.loc.gov/2016043615

Published by Mingei International Museum
1439 El Prado
San Diego, CA 92101
www.mingei.org

Published in association with
Princeton University Press,
Princeton and Oxford
41 William Street
Princeton, NJ 08540
USA

6 Oxford Street
Woodstock, Oxfordshire
OX20 1TR
UK
www.press.princeton.edu

Produced by Lucia|Marquand, Seattle
www.luciamarquand.com

Managing editor Christine Knoke Hietbrink
Principal photography by Steve Oliver and iocolor, Seattle
Edited and indexed by Jean Patterson
Designed by Jeff Wincapaw
Typeset in Slate by Tina Henderson
Proofread by Ted Gilley
Color management by iocolor, Seattle
Printed and bound in China by C&C Offset Printing Co., Ltd.

10 9 8 7 6 5 4 3 2 1

Mingei International, Inc. is a non-profit, public corporation, 501 (c)(3), dedicated to furthering the understanding of art of the people (*mingei*) from all eras and cultures of the world.
Accredited by the American Alliance of Museums

The exhibition and publication are supported by Mingei International Museum with additional funds provided by:
Gordon J. Brodfuehrer
The Donald C. & Elizabeth M. Dickinson Foundation
Helmstetter Family Foundation
Ellen Merewether
Royal Little Family Foundation
Bruce D. Silverstein, M.D. FACP

Front cover: *Mokei kanban for tobacco shop*, late nineteenth century. Wood, pigment, lacquer, 20¼ × 15 in. (51.4 × 38.1 cm). Private Collection.
Page 1: *Mokei kanban for brush shop*, nineteenth century. Wood, bamboo, pigment, cotton cord, 43 × 7½ in. (109.2 × 19.1 cm). Mingei International Museum, Gift of Jeaninne and Richard Helmstetter, 2000-04-003.
Page 3: *Circular shitta kanban for pharmacy selling Adora eye drops*, early twentieth century. Wood, gold leaf, pigment, 24 in. (61 cm) in diameter. Private Collection.